Discourse Analysis in
Chinese Composition

《篇章結構學》

陳滿銘／原著

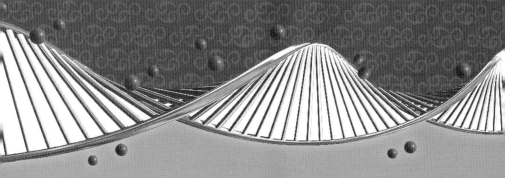

Written by
Man-Mian Chen（陳滿銘）

Supervised and edited by
David Wei-Yang Dai（戴維揚）

Translated by
Paul Tseng（曾貴祺）
Stephen Paul Ohlander（歐斯迪）
Yu-Hsien Tai（戴育賢）
Szu-I Yu（于嗣宜）
Kuo-Ping Tai（戴國平）

Co- Published by National Institute for Compilation and Translation, Republic of China (Taiwan)
and Wanjuan Lou Books, Ltd

Discourse Analysis in Chinese Composition

《篇章結構學》

Written by Man-Mian Chen（陳滿銘）

Surpervised and edited by David Wei-Yang Dai（戴維揚）

Translated by Paul Tseng（曾貴祺）, Stephen Paul Ohlander（歐斯迪）, Yu-Hsien Tai（戴育賢）, Szu-I Yu（于嗣宜）, Kuo-Ping Tai（戴國平）

©2010 by National Institute for Compilation and Translation, Republic of China（Taiwan）

E-mail:service@mail.nict.gov.tw

TEL:886-2-33225558

Published in 2010 by Wanjuan Lou Books, Ltd.

F-3, No.41,Sec.2,Roosevelt Rd.,Taipei,Taiwan,R.O.C

Printed in Taiwan

原　　著：陳滿銘

審　稿　者：戴維揚

譯　　者：曾貴祺、歐斯迪、戴育賢、于嗣宜、戴國平

著作財產人：國立編譯館
　　　　　　地址：10644 台北市大安區和平東路一段 179 號
　　　　　　網址：http://www.nict.gov.tw

出　版　者：萬卷樓圖書股份有限公司
　　　　　　臺北市羅斯福路二段 41 號 6 樓之 3
　　　　　　電話(02)23216565・23952992　傳真(02)23944113
　　　　　　劃撥帳號 15624015

發　行　人：陳滿銘

出版登記證：新聞局局版臺業字第 5655 號

網　　址：http://www.wanjuan.com.tw

E－mail：wanjuan@seed.net.tw

展　售　處：國家書店松江門市　地址：104 台北市中山區松江路 209 號 1 樓
　　　　　　電話：02-2518-0207（代表號）
　　　　　　國家網路書店　http://www.govbooks.com.tw
　　　　　　台中五南文化廣場　　地址：400 台中市中區中山路 6 號
　　　　　　電話：04-22260330　傳真：04-22258234

定　　價：600 元

出版日期：2010 年 11 月初版

GPN 1009904028

ISBN 978-957-739-680-8

Acknowledgements

It is our great privilege and pleasure to express our uttermost gratitude to National Institute for Compilation and Translation (國立編譯館) and Wanjuan Lou Books Publishing Company (萬卷樓) for providing us the amazing opportunity of translating the well-known Chinese scholar 陳滿銘 Chen, Man Mian's *Discourse Analysis in Chinese Composition*《篇章結構學》.

Dr. Paul Tseng (曾貴祺) is responsible for translating chapter one, chapter two, chapter three and appendix, while Prof. Stephen Paul Ohlander helps with proofreading and polishing them. Dr. Yu, Szu-I (于嗣宜) is responsible for translating chapter four, and Dr. Tai, Yu-Hsien (戴育賢) and Tai, Kuo-Ping (戴國平) are responsible for translating chapter five. Thanks also for the publication arranged and managed by Miss Chen, Hsin-Hsin (陳欣欣) and Yeh, Shu-Yin (葉書吟) for helping us through the final stages.

Overall, the translation and publication are supervised and edited by Dr. Dai, David Wei-Yang (戴維揚).

Preface

In terms of thinking, expression and the composition consist of three components, that is, "image thinking," "logical thinking," and "synthetic thinking." These three major ways of thinking are explained as follows. Ifwe associate the feelings or logic intended to be expressed by a composition as well as its expressions with all kinds of subjective associations and the imagination, or selected landscapes and things, or if we carve out expressive skills designed specifically for certain "feelings," "logic," "landscape," and "things," this is "image thinking." This, of course, is related to materials selection and diction, which are the subjects researched by the study of images, the study of words, and rhetoric. Second, if we make the materials such as landscapes and things correspond to natural laws, or if we associate these materials with objective associations and the imagination, and logically arrange them by the principles of order, change, consistency, and unity, these belong to the category of logical thinking. This is related to material employment, layout, and expression construction, and these indeed are the research subjects of grammar. Third, synthetic thinking combines "image thinking" and "logical thinking," researching the wholeness of their attributes. This is related to "intention," and "the whole attributes," which are the subjects researched by the study of main themes, the study of genres, and the study of styles. And all of these can be called a study of expressions and composition. Therefore, in terms of academic fields, the contents of expression and composition mainly include the study of images, the study of vocabulary, rhetoric, grammar, the study of the art of composition, the study of themes, the study of genres, the study of styles, etc. All of these are the valuable fruits of the study of expressions and composition.   As to the study of the art of composition, because it is designed largely to discuss the logical structure of the contents of the composition, it is associated with the meaning, intention, and style of the composition. So, from the angle of thinking, in addition to logical thinking, the art of composition is related to thinking of images and synthetic thinking.   In other words, the structure of composition puts emphasis on images (image thinking), and the art of composition (logical thinking).   Attached to the structure of the composition are its main themes, styles (synthetic thinking).   And, overall, the logical structure of "many, two, one, and zero" is used to account for the art of composition.

Therefore, this book is called *The Study of the Structure of the Composition and Paragraphs*, according to which chapters and sections are arranged.   The first chapter is "A General Introduction to the Structure of Composition and Paragraphs.   Here, the contents of the structure of composition are addressed in terms of the relation between "composition", image thinking, logical thinking, synthetic thinking, and the logical structure of "many, two, one (zero).   The second chapter is "The Image Contents of the Structure of Composition."   Here, "meaning" and "material" are the focal points, which later are combined with "the vertical (image) structure" to echo the first chapter in addressing the image contents of "the structure of composition."   The third chapter is "The Logical Contents of the Structure of Composition."   We   emphasized are the "types of the art of composition," and "the rules of the art of composition," both of which are combined with "the perspectives on the analysis of the art of composition," and "several kinds of special art of composition" to echo the first chapter in addressing the logical contents of "the structure of composition."   The fourth chapter entitled "The Synthetic Contents of the Structure of Composition" puts its emphasis, at the very beginning, on "the topics and guidelines" and "the manifested and hidden topics."   Then, this chapter provides a discussion on "a few basic types for arranging topics or guidelines," echoing the first chapter in addressing the issues related to the synthetic contents of the structure of compositions. The fifth chapter entitled "The Contents of Logical Structures, 'Many, Two, One/Zero," first discusses the formation of the logical structures, then it explains the styles and aesthetics of the logical structures in order to echo the first four chapters by talking about the main contents of these logical structures. Moreover, included in the appendix is the article entitled "Linguistic Competence and a Study of Expressions and Compositions—in Terms of the Spiral Structure of Many, Two, One/Zero." This article aims to point to map linguistic competence to the study of phraseology and composition in both directions, so as to reveal the inseparability of the two and to highlight their close relationship and its importance. This will then compensate for the inadequacy of the main text.

Recently, the structure of composition has been taken into serious consideration in instruction on the listening, speaking, reading and writing of Mandarin to such an extent that it has been explicitly included in teaching outlines of Mandarin courses at all levels of schools. However, owing to the insufficiency of study on the structure of composition, linguistic competence, and expression and composition, the promotion of discourse analysis in Mandarin teaching more often than not lacks substantial results. Recently, studies in this field have been booming and a series of theises and books have been produced. And in universities certain courses such as the study of composition (for undergraduates) and the advanced study of composition (for graduate institutes) have already been started. In addition, research results in linguistic competence and discourse studies have been used to design the contents and criteria of assessments. For example, consider the MOE qualification exams for school and kindergarten teachers, where the multiple choice questions in the Mandarin proficiency test section consists of "word shapes, word sounds, word meanings," "vocabulary," "grammar and rhetoric," "structures of composition," "appreciation of styles," "the main ideas of contents," "common Knowledge for Mandarin and applications" and "synthetic questions." Accordingly, this assessment method, mainly based on linguistic competence or contents of expression and composition, is the first time for both sides of the Taiwan Strait.

Some people hold that if a composition is analyzed in terms of its multiplicity of linguistic competence and contents, this will damage the wholeness of the composition, destroying its aesthetics. Indeed, this is controversial. For creative writing produces concrete images out of abstract meanings. The creative ability is natural and even spontaneous. On the other hand, critical reading aims to interpret meanings derived from images. This is based on scientific theories, which can objectively evaluate and criticize literary works. Therefore, analysis, in a sense, is an effort to reconstruct the author's meanings. Without scientific analyses, the critique would be so subjective that they could not understand how abstract meanings are transformed into concrete images, failing to grasp the wholeness of aesthetics. Actually, reconstruction is a key factor in appreciating literature. And without scientific analyses, reconstruction is baseless.

Discourse, analysis of Chinese composition is both vital and many- faceted. Currently, a good introductory book on the analysis of composition is an urgent necessity. This book can serve as a self-study book or a textbook for college students. Hopefully, this book will help readers enhance their ability to analyze Chinese compositions, reconstructing the creative processes, and thus understanding Chinese aesthetics in its entirety.

in study room 835 at Chinese Department of
National Taiwan Normal University
March 6, 2005.

Contents

Synthetic Contents of Structures of Lexical Composition

Chapter Five --- ❖369

Logical Structures of "Many, Two, One/ Zero"

Researches on Language Proficiency and Lexical Composition

-- In Terms of the Spiral Structure of "Many, Two, One/Zero"

Chapter **1**

An Introduction to the Structure of Composition and Paragraphs

The study of composition structure is a subject in the study of expressions and compositions with the contents and organization of composition. Since this subject is inclusive of paragraphs and compositions, the first thing we have to do is to clarify the relationships between the two and to identify contents of each concept.

I. The Relations between Paragraphs and Compositions

Expressions and compositions are based on words, sentences, paragraphs, and compositions. According to "Paragraphs and Sentences" in *The Literary Mind And The Carving of Dragons,* "In order to express what one has to say, one needs to form sentences from words, to organize sentences into paragraphs, and to organize paragraphs into completed compositions. The brilliance of a literary piece depends on faultlessness of each paragraph; the clarity of the paragraph depends on the flawlessness of each sentence; and the purity of the sentence depends on a good choice of words. For when the stem stands up, the branches naturally follow; and when one understands a unifying principle, he understands all about ten thousand [phenomena subsumed under that principle]." Thus, the formation of an article is based on such morphemes as word, sentence, paragraph and composition. Among these, paragraph and composition are the biggest units used to unify the whole article. Despite their different size, a paragraph often "includes" a composition, and a composition, on the other hand, includes a paragraph. Their relations are inseparably close. And this close relation can be clearly seen by a table of structure. Take Su-Shih's "A Record of Transcendental Platform," for example. In terms of paragraph and composition, its structure is analyzed to explain the content and form.

The structures of this article can be divided into "paragraph" and "composition," both of which can combine to form its contents and organizations. These structures can also be illustrated as below.

1. The Structure of Composition

In terms of composition, this article's structure is in the sequence of argument first, and later, narration. In addition, in terms of paragraph, the structure is in the order of "positive" first, and later "negative", or "sequential" first, and later, "complementary."

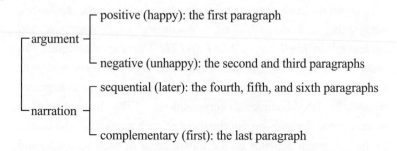

positive (happy): the first paragraph

argument

negative (unhappy): the second and third paragraphs

sequential (later): the fourth, fifth, and sixth paragraphs

narration

complementary (first): the last paragraph

This article can be divided into seven paragraphs. The first, second, and third paragraphs are arguments (for logic), while the fourth, fifth, sixth, and seventh ones are narrations (of things). In the part of argument (for logic), the positive side of "being happy" is first written, and then the negative side of "being unhappy" is written. In this way, the part of narration (of things) is initiated. In addition, in the part of narration (of things), he used his experiences of moving to Mi State to serve as an official from Hang State to describe "better not to be happy,"[1] and then he sequentially described the positive side, that is, "expressing joy outside."[2] In this way, the method of complementary narration was employed to explain the name of the platform as well as the reason why it was named to echo the previous section of this article.

2. The Structure of Paragraph

Since this article's structure is based first on argument and then on narration, these two major parts will be further discussed as follows.

(一) The Part of "Argument"

This part included the first, second, and third paragraphs. Here, the author first described the positive side of "being able to rejoice," and then he described the negative side of "being unhappy," thus initiating the part of "narration."

1. In terms of the positive side, the original text is translated as follows.

凡物皆有可觀 (Common things all have something worth being seen;)；苟有可觀 (if there is something worth being seen,)，皆有可樂 (there will be something worth rejoicing.)，非必怪奇偉麗者也 (It is not necessarily strange and spectacular.)。餔糟啜

....

1 As to 人固疑余之樂也。(people must think that I was happy), Lin Yun-ming makes such comments: "it's not forsaking happiness and choosing sadness. Indeed, there is nothing worthy of happiness." See *Collection of Analysis of Ancient Prose.* 《古文析義合編》 (Taipei Kungwen Bookstore, Oct. 1965) p.317.

2 Lin Yun-ming added a note for the sentence—"the white hairs were turned black in day time." "Joy was expressed outside, which was evidenced in this way." This is the same as the first note.

醨，皆可以醉 (All can make man drunk;)；果蔬草木，皆可以
飽 (fruits, vegetables, grass, and tress all can make man full;)；
推此類也 (Everything is valid for a perspective itself.)，吾安往
而不樂 (In this way, I will never be unhappy wherever I go.)？

In this way, we can enjoy ourselves in common things.
Common drinks are enjoyable, so does common food.   No
matter what circumstances we are in, we can enjoy ourselves.

This paragraph is written directly from the positive side, using a
key word "enjoy (happiness)" to unify the whole thing.[3]   Its
structure, sequentially speaking, is in the order of "generalization,
specification, and generalization."

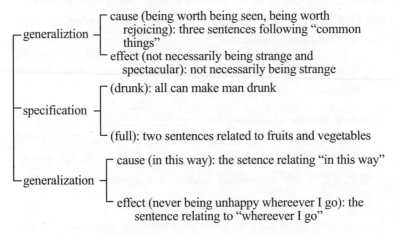

generaliztion
- cause (being worth being seen, being worth rejoicing): three sentences following "common things"
- effect (not necessarily being strange and spectacular): not necessarily being strange

specification
- (drunk): all can make man drunk
- (full): two sentences related to fruits and vegetables

generalization
- cause (in this way): the setence relating "in this way"
- effect (never being unhappy whereever I go): the sentence relating to "whereever I go"

This is the first paragraph connected with「在物」(on object).[4]

....

3   Wang Wen-ju pointed out that "the word "joy" is the main idea."   See
Comments on Anthology of Ancient Prose. 《精校評注古文觀止》 Vol.11
(Taipei: Taiwan Chunhua Bookstore, Nov. 1972.) p.7.
4   Lin Yun-ming makes a comment on「非必怪奇偉麗者也」(It is not necessarily

The first four sentences explained that common things ordinary, strange, or spectacular, do contain some elements worth being seen and rejoicing.   And then, in terms of 「處物」,[5] the following four sentences use examples to interpret this philosophy.   And then, "in this way" is used to deduce the concluding sentence—"I will never be unhappy wherever I go."   Thus, it can be seen that "happy," the key word is employed to connect the whole composition.

   2. In terms of "the negative side," the paragraph goes in this way:

夫所謂求福而辭禍者（The reason why man seeks blessings and escapes from disasters）以福可喜而禍可背也（is that blessings make man happy, while disasters make him sad）人之所欲無窮（man's desires are countless）而物之可以足吾欲者有盡（the things I desire are limited in every way）美惡之辨戰乎中（the spiritual war of telling beauty from evil is in my mind）而去取之擇交乎前（the choice is before my eyes），則可喜者常少（the things making us happy are few），而可悲者常多（The things making us sad are many.）是謂求禍而辭福（This seems to seek disasters and escape from blessings），夫求禍而辭福（seeking disasters and escaping from blessings），豈人之情也哉？（Is this man's original intention?）物有以蓋之矣（They are suppressed by desires for materials.）彼游於物之內（They are limited in the material world.）而不游於物之外（They cannot get rid of desires for materials.）物非有大小也（Objects are the same in size.）自其內而觀之（viewing them from inside）未有不高且大者也（They are all both tall and big.）彼

....

strange and spectacular): "joy is the main idea.   The four lines speak about objects."   Same as note 1.

[5]   Lin Yun-ming make a comment on 「吾安往而不樂」(No matter what circumstances we are in, we can enjoy ourselves): the six lines talk about dealing with objects.   Same as note 1.

挾其高大以臨我（They appear before us tall and big.）則我常
眩亂反復（I am left in confusion.）如隙中之觀鬥（It's like
observing a fight from a small hole.）又焉知勝負之所在？
（How can we know the final result?）是以美惡橫生，而憂樂
出焉（Thus, beauty and ugliness are produced; happiness and
sadness are perceived.）可不大哀乎！（This indeed a great
pity.）

This part can be divided into two paragraphs, that is, the second
and third paragraphs. It is framed by the structure of "first man
(desire) and then heaven (object)."

```
                  ┌ cause（求福辭禍）：two lines following「夫所謂」
  ┌ man (desire) ─┤         ┌ cause（所欲無窮）：six lines followng「人之所欲」
  │               └ effect ─┤
  │                         └ effect（求禍辭福）：「是謂求禍」
  │               ┌ effect（求禍辭福）：two lines following「夫求禍」
  └ heaven (object)┤ cause（游於物內）：ten lines following「物有以」
                  └ effect（求禍辭福）：「是謂求禍」
```

In the second paragraph, following the word 「樂」(joy), the
two lines of 「夫所謂求福而辭禍者」(The reason why man seeks
blessings and escapes from disasters) are used to directly point out
that the reason is that blessings are joyful and disasters are sad.
And the six lines following 「人之所欲無窮」(man's desires are
countless) deduce the result of desires—happy endings are few,
while sad results are numerous. In addition, the line--「是謂求禍而
辭福」(This seems to seek disasters and escape from blessings）--
echoes the first line, explaining why man is unhappy and paving a
way for the following lines. In the third paragraph, following the last

line of the previous paragraph, the two lines following 「夫求禍而辭福」（Seeking disasters and escaping from blessings）reveal that this phenomenon is against human wishes. And then, the line--「物有以蓋之矣」（They are suppressed by desires for materials.）is used as a general assumption. Furthermore, the two lines following 「彼游於物之內」（They are limited in the material world.）point out that the fruit results from the suppression of man's heart. And the seven lines following「物非有大小也」（objects are the same in size）portray the phenomenon of man's suppression by materials, big and small. In addition, the two lines following 「是以美惡橫生」（thus, beauty, evil, happiness and sadness are produced）point out its result. Finally, the work ends in「可不大哀哉」（This indeed a great pity.）In this way, from an opposite side, it is revealed that「游於物之外，則無所往而不樂」(Surpassing the desires for materials, one can be always happy).[6]

（二）The part of "narration"

This part includes the fourth, fifth, and sixth paragraphs. Here, the author first from the opposite side talks about 「宜不能樂」(better not rejoice), and then from the opposite side he discusses 「樂形於外」(Joy is expressed outwardly). And then, he further points out how the platform was named.

1. In terms of "in order," the part is as follows.

余自錢塘移守膠西 (1 moved from Hanchou to Michou)，釋舟楫之安 (forsaking the ease and comfort of boats)，而服車馬之勞(experiencing the discomfort of horses and carts)，去雕牆之美而蔽采椽之居 (leaving fine houses and then live a humble house)，背湖山之觀 (bidding farewell to the spetaculous scene

---

6 See *Comments on Anthology of Ancient Prose.*《精校評注古文觀止》p.8.

of mountains and lakes)，而適桑麻之野。(coming to the field of plants)。始至之日 (when I first came in office)，歲比不登 (for years the harvest yield was barren)，盜賊滿野 (thieves and robbers were everywhere)，獄訟充斥 (suit filings were many)，而齋廚索然 (food was insufficient)，日食杞菊 (I ate wild vegetables every day.)，人固疑余之不樂也。(People must think that I was unhappy)，處之期年 (after a year)，而貌加豐 (my countenance became nicer)，髮之白者，日以反黑。(My white hair gradually turned black.)，余既樂其風俗之淳，(I loved this place whose customs were pure and good.)，而其吏民亦安余之拙也，(The officers and inhabitants got used to my awkwardness.)，於是治其園圃，(Therefore I cultivated the gardens.)，潔其庭宇 (cleaned yards)，伐安丘、高密之木 (cut the high and dense trees of hills)，以修補破敗，(repaired broken parts)，為苟完之計(making them complete)，而園之北 (the northern part of the garden)，因城以為臺者舊矣 (The platform along the city was old.)，稍葺而新之 (I renewed it) 時相與登覽 (I frequently went up for a view.) 放意肆志焉 (My horizon was thus broadened.) 南望馬耳常山 (On the platform, I looked south to Maerh Mountain and Chang Mountain) 出沒隱見 (Sometimes they were not visible.) 若近若遠 (the distance was unpredictable) 庶幾有隱君子乎？(perhaps there were hermits in the mountains) 而其東則盧山 (In the eastern side was Lu Mountain) 秦人盧敖之所從遁也 (Lu Ao of the Ching Dynasty lived there as a hermit) 西望穆陵 (looking west to Mulin) 隱然如城郭 (it looked like a city) 師尚父齊威公之遺烈猶有存者 (legacies of Chiangtaikung and Chihuankung remained there) 北俯濰水 (looking north to Weishui) 慨然太息，思淮陰之功 (remembering Han Sin's achievements, I sighed.) 而弔其不終 (for his unfortunate end of life) 臺高而安 (the platform was high and stable) 深而明 (deep and bright) 夏涼而冬溫 (summer was cool and winter was warm) 雨雪之朝

(in the morning of snow places) 風月之文 (in nights of winds and moon) 余未嘗不在 (I was always on the platform) 客亦未嘗不從 (friends also followed) 擷園蔬 (picking up vegetables in the garden) 取池魚 (fishing in the pond) 釀秫酒 (making wine) 瀹脫栗而食之 (cooking rice to eat) 曰：樂哉遊乎！(I said, "the travel was so happy!)

These three paragraphs are framed by the structure of "first negative and then positive."

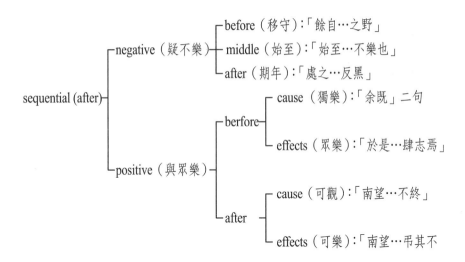

In terms of the part of negativity, this part begins with the first line of the fourth paragraph, ending in 「人固疑余之不樂也」(people must think that I was unhappy). Here, the author uses four lines following 「余自錢塘移守膠西」(I moved from Hanchou to Michou) to describe how he deserted the life of joy and prosperity and chose to live a life of hardships and difficulties. And the line--「始至之日」(when I first came in office)—is used as a connection to introduce five lines following 「歲比不登」(for years the harvest yield was scare) , which described the early difficult days in Michou. And then, the line--「人固疑余之不樂也」(people must think that I was unhappy)—echoing the negative parts of the second and third paragraphs discloses that in the eyes of outsiders this kind of experiences must be unhappy.   Thus, it makes a contrast to the following 「樂形於外」(Joy is expressed outwardly).[7]   And then, in terms of the positive part, this part includes the second half of the fourth paragraph, the fifth and sixth paragraphs.   In the second half of the fourth paragraph, the line--「處之期年」(after a year)—is used to link the previous line--「始至之日」(When I first came in office), thus introducing the three lines following 「而貌加豐」 (my countenance became nicer), which prove his happiness by the countenance change. And then, the two lines following 「余既樂其風俗之淳」(I loved this place whose customs were pure and good) are used to generally describe how offices can get along with inhabitants.[8]   The positive description paves a way for the following lines-「時相與登覽」(I frequently went up for a view) and 客亦未嘗不從 (friends also followed). Moreover, the eight lines following 「治其園圃」(therefore I managed gardens) are used to describe how the joy spread from gardens to the platform and how they were managed. And then, the two lines following 時相與登覽 (I frequently went up for a view) are used to explain that the purpose of fixing gardens and the platform is to have officers and inhabitants enjoy the view together.   In this way, they can keep happy exceeding the material bondage.   In the fifth paragraph, these wordings such as 南望 (looking south) 而其東 (to the east) 西望

....

7 Wang Wen-ju, *Comments on Anthology of Ancient Prose.* 精校評注古文觀止》 「人固疑予之不樂也」(people think that I am unhappy) indeed serves to link the next lines. pp.8-9.

8 See Wang Wen-ju, *Comments on Anthology of Ancient Prose.* 《精校評注古文觀止》Vol.11, p.9.

(looking west) 北俯 (looking north) are used to in turn describe the views in the space. And then, in the last paragraph, the three lines following 臺高而安 (The platform was high and stable) are used to describe the feature of the platform. In addition, the four lines following 「雨雪之朝」 (in the morning of snow places) are used to describe the happiness of enjoying the view. Furthermore, the four lines following 「擷園蔬」 (picking up vegetables in the garden) are used to describe the tool for enjoying the view. In this way, the line-「曰樂哉遊乎」 (I said, "the travel was so happy)—is introduced to echo the first paragraph, explaining 「苟有可觀，皆有可樂」 (If there is something worth being seen, there will be something worth rejoicing.)

2. In terms of "supplement," this part is the final paragraph.

方是時 (at that time)，余弟子由適在濟南 (My younger brother came over to Chinan) 聞而賦之，（Hearing of these ,he wrote an article.）且名其臺曰「超然」（He called this platform "supreme".）以見余之無所往而不樂者（explaining that I might be happy everywhere）蓋游於物外也。（Because I could live outside the world and enjoy the world.）

The structure analysis diagram can be as follows.

This paragraph is framed by the structure of "first dot and then dye."[9] First, 「方是時」 (at that time) is used as a linkage. And then, the line 「余弟子由適在濟南」 (My younger brother came over to Chinan) introduces four lines following 「聞而賦之」 (Hearing of these ,he wrote an article.), revealing why the platform is named.   In this way, the joy outside the world is underlined.   So, Wan Wen-ju holds that "the meaning of supremacy ends in this skillful way."[10]

Accordingly, the author points out joys from a positive side. And the word "joy" serves as the main idea of this work. Furthermore, the author infers from an opposite side that man's unhappiness indeed results from the fact that he can not surpass the material world.   And then, based on his own personal experiences and the scenes and happiness related to the platform, he points out that by surpassing the outside one can live happily under all kinds of circumstances.   Just as Wu Chutsai put it, "First, this work

....

9 "Dot and dye" is originally used in painting, referring to basic skills. And it was first used by Liu Si-dai to interpret the compostional art. His usage of "dot and dye" refers to feelings (dot) and landscape (dye). This is very similar to the "feelings-landscape" type in the family tree of compositional art.   The "dot" refers to a certain point in space and time, which is used to narrate events, describe landscapes and express feelings, and which is also used to introduce, conncet, or end reasoning. And "dye" refers to the mainbody practically used to narrate events, describe landscapes, or explain reasons.   In other words, "dot" serves as a point of departure, while "dye" refers the content. This compositional type can be transformed into "first dot and then dye," "first dye and then dot," "dot, dye, dot," "dye, dot, dye," producing the functions of order, change, consistence.   See Chen Man-ming's *Several Special Compositional Types*. 〈論幾種特殊的章法〉 (Taipei: Taiwan Noramal University, Chinese Journal, 《國文學報》 June 2002) pp.181-187.

10 See Wang Wen-ju, *Comments on Anthology of Ancient Prose.* 《精校評注古文觀止》Vol. 11, p.10.

underlines the meaning of supremacy, and then mentions the event. In its narration of events, he talks about spectacles in space and sceneries in four seasons.　All of these refer to the joy beyond the world."[11]　Therefore, in terms of comments, narration, sequence and complement, this work is wholly consistent.　And from the angle of materials employment and paragraph arrangement, the style is consistent despite the variations, showing the talents of the author.

According to the above analysis, the structure of a text can be divided into "composition" and "paragraph." And in terms of length and structural units, the paragraph can be divided into certain parts. In addition, all literary works, through a structural analysis, can reveal the laws of order, consistence, change and unification. This can integrate content and form and unify truth, goodness, and beauty.[12]

II. The contents of the structure of composition and paragraphs

Rhetoric cannot deviate from content and form, rhetorical study being research in rhetorical contents and forms.　Zhang Zhe Gung thinks it is a study of linguistic art with ethnic characteristics (*The Learning of Compositions and Expressions*).[13]　This definition seems limited to the artistic presentation of rhetorical expressions and leaves out its contents.　However, the contents must be presented

....

11　See Wang Wen-ju, Wu Chu-tsai, *Comments on Anthology of Ancient Prose.* 《精校評注古文觀止》　Vol. 11, p.7-8.

12　See Chen Man-ming, Four *Major Laws of Compositiona Types, Paper Collections of Compositional Art.* 〈論辭章章法之四大律〉,《辭章學論文集》　(Fuchou: Seatide Photo Art Publishing Company, Dec. 2002) pp.68-77.

13　See Cheng Yi-shou, *Reflection and Prospect of the Study of Compositonal Art.* 〈辭章學研究的回顧與前瞻〉　(Taipei: *The World of Chinese Language and Monthly-Literature* 《國文天地》　Aug. 2003) p.87.

in a certain form and the form must have contents.　Therefore in a rhetorical composition, contents and forms are dependent on each other and not separable.[14]　The discussion of this section will first delve into the text of the structure and try to define the structure of the context, and then move to the abstractness of the forms and the logical thinking behind the components of the composition. From sections to chapters, gradually the focus and concept which the composition is trying to convey will become clear.　The structure of the text can be analyzed through the relations between the contents and the forms of the entire composition.

1. The definition of structure of compositions and paragraphs

Text structure is the most important part of rhetorical study.　In order to understand the text structure, the contents of the text must be understood first; yet, before understanding the contents, the rhetorical composition must be understood. As a general rule, the rhetorical composition consists of "image thinking", "logical thinking" and "composite thinking".[15]　Each of the thinking types has its own identity. When a composition intends to express certain emotion or reasoning by combining the scene or ongoing events with subjective association and imagination,[16] or the illustration of

....

[14] See Liu Hsieh, *Liteary Mind and Carved Dragon,* 《文心雕龍・情采》 "the function of literary decorativeness is to adorn discourse, and beauty of eloquence is based on real emotion.　Thereofore, emotion is the warp of literary pattern, linguistic form the woof of ideas.　Only when the warp is straight can the woof be rightly formed, and only when ideas are definite can linguistic form be meaningful.　This is the fundamental principle in literary creation." (Beijing: Chunhua Bookstore, Aug. 2000) p.415.

[15] See Wu Yin-tien, *Compositional Structuralism.* 《文章結構學》 (Beijing: Chinese People University Publishing Company, Aug. 1989) p.345.

[16] See Peng Yi-lien, *Fun in the Logic of Classic Poetry and Tzu* 《古典詩詞邏輯趣談》 (Shaghai: Shanghai People Publishing Company, Sept.2001) p.13.

the author's descriptive skill by description of a certain emotion, reasoning, scene or event, it falls into the realm of "image thinking". These aspects involve "conceptualization", "materialization" and "wording", and the studies associated with these aspects are imagology, lexicology and rhetoric.   If materials in scenes or events are combined with emotion and reasoning and expressed by objective associations with natural rules and the imagination, and arranged based on the principles of order, variation, consistency and unification, all this can be regarded as "logical thinking". This process involves the gathering of materials, composition layout and word structuring.   Study in these areas is a study in grammar and composition stylistics.   "Composite thinking" is a process entailing the combination of "image thinking" and "logical thinking" in search of an entity's characteristics, which involves conceptualization and character establishment. The study of these aspects would be thematology and stylistics.   The study of the whole or partial subject in these fields is rhetorical composition or essay study.   And the relation between them is:

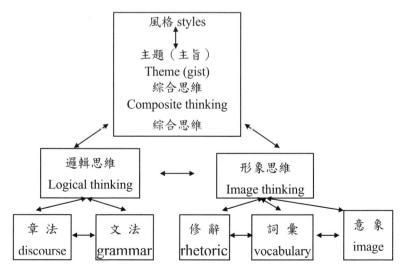

Rhetoric composition consists of contents that can be studied , as in the fields of academic studies, imagology, lexicology, rhetoric, grammar, composition stylistics, thematology and stylistics ... etc, which will be further explained as follows.

First, imagology is one aspect of image study in terms of rhetorical composition. The image aspect in the Chinese literature had been noted for a long time. It had been regarded as the "first component in writing, most important in composition" (*The Literary Mind and the Carving of Dragons*, mind searching).   Huang Yung Wu explains "image" as "the intersection of author's senses and the display of external objects, brewed by observation, thinking and beautification, manifested as a vivid description of scene and state of mind. [17]   The object described, as explained by Chu Xi, includes events that are happening in the surrounding environment. Scenery is motionless space (static) and events are motions in time (dynamic). A complete work of literature usually consists of multiple images. Image thinking is applied during the formation of the individual image.

Next lexicology, which is a linguistics discipline that deals with the lexical composition of a language and its historical development. Zhuang Wen Chung said: "If language is a building, then text is the construction material of this building--just like thousands of bricks and prefabricated building blocks which compose this spectacular building of literature."   Chang Zhe Gung said: "The foundation of language is text.   The functions of language (tool of socialization, tool of information propagation, tool of thinking) depend on the text to materialize.   He also said: "From the perspective of teaching, learning and application, text is important, text is difficult." [18]   From

....

17 See *Chinese Poetics, Part of Design.* 《中國詩學・設計篇》 (Taipei: Chuliu Publishing Company, June 1999) p.3.

18 See *Middle School Language Teaching Study.* 《中學語言教學研究》

these descriptions we may see text as the first steps in transforming emotion, reasoning, scene and events into writing notations, which is fundamentally important in the study of rhetorical composition.

Next is the study of rhetoric. Master of rhetoric Chen Wang Tao said: "Rhetoric is a way of expressing with emphasis on reasoning and emotion. Rhetoric is simply an effort to adjust the contents of a text such that they are expressed appropriately." [19] Huang Ching Shuan thought that "the contextual substance of rhetoric is the image formed by the author." "The way of rhetoric is to design and readjust", "the principle of rhetoric is to be accurate and vivid". [20] It can be said that the rhetoric emphasizes individual expressions by the objective design and adjustment of the author, making it accurate and lively to intensify the appealing and persuasion of the text. This is obviously a process based upon image thinking.

Then we have the study of grammar, or syntax, which investigates the structural patterns of a language. It includes the composition of words and their variation, the organization of phrases and sentences. Yang Zhu Shue combined the hypotheses of such scholars as Lu Shu Shiang, Chao Yuan Zhen and Wang Li in the revised edition of "The ABC of Grammar": "What is grammar? Simply put, grammar is the organization principle of a text. There is no set formula for this principle. Instead, there are regularities extracted from analysis of the words of the language. This principle also includes the internal structure of words and the integration of words into sentences. Therefore grammar is the set of rules governing the linguistic structure and sentence making. [21] Given these arguments, when

....

(Kuangchou: Kuangtung Education Publishing Company, Jan. 2001) pp.29-30.

19 See *Retorics*, 《修辭學發凡》 p.5.

20 See *Retorics*. 《修辭學》 (Taipei: Shanming Bookstore, Oct., 2002) pp.5-9.

21 See *Grammar ABC*. 《文法 ABC》 (Taipei: Wanchunlo Publishing Company, Feb., 2002) pp.1-2.

these principles are applied to the formation of concepts and images, they are directly related to logical thinking.

Next, the composition stylistics. The so called stylistics is a search of the logical structure of a composition. In other words, the organization of making words into sentences, combining sentences into paragraphs, and paragraphs into an essay. Although researchers have long noted the stylistic regularities in compositions, it is note until recently that the findings are collected and the scope, contents, and principles are determined to form a system and become a discipline.[22] At the present time, there are approximately forty rules of stylistics which can be explained clearly.   These rules evolved from the common principles of human discipline and were formed by logical thinking, all of them serving the functionality of forming order, diversifying, interconnecting, and achieving ultimate unification. Order, diversity, connection and unification are referred to as the four rules of composition stylistics.   Among them, order, diversity and connection are related to the application of materials, and the emphasis is on analysis; unification, on the other hand, is associated with the expression of emotion, and the focus is on continuity. This method of considering partial (material) analysis

....

22 Cheng Yi-Shou said, "It's fruitful for Taiwan's establishment of the discipline of compositional art.   The representative work is *New Design of Compositional Art* by Chen Man-ming.   A series of works are also done by his students including Chou Hsiao-ping and Chen Chiao-chun.   The system and science of taiwan's compositional art might well become a discipline." (Suchou: Conference on Cross-Strait Chinese Traditional Culture and Modernization, 《海峽兩岸中華傳統文化與現代化研討會文集》 May 2002) pp.131-139. Wang Si-chieh also said, "Compositional art is a practical discipline with high academic value.   It is intimately associated with rhetorics, pragmatics, aesthetics, logic.   And Chen Man-ming has initially established its system." "Small Talks on Compositonal Art" 〈章法學門外閒談〉 (Taipei: The World of Chinese Language and Monthly Literature 《國文天地》 Oct.2000) pp.92-95.

and the continuity (emotion) of the entire setup, is very comprehensive.[23] The logical thinking of the composition and wording should be consistent.

Then we come to thematic studies. Chen Peng Shiang stated in his "Theory and Practice of Thematology": "Thematology is a field of study in Comparative Literature. Ordinary thematic studies are studies in a single layer of the multiple layers involved in any literature creation. The objective of thematology is the study of identical themes (including lexis, imaging and topics) in the hands of various authors at different times in an effort to understand the characteristics of an era and the intention of the author, whereas the ordinary thematic studies will concentrate on the illustration of a certain singular theme."[24] From this description we may see that theme includes "lexis," "imaging" and "topics." In the scope of one single chapter, i.e., the expression of a particular topic, it means the language of emotion, the language of reasoning, imagery and purposes (including the abstract). The language of emotion and reasoning are used to illustrate the purposes (including the abstract) and should be regarded inclusively. Where the theme of a chapter is concerned, it usually means the purposes (including the abstract) and imagery (generalized), which is a composite of image logic and thinking logic.

Finally, stylistics. Generally speaking, there are multiple aspects of styles, and this is especially true for literal styles. Differences exist in writing styles, author, school, time, region, ethnicity and creativity. Looking further into a composition, it has contents and appearances (artistic), the content by itself being related to theme

....

23 See Chen Man-ming, *On Compositional Art.* 《章法學綜論》 (Taipei: Wanchunlo Publishing Company, June 2003) pp.17-58.

24 See Chen Pen-siang, *Theory and Practice of the Study of Themes.* 《主題學理論 與實踐》 (Taipei: Wanchunlo Publishing Company, May 2001) p.238.

(topic, image) whereas appearance is closely related to grammar, rhetoric and order. The style of a composition is an integral presentation which is composed of content and appearance.[25] This is a combination of the author's logic and image thinking, which drives the theme with individual characteristics in grammar, rhetoric and composition for the presentation of an integrated appearance.

The above describes the major contents of the rhetorical composition. All of these contents are closely related to image thinking or logical thinking. The ones that relate to wordings (surface structure) are images (individual), verbiage, rhetoric and grammar. The ones which concern chapter and article are logical thinking (deep structure; whole body) and order of chapters. Topics and styles have something to do with the writing in question. Therefore the rhetorical composition has images (from individual to whole body) and text regularity (or patterns of composition) as its contents and is connected by topics and styles in the total presentation.

We may therefore conclude that the text structure is a major branch of rhetorical composition, which is a study of the images of a chapter (image thinking), text regularity logical thinking, topics and stylistics (deep composite thinking).

2. Textual contents mainly concerning image thinking

Imagery is the most important and the key to the contents of image thinking. Imagery is a product of sense and appearance, and linking parts of rhetorical composition.

However, its definition differs in a broader sense and a narrower

....

25 Ku Chu-chun said, "the causes of style are not necessarily individual elements of the work, but an overall aesthetic view of the organic content and form of the literary work." See *New Interpretation of Literary Principles*. 《文學原理新釋》 (Beijing: People Literature Publishing Company, May 2001) p.184.

sense.   It often means the entire contents of the whole body in a broader sense, and can be subdivided into sense and appearance. The narrower sense refers to the individual, usually the partial and sense and appearance are treated as one.   Since the entirety is the integration of partials and the partial is a part of the entirety, the two have inseparable relations. Nevertheless, in the narrow sense, even though sense and appearance are a combinational representation, often the partial meaning could be adopted. For example, the sensing images of grass and wood or peach blossom all lean toward the sensing parts, since grass and wood or peach blossom lean toward the "images" by themselves.   One of the representations of the peach blossom is love, and love could be a sense.   The sensing image of reunion or wandering lean toward "image". One image of wandering is the cloud, and the cloud could be an "image".   The former may be one image with multiple senses and while the latter may be one sense and multiple images.   Despite their differences, they are all "sensing images"

As a whole, the main contents of rhetorical composition consist of emotion, reasoning, events and objects (scene).   Emotion and reasoning are senses and the core of the composition.   Events and objects (scene) are peripheral components and the forms of the composition, which can be demonstrated by the following tree diagram.

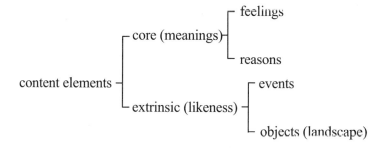

As regards the rhetorical composition of this combination of emotion, reasoning and events, and objects (scene), it is "sense" in terms of emotion and reasoning; while it is "form" in terms of events and objects.

Since the core of the composition is emotion and reasoning, the center of the entire writing is the affection which the author is trying to project.   It involves the various images made from imagery and logical thinking, but will be skipped for this moment as we concentrate on the so-called peripheral components, which are various images and forms respectively. The peripheral components are descriptions of events or objects (scene). In other words, the peripheral structure is formed by materials no other than events and objects.

First, the objects.   Anything that exists between heaven and earth in the universe can become the objects of a composition.   From the larger objects such as heaven (empty), earth, man, the sun, the moon, stars, mountains (land), water (stream, river, creek), cloud, wind, rain, thunder, electricity, smoke, haze, flower, grass, bamboo, wood (tree), spring, stone, bird, animal, insect, fish, house, gazebo, pearl, jade, morning, evening, day, night, wine, food. Individual objects can be peach, apricot, plum, willow, chrysanthemum, orchid, lotus, tea, wheat, pear, date, crane, goose, oriole, gull, egret, shrike, partridge, cuckoo, cicadas, frog, bass, mosquito, ant, horse, monkey, flute, bassoon, banjo, harp, guitar, boat, flag, palanquin …and so on. Objects are full of wonders and are numerous.   Mostly, when authors handle these contents, they will organize objects into a structure. For example, in the "Inscription of West Lake" by Ma Zhi Yuan:

暖日宜乘轎，warm days suit riding on a sedan chair
春風堪信馬，springtime, a tame horse

恰寒食有二百處秋千架。just by our humble fare are two
hundred swings
向人嬌杏花，toward us waft the delicate apricot blossoms
撲人衣柳花，alighting on our clothes fall the willow blossoms
迎人笑桃花。welcoming us, the laughing peach blossoms
來往畫船遊，to and fro travel the painted boats
招颭青旗掛。pure-blue banners hang beckoning in the wind

This is a Yuan poem of a spring scene, from the manmade artifacts of horse palanquin, swings, pleasure boats, green flags, blended with the natural scenery of apricot, willow and peach, which make the scene bustling and animating. The analytical structure of this Yuan poem is:

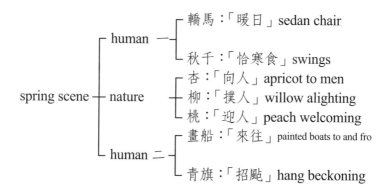

The horse palanquin, swings, pleasure boats, blue banners, apricot, willow and peach are objects of the poem, which bring out a sense of joy and unification from the external objective portions of the composition. Taking another poem for example from the same author "Meditation on Autumn"

枯藤、老樹、昏鴉。小橋、流水、人家。古道、西風、瘦馬。夕陽西下。斷腸人在天涯。

Withered vine, old tree, bleak raven, small bridge, flowing water, human hut, ancient path, west wind, gaunt horse, sunset in the west, the saddest soul at the fringe of the earth.

The purpose of this Yuan poem is to describe the hardship endured from wandering to the edge of the world.   It started with the space, using "withered vine" to describe what was seen at the roadside, using "ancient roadway" to portray what was on the roadway. Then followed the time frame, using "setting sun" to point out the time was dusk, to enhance the emotional effects.   Lastly, it changed from scenery to sentiment, exposing the sadness of the mindset of the traveler who felt "life was short" "wandering without destination," [26] and then ended with "broken hearted". The analytical structure of this Yuan poem is:

Nature：「枯藤老樹」withered vine; old tree

beside roads

human：「小橋流水人家」small bridge; flowing water; human hut

horse：「古道西風」ancient path ; west wind

in roads

man：「夕陽西下，斷腸人在天涯」sunset in the west; the saddest soul at the fringe of the earth

This Yuan poem contains abundant materials. But with simple sorting, its intention can be seen.   Obviously, it uses the sentiment

....

26 See Yang Tung, *Selections of Chinese Classic Literary Works*.《中國古代文學 名篇選讀》 (Tienchin: Nankai University Publishing Company, March 2001) p.62.

of "broken hearted" to summarize the "scene" observed on and by the roadway.

For the scenery of events, anything that has happened between heaven and earth could be materials for composition. From abstract events such as give and take, public and private, in and out, together and farewell, gain and loss, receiving and outgoing, to serve and to retire, sad and happy, suffer and enjoy, sing and dance, come and go, success and failure, vision and hearing, sober and drunk, dynamic and static, even dreaming, condolence over ancient events, mourning over recent events, home living, traveling, sighs over current events, sadness over separation, revenge, hatred, self improvement, home management, national politics, global events, common discussion, to eye witnesses, experiences, results... etc to more specific events such as on board a ship, picking a lotus, pacing around a room, reading, getting drunk, leaving the hometown, going home, invitations, going to an appointment, being sick, eating rice bran, touring a mountain, shedding tears, playing the zither, leaning on a cane, listening to cicadas, receiving a letter, opening a letter, buying liquor, preparing a meal, even filial duty, brotherly love, respect, trust, grace ...etc. These materials are everywhere and cannot be counted. Authors will usually choreograph with a specific event, and summarize with invisible abstract events. For example, the "Official in She Hao", a poem by Tu Fu:

暮投石壕村，(there, where at eve I sought a bed)
有吏夜捉人。(a pressgang came, recruits to hunt)
老翁踰牆走，(over the wall the Goodman sped)
老婦出看門。(and left his wife to bear the brunt)
吏呼一何怒，(ah me! The cruel serjeant's rage!)
婦啼一何苦。(ah me! how sadly she anon)
聽婦前致詞：(told her story's mournful page)
「三男鄴城戍，(how three sons to the war had gone)

一男附書至，(how one had sent a line to say)
二男新戰死。(that two had been in battle slain)
存者且偷生，(he, from the fight had run away)
死者長已矣。(but they could ne'er come back again)
室中更無人，(she swore 'twas all the family)
惟有乳下孫。(except a grandson at the breast)
有孫母未去，(his mother too was there, but she)
出入無完裙。(was all in rags and tatters drest)
老嫗力雖衰，(the crone with age was troubled sore)
請從吏夜歸。(but for herself she'd not think twice)
急應河陽役，(to journey to the seat of war)
猶得備晨炊。」(and held to cook the soldiers' rice)
夜久語聲絕，(the night wore on and stopped her talk)
如聞泣幽咽。(then sobs upon my hearing fell)
天明登前途，(At dawn when I set forth to depart,)
獨與老翁別。(Bid farewell to the old man alone)

The purpose of this poem is to record the brutality of the officials in She Hao, to reflect the suffering of the people and the darkness of the politics. The poem was composed in 759 A.D. during the era of Emperor Tang Su Zong.　The author was passing by Tung Kwan from Lo Yang on his way to Hua Zhou.[27] The poem opens with the first two lines to briefly point out what has happened, then it follows with an "old man escaped by jumping over the wall" and then 20 lines to lay out the facts, i.e., that the old man escaped and an old lady was detained.　Since it was the old lady that was detained, the poem uses only one line to mention what happened to the old man and nineteen lines to depict the detaining of the old lady.　Four of the nineteen lines are used to describe the plea she made to the

....

27 See the analysis of Ho Sung-lin, *Anthology of Tung Poetry.* 《唐詩大觀》
    (Hong Kong: the Commercial Bookstore, Jan.1986.) pp.483-484.

official, thirteen lines to reveal the contents of the plea.   From the three sons drafted by the military, with two sons killed in action, the grandson still being breast-fed, the daughter-in-law not having a fitting dress to go out of the house, to how and why it was only the old lady herself who could answer the morning kitchen duties of the military--step by step, it tells of the tragic suffering of that family. Two lines about the "long night" are used to imply that the plea was ineffective and the old lady was still being detained.   The "morning dawn" of the last two lines is used to subtly conclude the episode and also responds to the situation in the first three lines, stating that she would bid farewell to the old man alone at the dawn of the next morning.   These two lines look as if they are concluding the story with emphasis on the old man.   In reality, it includes the old lady.   From "Principles of Tang and Sung Poems" by Kao Pu Ying, "the ending with a farewell to the old man, being exit of the two opening lines, said more than the return of the old man." [28]   It was also pointed out in the article of "Tu Fu" by Liu Kai Yang, "The ending disclosed that the author 'back to continue the journal, bid farewell to the old man alone', it being obvious the old lady had been detained." [29]   With the ending by implying, the effects of subtlety and skills can be achieved.   The structure analysis is as follows:

.

[28] See *Major Tung Sung Poetry*. 《唐宋詩舉要》 (Taipei: Hsiehhai Publishing Company, Feb., 1973) p.68.

[29] See *Du-fu*《杜甫》 (Taipei: The World of Chinese Language and Monthly Literature, July 1991) p.58.

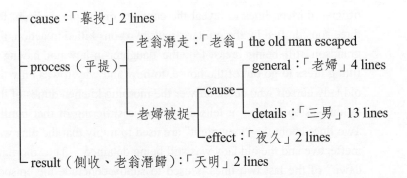

It can be said that events such as "the official arrests at night", "official screams", "a woman's cries", "voices subsiding", "weeping silently" and "farewell to the old man" form the images of the story and portray the sentiment behind the brutal acts of the local officials and suffering of the villagers. The structure is orderly and the contents easy to grasp.   From the "Book of Filial Piety: Amplification of 'The All-embracing Rule of Conducts'", whose purpose is to discuss the effects of the practice of filial duty.   Its structure is "to start with ease then hint from the sides."

教民親愛，(In teaching people to love each other) 莫善於孝；(filial piety is most important) 教民禮順，(In teaching people to know etiquette and to be compassionate) 莫善於悌；(respecting and loving elder brothers is best) 移風易俗，(In improving customs and tradition) 莫善於樂(music is best)；安上治民，(In making the ruling class properly and adequately rule people) 莫善於禮。(etiquette is best).

The starting point is: from "For teaching the people to be affectionate and loving"; the ending: "there is nothing better than the rules of propriety".   The thesis: to discuss filial piety and fraternal duties from the perspective of family order, then expand the scope to the ruling of the country by the discussion of music and propriety. From the "The Analects of Confucius, Chapter of Xue Er": "Filial piety and fraternal submission - are they not the root of all benevolent actions?" And from the text of "Ba Yi": "If a man be without the virtues proper to humanity, what has he to do with the rites of propriety? If a man be without the virtues proper to humanity, what has he to do with music?"--which identify the source of propriety and music as filial and fraternal duty, and that the results of practicing filial piety can be observed. The table of its structural analysis is:

```
                                    ┌─孝：「子曰」3 lines→ filial piety
        ┌─齊家 (ruling the family) ─┤
        │                           └─悌：「教民」2 lines→ fraternal
        │                                                   friendship
        │                           ┌─樂：「移風」2 lines→music
        └─治國 (ruling the country) ─┤
                                    └─禮：「安上」2 lines→rites
```

The author attempted to step away from the "events" of "filial piety" and "fraternal duties" toward "music" and "propriety" so as to demonstrate the "affections" that the core success of ruling a country stems from "home management", and "home management" starts with filial behavior. The content was exposed in such an order for the reader's ready understanding.

The physical materials in the examples above were mainly used to describe "scene (objects)", and the materials were used for descriptions of events. Whether the description was scenery or events, they all had their own "image" to portray. In this way, the congregation of individual texts came to make up a whole volume, while the core could be fused with the peripherals to form an integral composition.

3. Textual contents mainly concerning logical thinking

The contents of the sections and chapters that are based on logical thinking make up the order of the chapter. The chapter here is identical to the definition given by Liu Shie in his *The Literary Mind and the Carving of Dragons*, which was a portion of an episode. And the order of the text is based on the principle of the opposing characteristics of yin and yang, which deals with the logical relations among the contents within the composition [30] --namely, the organizational rules which combine sentences into a phrase, phrases into a paragraph and paragraphs into a chapter. There are about forty types of text regularity, such as present and past, permanent and temporary, far and near, in and out, left and right, high and low, large and small, change of angles, time and space chiasmus, change of conditions, transformational sense relations, beginning and end, shallow and deep, cause and result, parallel, situational, argumentative, panel discussion, trueness or falseness of space, trueness or falseness of time, supposition and facts, common vision, details and brevity, host and guest, positive and negative, established and uprooted, up and down, question and answer, frontal and sideways, expanded and extracted, tight and loose, intersection, complementary, part and whole, dye and point, heaven and human, the figure and background, and knocking ideas about or around. All these pairs and methods evolved from the common principles of human thinking which formed the rules for logic of thinking. They all carry the functional characteristics of forming order, variation,

....

[30] See Chen Man-ming, "On Compositional Art and Logical Thinking," *Papers of The Fourth Chinese Rhetoric International Conference.* 《第四屆中國修辭學國際學術研討會論文集》 (Taipei: Fu-jen Catholic University, May 2002) pp.1-32.   Also see Chen Man-ming, *The Philosophical Thinking of Compositional Art, Papers of Compositional Art.*   pp.40-67.

connection to further progress into a unified expression.   This so-called order, variation, connection and unification are the four principles of the chapter order.   Order, variation and connection are more analytical when associated with the usage of the writing materials.   And unification is used in affective expression that emphasizes connecting the emotion throughout the entire chapter. We shall discuss them as follows:

3.1 The law of order

The meaning of order is the arrangement of the materials in an orderly fashion.   Any text regularity can follow this rule with "fixation" (ascending, descending) to determine the order of priority. From the most common applications used, we may observe that the structure of the text can be formed from determining the order of priority. In the method of present and past, there is "present then past" (descending), "from past to present" (ascending).   In the "fiction or reality" method, "from fiction to reality" (ascending), "from reality to fiction" (descending).   In the "host and guest" method, "from guest to host" (descending), "from host to guest" (ascending).   The structures which are formed by these movements of ascending or descending orders can be seen everywhere.

For instance, the "A March, Short Song" by Cao Cao

對酒當歌 (Bringing up wine cups and happily singing)，人生幾何 (How many days can we have in our life)？譬如朝露 (Life is as short as morning dew)，去日苦多 (I am worried that so many days passed)。慨當以慷 (my mind can not be calmed.)。幽思難忘 (sad thoughts are lasting)。何以解憂 (how to get rid of sadness)？唯有杜康 (the only way is to drink wine)。青青子衿 (decent gentlemen)，悠悠我心 (I have missed you so long)。但為君故 (for your sake),沈吟至今 (I have been missing you)。呦呦鹿鳴 (deer cry),食野之苹 (when eating grass in wilderness)。我有嘉賓 (I have fine guests),鼓瑟吹笙 (so I play musical instruments)。明明如月 (under the bright moon),何時可掇 (when can I pick it up)?憂從中來 (sadness surges from my heart),不可斷絕 (it is ceaseless)。越陌度阡 (you travel a long way to visit me),枉用相存。契闊談讌 (we happily gather together and enjoy a party),心念舊恩 (my heart can not forget your grace of old days)。月明星稀 (the moon is bright and stars are scarce),烏鵲南飛 (birds fly south)。繞樹三匝 (they fly around the tree three times),何枝可依 (they do know which branch they can rely on)?山不厭高 (mountains can be enormously high),海不厭深 (sea can be enormously deep)。周公吐哺 (Choukung spat out meat),天下歸心 (I will win the heart of the world)。

The theme of this poem is to express the disappointment the author felt that there had been no capable talent to help him unify China. Fu Gung Sheng thought it "meant principally to recruit talent." [31] With the structure of "from cause to result," for the "result", from the beginning to "which branch to rest" at the end, it follows the same sequence of " from result to cause". It uses the first eight lines of "facing liquor" to express sadness because life is short (cause), so only liquor can relieve its worrisome anxieties. The following eight lines from "the green lappet of your gown" are the facts, to show those intellectuals who had not submitted their services to the author how much he desired their contribution (negative, passive). It also reiterated how much he welcomed and was thankful for those who had already joined him, and he would

....

31 See Fu Ken-shen, *Appreciation of Chinese Literature.* 《中國文學欣賞舉隅》 pp.66-67.

continue his courteous treatment of them (positive, aggressive). The next eight lines from "bright as the full moon" were abstract, expressing the complex contrast of anxiety about when he might acquire the services of the intellectuals and how he would realize his ultimate goal.   The last four lines, which use the scene in which the crows could not find a branch to rest upon under the moonlight reveal how pitiful he felt those intellectuals were who had not had a master.   These twenty lines start with sentimental expression and follow by description of the scenery.   The fusion of sentiment and scenery are the cause.   The four lines from "a mountain will not regret being mighty" are metaphor (abstract), while the story of Chou Kung is used to declare the author's tireless eagerness to seek the services of the wise.   It also shows the vision the author had after the world had been unified (fact).[32]   The manipulation of these methods of "from result to cause", "from cause to result", "from negative to positive", "from sentiment to scenery", "from facts to the abstract" and "from abstract to facts" successfully exhibit the author's concerns for intellectuals and his desires for unification. The diagram of the structural analysis is as follows:

....

[32] See *Dictionary of Poems of Han Wei Chin and Sue Dynasties*.   (Taiyun: Shansi People Publishing Company, March 1989) p.123.

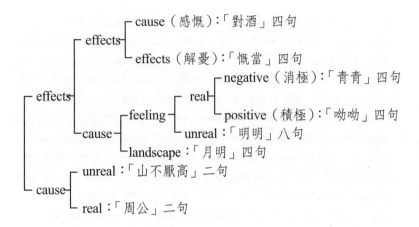

These "orderly" structures, whether they are complaisant or contrary, are the materials which the author has arranged and organized by following the human characteristic of perusing the order and the process of logical evaluation. This type of combination is referred to as "repetition", and is a form of "unification". Chen Xue Fan said in his article:

The simplest form is repetition, which means that a thing repeats itself again and again. In terms of other constituencies, repetition is uniformity. Accordingly, the rule of repetition is the one of uniformity. Originally, the rule of uniformity or repetition is an extremely simple form. However, it can be applied everywhere in order to gain simple pleasure.[33]

"So-called formality is entirely the relevant union among matters,[34] say 'from A to B', and the orderly union (same matter)

....

33 See *General Introduction to Aesthetics*. 《美學概論》 (Taipei: Wenchin Cultural Business Company, Dec. 1984) pp.61-62.

34 See *General Introduction to Aesthetics*. 《美學概論》 p. 60.

between A and B. Thus it can be seen that the order in the text, if seen from a different perspective, is repetition and unification, which is very common in logical thinking."

3.2 Law of Change

So-called variation is to break the sequential order of materials in the text. The order of every text may be applied following this rule, with the effects of crisscrossing achieved by alternating orders.   We can observe these arrangements from what we have seen from the examples above, such as in the methods of positive and negative: "positive, negative, positive", "negative, positive, negative", "constructive, destructive, constructive", "destructive, constructive, destructive", "cause, result, cause", "result, cause, result".   These alternating structures by crisscrossing orders are fairly common. For example, from Su Shi's "Magnolia":

雙龍對起 (Two pines stand like dragons)。白甲蒼髯煙雨裏 (in foggy rains pine branches are like hairs of the dragon)。疏影微香 (shadows of the pine branches are interwoven and fragrance can be smelt)。下有幽人畫夢長 (the day dream of men are long)。湖風清軟 (on the surface of the lake winds are clear and soft)。雙鵲飛來爭噪晚 (birds fly making noise)。翠颭紅輕 (red flowers and green leaves)。時下凌霄百尺英 (so high, quivering in the wind)。

This Cu poem was composed in Sungshentsung's seventh year (in 1074) ,[35] There was a monk poet living in West Lake.   Before his house were two ancient pine trees.   He often slept under the trees.   One day when I passed by, pine winds flew and flowers fell

....

35 See Chou Tung-chin, Wang Chun-tan, *Su Shih's Cu Notes.* 《蘇軾詞編年校注》 (Beijing: Chunhua Bookstore, 2002). p.63.

so beautifully that the monk asked me to write a poem for this. The first three lines are about the scene of the two ancient pine trees, which serves as a first "guest." And then, the line depicting the sleeping monk functions as "master." Finally, the four lines following 「湖風」 (lake wind) depict the scene of flying birds on the tree, which serves as another "guest." Apparently, the ancient pine trees and fallen flowers serve as "guest," while the monk serves as "master." So, the Cu poem is framed by the structure of "guest, master, guest." The structure analysis diagram is as follows.


```
            ┌ real（樹身）:「雙龍」二句
┌ Guest —（古松）┤
│            └ unreal（影香）:「疏影」句
│
├ Master—（幽人）:「下有」句
│
│            ┌ cause :「湖風」三句
└ Guest —（落花）┤
            └ effects :「時下」句
```

This regularity among variation actually has its basis in human psychology.　Chen Xua Fan says in his "Staring at the Way":

Humans by nature like the stimulus of variety. Generally speaking, evoking consciousness needs variety. And it also needs variety to keep consciousness awake. If stimuli are too uniformed and lack variations our consciousness will become slow in responding, or even stop reacting to them completely.　In terms of this basic human nature, the form of repetition has apparent weakness. Indeed, repetition serves as events which repeatedly stimulate us. In case of excessive repetitions, consciousness would become dull, turning to another stimulus of variety and change.[36]

....

36 See *General Introduction to Aesthetics.* 《美學概論》 pp. 63-64.

"the analysis and grasp of variation of the structure brings closer understanding of the author's thought"

3.3 Law of Consistency

So-called "consistency" refers to the linkages and responses among materials, which is also called "linkage",   It does not matter which chapter order is used, linkage and response can be established by creating a partially harmonized or contrastive environment, the effects thus being connected. In the forty or so methods, with the exception of noble and humble, blood relatives and unrelated, positive and negative, depressed and uplifted, constructive and destructive, numerous and few, detailed and brief, compressed and loose …etc, with which it is relatively easy to form a "contrast"; with others, such as "now and then", "far and near", "large and small", "high and low", "shallow and deep", "host and guest", "virtual and actual", "release and receive" …and so on, it is easier to form a harmonized relation.   Some relations can only be clarified by examining the chapter structure. In the "Song of Midnight" by Mr. Anonymous:

儂作北辰星 (I am a star in the North)，千年無轉移 (never moving for a thousand years)。歡行白日心 (your departure showed your heart as the morning sun)，朝東暮還西 (rising in the east and falling in the west)。

This poem aims to describe the feelings of regret.   It begins with the positive side, comparing her feelings to 「北辰星」 (a star in the North).   And then, from the opposite side, the author compares her beloved person's departure to 「白日」 (morning sun). In this way, a strong contrast is made to show the strong feelings of dissatisfaction. 」[37] : And the contrast makes the poem consistent and unified.   The structure analysis diagram is as follows.

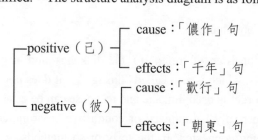

Actually, harmony and contrast are not always rigid.   Harmony, observed from a certain angle, refers to the state of unification before contrast.   And contrast, if seen from a post event situation, it would form a harmonized and unified state. These two can be constantly interacting and circulating and form a spiral structure, as stated by Chiu Ming Cheng:[38]

The principle of oppositions penetrate the whole psychological movement of evaluating and creating beauty. It is omnipresent. However, the psychological movement of aesthetics is paradoxically contradictory and unified. Through conscious or unconscious self adaptation, which might compromise all kinds of contradictions, the contradictions and oppositions might become unified and harmonious in psychology of subjective aesthetics. For example, the adaptation of the subjective to the

....

[37] See La Shao-pa, Si Man-chun's analysis, *Dictionary of Appraisals of Classic Poetry.* 《古詩鑑賞辭典》 (Beijing: Chinese Women Publishing Company, Dec. 1998) p.1126.

[38] Two opposite things will produce interaction, cycling and elevation, resulting in a spiral structure.   See Chen Man-ming, "On the Spiral Structure of Confucius Thoughts Systems," (Taipei: Taiwan Normal University, Chinese Journal, June 2000) pp.1-34.

objective is a process of transforming contradictions to unification. Even if the subjective mind still cannot adapt themselves to the objective reality, or even feels repulsion, the psychology of the subjects is in a state of harmony. The principle of opposition and unification reflects the fact that despite opposition and rejection, the two contradictory parties mutually transform and unify the contradictory movement rules. The common rules of opposition and unification of the whole universe reflect themselves on the aesthetic psychology.[39]

Analysis and appraisal are descending processes trod from the end toward the source (psychology, conceptualization) whereas creation acts oppositely, being an ascending process starting from the source and moving toward the end.   The principals involved are identical; if the order of the chapter can be analyzed for appraisal, the mindset of the author when composing this article can then be understood. Order and variation follow this rule, so do harmony and contrast, which form the connection.

3.4 Law of Unification

So-called unification means the emotional consistency of the materials.   Usually, achieving unification of rhetorical composition must be done through topic (sentiment) and guidelines (referring to the materials used).   Any rhetorical composition, despite its types, may use this method to unite its themes.   In Shen Fu's "Memories from Childhood":

余憶童稚時 (I recollected my childhood)，能張目對日 (I could open my eyes to stare at the sun)，明察秋毫 (I can even

....

[39] See *Psychology of Aesthetics.* 《審美心理學》 (Shanghai: Futan University Publishing Company, April 1993) pp. 94-95.

observe the tiniest thing)。見藐小微物 (in seeing the tiny things)，必細察其紋理 (I always observed their constructive structures)，故時有物外之趣 (So, I often had fun outside the material world)。

夏蚊成雷 (in summer, mosquitoes flied in groups)，私擬作群鶴舞空 (I personally compared them to cranes flying together in the sky)，心之所向 (as my heart goes)，則或千或百 (hundreds or thousands of mosquitoes)，果然鶴也 (were really like cranes)；昂首觀之 (I looked up)，項為之強 (my neck was sore for this)。又留蚊於素帳中 (and I let mosquitoes stay in the white)，徐噴以煙 (I slowly let out cigarette smoke)，使之沖煙飛鳴 (making them rush to smoke making noise)，作青雲白鶴觀 (I imagined them to be cranes on white clouds)；果如鶴唳雲端 (they were like cranes crying on the clouds)，為之怡然稱快 (I was so happy for this)。又常於土牆凹凸處 (I often on the crooked places of mud wall)，花臺小草叢雜處 (on the places of flourishing flowers and grasses)，蹲其身 (lowered down my body)，使與臺齊 (making it as high as the flower stadium)；定神細視 (I concentrated my mind to make observations)，以叢草為林 (considering grass to be forests)，蟲蟻為獸 (considering worms and ants to be animals)，以土牆凸者為丘 (considering high places of mud walls to be hills)，凹者為壑 (considering low places of mud walls to be valleys)；神遊其中 (imagining myself travelling there)，怡然自得 (I did enjoy myself)。

一日 (one day)，見二蟲鬥草間 (I saw two worms fight each other on grass)，觀之 (when I was watching this)，興正濃 (I was so intensely interested in this)，忽有龐然大物 (suddenly a huge monster appeared)，拔山倒樹而來 (it seemed to pull mountains and crush trees)，蓋一癩蛤蟆也 (it turned out to be a frog-like animal)。舌一吐而二蟲盡為所吞 (it stuck out its tongue eating two worms)。余年幼 (I was so small)，方出神 (I forgot myself)，不覺呀然驚恐 (I was so astonished)。神定

(and then, I came back to myself)，捉蛤蟆 (I caught the toad)，鞭 數 十 (I severely punished it)，驅 之 別 院 (forcing it outside)。

The purpose of this writing is to recall the joy gained beyond the boundaries of physical limitations. The structure used is of the type "from summary to list". The summary is the first paragraph of the article, the author directly recalling, from cause to result, and pointing out the topic of "joy gained beyond the boundaries of physical limitations" that connects the entire writing. The listings make up the second, third and fourth paragraphs. In the second paragraph, the author uses a swarm of mosquitoes as an example. He analyzes their texture and portrays them as cranes, describing how they fly in the sky and how their calls could be heard above the clouds. The author is so attracted by what he has seen that his neck muscles grew tense, and he has definitely enjoyed going beyond the boundaries of physical limitations. In the section on "cranes dancing in the sky", while the "summer mosquitoes loud as thunder" is within the physical boundaries, from the "cranes dancing in the sky" to "they were actually cranes flying" goes beyond the boundaries. The part "pretending as" is used as a bridge to connect to the parts that comes after. The part about "joy beyond physical limitations" is connected by "tilt my head and observe" and then "until my neck stiffened" with what he means by "joy beyond physical limitations". In the section with the "crane calls above the clouds", from "the mosquitoes stay" to "fly up as smoke rising" is within the boundaries, the following two lines from "blue clouds" were beyond boundary. With the bridging word "make", this makes up the part about "observing details". As to the theme of "joy beyond boundaries of physical limitations", the bridging word is "being" and the enjoyment is seen in the "happily cheerful" part. In the third section, the author takes the weeds by a dirt wall and the wandering insects as targets of fantasy. He portrays the thick grass as jungle and the insects as wild animals, and this is where the author gains his "joy beyond the boundaries of physical limitations", and this is listing number two. In the part about "observing details", from "I always went to" to "even with the platform" is the part within the boundaries, while the worms and ants that from "inside the weeds" to "pretend the dent is a ravine" is the part outside the physical boundaries, the bridge being "concentrate and observe". The "joy beyond the boundaries of physical limitations" is denoted by "happily cheerful". In the last section, there are two bugs and a toad in the grass, the toad being portrayed as a humongous monster who swallows the two bugs with a slurp of the tongue. The author then catches the toad, punishes it with 10 whip lashes, exiles it to his backyard and gains his "joy beyond the boundaries of physical limitations", this being listing number three. The part about "observing details" starts with "one day" and is followed with two lines from "within the boundaries", the two lines from "observing" being the bridge and the lines from "all of a sudden" to "unconscious" being a description of "outside the physical boundaries". The part "It was a toad" is the bridge and "focused attention" is the connecting phrase while the three lines from "apprehending the toad" are the "joy beyond the boundary of physical limitations". One special note: this "joy beyond the boundaries of physical limitations" carries us back to the beginning of the events "within the physical boundaries". It is very obvious that the entire writing is connected by the sense of "joy beyond the limitations of physical boundaries" and never deviates from the word "joy", being crisscrossed with "cause and result" to maintain consistency throughout the whole composition. The structural table of analysis is as follows:

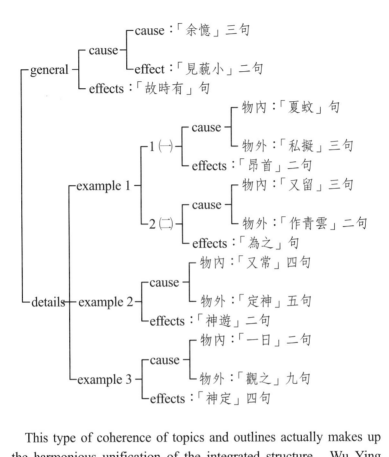

This type of coherence of topics and outlines actually makes up the harmonious unification of the integrated structure. Wu Ying Tien stated in his book *The Structure of Literature*:

> In addition, there are the unification of viewpoints and materials, and the unification of perspectives and evidence. This is the problem of logical thinking, also taking care of the psychological factors of harmony.[40]

....

40 See *Compositional Structuralism,* 《文章結構學》 p.359.

Even though this style is for argumentative prose, it can be utilized by other types of writing. This "union of perspectives and materials", in a broader sense, is the union of the topics or the guidelines with the materials of the whole article. This kind of unification, when consolidated with the unification at the level of text structure, will help push the text as a whole towards the highest level of harmony. This harmony is achieved through a combination of contents and form. It may be regarded as the result of applying composite thinking. Wu Ying Tien also stated:

Actively engaging in synthetic thinking can help the content and form of a text to rapidly reach a high degree of unification. Furthermore, this can serve the purpose of knowing the ordinary and being able to cope with the extraordinary. [41]

We can see the importance of logical thinking and composite thinking.

It is said, "all people think in the same way and all thoughts share the same principle." This principle, is sincerity from another aspect. When reflected philosophically it becomes the principle of philosophy and when reflected in the realm of the arts (music, painting, film, etc.) it becomes the principles of the arts. When it is projected into literature, it naturally becomes the principles of literature. If we take one step further, when this principle is projected into the order of chapters, it becomes the principles of the chapter order, which are order, variation, connection and unification. These four principles can form the basis of psychology and present elements of "truth". They also serve as the basis for rules of composition and present a sense of "perfection". In terms of aesthetics, they help achieve the effects of "beauty". This is the

....

[41] See *Compositional Structuralism*, 《文章結構學》 p.353.

most reasonable way to regard these four principles.

4. Textual contents mainly concerning composite thinking

This basically means the combining of the sources of the entire imagery with the theme and style. Thematology, from what was quoted in the last section from *The Principles and Practices of Thematology* by Chen Peng Shian, ordinary themes include lexis, imagery and topic. In a single chapter, from the perspective of single topics, this means language of sentiment, language of reasoning, imagery, and topics (guidelines included). Since the function of sentimental and reasoning language is to highlight the topics, they can be treated as one. Therefore, the themes of a chapter basically include the topics and the images, which are a composite of image thinking and logical thinking. It has multiple aspects as far as the style of the chapter is concerned. From the perspectives of true literature, as stated in the last section, this includes stylistics, author, school, time frame, region, ethnicity and creativity. Regarding a composition, its style can be observed from its contents and formation (art). Contents involve the theme (topics and imagery), and the formation (art) has to do with grammar, rhetoric and order. The characteristics of a creation is the illustrated beauty of the integrated entity of contents and formation; this is how the author pulls his logical and image thinking together to control the theme, rhetoric, order and other specifics to portray the characters of the writing as one unit.

Two aspects of the theme need to be given attention; they are the topics and the guidelines. Since the two belong to the same premises of the theme, there is a common point between the two, which is that they both must be consistent and coherent throughout the entire composition. The difference is the topic is the center of expressions of the entire composition and the guidelines are the veins to connect the materials of the composition. Using a string-of-pearl necklace as an example, the various sizes of the pearls are the materials, the string that keeps the pearls together with the guidelines; the main purpose of the pearl necklace is to decorate. This ultimate purpose is like the theme of a composition.

There are two points that need to be given more attention: "the transparency or opacity of the topic", and "the position where the topic appears". The transparency or opacity of the topic concerns whether the topic is clearly pointed out in the composition, and based on this point, there are situations that can be developed: "total transparency of the topic", "total obscurity of the topic" and "obscurity among the transparency of the topic". These examples can be seen in "Petition for Mercy" by Lee Mee, "Answer for a Good Horse" by Yue Fei and "Discourse of the Six Kingdoms" by Su Shuen. There are four positions where the topic may appear: it may appear in the beginning, in the middle, at the end, and it may appear outside the context. These situations can be observed in the examples, "Admonishment against Eviction of a Guest" by Lee Si, "Song of a Pi-pa Player" by Bai Ju Yi, "Record of the Yue Yang Building" by Fan Zhong Yen and "Farewell with Meng Hao Zen at the Huang He Building" by Li Pao.

As for the guidelines, the tracks of the composition are determined by the number of its veins. Supposed the topic of a composition is "industriousness and laziness", then there are two tracks for the guidelines, industriousness and laziness, the topic may have something to do with being industrious. If the topic of the composition is "yesterday, today and tomorrow", then yesterday, today and tomorrow will be the three tracks of the topic and the main topic could be related to cherishing one's time. Thus the outline can be a monorail, double tracks, triple rails or even multi-tracks. An example of a monorail is the "picking of mulberry" in "Beauties of West Lake"; an example of a double track can be seen in "An Old Horse Knows Its Way" in "Guan Zhong, Shi Peng" by

Han Fei Zi, and an example of a triple track is "Waiting for the moon to rise while touring six bridges at evening" in (spring, moon, morning and evening clouds) by Yuan Hung Dao.[42]

Usually, the topic and the guidelines coincide, such as in "Memories from Childhood". However, there are times when this is not true, which can be seen in "Records of the Grand Historian: The Analects of Confucius":

太史公曰（Taishihkung said）:《詩有之》（there were two lines in Shihching）。「高山仰止」（people can look up to mountains），「景行行之」（people can walk on wide roads）。雖不能至（although we cannot as great as Confucius）；然心鄉往之（my heart admired him）。余讀孔氏書（I read his book），想見其為人（I wanted to know his personality）。適魯（I went to Lu Nation），觀仲尼廟堂，車服，禮器（I observed his temple, carts, clothes and vessels）。諸生以時習禮其家(students regularly came here to learn etiquettes)，余低回留之（I lingered there），不能去云（I could not leave）。天下君王至於賢人眾矣（kings and able men were many in the world），當時則榮（they were glorified in the world），沒則已焉（embracing nothing after death）。孔子布衣（as a ordinary citizen, Confucius），傳十餘世（has been remembered for generations），學者宗之（scholars admired him）。自天子王侯（emperors and princes），中國言六藝者（when it comes to six arts）折中於夫子（confucius was a standard），可謂至聖矣！（He was indeed a holy man!）

This work is framed by the structure of general/guideline, details, general/topic." The first part of "generalization/guideline" from the first line to 「然心鄉往之」(my heart admired him) uses the

....

[42] The above-mentioned guidelines, tasks, and topics can be seen Chen Man-ming's *Views of Compositional Art*. 《章法學綜論》 pp.1-506.

two lines--「高山仰止，景行行止」(people can look up to mountains; people can walk on wide roads)—to introduce 「鄉往」 (admire) as a guideline for the following lines. For the part of "details," the lines from 「余讀孔氏書」 (I read his books) to 「折中於夫子」 (Confucius was a standard) use the method of "from small to big" to explain the meanings with three sections. In the first section, he wrote about what he thought and saw in 「讀孔氏書」 (reading his books) and 「觀仲尼廟堂」 (observing his temple). In addition, the author uses the lines--「想見其為人」(I wanted to know his personality) 與「低回留之，不能去云」(I lingered there; I could not leave)—to express his admiration of Confucius. In the second line, he contrasts Confucius with 「天下君王至於賢人」(kings and able men). And then, he uses 「學者宗之」(scholars admire him) to express how the scholars of Confucialism admire Confucius. Furthermore, in the third section, he uses 「折中於夫子」(Confucius was a standard) to express scholars' universal admiration of Confucius. And for the second part of "generalization" (topic), he uses the line--「可謂至聖矣」 (he was indeed a holy man) to reveal the topic, echoing the beginning lines. The structure analysis diagram is as follows.

```
┌ general (guideline)：「太史公曰」六句
│            ┌ detail 1（自身）：「余讀」八句
├ details ┤ detail 2（孔門學者）：「天下」六句
│            └ detail 3（天下讀書人）：「自天子」三句
└ general (topic)：「可謂至聖矣」
```

It can be seen that the author uses 「鄉往」(admiration) as a guideline, and employed his own, Confucius' students', and all other scholars' universal admiration of Confucius to praise Confucius greatly. Despite its brevity, the meaning is so profound that the feelings of admiration seem to linger forever.

Accordingly, this work uses topic (holy man) and guidelines (admiration) to unify the images (events) of the whole work.   In addition, the author puts the guideline at the beginning of this work, placing the topic at the end.   This underlines the feature of the author's synthetic thinking.

In terms of style, the "hardness" and "softness" formed by "binary oppositions of Yin and Yang" can be said to be the mother of all kinds of styles.   In deed, it is not until Yao Ni of the Qing Dynasty that "hardness" and "softness" were clearly explained and used to generalize all kinds of styles. He divided styles into "hardness" and "softness".   The styles such as spacious, active, open, and awesome belong to the type of "hardness." In addition, the styles such as conservative, indirect, decent, and opaque belong to the type of "softness." [43]   And, the presentation of "hardness" and "softness" mainly depends on the compositional types formed by "binary oppositions." [44]   Take Wang Wei's poem, for example.

萬壑樹參天 (in countless valleys trees soar to the skies)，千山響杜鵑 (a thousand peaks resound with cuckoos' cries)。山中一夜雨 (a heavy rain in the mountains all night)，樹杪百重泉 (brings cascades from the tree-tops on the height)。漢女輸橦布 (with "tong" flower cloth Han women pay tribute)，巴人訟芋田 (on taro fields Ba people may dispute)。文翁翻教授 (Instruct the people like the ancient sage)，不敢倚先賢 (in glory only for the bygone sages)。

....

43 See Chou Chen-fu, *Examples of Literary Styles*. 《文學風格例話》p.13.

44 Compositional art can be soft, hard, yin, and yang through the analyses of order, position, blending, contrast.   See Chen Man-ming, "On the Styles of Compositional Art." *Papers Collection of Rhetoric.* 《修辭論叢》 (Taipei: Hungye Cultural Business Company, Nov. 2003.) pp.1-51.

This is a poem of gift for a friend which describes the local scenery and the customs, and contains hidden praises.[45] The structure of the poem is "from reality to the virtual". The first three paragraphs are a description of the actual scene. The first four lines are about the scenery surrounding "Zi Zhou"; the following two lines, from "Han girl," concern the local customs of Zi Zhou. The two lines from "Thousands of valleys" are a visual as well as an acoustical sensation of the scenery seen from afar. The two lines from "in the mountain" use the structure of "from long term to temporary" to describe the nearby scenes. The two lines from "Han girls" use the order of "from positive to negative" to describe the local customs. The last two lines are the "virtual" part to praise the host at the end. This is a very skillful writing which covered location, events and personnel. Yu So Zhen stated in his detailed analysis:

The first four lines of this poem are an remembrance of Zi Zhou's marvelous scenes. This refers to "places". In addition, the repeated usage of「山樹」(mountain trees) indeed follows the expression of「千山萬壑」(a thousand peaks and countless valleys) .This emerges as a typical example of repeated expressions in a poem. Moreover, 「巴人漢女」(Ba people and Han women) is used to describe the customs of Shuchun. This refers to "events." Finally, the instruction of the people refers to "people". In the final two lines, it can be seen that despite their poverty these people still can be instructed. The policy of teaching is sustainable. Indeed,these inhabitants are obedient to orders.[46]

....

45 See Yu Shou-chen, *Detailed Analysis of Tung Dynasty Three Hundred Poems.* (Taipei: Taiwan Chunhua Bookstore, April 1996) p.147.

46 See *Analysis of Tung Dynasty Three Hundred Poems.*《唐詩三百首詳析》

This is a very deep analysis and helps the readers to understand the poem. The following is a table of its structural analysis:

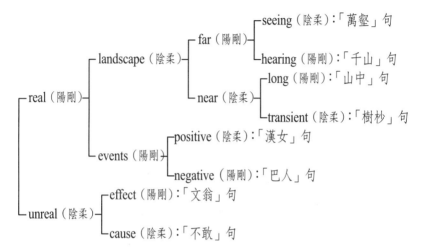

For an illustration of the degrees of "sublime" and "beauty" of its structure, see the following table:

Top level	second	third	bottom

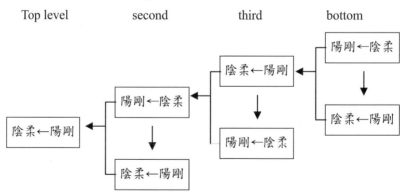

The structure of this poem consists of four layers. The topmost layer, "from reality to the virtual" (opposite of movement) is the core of the structure. Its trend proceeds from masculine to feminine. The next layer consists of a two "movement" structure one is "from scene to events" (docile) and the other "from result to cause" (opposing), with its trend moving from "masculine to feminine" and "masculine to feminine". The third layer has a two "movement" structure as well. One is "from far to near" (opposing) and the other "from positive to negative" (docile, contrast), with the trend advancing as "masculine → feminine" → "feminine → masculine". The bottom layer consists of a two "movement" structure of "from visual sensation to acoustical sensation" (docile) and "from long-term to temporary" (opposing) with a trend of "feminine→masculine" →"masculine→ feminine". In summary, the trend of this poem has four feminine structures and three masculine structures. We can observe that while the feminine lines are the major one and more aggressive, the masculine lines are the minor and more passive. Especially in its core structure, [47] the topmost layer ended with feminine lines. We can therefore conclude that this poem has feminine characteristics. [48] Chou Zhen Fu analyzed this point as follows:

....

[47] See Chen Man-ming, "On the Core Structure of Many, Two, One/Zero." (Taipei: *Taiwan Normal University Journal*, 《師大學報》Dec. 2003) pp.71-94.

[48] This poem is structured by four levels. On the top level is the core structure of "first real and then unreal" (reverse, changing position) with the symbolic number of "yin 16, yang 8." On the second level is two position changing structure—"first landscspe and then event" (sequential), and "first effect and then cause"—with the numbers of "yin 19, yang 14." On the third level are two changing position structures—"first far and then near" (reverse), and "first positive and then negative" (sequential, contrast)—with the numbers of "yin 12, yang 12." On the bottom level are two changing position structures of "first seeing and then hearing" (sequential), and "first long and then transient" (reverse)—with the numbers of "yin 5, yang 4." Totally speaking, the sum of the numbers is "yin 58, yang 42." This is close to a "soft" style. See Chen Man-ming's "On Compositional Styles." p.28.

Chi Yun's comments on the first four lines of Wang Wei's poem is "it's as high as rising clouds." And Hsu Ying-fang describes them as" "of great power." So, the style is of strength and sublime. Furthermore, it is worth attention that Hsu Ying-fang views this poem as clear, high, strong and spacious. In terms of sense, it is clear and high. Trees in countless valleys soar to the skies. A thousand peaks resound with cuckoos' cries. And a heavy rain in the mountains all night brings cascades from the tree-tops on the height. These are the sublime scenes of mountains. Cleanness does express a clear and high sense. However, in terms of natural scenes, this poem is of great power. Without the appreciation of the clear and high sense, we cannot praise the natural scenes or express the sublime style. This is worth our discussion.[49]

The sentiment underlying the contents, the "taste", from the perspective of a rhetorical text, is the determining force behind everything. Since this poem has a fresh, long-lasting flavor in taste and the scenery is majestic, then suffice it to say this poem is basically fresh (feminine) with traces of majesty (masculine). If this assumption is acceptable, this phenomenon can be explained by the masculine and feminine lines that emerge from the "logical structure of the contents" (structure of the text's order). As a whole, even the trend of this poem inclines toward the feminine, but it is very near a state of equilibrium between the feminine and masculine, which is on the highest plateau of aesthetics.[50]

Since this poem has a fresh, long-lasting flavor in taste and the scenery is majestic, then suffice it to say this poem is basically replete fresh (feminine) with traces of majesty (masculine). If this

....

[49] See *Examples of Literary Styles.* 《文學風格例話》 p.49.
[50] See Chen Wan-hen, *History of Chinese Classic Aesthetics.* 《中國古典美學史》 (Changsha: Hunan Education Publishing Company, Aug. 1998) p.202.

assumption is acceptable, this phenomenon can be explained by the masculine and feminine trends that emerge from the "logical structure of the contents" (structure of the text's order). As a whole, even the trend of this poem inclines toward the feminine, but it is very near a state of equilibrium between the feminine and masculine, which is on the highest plateau of aesthetics, which combins meanings and morphemes.

Be it the topics or the stylistics of a composition, it cannot deviate from "semantic imagery", a result of "composite thinking" and a combination of "image thinking" and "logical thinking".

5. The "many, two, one/zero" structure of expressions and compositions

Both in philosophy and in aesthetics, the concepts of "unity in opposition", "unity in multitude", "two in one" or "from multiple to one" are very important. They are always regarded as the principal changes in aesthetics and seem to leave no more room for further discussion. However, with appropriations from the ancient books, *The Book of Changes and of Lao-tzu*, it can be made more accurate and complete. Not only can a more "multitude, two, one (0)" be reversed structure can be found from "vividness" to "void", a more forward structure of "(0) one, two, multitude" can be found as well. In *Lao-tzu*, Chapter Forty states: "Repetition is the moving force of the Tao", and in Chapter Sixteen "Even though there are numerous things in the world, they all have to return to their roots in the end"; also in *The Book of Changes*, in the chapter on "the orderly sequence of the Hexagrams" the discussion of "already" and "not yet", the connection between the forward and reversed structures not only unfolds in sequence, it becomes a repeated and endless rising spiral structure in the reflection of the never-ending lives of the universe.[51] This type of rule or structure can be used in philosophy, literature, aesthetics and many other subjects, or everything to which it is applicable.   When used in literature or aesthetic creation, the "(0), one, two, multitude" may illustrate the forward process of creation, whereas "multitude, two, one (0)" illustrates the reversed process of aesthetics.   The same can be applied to rhetorical order.

The four major rules of rhetorical order fall in lines with the structure of "multitude, two, one (0)".   "Order and variation" would be "multitude"; connection is basically "two" (yang and ying), and union "one (0)".   This sequence of multitude, two, and one, highlight the relations formed by the four rules and are not parallel but a "many, two, one (0)" logical structure.

When this "multitude, two, one (0)" structure is applied to rhetorical composition, all the other structures other than the core structure, belong to "multitude".   The "two opposing elements" that form the core structure, being opposing yet attracting, and connected through up and down, with harmonious and contrasting characteristics, are two.   Conversely, the topic or the style (taste, atmosphere, level), formed by unification, would be "one (0)".   What is more, the use of (0) for style to represent the abstract power of rhetorical composition would be very appropriate.[52]

If we expand the discussion to rhetorical composition, there is the same spiral structure of multitude, two and one (0). The multitude would be the artistic representation of rhetoric, grammar, imagery and text order.   "Two" means the image thinking (feminine) and

....

51 See *Laotze*,"Word Born One." Taichi of Yingchuan is "one/zero." Laotze , two "born by one"; Liangyi of Yingchuan is "two." *Laotze*'s "three gives birth to all creatures." "Four Hsiang gives birth to eight Kua" means "many." See Chen Man-ming, "On Many, Two, One/Zero, A Spiral Structure—Focus on Chouyi and Laotze." (Taipei: Taiwan Normal University Journal, April 2003) pp.1-19.

52 See Chen Man-ming, *Views of Compositional Art.* 《章法學綜論》 pp.227-270.

logical thinking (masculine), and the reaction attained with the up and down connection. The "one (0)" is the "topic" and the "style" highlighted by this structure. This is the sincerity stated in *The Book of Changes*, "sincerity established by rhetoric", being the core of rhetorical composition. When rhetorical composition is dissected by "multitude, two, one(0)", the buffer effect of "two" ("image thinking"[feminine] and "logic thinking"[masculine]), the multitudes (image, lexis, rhetoric, grammar, order) may be unified with "one" (topic and style).

The buffering "two", namely "image thinking" and "logical thinking" may be integrated by "sense imaging"(whole entity). Viewed from the formation and behavior of "sense imaging", we find that it has to do with "image thinking". The elements involved with image thinking are "sensing" (sentiment, reasoning) and "imaging" (events, scenery) and the impression given by the combined effects of the two. The fields that discuss the union of "sensing" (sentiment, reasoning) and "imagery" (events, scenery) are lexicology and imagology (narrow sense). The discussion of the performance of sensing and imagery is rhetoric. When looked at from the perspectives of the organizational and sequential order, we find that it has to do with logical thinking. And the elements of logical thinking are the arrangements of "sensing and imaging" (sense and sense, image and image, sense and image, sense images and sense images). The field that involves the order of chapters is composition stylistics, and its major role is to seek the arrangement of sensing and imaging. The area that involves imagery and lexical grammar would be grammar, and its major role is to seek organizational order among the conceptions. From these arguments we may see that image thinking, logical thinking and the other major contents of rhetorical texts, cannot deviate from "sense imaging". Topics and styles are highlighted by this aspect. The relationship can be summarized by the following table.

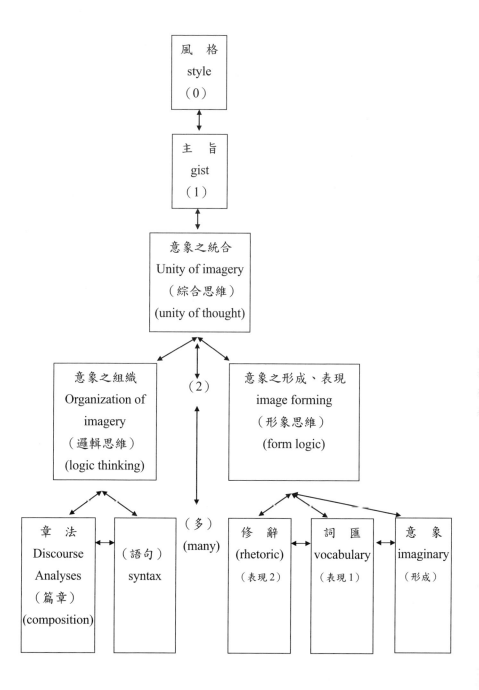

Thus we can see that rhetorical composition cannot depart from "sense imaging". The same can be said about topic and style, because topic is the sentiment underlying the core and style is the abstract summation, presentation and organization of all images under topic.   This is why rhetorical composition is dependent on sense images and if an originating source is sought, it should be the statement of Confucius: "Establish an image to complete the expression" in *The Book of Changes*.   Yeh Long explains this quote from an artistic angle in his *Chronicle of Aesthetics in China*:

"Likeness" is concrete, intimate, expressive and variable. In addition, "meaning" is profound and obscure. Here this passage points out that artistic images express generalization by individuality, showing abundance by simplicity, presenting infinity with limitations.[53]

So from this "express abundance with simplicity, and infinity with limitations", an artistic sense is derived.   Chang Hung-yu said in "Aesthetic of Writing":

Aesthetics comes from emotion stirred up. This, more often than not, is consistent with the types of objects and events. Aesthetics if often attached to certain things.[54]

He pointed out further: "The reason why some events can be agents of passion is that they touch the emotions of people's aesthetic sense and stir this aesthetic sense.   Hence our imitation of

53 See *Outline of Chinese Aesthetic History.* 《中國美學史大綱》 (Taipei: Changlan Publishing Company, Sep. 1986) p.26.

54 See Chang Hung-yu, *Writing Aesthetics.* 《寫作美學》 (Kaohsiung: Liwen Culture Publishing Company, Oct. 1996) pp.311-314.

matters is actually an imitation of the vibrating waves of our aesthetic sense, a necessary method for carving out the aesthetic senses. Therefore, so-called static or dynamic imitation does not prescribe a mimetic reproduction of lifeless forms or an superficial repetition of movements; it is a search for its deepest meaning and the most vivid contents for a confident expression of this vibrating sense of aesthetics."[55]

The "vibration of emotion" is the sense of the main body. And the "deepest meaning and most vivid contents" are the image of the peripheral contents. This relationship between sense and image has been explained by Gestalt psychologists as "like form like structure" or "different mass same structure". Lee Zhe Ho said in "Aesthetic and Formality".

It's not only a linkage between materials (sound, color, shape, etc.) and acoustic senses. More important, it is also associated with human movements and senses. Indeed, objects and the mind, material worlds and spiritual worlds are in constant motion. Even a still thing is inclusive of factors of motion…there is a sophisticated corresponding relation and influencing function existing in the structure and form…. Psychologists think that this phenomenon is a tribute to the sameness of forms and structures of the external/physical power and internal/psychological power. And this phenomenon can be said to be "different in quality and the same in structures." The electric impulses they stir up in brains are the same. Therefore, this results in the harmony between objects and subjects, external worlds and inner feelings, creating the aesthetic pleasure of symmetry, balance, rhythm, order and harmony.[56]

....

55 See Chang Hung-yu, *Writing Aesthetics.* 《寫作美學》
56 See *Li Cheho's Philosophical and Aesthetic Articles.* 《李澤厚哲學美學文選》

It can be seen that aesthetic sensibilities can be created by the reaction of "different materials, same structure" to "sense" and "image". We shall use "Endless memory of love" by Bai Ju Yi as an example:

汴水流 (The Pien river flows)，泗水流 (The Szu river flows)，流到瓜州古渡頭 (Flowing onto Guachou harbor it goes)。吳山點點愁 (My sorrow is as spacious as the mountains)。思悠悠 (Thoughts are immensely long)，恨悠悠 (Hatred is immensely deep)，恨到歸時方始休 (Hatred will not end until I go back home)。月明人倚樓 (I look forward to my hometown under the moonlight)。

This poem depicts the strong emotion of separation of a wandering traveler, with the structure of "image (scenery), sense (emotion), image (scenery, event)".

For the image (scenery) part, the first three lines record the water scene (image one), the long flowing of the two rivers accentuating his lasting dismay. The two lines from the "flowing of Bien River" with the structure of "from host to guest" provided a description of the events. When put together, enhanced, lasting and lingering effects are achieved. The usage of the water scene to depict emotion has been a favorite of poets for generations. From "Early autumn of Taiyuan" by Lee Bai:

思歸若汾水 (thinking to return is like water flowing)，無日不悠悠 (every day my thinking endures long)。

Or take "Farewell to Mr. Wang Ba one night in Baling" by Gia Zhe:

....

(Taipei: Kufan Publishing Company, May 1987) pp.503-504.

世情已逐浮雲散 (Feelings of the mundane world have faded away like floating clouds)，離恨空隨江水長 (hatred for departure is as long as the running river)。

Furthermore, the author uses "flowed to the ancient pier of Guazhou" to continue the line with "Si River flows". The succeeding method is used to emphasize the emotional expression. The same rhetoric can be seen in many compositions.　For example, in "Book of Poems"

威儀孔時，君子有孝子 (Among Conficius days, there were men of filial piety)。孝子不匱 (they served as models for later generations)，永錫爾類 (we needed to promote the filial piety in the court)。

As stated in "Feeding a horse at the Great Wall" by an anonymous writer:

長跪讀素書 (I sincerely knelt down to read your letter)，書中竟何如？ (what was told in your letter?)

In this way of modifying with the succeeding method, the two lines are connected seamlessly for a unified lingering effect. Moreover, the word "flow" is used three times in three consecutive lines, which makes the flow of the river even more endless, and thus the special lingering effect.

After the author describes watery scene in such fashion, he uses "tiny bitsy glooms of the Wu hills" to portray the hills as seen through his eyes (scene two).　Here, the author uses "from host to guest" to express the scenery mixed with his mood.　The words "tiny bitsy" being used to paint the not-so- tremendous but numerous hills of Jiang Nan, they were also used to express the gloomy mood felt by the author.

楚天千里清秋 (on the immense land of the southernnation autumn arrives)，水隨天去秋無際 (waters flow to the horizon of heaven, and the autumn scene is so spacious)。遙岑遠目 (looking far into the sky)，獻愁供恨 (sorrow and hatred are presented)，玉簪（尖形之山）羅髻（圓形之山）(on small mountains)。

Xin Qigi of the Southern Song Dynasty states in his poem, "Chant of the Water Dragon"
琵琶起舞換新聲 (with the new music of the string instrument)，
總是關山離別情 (the music stirred up the feelings of homesickness)。

In this way, the gloomy mood is enhanced by the long and slow-flowing waterways, and multiplied by many a "tiny bitsy" of them; the so-called "hills hang with a separating dismal and broken heart, the gurgling water carries the sound of farewell and flows into a dream" (Lo Yin, poem for the Tsai brothers at Mien Valley), the emotional expression thereby making an even deeper impression.

Next, looking at the role of sentiment (emotion), it uses the three lines from "lingering thoughts" to express the emotion underyling the scene, i.e., to describe the lingering gloomy mood after viewing the scenery. In the two lines from "lingering thoughts" the author uses overlapping characters [words] and repeated rhymes to correspond with the flowing of Bien river, Si River and the "tiny bitsy" of the Wu hills in order to create the integrated effects of "lingering". The use of "thought" (meaning emotion, a gloomy mood) and the gloomy mood draws out the dismal thinking (sentiment) previously mentioned. And "this dismay [that]will not end until the time to go home" not only reacts to the previous two lines to enhance the lingering dismal mood, but also pushes the time frame from present (reality) to future (virtual), which escalates the feeling of gloom. We can see the same method used by Jimmy Tu in his poem, "Moonlit night":

何時倚虛幌 (When can we both stand leaning by the gauzy veils)，雙照淚痕乾 (our faces'll shine with tears that have become dry trails)。

These two phrases which describe the elation of reunion in the future (virtual) to compliment the bitterness of the present suffering from love (reality), match exactly the mood described by "this dismay [that] will not end until the time to go home". Bai Ju Yi expanded the time frame into the future, achieving the same effect as Tu, the emotion aspect of the poem having been strengthened.

Finally, the "image (scenery, event)" portion will be discussed. There was only one sentence, "a man is leaning on a building under the bright moonlight". From a grammatical perspective, this sentence contains the attitudinal statements of "bright moonlight" and the narrative sentence of the "man leaning on the building" with the same structure of "from subject to predicate", only the predicate of the latter contains the predicate and the premised object, and there is only a slight difference. And even though "a man is leaning on a building under the bright moonlight" is only one sentence, it controls the entire poem. It makes the reader see the author as this "man" leaning on a building under the bright moonlight, facing the scenery of the waterways and far hills, while thinking thoughts provoked by his gloomy, dismal mood. This greatly demonstrates the sentiment brought forth by this scene (event). Everybody knows that one of the best ways to conclude a rhetorical composition is to combine the emotion with the scenery. For instance, take the "auspicious dragon chant" by Chow Ban Yen: "Spring field trips are full of the sadness of departing", which concludes the field trip on a spring day. It continues with the following poem after pointing out the topics:

官柳低金縷 (the willow tree besides the path bow down)，歸騎晚 (I rode a horse coming late)、纖纖池塘飛雨 (slim rain is flying upon the pond)，斷腸院落 (I am so sad in the empty yard)，一簾風絮 (wind blows through willow trees and lonely curtains.)。

It is obvious that the evening scene in late spring (objects) is used to highlight the sad feelings for departure (meaning). In this way, the objects express the feelings (meanings) which will certainly generate a sense of sadness.   Therefore, the fact that Pai Chu-yi concludes the poem with 「月明人倚樓」(under bright moonlight man leaned against the building) can indeed add emotional attraction to his work. Here, the moonlight (object) is used to highlight the meaning of hatred. For ages, moon has been used to highlight "memory" (feelings for departure).   Also, take Li Pai's poem, for example.

我寄愁心與明月 (I gave my feelings to tonight's bright moon)，隨風直到夜郎西 (hopefully, my feelings could fly on wind to a foreign nation in the West)。

Another example is from the poem "Good Bye by the Ancient Road" by Meng Jiao

別後唯所思 (after departure we missed each other)，天涯共明月 (although we lived so far apart, we shared the same bright moon)。

There are numerous examples similar to this.

The author uses the structure of "image (scene), sentiment (emotion), image (scene-event)", to arrange the sequence of "water", "hills", "moon", "man"--namely the scene he had seen under the moonlight, and the feeling that had arisen from seeing such a scene, making a special impression that lingers on and on.　Some people suggest that this poem actually describes the feelings of a lonely woman. This is possible but, even so, the aesthetic value of the poem is not affected.　The following is the structural analysis:

```
                       ┌likeness1（水－low）:「汴水流」三句
        ┌Likeness（景）┤
        │              └likeness2（山－high）:「吳山點點愁」
        │                      ┌meaning1（real－present）:「思悠悠」二句
        ├Meaning (feeling) ┤
        │                      └meaning2（unreal－future）:「恨到歸時方始休」
        │                            ┌likeness3（月－high）:「月明」
        └Likeness (landscape, event) ┤
                                     └Likeness4（人－low）:「人倚樓」
```

Generally　speaking,　from　individual　semantic　imagery perspective, this poem used images such as "water flow", "tiny bitsy hills", 'bright moon light" and "a man leaning on a building" and integrates them with "long lingering" "dismal", resulting in with a huge effect by "different materials of identical structure".　From the perspective of "imagery and phrase", the different phrases were formed by the emotions felts (sentiment) and scenery seen (event) (image).　From the aspect of rhetoric, the watery ways were presented by a succeeding method and the hills were portrayed with personification, which made the water and hills filled with lingering sentiment to enhance the affections of this literary work.　The author's image thinking can be seen from these points, and from the distinguishing characteristics of the forming and presentation of the sensing image.　From the perspective of grammatical analysis, all of the phrases used were of the subjective predicate structure, which organizes the individual concepts to form different images in a presentation of imagery of logical structure. From the point of chapter order, the entire poem has used methods of "scene sentiment", "high- low" and "reality and the virtual" to sequentially string the images together and form the logical structure of the chapter order. From the point of topic and style, the methodical arrangements in "image"(individual), "imagery", "rhetoric", "grammar" and "order" fully illustrated the theme of "lingering dismay" with the style of a "fine- tuned musical, smooth flowing as a pearl", [57] which helps the readers to understand the beauty within. All of these were a composite thinking and an integration of image thinking and logical thinking.

From all these examples we may discover that rhetorical composition cannot depart from the forming, presentation and organization of coining images, which is "multitudes". The integration of "image thinking" and "logical thinking can be "two". And the topic and style magnified is "one(0)". This type of structure is similar to a tree: the entity is a formation of individual branches, boughs, leaves and forms, all the structures and auras being closely knitted and inseparable.

From the discussion above, the contents of a rhetorical composition basically contain "sense images" (from individual to the whole body), order, topic and style. The sensing order is formed from image thinking and the order is formed by logical thinking. The topic and style are highlighted by composite thinking, which integrates the phrases, verbal expressions, and

....

57 Chao Jen-kuei, Li Chenyin, Du Yuan-ping, "the Tze, as a whole, uses flowing water to express feelings.   And repeated words make the acoustic effect beautiful."   See *Tang Wu Tai 300 Tze Translation and Analysis*. 《唐五代詞三百首譯析》(Changchun: Chilin Literature and History Publishing Company, Jan. 1997) p.148.

images and logical thinking of the entire work. From a perspective of the whole, the rhetorical composition contains a multitude of "verbal expressions", "rhetoric", "grammar" and "order". And the "two," "image thinking" (yin) and "logical thinking"(yang), controls the "multitudes" and communicates with the "one(0)". And the topic of "one(0)" is the central nerve of the composition that integrated the "multitudes" and the "two" and forms the style and character of the work. It seems to be clearer and more reasonable to analyze rhetorical composition and structure from these various perspectives.

Chapter **2**

Image Contents of Structures of Conception and Composition

The contents of compositional structures are a combination of two things- "the formation of conception and likeness" categorized as "image thinking," and "the organization of conception and likeness" categorized as "logical thinking." In this chapter, for the former item, the related discussion will be carried out in the light of "conception and likeness," and "vertical structure."

I. Conception (essence) and likeness (materials)

In terms of composition, "conception" refers to "essence," while "likeness," to "materials," Here, in terms of "conception and likeness" (essence, contents), we'll explore their philosophical significance and literary application.

1.The philosophical significance of conception and likeness

Conception and likeness, in a sense, are based on philosophy.

In terms of philosophy, conception and likeness are associated with a union of hearts and objects. Here, we'd better directly embark upon a discussion of "conception" and 「象」（Hsiang）/likeness, omitting the past controversial discussions. Indeed, the most essential discourse related to conceptual meanings and 「象」 (Hsiang)/likeness is 《易傳》Yichuan of which〈繫辭上〉(Hsitzu) said,

聖人有以見天下之賾 (Saints observe the objects of the world.)，而擬諸其形容 (They intend to describe them,)，象其物宜，是故謂之象 (The proper imitation and description of the objects being likeness or image.)。

In addition, An Interpretation of *The Book of Changes* said,

《易》者，象也。(Yiching's contents are Hsiang)
象也者，像也。(Hsiang is likeness)
……是故吉凶生而悔吝著也。(Peace and disasters will arise; and repentance and meanness will appear.)

In *Analysis of Chouyi*, Kung Yin-ta makes such comments,

《易》卦者，寫萬物之形象，(Yiching describes images of all creatures)故《易》者，象也。(So, Yiching is Hsiang) 象也者，像也，(Hsiang is likeness.) 謂卦為萬物象者，(The Yiching is a likeness of all creatures) 法像萬物，猶若乾卦之象法像於天也。(The Hsiang of the Yiching is indeed the likeness of all creatures.)[1]

Judging from this, we can see "likeness" comes from objects far or near, which signifies peace, disaster, repentance and meanness. Broadly speaking, concrete objects are used to express abstract phenomena.

This serves the purpose of symbolism. Therefore, Chen Won-hen said in *A History of Chinese Classic Aesthetics*.

According to Yiching, "observing creatures to gain images," and

---

1 See *Analysis of Chouyi*. 《周易正義》Vol.8 (Taipei: Kuanwen Bookstore, Jan.1972.) p.77.

"Hsiang being likeness" pointed to symbolism rather than imitation. This made a profound impact on the character of Chinese arts.[2]

In terms of expression, "symbolism" is a sign. Therefore, Fan pointed out in *A Collection of Articles of Fan Yu-nan.*

According to 〈繫辭傳〉(Hsitzuchuan), "Changes are images is Hsiang." Also, "The saints described the images of all creatures. So Hsiang is a kind of likeness." Accordingly, "Hsiang" is an imitation of the complicated state of the objective world. In addition, Hsiang is indeed an image of the objective world. However, the imitation and images are not like taking or drawing pictures. Actually, it uses symbols to represent the doctrines of the world. 64 卦 and 384 爻 are such symbols and signs.[3]

In his *An Outline of the History of Chinese Aesthetics,* Yeh-nan explains the doctrines expressed by signs. He holds that according to Hsitzuchuan, *the Yiching* as a whole is " likeness." The book uses images to express doctrines.[4] In addition, likeness is related to doctrines, which are expressed by likeness. According to Hsitzu,

子曰：「書不盡言，言不盡意。」(Confucius said, "Books cannot conception express words, which also cannot fully express meanings." 然則，聖人之意，其不可見乎？(However, are

....

2 See Chen Wan-hen, *History of Chinese Aesthetics.* 《中國古典美學史》(Tsaisa: Hunan Education Publishing Company, Aug. 1998) p. 202.

3 See *Collection of Fan You-nan's Articles.* 《馮友蘭選集》(Beijing: Beijing University Publishing Company, July 2000) p.394.

4 See *Outline of Chinese Aesthetic History.* 《中國美學史大綱》(Taipei: Tsailan Publishing Company, Sep. 1986.) p.66.

meanings, according to saints, unfathomable?) 子曰:「聖人立象以盡意 (Confucius said, "Saints established images to express meanings;), 設卦以盡情偽 (They designed symbols to manifest truths;), 繫辭焉以盡其言 (they employed expressions to disclose words;);變而通之以盡利 (they kept flexible to produce advantages;),鼓之舞之以盡神 (they encouraged people to do everything in a good spirit.")。

Generally speaking, in expressing thoughts and feelings, language, in a sense, is confined. That is, words cannot fully express the meanings. However, Hsitzuchuan pointed out that likeness can express meanings, and that expressions can be expressive of words. In《周易略例.明象》(Brief Examples of Chouyi, MinShan), Wang Bi said.

夫象者,出意者也 (Hsiang is designed to express meanings.);言者,明象者也 (Words are used to manifest Hsiang.)。盡意莫若象 (Hsiang is most instrumental in expressing meanings.),盡象莫若言 (Words are the most useful for disclosing Hsiang.)。言生於象 (Words are produced by Hsiang;),故可尋言以觀象 (therefore, words can be searched in order to observe Hsiang.);象生於意 (Hsiang is produced by meanings;),故可尋象以觀意 (therefore, Hsiang can be searched in order to observe perception.)。意以象盡 (Meanings can be expressed by Hsiang.),象以言著 (Hsiang is revealed by words.)[5]。

Therefore, thoughts and feelings can be substantially expressed by words and images. And thoughts and feelings serve a purpose, while

....

5   See "Chouyi's Brief Example, Mingshan"《周易略例・明象》 in *Collections of Yiching.*《易經集成》 (Taipei: Wenchien Publishing Company, 1976) pp.21-22.

words and images function as a tool. Chen Wan-hen said in *A History of Chinese Classic Aesthetics*,

> Wang Bi put "language," "likeness," and "conception" in order, holding that "language" originated from "likeness," and that "likeness" stemmed from "conception" Therefore, a search of languages is for the observation of "likeness," which in turn is for the production of meanings. In the linear order of "language," "likeness," and "conception" the former is the means of the latter, while the latter is the purpose of the former.[6]

Here, the linear relations among "meaning," "likeness," and "language" are comprehensively clarified. However, his explanation of "language→likeness→meanings" is based on the role of reading, evaluation, and appreciation. In terms of creation, the linear order should be "meanings→ likeness→ language." In addition, *An Outline of the History of Chinese Aesthetics,* Yeh Lan concisely and clearly interpreted "likeness" and "meaning" from another angle.

> 「象」 (Hsiang) is concrete, close, open and variegated.
> On the other hand, "meaning" is profound and obscure.
> These words show three characteristics of artistic images--using individuality to show generalization; using simplicity to show abundance; using limitation to show infinity.[7]

So-called "simplicity" 「象」 (Hsiang) and "abundance" (meanings), "limitation" 「象」 (Hsiang) and "infinity" (meaning) mean the

....

6 See Chen Wan-hen, *A History of Chinese Classic Aesthetics.* 《中國古典美學史》 As in note 2, p. 207.

7 See *An Outline of the History of Chinese Aesthetics.* 《中國美學史大綱》 As in note 4, p. 26.

relation between 「象」 (Hsiang) and "meanings."

Judging from the above, the philosophical level of "meaning" and 「象」 (Hsiang) was based on this, and aesthetics was also produced out of this. Just as Chang Hung-yu said in *Aesthetics of Writing:*.

Aesthetics is produced when emotion is stirred up. This is consistent with the types of things. Aesthetics is always attached to certain things.[8]

He further pointed out that "The reason why things can stir up emotion is that they can stimulate people's aesthetic emotion, stirring up aesthetic emotion. Accordingly, our imitation of things is indeed that of stirred-up aesthetic emotion. This is a necessary means of carving out aesthetic emotion. Therefore, the so-called imitation of a static state as well as a moving state is not necessarily a production of shapes of lifeless things, or an imitation of the moving surface of things. It aims to explore the contents which are more essential and visual, which can find an outlet for aesthetic emotion.[9]

His "stirred-up emotion" is the subjective "conception" In addition, "the more essential and visual contents" of things are objective 「象」 (Hsiang). For this formation of conception and 「象」 (Hsiang), psychologists used "sameness of shapes and structures" and "differences of qualities and sameness of structures" to interpret a phenomenon. Just as Li Che-hou said in "Aesthetics and Sense of Forms,"

The connection between materials and people's exercising of the

....

8 See Chang Huang-yu, *Writing Aesthetics.* 《寫作美學》 (Kaohsiung: Liwen Culture Publishing Company, Oct. 1996). p.311.

9 See Chang Hung-yu, *Writing Aesthetics,* 《寫作美學》 pp.311-314.

senses is more important than the one between materials (sound, color, shape, etc.) and the visual and acoustic senses. Objects (guest) and feelings (master), just like the material world and spiritual world, are in a constant process of motion. Even objects in stasis have factors of motion...there is a sophisticated corresponding relation and influence between forms and structures. Some psychologists hold that this is to be attributed to the "sameness of forms and structures" existing in external power (psychology). In other words, in the case of "different materials and the same structures," electric pulses are produced. In brains it will be the same. In this way, "master" and "guest" can be in harmony; "object" and "I" will become one. In addition, in case of a unity of external objects and internal feelings, the pleasure of aesthetics will be produced by a corresponding symmetry, balance rhythm, order, harmony, etc.[10]

This concisely explains the reasons why the formation of "conception" and "likeness" can be unified and produce aesthetics in terms of reasons, processes, and results.

2. The literary application of meanings and materials (likeness)

The conception of compositions is abstract, while the materials (likeness) selected are concrete. The composition can be most convincing and powerful by selecting concrete materials to express abstract concepts. And generally speaking, the selected materials can be divided into two major categories—"matters" and "objects." Accordingly, we see how the meanings of the composition can be closely related to the selection of materials.

....

10 See *Collection of Li Tzeho's Philosophy and Aesthetics.* 《李澤厚哲學美學文選》(Taipei: Kufan Publishing Company, May 1987) pp.503-504.

2.1 Selecting "things" as materials to manifest "meanings"

The so-called "things" can be fact or fiction.   In terms of facts, the "past facts" via allusions are largely used.   Take Lobinwan's "Claiming a War," for instance.

霍子孟之不作 (Figures like Huokuang in the Han Dynasty never appeared again;)，朱虛侯之已亡 (Figures like Liuchang, who destroyed Lushih, also never reappeared.)。

In the first line, the author uses the story of Hokung's helping the prince Hanshandi to continue the Han dynasty to show that nowadays there is no faithful subject like Hokung to help the prince Tanchunchung.   In the second line, the author uses the story of Liuchang's eliminating the queen's relatives to stabilize the country so as to show that the current situation is a similar case.   Therefore, it can be seen that stories are employed to manifest the textual meanings.   In addition, take a passage of Su Chih's "Writing on Supreme Platform" , for instance.

南望馬耳常山 (Looking south to Maerh mountain and Chang mountain)，出沒隱見 (sometimes they are visible; but sometimes they are invisible)；若近若遠 (sometimes they seem far, but sometimes they seem near.)，庶幾有隱君子乎 (Perhaps there are hermits in the mountains)？而其東則盧山 (Lu Mountain is in the eastern mountains;)，秦人盧敖之所從遁也 (It's the place where Lu Aao, a hermit in the Chin dynasty, lived.)。西望穆陵 (Looking west to Mu Lin)，隱然如城郭 (looming like cities)，師尚父齊威公之遺烈猶有存者 (the legacy of two great ancient men remains.)。北俯濰水(Looking north to Wei Water,)，慨然太息 (I sigh and show sympathy,)，思淮陰之功 (remembering Hansin's achievements,)，而弔其不

終 (mourning over his tragic death.) 。

Moreover, he uses Lu Aao's case to express his wish of becoming a hermit.　And then, he uses 「西望」 (looking west) and the historical facts of two great ancient men to show that he wishes to help the emperor to conquer the world.　Furthermore, he uses 「北俯」 (looking north) and the tragic end of Hansin's life to disclose his worries about the future.　However, such worries will not discourage the author.　For judging from the arrangement of the paragraph, we can finally see that his eagerness to serve the emperor overshadows his concern and worries.　Concerning this point, we can sense something from a Ci entitled "Suediaoketo."

In this paragraph, the author uses 「南望」 (looking south) 、「而其東」 (in the east) to tell us about 「隱君子」 (a hermit).

吾欲乘風歸去 (I want to ride on winds and return to the moon palace.) ,
但恐瓊樓玉宇 (I'm worried that, living in the distant moon palace,) ,
高處不勝寒 (I cannot resist the cold at height.) 。
起舞弄清影 (I rise up to dance with my own shadow.) ,
何似在人間 (Isn't the moon palace better than the mundane world!) !

Here, he compares himself to a fairy in exile, seeing the moon palace as an ideal reclusive place. The reason for his wish to return is apparently to be associated with certain Wu Tai legal poetry cases. In addition, his younger brother also advised him to retire decently right away. However, judging from 高處不勝寒 (I cannot resist the cold at height), we can sense that he could not get used to his retirement. Therefore, in the two lines following 「起舞」 (rise up to dance), we can see that he wanted to go his own way after retirement.

This indeed echoes "Writing on Supreme Platform". [11] Here, we can also take Chui Hao 's poem entitled "Yellow Crane Building," for example.

晴川歷歷漢陽樹 (By the sun-lit river Hanyang's trees can be counted one by one.)，
芳草萋萋鸚鵡洲 (On Parrot Islet the sweet green grass grows fast and thick.)。

In these two lines, the author shifts from Hanyang, located in the northeastern part of the yellow crane building, to Parrot Islet, located in the southeastern part of Hanyang, expressing deep feelings of fatalism. When it comes to Parrot Islet, we should remember the proud Mi Hen, who was not blessed in his career. According to histories of the Han Dynasty, Mi Hen was eloquent, but proud.

Although he was respected and loved by Kungju,he was rejected by Tsaichao, and Liubiao was killed by Hungju. And then, he was buried on Parrot Islet, famous for the "Parrot Islet Song." It can be seen that the author uses allusion to express his depression. Perhaps the meanings seem contradictory to the topic of homesickness. But, actually fatalism and homesickness are like twins. In Tu Fu's poem entitled "A Night in Travel," he says, "名豈文章著 (Famous for my composition), 官應老病休 (I need to retire due to my age and sickness). These two lines refer to fatalism. And then, he says, "飄飄何所似 (Can I compare myself), 天地一沙鷗 (to a bird flying in the sky)." These two lines point to homesickness. From this, we can see that fatalism and homesickness can coexist naturally in narration. Here, take Sin Chihji's "Yungyu Poem", for instance.

....

11 That is the expression of the thoughts of retirement. See Chen Man-ming, *Papers on Su, Sin's Tzus.* 《蘇辛詞論稿》 (Taipei: Wenching Publishing Company, Aug. 2003) pp.51-53.

千古江山 (In the eternally unchanged mountains and rivers)，英雄無覓，孫仲謀處 (There is no place where we can find heroes like Sun Chungmou.)。舞榭歌臺 (On platforms for singing and dancing)，風流總被，雨打風吹去 (The legacies of heroes have been washed away by wind and rain.)。斜陽草樹，尋常巷陌 (In common alleys with grass and trees under sunset)，人道寄奴曾住 (people said that 劉裕 lived there,)。想當年(Reflecting on past years.)、金戈鐵馬 (His weapons shone like gold and his horse was as strong as iron,)，氣吞萬里如虎 (His spirits, like a tiger's, seemed to devour the immense land.)。元嘉草草 (An emperor of the Sung Dynasty in a rush)，封狼居胥(waged a war.)，贏得倉皇北顧 (He looked to the north full of worry.)。四十三年，望中猶記 (43 years ago, I passed through Yangchou in the war zone.)，烽火揚州路 (Wars raged in Yangchou.)。可堪回首 (It's remembered)，佛貍祠下，一片神鴉社鼓 (for its crying ravens and banging drums in front of the temple of a deceased emperor.)。憑誰問，廉頗老矣，尚能飯否 (Who would ask me, "can you, as old as Lienpo, continue serving your country?")。

This Tzu (a poem of irregular rhythm) is full of allusions. In the first six lines, the author uses the allusion to Sun Chuan to explain that there are no heroes of today who can defeat the enemy. And then, in the five lines from 斜陽(sunset), the allusion to Liu Yu is used to describe the sad fact that no one can march north to fight their enemies. In addition, three lines from Yuanchia advise the authorities not to attack their enemies in a rush. For the emperor of the Sung dynasty failed in a war waged in a rush. Furthermore, three lines from 43 point out that he had once seen enemies burn Yanchou 43 years ago. This serves as strong evidence for the warning issued in the above three lines. The three lines from 「可堪」 (it's remembered) further point out that since their enemies were still strong, the government could not neglect them. Meanwhile, the historical fact that the emperor built a palace on Fuabu Mountain is presented to prove the prevailing strength of their enemies. Furthermore, the three lines from「憑誰問」(who could ask me) uses the allusion to Lien Po to illustrate that like the old Lien Po he was still so useful that he could bear the responsibility of recovering the former country. By these allusions, the author expresses his conception in a sophisticated way.[12] When it comes to fiction, the allegory is most frequently seen. Take a story in *Hanfeitze* for an example.

鄭人有欲買履者 (In the Cheng nation, there was a person who wanted to buy a pair of shoes.)，先自度其足 (First he measured his feet)，而置之其坐 (and then he put his recorded measurements down on his seat.)。至之市 (After that he went to the market)，而忘操之 (where he found he had forgotten to take the record.)；已得履 (When he found the shoes he liked,)，及曰 (he said,)：「吾忘持度。」("I forget my size.") 反歸取之 (So he went back home to get the record of his size.)。及反 (When he got back to the market,)，市罷 (the market had closed.)，遂不得履 (He could not buy the shoes.)。人曰：(People asked,)「何不試之以足？」("why did you not try on the shoes?")曰：(He said,)「寧信度，無自信也。」("I would rather trust the measurement than trust myself.")

Here, the author tells a fictional story: a person in the Cheng nation wanted to buy a pair of shoes. However, instead of believing his own feet, he insisted on his previously measured size. Thus, he lost an opportunity to buying a pair of shoes. Indeed, the moral lesson is that a person cannot neglect roots in pursuing ends.

....

12 See Chen Man-ming, *Papers on Su, Sin's Tzus*. 《蘇辛詞論稿》 pp.114-115.

The fictional story was more convincing than an ordinary argumentative compositions. Also, take *Chungtze*, for example.

莊子行於山中 (Chuangtzu was walking in the mountains)，見大木枝葉盛茂 (when he saw a flourishing tree.)，伐木者止其旁而不取也 (A log cutter had stopped beside it but would not cut it into a log.)，問其故 (He asked him why.)，曰：(He said)「無所可用。」(it was useless.) 莊子曰：(Chuangtzu said,)「此木以不材得終其天年。」(This tree could enjoy its remaining lifespan for it was useless.) 夫子出於山 (As Chuangtzu was walking out of the mountains,)，舍於故人之家 (he stopped at his friend's house,)，故人喜 (who was happy [to see him].)，命豎子殺雁而烹之 (When he ordered his servant to kill and cook a goose,)。豎子請曰：(the servant asked his master,)「其一能鳴，("one goose can cry,) 其一不能鳴 (the other cannot:)，請奚殺？(which goose should I kill?")」主人曰：(The master said,)「殺不能鳴者。」("You'd better kill the one which cannot cry.")

This story tells us that useless trees can live long, while useless geese cannot. Through this fictional story, the author explicitly expresses that "there is no fixed rule for dealing with everything." In addition, take the story entitled " A stupid Old Man Removes Mountains in *Lietze*, "for an example.

太形、王屋二山 (Taihsing Mountain and Wangwu Mountain)，方七百里 (with a girth of seven hundred kilometers)，高萬仞 (were extremely high) 本在冀州之南 (and originally located in the south of Chichou.)、河陽之北 (In the north of Hoyang)。北山愚公者 (there was a stupid old man at the northern mountain.)，年且九十 (His age was ninety years.)，面山而居 (He lived in front of the two mountains)。懲北山之塞 (hindered by a portion of the northern mountain.)，出入之迂也 (Travel was not efficient.)，聚室而謀曰：(He gathered together his family members, saying:)「吾與汝畢力平險 ("You and I will do our best to eliminate the barriers of the mountains,)，指通豫南 (and then, we can directly go south to Yuchou,)，達於漢陰，(to the south of Han river.)可乎？」(Can we not do that?") 雜然相許 (They unanimously agreed.)。其妻獻疑曰：(But his wife still doubted,)「以君之力，("your strength) 曾不能損魁父之丘，(cannot reduce a small hill like Kueifu.) 如太形、王屋何？(How could you level these two huge mountains,) 且焉置土石？」(and where to put the mud and stones?") 雜曰：(They all said,)「投諸渤海之尾 ("let's toss the mud and stones at the end of the Po Sea) 隱土之北。(north of Yintu.")」遂率子孫荷擔者三夫，(Thus, he led forth his family members; three of them bore the gear for carrying the mud and stones,) 叩石墾壤，(after breaking up the stones and dig the mud,) 箕畚運於渤海之尾；(to carry them to the end of the Po Sea.) 鄰人京城氏之孀妻有遺男，(A son of the widow living next door,) 始齔，(who was just seven or eight years old,)跳往助之；(earnestly wanted to help him.) 寒暑易節，(Come summer and winter) 始一反焉。(he would go back home to rest for a while.)

河曲智叟笑而止之曰：(A wise old man in Hochu laughed, intending to stop him:)「甚矣，("you go too far,)汝之不慧！(you are so unwise!)以殘年遺力，(Your longevity and strength are limited.)曾不能毀山之一毛，(You cannot destroy even the grass of these mountains.) 其如土石何？」(How can you deal with the mud and stones?") 北山愚公長息曰：(The stupid old man of the northern mountain sighed and said,)「汝心之固，("your heart is so stubborn) 固不可徹，(and so unreasonable.) 曾不若孀妻弱子。(You are less reasonable than a widow and an orphan.) 雖我之死，(If I die,) 有子存焉；(my descendants will still live on.) 子又生孫，(My sons will have children,) 孫又生子；(these grandchildren will have children,) 子又有子，

(their sons will have sons) 子又有孫；(and their sons will have children.) 子子孫孫，(Of sons and grandchildren) 無窮匱也。(There is no end.) 而山不增，(The height of the mountains won't increase.) 何苦而不平？」(How can the mountains not be leveled?") 河曲智叟亡以應。(The wise man had nothing more to say.)

操蛇之神聞之，(The snake-handler god heard of this,) 懼其不已也，(fearing that he wouldn't stop.) 告之於帝，(The god reported it to the Supreme God.) 帝感其誠，(Moved by the stupid old man's sincerity,) 命夸娥氏二子負二山，(He ordered his two sons in Kuaerhshih to bear off the two mountains,) 一厝朔東，(putting one in the east of Shuofan,) 一厝雍南。(the other in the south of Yungnan,) 自此冀之北、(from north of the Chichou) 漢之陰，(to the south of the Han river,) 無隴斷焉 (where there were no highlands or stones.)。

In this well-known allegory, the author expresses two moral lessons—"God helps those who help themselves"; "Where there is a will, there is a way." According to the first paragraph, considering that two mountains hindered transportation between the north and the south, the stupid old man made up his mind to remove them. And he got his family's approval. This serves to point out that "he had a will." In addition, in the second paragraph, the stupid old man chose a location for the disposal of mud, and he got his descendants and neighbors to help remove the mountains. This refers to "God's help" (including self help). Furthermore, in the third paragraph, we can see that the stupid old man braced himself for the wise old man's laughter, yet he firmly believed that if he kept struggling he would succeed someday. This story is especially written to explain the meaning of "will" and "God's help." Moreover, in the final paragraph, we can see that the spirit of the stupid old man touched both earth and heaven, resulting in God's help.   So, his will could be fulfilled.   This actually belongs to the part about "God's help" and "there is a way."   In this way, the author employs a simple story to help readers understand the existing philosophy.[13]

This can be said to be a unique and universal characteristic of allegories, when compared to other genres.   Actually compared with *Chungyun*, the efforts of the wise old man, his family members and neighbors speak of self integrity, which might lead to God's help. This is the essential meaning of *Chungyun*.[14]   Of course, the author's interpretation is not necessarily absolute.   But we are likely able to embrace such understandings existing between the lines.   Indeed, this is an advantage of allegory:

2.2 Taking "objects" as materials to manifest meanings

In addition to taking " things" as materials to express the contends, many specialists of compositional art like to take "objects" as materials to express not only meanings but feelings.

"Objects" are without feelings but the specialists of compositional art are fond of imposing feelings on them.

In this way, the objects can produce images, which are integrated with inner feelings. That is, feelings and landscapes become a union, just as Wang Kue-wei said, "All words about landscapes are words of feelings."[15]   Take Yenchu's Poem, entitled "Wansisa," for example.

....

13 See Chou Jung-yuan, Shu Yin-pei, *A Dictionary for the Appreciation of Ancient Prose* 《古文鑑賞辭典》   (Nanking: Chiangsu, Literary Arts Publishing Company, Nov. 1987, first edition) p. 136.

14 See Chen Man-ming, *New Design for Learning the Meanings of* Chungyun   《學庸義理別裁》(Taipie: Wanchunlo Publishing Company, Jan. 2002, first edition), pp. 393-403.

15 See Wang Kuo-wei, *Tzus of the Mundane World. , Collection of Tzus.* 《人間詞話刪稿》,《詞話叢編》   (Taipei: Sinwenfasn Publishing Company, Feb. 1988)

無可奈何花落去，(It's a pity that flowers wither.)
似曾相識燕歸來。(The swallows returned as familiar friends.)

The two lines were so well-known for they have been widely read since the Sung dynasty. Besides the parallel and rhythm, the natural scenes of withered flowers and returning swallows are integrated with the emotion of pity and familiarity. In this way, "flowers" "swallows" and human affairs are combined, creating a sense of transience and uncertainty. Indeed, "flowers" are symbolic of the good old days, and "swallows" can indirectly hint of the loneliness of a single man. Therefore, the scene of withered flowers will stimulate sentiments of the good old days, and returning swallows can result in hatred of the absence of beloved persons. Thus, inner feelings can be connected with outside landscapes. Take Fan Chungyen's Pem, entitled *Sumuche*, for example.

山映斜陽天接水，(Mountains are reflected in the sunset.) 芳草無情，(Merciless grass) 更在斜陽外。(extends beyond the sunset.)

These three lines of the "Sumuche" describe scenery that gradually extends from "mountain," "sunset," "water," to "beyond the sunset." Although, indeed, "grass" is immune from feelings, it is personalized and described as "merciless", for it ignored the pains of departure and grew wildly on its own. So, was it merciless? This kind of description makes people mentally downcast. Furthermore, the personalization of "grass" results in the fact that wild grass, in the eyes of travelers, highlights the infinite sorrow of departure. Therefore, writers prefer to use the image of grass to highlight feelings of departure. Take Wang Wei's "Seeing You

p.4257.

Off," for instance.

春草明年綠，(Next year when the grass turns green in the spring,) 王孫歸不歸？(I don't know whether you will come back.)

In addition, take Lu Luen's poem, for example.

故園衰草遍，(My hometown is covered with flourishing grass.) 離別正堪愁。(I bade farewell and felt sad.)

And take Li Lee's Poem, for instance.

離恨恰如春草，(Hatred of departure is like spring grass) 更行更遠還生。(The farther I travel, the longer it grows.)

Such kinds of examples are numerous. Judging from this, we can see that "grass" is commonly used to highlight feelings of departure. Take Wen Ting-yun's Poem, entitled "Kenlotze," for instance.

玉爐香，(A fine urn spread ash and smoke.) 紅蠟淚。(Red candles seemed to shed tears.) 偏照畫堂秋思。(Light projected on someone sorrowful over autumn.) 眉翠薄，(Her decorated eyebrows grew thinner,) 鬢雲殘，(her hair in disarray.) 夜長衾枕寒。(The night was so long that the bed turned cold.) 梧桐樹，(The trees stood still;) 三更雨，(it rained at midnight.) 不道離情正苦。(The sadness of departure was untold.) 一葉葉，(Leaves fell.) 一聲聲，(Raindrops broke the quiet) 空階滴到明。(as they dropped on the empty steps until dawn.)

This is a work expressing feelings of departure. The initial two lines describe the scene in which a beautiful woman felt sad over autumn while facing urn smoke and the candle's "tears" in her chamber. And then, the three lines from 「眉翠薄」 (her decorated eyebrows grew thinner) uses thin eyebrows, hair in disarray, and insomnia to start the description of images. And then, the following six lines further describe feelings of departure, that is, sadness over autumn by expressing a scene in which the beautiful woman remains alone listening to the raindrops dropping on the empty steps until dawn. In this way, feelings of departure are substantially expressed by concrete images such as raindrops, urn ash, candle tears, cold beds, and thin eyebrows. This Poem was thus soaked in powerful feelings which find expressions in concrete images. Here, let's take Tu Shen-yen's "In Reply to Magistrate Lu's Poem: An Excursion in Early Spring," for example.

獨有宦遊人 (Only to officials away from home,) 偏驚物候新 (The shock of beautiful woman ever new will come) 雲霞出海曙 (Of rising clouds at dawn above the sea) 海柳渡江春 (Of Spring at far streamside and willow-tree).
淑氣催黃鳥 (Orioles are urged to sing in warm air,)
晴光轉綠蘋 (And green clover ferns in clear light wax fair.) 忽聞歌古調 (An old tune suddenly sung to my ears) 歸思欲霑巾 (With home Sick homesick, my eyes with tears.)

This poem is framed by the structure of "first generalization and then details" As for the role of generalization, the first line introduces the second line. The two tracks of 「偏驚」 (shock) and 「物候新」 (beautiful woman ever new), are used to control the third line, which belongs to "details" In addition, the fresh beautiful woman of spring is substantially described. Here, the author uses 「雲霞」 (clouds), 「梅柳」 (plum and willow-tree), 「黃鳥」 (orioles) and 「蘋」 (duckweed) to describe 物 (objects) and then, 「曙」（dawn）,「春」（spring）,「淑氣」（warm air）,「晴光」（sun）are employed to describe 「候」（the climate）. Furthermore, 「出海」（over the sea）,「渡江」（over a stream）, 「催」（urge）,「轉綠」（green）are used to describe 「新」（new）. In this way, 「物候新」new objects and the climate are depicted by concrete images, creating strong feelings to reinforce the feelings of homesickness in the last line. Actually.「雲霞」（clouds）,「梅柳」（plum and willows）,「黃鳥」（orioles）and 「蘋」（clover ferns）are connected with homesickness. Take 「雲霞」（clouds), for example. They are frequently used to signify travelers, for they drift unpredictably. As for the usage of the symbol of 「雲」（clouds）, we can view Du Fu's "Dreaming of Li Po."

浮雲終日行，(The floating clouds are strolling all day long.)遊子久不至。(You wanderer for a long time have gone.)

Take Wei Yinwu's poem, for example.

浮雲一別後，(Like drifting clouds we parted then)
流水十年間。(Ten fleeting years stream by, without regret.)

Concerning sunset, take Ho Tzechang's poem, for example.

綠水殘霞催席散 (The feast ended with green waters and rosy clouds.)，畫棲明月待人歸 (The bright moon above the attic was awaiting the traveler returning home.)。

In addition, take Chien Chi's poem, for example.

海月低雲旆，(The bright moon above the sea shone on the cloud flag.) 江霞入錦車。(Rosy clouds above the river dyed the carts red.)

As to "plum and willow," "willow" has been closely connected with feelings of departure for generations thanks to one of Changan's customs in which people broke willow branches in bidding farewell to others. Take one of Sung Tzuwen's poems, for instance.

故園斷腸處 (Remembering our hometown so much)，
月夜柳條新 (Willow branches seemed to turn greener)。

Wang Changlin's "Chamber Hatred" is another example.

忽見陌頭楊柳色
(Suddenly seeing green willows by the roadside)，
悔教夫婿覓封侯
(She regrets for her husband seeking fame far away)。

Plums have been associated with feelings of departure due to the story of Fanye and Lukai in the Nanpei dynasty. According to the *Chinchou Journal*, Lukai once met a messenger of the capital city of Chiangnan, and he broke a branch of the plum tree as a gift for Fanye, then living in Changan. Meanwhile, he wrote a poem as a gift.

折梅逢驛使，(I met a mailman while breaking plum branches.)
寄與隴頭人。(I wanted to mail plums to my good friend.)
江南無所有，(There was nothing special in Chiennan.)
聊贈一枝春。(I could only send you a message of early spring.)

From then on, the"plum" was used by authors to describe feelings and memories. Take Sung Tzewen's "On North Station of Tayu Mountain," for example.

明朝望鄉處，(Tomorrow from the peak one more look homewards I'll cast.) 應見隴頭梅。(There, in the warm air some plum blossoms I may find at last.)

Han Wo's "After the riots I walked past a wilderness pond on a spring day" is another example.

世亂他鄉見落梅，(In a chaotic world I saw plums falling in strange lands.) 野塘晴暖獨徘徊。(Beside the wilderness pond under the sunshine, I strolled around.)

Moreover, when it comes to orioles, we've got to mention Chin Chanshu's poem.

打起黃鶯兒，(Drive the young orioles away,) 莫叫枝上啼。(nor let them on the branches play.) 啼時驚妾夢，(Their chirping breaks my slumber through) 不得到遼西。(and keeps me from dreaming of you.)

Judging from this poem, orioles and their crying are connotations of homesickness. Take one of Kao Shi's poems, for example.

黃鳥翩翩楊柳垂，(A yellow bird tenderly flew over the willow tree.) 春風送客使人悲。(I felt sad while seeing visitors off in spring wind.)

Furthermore, take Bei Chuyi's poem, for example.

柳絮送人鶯勸酒，(Willow leaves see men off, and orioles urge people to drink.) 去年今日別東都。(Last year on the same day I left the eastern capital.)

Considering such expressions as 「黃鳥翩翩」 (a yellow bird tenderly flew) and 「鶯勸酒」 (orioles urge people to drink), we can see these expressions did deepen the feelings of homesickness. In addition, 「白蘋」 (the plane tree) is frequently used as a symbol of wandering. Take Liu Changching's poem, for example.

誰見汀洲上，(Who saw me standing here?) 相思愁白蘋。 (Looking at the plane tree, my heart was full of sorrow over missing you.)

In addition, take Chang Chi's poem, for example.

送人發，(I saw my friend off.) 送人歸，(I had to come back.) 白蘋茫茫鷗鴣飛。(The white flowers on the river were so dense that I could not see the ferry, only hear the flying birds crying.)

Here, 「白蘋」 (white flowers) are undoubtedly used to describe the feelings of departure. It can be seen that Du Shen-yen selected such scenes of early spring as 「雲霞」 (clouds), 「梅柳」 (plum and willow), 「黃鳥」 (yellow bird) and 「蘋」 (plane tree) to deliberately highlight homesickness. In this way, the objects were selected as materials to strengthen its impact. Take Chang Ke-jeou's "Wuyeerh", 梧葉兒 for example.

薔薇徑，(The small path was covered with roses,) 芍藥闌， (the railings also covered with flowers.) 鶯燕語間關。(The birds' crying sounded pleasing.)小雨紅芳綻，(A little rain made the red flowers more beautiful.) 新晴紫陌乾。(When the sky became clear, the paths in the wilderness turned dry.)日長繡窗 閒，(The day was so long and the women within the window had nothing to do.) 人立秋千畫板。(They left their room and played on the swings.)

This work depicts the scenes of springtime, which include 「闌」 (railings), 「薔薇」 (roses) and 「勺藥」 (flowers) beside the path, 「鶯燕」 (birds), 「紅芳」 (red flowers) and 「紫陌」 (the paths in the wilderness), silence 「繡窗」 (the window), and persons on 「秋千」 (the swings). The author uses these expressions to describe feelings of isolation, which are expressed by red flowers, birds and swings. For, in addition to expressing a wonderful time, flowers are used to symbolize the persons being missed. Moreover, single birds can signify homesickness and feelings of departure. As to swings, they are associated with the persons who played on them. Thus, these materials might well portray the feelings of missing beloved persons.

Accordingly, the meaning of literary works is intimately associated with material selection. Although certain works pinpoint their topics (thoughts and feelings) within the text, the abstract topics still need to be portrayed by concrete objects. In addition, some works put the topics outside the text. Under such circumstances, we need to trace the textual meanings by observing the materials the author has used. In short, we have to trace meanings by observing outward materials (likeness).

II. Vertical structure

Whatever the type of a composition, we need to examine its structure in both vertical and horizontal ways. In terms of compositional types, the horizontal relations are represented by far-near, big-small, root-end, deep-shallow, guest-master, real-unreal, positive-negative, flat-side, release-catch, cause-effect, etc.[16]

....

16 See Chen Man-ming, "On Major Contents of Compositional Types." 〈談詞章章法的主要內容〉 (Taipei: *The World of Chinese Language and Monthly Literature,* Dec. 1997. Jan.1998) pp.84-93, pp.105-117. Also see Chou Hsiao-

However, a complete structure is indeed organized in both horizontal and vertical ways. Thus many years ago, I claimed that in analyzing compositions, we have to make clear such components as "feeling" "reason," "landscape-object," and "things," Furthermore, we can take advantage of compositional types to grasp their logical structures.[17] Meanwhile, I wrote essays using these components as perspectives to explicate structures of compositions.[18] However, at that time, I did not directly discuss the vertical issues. Therefore, I will discuss them here. First, the organizational types of structural contents of compositions can be shown as follows:[19]

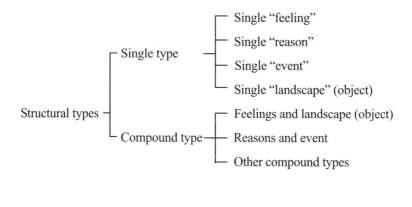

ping, *Types of Compositional Structures.* 《篇章結構類型論》(Taipei: Wanchenlo Publishing Company, Feb. 2000) p.620.

17 See Chen Man-ming, "How to Draw Chinese Text Structure Analysis Diagram" *Chinese Teaching.* 《國文教學津梁》 (Taipei: Taipei City Teachers Study Center, June 1900) p.65.

18 See Chen Man-ming, "On Compositional Structures."(Taipei: *The World of Chinese Languagse and Monthly Literature*, Oct. and Nov. 1999) pp. 65-71, pp.57-66.

19 See Chen Chiao-chun, "On Single Types of Compositional Structures—Focus on Applicable Compositional Types." *Paper Collection of Rhetoric.* 《修辭論叢》 Vol.4. (Taipei: Hungyei Cultural Business Company, June 2002) p.670.

1. Single types

The so-called "single" is used to describe the individual components of the composition such as "feelings," "reasons," "landscape" and "event". Generally speaking, to grasp a compositional structure, we should start with the main components of the composition, making clear the structural levels of the composition. Whenever a level appears alone, it can be considered a single type. In terms of compositional art, it is "wholly real" (event or landscape) or "wholly unreal" (feelings or reasons).[20] This may be further explained as follows.

1.1 Single "thing" type

This refers to "paragraph" or "composition." It is mainly used for narration. The topics of these types of compositions, more often than not, are put outside the text. This can be interpreted "between the lines."[21] And this also echoes the Chinese expression「不著一字，盡得風流」"Elegance can be shown without words" or "Handsome as handsome does."[22] Take "The Stupid Old Man Removes Mountains," for example. As a narration, it is a remarkable example of "single-thing type." The structure analysis table is as follows:

....

20 That is the single usage of reality and fiction.   See Chen Man-ming, "On Several Basic Means of Employing Compositional Materials," (Taipei: *Middle School Education*. 《中等教育》 Oct. 1985.) pp.8-9.

21 According to Huze, "the poem is excellent, expressive between lines.   We can well see the sadness and sorrow."

22 According to Shih Kwon-tu, "few words express so many concepts.   A picture is worth ten thousand words."

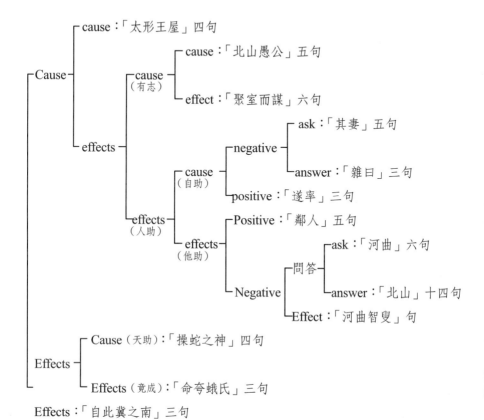

According to the table above in telling this fable, the author uses the cause-effect type, positive-negative type, and question-answer type to organize the texual matcrials in ordei to form a complete structure.[23]

齊景公遊於牛山之上，(When Chichingkung traveled to Cow Mountain,) 而北望齊曰：(he saw the nicely arranged houses in the capital, saying,) 「美哉國乎！(how beautiful the nation is!)

....

23 See Chen Man-ming, *On Compositional Structures.* 〈談篇章結構〉

鬱鬱泰山，(Green mountains and beautiful scenery!) 使古而無死者，(If there had not been so-called death since ancient times,) 則寡人將去此而何之？」(how could I leave this nation and die?") 俯而泣沾襟。(And then he cried.) 國子、高子曰 (Kuotzu and Kaotzu said,)：「然。臣賴君之賜，("We rely on our king.) 疏食惡肉，(Bad and rotten vegetables and meat)可得而食也，(we are willing to eat.) 駑馬柴車，(Bad horses and broken vehicles) 可得而乘也。(We are willing to ride.) 且猶不欲死，(In this way, we want to live forever,) 況君乎？(Not to mention our king.)」俯泣。(They cried.)

晏子曰：(Yentzu said,)「樂哉 ("happily,) 今日嬰之遊也，(on my trip today) 見怯君一 (I saw a scary king)，而諛臣二。(and two flattering subjects.) 使古而無死者，(If ancient men had never died,) 則太公至今猶存，(Kings of ancient times would be alive today.) 吾君方將被蓑笠而立乎畎畝之中。(And then you would be wearing farm clothes and laboring on farms.) 惟事之恤，(Under such labor) 何暇念死乎？」(You would never think of death.")

景公慚，(Chingkung felt ashamed.) 而舉觴自罰，(He thus punished himself by drinking a cup of wine.) 因罰二臣。(So did the two subjects.)

Take the story of 《韓詩外傳》 (*Hanshihwaichuan*), for example. According to this story, Yentzu criticized Chichingkung for his fear of death. At the outset, the protagonists and location are presented. And then, the five lines from 「美哉國乎」（how beautiful the nation is）are used to describe the sadness of Chichingkung, who mourned over 「使古而無死者，則寡人將去此而何之」(If there had not been so-called death in ancient times, how could I leave this nation and die). This indeed shows he did fear death. According to 《晏子春秋、內篇、諫》, "When Chingkung travelled to Dxen Mountain, in the face of his country, he said, while crying, "How can I die someday？"And the same historical fact can also be seen in *Lietze*. At that time, the subjects surrounding Chingkung should have advised him. However, to please him, Kuotzu and Kaotzu narrated seven lines from「臣賴君之賜」（We rely on our king）. Moreover,「俯而泣沾襟」（and then he cried.）. Under such circumstances, Yentzu had to offer advice. At that moment, he began with the line「樂哉！今日嬰之遊也」（Happily, on my trip today.）And then, he directly pointed out「見怯君一，而諛臣二」（ I saw a scary king and two flattering subjects）. Furthermore, concerning Chingkung's sigh, he used eight lines from「使古而無死者」（if ancient men had never died）to indirectly disclose that if "kings in ancient times were still alive today"「太公至今猶存」, he would not have gained his crown and would have even become sad for his country. These words worked. So, Chingkung felt ashamed. And he thus punished himself by drinking a cup of wine. Yentzu often used soft but wise words to offer advice. This is just one of the examples. The structure analysis table is as follows:

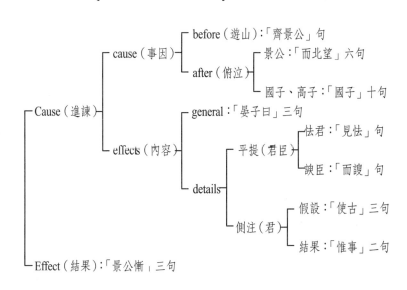

According to the diagram above, the author mainly uses such compositional types as "cause and effect" "present and past" "general and detail" and "flat and side" to organize its textual materials, forming its compositional structure. The textual logic is remarkably clear.

1.2 Single "landscape"(object) type

This means that the "composition" or "paragraph" of a work is mainly used for describing "landscape"(object). The main idea of this compositional type is totally put outside the work. However, inside the work, the topic is highlighted by "landscape"(object). Just as Wang Kuo-wei pointed out "all words of landscapes are words of feelings." [24] Take Ouyang Hsiu's Poem entitled 〈采桑子〉 ("Chaishantzu"), for example,

春深雨過西湖好(In late spring, with raindrops ceasing, the scenery of West Lake is so beautiful) 百卉爭妍(All kinds of flowers are blossoming) 蝶亂蜂喧(Butterfiles wildly fly and bees utter voices) 晴日催花暖欲然 (Warm sunshine seems to burn flowers) 蘭橈畫舸悠悠去 (Wooden boats slowly pass by) 疑是神仙 (It seems that fairies are on the boat) 返照波間 (Sunset is reflected on waves) 水濶風高颺管絃 (On vast waters and in breeze, music is spreading)

This is one of the thirteen songs written by the author to praise West Lake. It aims to describe his easy mind by praising the marvelous scenery in late spring. Here, the first line-「春深雨過西湖好」(In late spring, with raindrops ceasing, the scenery of West Lake is so beautiful）is used as a general introduction. And then, the

....

24 See Wang Kuo-wei, *Tzu in the Mundane World.* 《人間詞話刪稿》

three lines following 「百卉爭妍」（ All kinds of flowers are blossoming ） use such scenes and objects as flowers, bees, butterflies and sunshine to describe the beautiful scenery of late spring on West Lake. In addition, four lines following 「蘭橈畫舸悠悠去」（ wooden boats slowly pass by ） use boats, sunshine reflection, vast waters, winds and music to mix natural objects with personnel in order to describe the beautiful scenery of late spring on West Lake. The narration is in the order of "from general to details" vividly depicting the marvelous scenery. The structure analysis diagram is as follows:

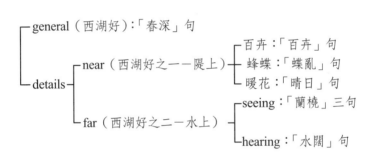

According to the diagram above, the author uses such compositional types as "general and details" "far and near" "consciousness shifting" to organize its textual materials, forming its compositional structure. The narration is in a strict order.[25]

Take Chou Mi's poem entitled 〈聞鵲喜、吳山觀濤〉（ Joyously Hearing Birds and Watching Sea ）, for example.

天水碧 (waters on the horizon are blue) 染就一江秋色 (Autumn sceneries on the river are colored) 鰲戴雪山龍起蟄

....

25　See Chou Hsiao-ping. *Types of Compositional Structures.* 《篇章結構類型論》 pp.148-161.

(sea-tortoises cap the snow mountain and dragons wake up) 快風 吹海立 (Swift winds blow and sea waves stand) 數點煙鬟 青滴 (Smoke roll up) 一杼霞綃紅濕 (Sunset is red and wet) 白鳥明邊帆影直 (White birds fly along the river, and sails are up)隔江聞夜笛 (across the river, night sirens are heard)

This poem aims to describe the tides of Chantan River. In terms of time, it begins with tides moving, ending in tides ceasing. The first half of the poem describes the rolling tides. In the beginning, the first two lines are used to describe the autumn scene in which the blue river and sky serve as a setting for the rolling tides. And then, the two lines following 「鰲戴」 (sea-tortoises cap) are used to depict the shocking scene of the rolling tides. Here, in addition to capping sea-tortoises and swimming dragons, 「快風」 (swift winds) are employed to describe the sea waves which seem to stand high. Moreover, the ceasing tides belong to the second half of the Tzu. First, the two lines following 「數點」 (several dots) are used to describe the mountains and sunset, which turn green and red on smoky waters. And then, the two lines following 「白鳥」 (white birds) are used to describe the sea gulls flying around sails. This belongs to the part of visions. Moreover, the acoustic sounds come from the night sirens across the river. In this way, the author uses peaceful, calm scenes, which make a strong contrast to the marvelous scene of rolling tides of the first half of the Tzu. The best highlighting effect is thus created. According to Li Cho-tang. "the first half of the Tzu presents the vision of rolling tides from far to near. And then in the second half, the previously vibrating movements turn calm and quiet." In addition, in terms of the second half, he comments as follows: "Such calm can be experienced only after the rushing and rolling tides cease. Indeed, this does highlight the spectacle of the waves of the river. In depicting tides, the author uses the constrastive and transitional effects to create a remarkable effect despite concise language."[26]   The structure analysis diagram is as follows:

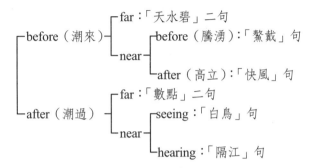

According to the diagram above, the author uses such compositional types as "present and past" "far and near" "consciousness shifting" to organize its textual materials, forming its compositional structure. This is very powerful and influential.

1.3 Single "reason" type

This means that the "composition" or "paragraph" of a work is mainly used to explain "reasons" Generally speaking, in both arguments and explanations, the "reasons" frequently cite "events"[27] as examples. Therefore, the long composition or paragraphs purely written for explaining reasons are rare. Here, take 〈紀孝行〉 ("Recording the Behaviors of Filial Piety") of 《孝經》 (*Doctrine of Filial Piety*), for example.

....

26 See *Anthology of Tzus.* 《詞林觀止》 (Shanghai: Shanghai Ancient Books Publishing Company, April 1994, 1st Edition) p.694.

27 See Chen Man-ming, "On the Relation between Meanings and Materials." (Taipei: The World of Chinese Language and Monthly Literature, Nov. 1994) pp.44-47.

子曰：(Confucius said,)「子之事親也，(in serving his parents, a man of filial piety) 居則致其敬，(respects his parents in his daily life,) 養則致其樂，(supports his family with a pleasing heart,) 病則致其憂，(takes care of his sick parents with care,) 喪則致其哀，(buries his parents in sadness,) 祭則致其嚴。(sincerely offers memorial services.) 五者備矣，(He needs to do these five things well.) 然後能事親。(And then he will serve his parents well.)

事親者 (in serving his parents), 居上不驕 (don't be proud when placed in the leading class)，為下不亂 (sincerely behave when placed under the leading class)，在醜不爭(don't compete when placed in a despised condition) 居上而驕則亡 (He who is proud for a high position will perish)，為下而亂則刑(He who doesn't behave in a lower class will be punished)，在醜而爭則兵(He who competes in a despised condition will lose peace)，三者不除 (without preventing the three things) 雖日用三牲之養(Even though serving his parents with abundant material supplies) 猶為不孝也 (that is not filial piety)。

This passage originally belongs to the tenth chapter of 《孝經》 (*Book of Filial Piety*), which aims to discuss the behaviors of a man of filial piety. And it is composed in the order of " from inside to outside." In term of "inside," the lines from「孝子之事親也」(a man of filial piety serves his parents) to「然後能事親」(and then he can serve his parents well) use the first six lines to explain that a man of filial piety is required to serve his parents in five aspects-「居」(housing),「養」(feeding),「病」(sickness),「喪」(burial) and「祭」(memorial service). And in dealing with these situations, a man of filial piety has to embrace the attitudes of respect, pleasure, care, sadness and seriousness. Furthermore, the two lines following 「五者備矣」(fives things are completed) serve as a generalization to explain how to serve parents inside the household. In addition, in terms of "outside" these lines were from 「事親者」 (the man serving his parents) to the last line. Firstly use the four lines following 「事親者」 (the man serving his parents) to extend filial piety from inside to outside. Initially, from the positive side, the proper behaviors when placed in 「居上」 (leading class), 「為下」 (in a lower class), 「在醜」 (in a despised condition) are explained. Moreover, the six lines following 「居上而驕則亡」 (He who is proud for a high position will perish) use the form of "first detail and then generalization" to mention, from a negative side, the improper behaviors when placed in 「居上」 (leading class), 「為下」 (in a lower class), and 「在醜」 (in a despised condition). And it is pointed out that these are without filial piety. In the opening of 《孝經》 (*Book of Filial Piety*), it is revealed that "The so-called filial piety begins with the service of parents goes through the service of the emperor, and ends with establishing oneself." The structure analysis diagram is as follows.

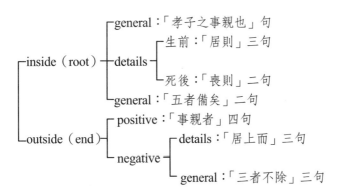

According to the diagram above, the author uses such compositional types as "root(inside) and end (outside)" "general and detail" "positive and negative" "present and past" to organize its textual materials, forming its compositional structure. Despite the shortness of the passage, the compositional types used are of a great variety. Take《禮記‧大學》(*Lichi. Great Learning*) for example.

大學之道：(The way of *Great Learning*)在明明德，(is to manifest one's own bright virtues,) 在親民，(is to endear oneself to the people,) 在止於至善。(is to make oneself perfect in goodness,) 知止而后有定，(And then, an individual can find a definite direction.) 定而后能靜，(A definite direction leads to a quiet mind.)靜而后能安，(A quiet mind leads to peace with one's own situation.) 安而后能慮，(Peace leads to delicate considerations.) 慮而后能得。(Delicate considerations lead to perfection.) 物有本末，(Every object has its root and tip.) 事有終始，(Everything has its beginning and end.) 知所先後，(Being able to distinguish beginnings from ends) 則近道矣。(almost justifies the way.)

古之欲明明德於天下者，(In ancient times among those who intended to manifest their bright virtues in the world,) 先其國；(first they had to manage their country.)欲治其國者，(While intending to manage their country,)先齊其家；(first they had to manage their families.) 欲齊其家者，(While intending to manage their families.)先修其身；(first they had to improve their own characters.)欲修其身者，(While intending to improve their own characters,) 先正其心；(they had to make their heart justifiable.) 欲正其心者，(While intending to make their heart justifiable,) 先誠其意；(first they had to make their intention sincere.)欲誠其意者，(While intending to make their intention sincere,) 先致其知；(first they had to enrich their own knowledge.) 致知在格物。(Enriching knowledge depends on figuring out the rules of the universe.) 物格而后知至，(Knowing the rules leads to complete knowledge.) 知至而后意誠，(Complete knowledge leads to sincere intention.) 意誠而后心正，(Sincere intention leads to a justifiable heart.) 心正而后身修，(A justifiable heart leads to perfection of character.) 身修

而后家齊，(Perfection of character leads to a well-managed family.) 家齊而后國治，(A well-managed family leads to a well-managed country.) 國治而后天下平。(A well-managed country leads to a peaceful world.)

自天子以至於庶人，(Both the emperor and common people) 壹是皆以修身為本。(should consider perfection of character the foundation.) 其本亂，(If we neglect the foundation,) 而末治者否矣；(a country cannot be well managed.) 其所厚者薄，而其所薄者厚，(If we confuse triviality and vitality,) 未之有也。(nothing can be done well.) 此謂知本，(In this way, we learn the basis of knowledge) 此謂知之至也。(This is true knowledge.)

This work generally talks about the aims and methods of *Tahsueh* (大學). The four lines following 「大學之道」（the way of Tahsueh）talk about the aims. This is, as Chutzu put it, "three pillars." (see composition and sentences of *Tahsueh*). As to the mehods, we can see these lines from 「知止」 to the final line. Here, in terms of the gradual steps, the author, on the one hand, explained how to realize "three pillars," and he, on the other hand, revealed how to implement 「八月」 (eight details). In composition and sentences of *Tahsueh*, Chutze commented on 「則近道矣」(almost can realize the way) -"this concluded the concepts of the two passages above."In addition, he commented on 「國治而后天下平」(Well-managed country leads to a peaceful world) 「修身」 (improve characters), it's to manifest bright virtues. Below 「齊家」 (manage families), it's the things of new residents, knowing rules leads to complete knowledge. Below 「意誠」 (make intentions sincere), it's an initiation of everything good."[28] It can be seen that this passage serves as a linkage in the contents of the text.

....

28 See *Notes on Four Books.* 《四書集註》 p.4.

Furthermore, the author pratically elaborated on "eight details" First, the author used thirteen lines following 「古之欲明明德」(in ancient times those who intend to manifest their bright virtues in the world) to explain eight details in reverse order. In addition, he used seven lines following 「物格而后知至」(knowing rules leads to complete knowledge) to elaborate on eight details step by step. And then, he indirectly concluded that 「修身」(improving characters) served as a basis. Moreover, he also explained the reasons for that. In composition and sentences of Tahsueh, chutze commented on "improving characters is the basis." "Above 「正心」(make hearts justifiable), these are related to 「修身」(improving characters)"[29] Moreover, he commented on 「未之有也」(nothing can be well done)- "character is the basis. And less important is the family. These two passages (from the line following 「天子」to 「未之有也」(nothing can be well done)) concluded the above two passages (from 「古之欲明明德」(in ancient times those who intend to manifest their bright virtues) to 「國治而后天下平」(a well-managed country leads to a peaceful world)[30] In addition, in Explicating Lichi《禮記正義》,Kung Yingta commented on 「此謂知之至也」(this is true knowledge)- "Basis refers to character. Accordingly, knowing one's own character is the basis of knowledge and this is the uttermost knowledge.[31] So, it can be seen that these lines were indirectly reached by "lateral, circuitous and recipient" form that took a circular comprehensive recycle. In this way, these echoed the details, explaining the step and aims. This was intended to simplify the complicated text. The structure analysis diagram was as follows:

....

29 See *Notes on Four Books*. 《四書集註》
30 See *Notes on Four Books*. 《四書集註》
31 See *Notes on Thirteen Books, Lichi.* 《十三經注疏‧禮記》 (Taipei: Literature Printing Company, June 1965) p.984.

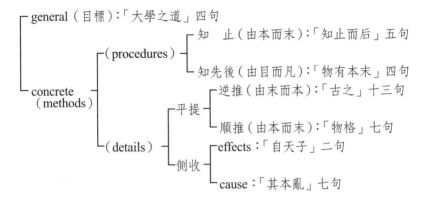

According to the diagram above, the author mainly uses such compositional types as "general and concrete" "Flat and side" "root and end" "general and detail" and " cause and effect" to organize its textual materials, forming its compositional structure. This is in accordance with the principles of order, change, consistence and unification.

1.4 Single "feeling" type

This means that the "composition" or " paragraph" is mainly used to express "feelings" since the "feelings" more often than not are highlighted by "landscape"(object) or "event" the works of which the whole composition or paragraph is used for a single purpose of expressing feelings are rare. These only can be seen in folk songs or other genres similar to them. Take《吳聲歌曲.子夜歌》之二十一 (21st of *Wu Voice Songs. Midnight Song*), for example.

別後涕流連 (I shed tears after departure.) 相思情悲滿 (My heart is full of sadness for missing you.) 憶子腹糜爛 (The memory of you makes my stomach decay.) 肝長尺寸斷 (Liver and bowels are thus broken to pieces.)

This poem mainly aims to express feelings after departure. *In Feelings Expression and Events Narration,* Hung Shun-lung points out that "the contents write about the girl's pains for missing her boy friend. This is also an admiration of feelings. Actually, the first two lines directly portray her mind. And then, the following two lines exaggerate the pains of missing her boy friend."[32] Such expressions as「涕流連」(shed tears).「腹糜爛」(stomach decay), and「肝腸斷」(Liver and bowels broken) are used to gradually expose her inner feelings. In addition, the line-「相思情悲滿」(My heart is full of sadness for missing you) serves as a holding center to connect the whole poem, forming the structure of "detail, general, detail" which clearly and directly expresses the hatred and feelings of a woman.

The structure analysis diagram is as follows.[33]

```
┌details（淺）:「別後」句
├general :「相思」句
│                  ┌一:「憶子」句
└details（深）┤
                   └二:「肝腸」句
```

From the diagram above, we can see that in this short song the author uses the compositional arts of "generalization and detail," and "parallel" to organize the contents, forming the compositional structure. This is easy to understand.

An anonymous author's poem, entitled "Looking to Chiangnan,"

---

32 See Hung Shun-lung, *Feelings Expression and Event Narration.* 《抒情與敘事》 (Taipei: Liming Cultural Business Company, Dec. 1998.) p.206.

33 See Chen Chia-chun. *On Single Types of Compositional Structures—Focus on Applicable Compositional Types.* 〈論辭章內容結構之單一類型——以其所適用之章法為考察重心〉P.672.

can serve as another example.

莫攀我，(Don't play with me!) 攀我太心偏。(I am only a plaything.) 我是曲江臨池柳，(I am a willow tree around a pond.) 者（這）人折了那人攀。(Men line up to play with me.) 恩愛一時間。(My love is very transient.)

This work voices the line-"I am only a play thing" from the perspective of a prostitute. In people's eyes, she is 「臨池柳」 (a willow tree around a pond), which everyone can play with. Therefore, it follows that 「恩愛一時間」 (love is very transient.) [34] The structure analysis table is as follows:

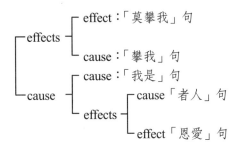

Accordingly, the author uses the cause-effect type to organize the texual materials, forming a complete structure. Moreover, the cause-effect type is rather basic. [35]

....

34 See Chang Si-hou's analysis. *Collection of Appraisal of Tang Sung Dynasty Tzu.* 《唐宋詞鑑賞集成》 (Hong Kong: Chunhua Bookstore, July 1987) p.15.

35 The structure of "cause and effect" has been frequently seen in the iron inscription of the West Chou Dynasty. See Chen Man-ming, "On the Nature of the Cause-Effect Compositional Type." (Taipei: The World of Chinese Language and Monthly Literature, Dec. 2002) pp.94-101.

2. Compound types

The so-called "compound type" refers to the combination of such major components as "feeling" "reason" "landscape/object" and "thing". This kind of combination belongs to the real-unreal compositional type, which also maintains a guest-master relation.[36] Among these components, "feeling" and "reason" are "master" while "landscape/object" and "thing" are "guest." Actually, this can be elaborated by Wang Kuo-wei's words-"All words about landscapes are words of feelings."

In other words, it was a means that the author used "landscape"(object), and "thing" to help with writing. However, it was his purpose to highlight "feelings" and "reasons" in this way[37] After fully understanding this point, we can comprehensively grasp what feelings and reasons the author intends to express. I will illustrate this below.

2.1 The compound type of "feelings" and "landscapes" (objects)

This type combines "feelings" and "landscapes"(objects) to form certain levels of structures of compositions and paragraphs. And this type can be divided into such minor types as "first landscape (object)

....

36 Wu Yin-tien, *Compositional Structuralism.* 《文章結構學》 (Beijing: Chinese University Publishing Company, 1989) p.311.

37 Chen Man-ming, *Analysis of Compositional Structures—as in the Textbooks of the Middle Schools.* (Taipei: Wanchunlo Publishing Company, May 1999) p.331.

and then feelings,""first feelings and then landscapes (object),"
"landscape (object) feelings, landscapes (object), and " feelings,
landscapes (object), feelings," Take Tu Fu's poem, for example.[38]

細草微風岸，(The breezes stroke lightly the grassy strands.) 危
檣獨夜舟。(The junk-mast tall and lone in the darkness stands.)
星垂平野闊，(The sparkling stars shine on fields wild and wide.)
月湧大江流。(The moon emerges from the rough river tide.) 名
豈文章著，(My pen has won me fame--heeds it my will?) 官應
老病休。(An official should not retire till old and ill.) 飄飄何所
似？(What am I who be everywhere wandering?) 天地一沙鷗。
(A gull between heaven and earth hovering.)

This poem was inspired by the sentiments of a lingering boat
along the grassy strands. In the first line, a single boat, grassy
strands, breezes were used to describe the loneliness of the river side.
And then, wide fields and river tide were used to describe the
spacious heaven and earth. This was the part of describing
landscapes, serving as a "reality" Furthermore, in the following line,
he mentioned his sickness and wandering. And in the final line, the
traveling boat and gull were implied to express his sadness for
wandering. This was the part of "expressing feelings," serving as
"fiction". The mixture of realities and fiction utterly expressed the
sad emotion.[39] The structure analysis diagram was as follows:

....

38 See Chao Hsiao-ping, *Types of Compositional Structures*, 《篇章結構類型論》
    pp.248-266.

39 See Fu Szu-chuan's analysis, *Collection of Tany Dynasty Poems*. 《唐詩大觀》
    (Hong Kong: the Commercial Press, Ltd., Jan., 1986) p.564.

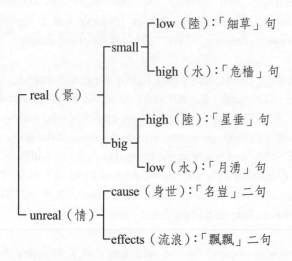

According to the diagram above, it can be seen that the author used such compositional types as "unreal (feeling) and real (landscape)" "big and small" "cause and effect" and "high and low" to organize its textual materials, forming the compositional structure.

The structure of "first feeling and then landscape (object)" can be illustrated by one of Li-Yu's poems.

多少恨，(How much sorrow and hatred) 昨夜夢魂中。(in last night's dream!) 還似舊時遊上苑，(I dreamed that I was playing in the garden.) 車如流水馬如龍。(Vehicles were like streams and horses were like dragons.) 花月正春風。(In the spring wind I enjoyed beautiful flowers and a bright moon.)

In the first two lines, the author directly poured out his hatred after waking up from a dream. And then, in the following line, he explained the reason for his hatred.[40] In addition, the three lines following 「還似」 were used to describe the world of the dream. Accordingly, the textual structure of "first feelings and then landscape" was employed to express his pains for the ruin of the nation.[41] The structure analysis diagram is as follows:

According to the diagram above, the author used such compositional types as "unreal (feeling) and real (landscape)," "cause and effect," "dot and dye," "heaven and man"[42] to organize the textual materials, forming its compositional structure. The structure of "landscape (object), feelings, landscape (object) can be seen in the following song.

· ·

40 See Wang Pei-ling and Fu Chen-ku's analysis. *Collection of Appraisal of Tang Sung Dynasty Tzus,* 《唐宋詞鑑賞集成》p.119.

41 See Wang Pei-ling and Fu Chen-ku's analysis. *Collection of Appraisal of Tang Sung Dynasty Tzus,* 《唐宋詞鑑賞集成》 p.120.

42 Heaven refers to nature, while man, to personnel. Both belong to materials. In depicting landscapes, it's common that in terms of materials "heaven" and "man" are presented in a parallel way, forming a structure. Thus, it's very reasonable to see "heaven and man" as a compositional type. Man Chih-yuan's song entitled "On West Lake" is a remarkable example. See Chen Man-ming, *Analysis of Compositional Structures—as in the Textbooks of the Middle Schools,* pp.295-297. Also see Chen Man-ming, *On Several Special Compositional Types.* (Taipei: Taiwan Normal University, Chinese Journal, June 2002) pp.187-191.

風飄飄，(The wind is blowing,) 雨瀟瀟，(the rain is falling.) 便做陳摶也睡不著，(I cannot sleep.) 懊惱傷懷抱，(Regret, hatred and sorrow pierce my heart.)撲簌簌淚點拋。(Tears fall.) 秋蟬兒噪罷寒蛩兒叫，(Insects continue their noisy ways.) 淅零零細雨灑芭蕉。(Tiny raindrops fall on the banana leaves.)

Kuan Han-ching had compsed a series of four songs called "Great Virtue Song,"which described a sentimental girl's memory of her beloved in four seasons respectively. This song was one of these four songs. In terms of its structure, it began with landscapes, ending in landscapes. And amid the song, the author used the method of inserted narration to express his feelings creating and landscapes a special effect of a union of feelings. The two beginning lines of 「風飄飄」（the wind is blowing）took advantage of fantastic winds and rains to usher in 「便做陳摶也睡不著」（I cannot sleep），which served as a bridge of expressing feelings. In addition, following the line of 「睡不著」（cannot sleep），the line of 「懊惱傷懷抱」（regret, hatred and sorrow hurt my heart）further described the sorrow of the master. This was the main body of expressing feelings. As to the final three lines, the author apparently used landscapes to highlight feelings. The tears of the master and the noises of insects and raindrops echoed the two beginning lines, utterly highlighting the sorrowful mind of the master. In this way, the abstract pains of 「傷懷抱」（hurt my heart）was concretely expressed. Indeed, the author expressed all of these in an extremely sophisticated way. The structure analysis diagram is as follows:

According to the diagram above, in this song, the author used such compositional types as "feelings and landscape," "cause and effects,""consciousness shifting," and "parallel" to organize these textual materials, forming its compositional structure.

As to the structure of "feeling, landscape, feeling," it can be illustrated by Tu Sheng-yen's poem entitled〈和晉陵陸丞早春遊望〉（The original text and its analysis can be seen in the first section）.The structure analysis diagram is as follows:

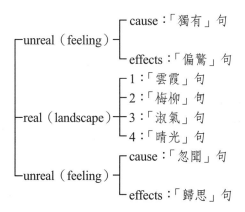

According to the diagram above, the author uses such compositional types as "unreal (feelings) and real (landscape)," "cause and effect," and "parallel" to organize the textual materials, forming its compositional structure.   In addition, there is also such structures as "landscape, feeling, landscape, feeling." Take Sin Chichi's poem, for example.[43]

2.2 The compounded type of "reason" and "thing"

This refers to a combination of "reason" and "thing," which forms certain structures of "compositions" or "paragraphs."   This type can also be divided into various structures such as "first thing and then reason," "first reason and then thing," "thing, reason, thing," and "reason, thing, reason."   The case of "first thing and then reason" can be seen in Liujung's "On Habits."[44]

蓉少時，(When I was young,) 讀書養晦堂之西偏一室。(I would read in my room.) 俛而讀，(First I would bow my head to read my books.) 仰而思；(Then I would look up to think over problems.) 思而弗得，(When I could not figure out the problem,)輒起，(More often than not I would get up.) 繞室以旋。(As I walked around the room,)室有窪徑尺，(a tiny piece of earth sank under the floor.) 浸淫日廣。(The sunken area was gradually expanded.) 每履之，(Whenever I stepped on it,) 足苦躓焉；(I feared that I would stumble.) 既久而遂安之。(As time passed, I got used to it.)

一日，(One day) 父來室中，(my father came to my room.) 顧而笑曰：(He took a look around and, laughing, said,)「一室之不治，("if you cannot keep your room well in order,) 何以天下

43 See Chou Hsiao-ping, *Types of Compositional Structures*, 《篇章結構類型論》 pp.260-261.

44 See Chou Hsiao-ping, *Types of Compositional Structures*, 《篇章結構類型論》 pp.267-288.

國家為？」(how can you bring order to a whole nation?") 命童子取土平之。(He ordered the servants to fill the hole under the floor.)

後蓉履其地，(After that I stepped on the filled-up hole.) 蹴然以驚，(I was surprised:) 如土忽隆起者；(it seemed that the spot had risen.) 俯視地，(Looking down at the spot,) 坦然則既平矣。(I noted that the ground indeed was flat.)已而復然；(And then the experience repeated itself.) 又久而後安之。(After a long time, I got used to it.)

噫！(Alas!) 習之中人甚矣哉！(Habits do affect men deeply.) 足履平地，(When I stepped on the flat ground,) 不與窪適也；(I could not get used to the hole.) 及其久，(After a period of time) 而窪者若平。(the hole seemed to become flat.) 至使久而即乎其故，(After a long time, when I stepped on the flat ground,) 則反窒焉而不寧。(I felt that I could not get used to it.) 故君子之學貴慎始。(Therefore, for a gentleman, learning is totally based on starting points.)

This work aims to explain how deeply a habit can influence a man in order to teach a moral lesson—"The beginning is vital for learning." Its structure can, in general, be divided into these main parts—"narration" and "commentary." "Narration" belongs to "details," while "commentary" belongs to "generalization." In the narration of "details," the seven lines from 蓉少時 describe the author's habit of "walking in a circle within the room" with the purpose of introducing the following tracks of words. And then, five lines, from 室有窪徑尺, tells us that in spite of suffering from the hole in the room, he got used to it. This is the first track. In addition, the thirteen lines, from 一日, tells us that due to his father's fixing the hole he was first stunned but later became used to it. This is the second track. And then, in the commentary or "generalization," the line--噫！習之中人甚矣哉—is used to express his feeling about the remarkable impact of a habit. Furthermore, four lines, from 「足履平地」, echoes the first track categorized as "detail," meanwhile making comments.　And then, two lines, from 至使久而即乎其故, echo the second track categorized as "detail," making further comments.　Finally, the line, 故君子之學貴慎始, turns from the subject of habit to that of learning, bringing the main idea into light.　Just as Sung ko said, this work uses "thought" to unify itself.　Owing to his "thoughts," the author "walks in a circle in his room," and then the subject is inductively and naturally explained.[45]　In this way, the main idea is more clearly explained, becoming quite convincing.　The structure analysis diagram is as follows:

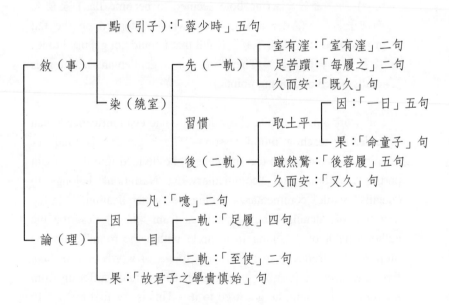

45 See Sung Kuo-yu, *Dictionary of Appreciating Ancient Prose*. 《古文鑑賞辭典》 (Shanghai: Shanghai Tze Book Publishing Company, April 1998.) p.2004.

According to the diagram above, the author uses such compositional types as "general and detail," "dot and dye," "cause and effect," "present and past" to organize its textual materials, forming its structure.

As to the structure of "first reason and then event," we can see Han yu's article.

大凡物不得其平則鳴。(Creatures will cry if not in balance.)草木之無聲，風撓之鳴。(Grass and wood are silent, but winds cause them to be heard.) 水之無聲，風蕩之鳴，(Water is soundless, but winds cause it to be heard.) 其躍也，或激之，(Water jumps for being stirred.) 其趨也，或梗之；(Water runs for being blocked.) 其沸也，或炙之。(Water boils for being burned.) 金石之無聲，或擊之鳴。(Gold and stone are soundless, yet make noises when being struck.) 人之於言也亦然。有不得已者而後言，(People's speech is a similar case.) 其歌也有思，(They sing of memories.) 其哭也有懷，(They cry from sadness.) 凡出乎口而為聲者，其皆有弗平者乎！(The speeches of people may result from an imbalance of mind.)
樂也者，鬱於中而泄於外者也，(Music is an outlet for people's inner feelings.) 擇其善鳴者而假之鳴(Proper musical instruments are chosen for making certain sounds)：金、石、絲、竹、匏、土、革、木八者，物之善鳴者也。(There are eight things, such as gold and stone, which are good at making sounds.) 維天之於時也亦然。擇其善鳴者而假之鳴(Heaven chooses those who are good at giving voice in various seasons.)：是故以鳥鳴春 (Therefore, in spring, birds give voice.)，以雷鳴夏 (In summer, thunder gives voice.)，以蟲鳴秋，(In fall, worms give voice.) 以風鳴冬，(In winter, winds give voice.) 四時之相推奪，其必有不得其平者乎！(The shifts in the four seasons may result from a kind of imbalance.) 其於人也亦然。(This can happen to a man.) 人聲之精者為

言，(The cream of man's voices is language.) 文辭之於言，又其精也，(Compositions and expressions are the cream of language.) 尤擇其善鳴者而假之鳴。(Men good at voicing are especially chosen to give voice.

其在唐虞，咎陶、禹，其善鳴者也，而假以鳴。(In the time of the Tang, Yu, Kaotao and Yu were used to voicing their times for they were good at giving voice.) 夔弗能以文辭鳴，又自假於韶以鳴。(Those who could not give voice through composition, did it by means of music.) 夏之時，五子以其歌鳴。(In the time of 夏 Taikang's five younger brothers gave voice (Those who were included in 詩、書、六藝 were good at voicing.) 周之衰，孔子之徒鳴之，(With the decline of the Chou dynasty, Confucius with his men voiced their times) 其聲大而遠。(Their voices were loud and far-reaching.) 傳曰：「天將以夫子為木鐸」(According to *Lunyu*, "Heaven will use Confucius as a wooden tool for warning and teaching the public.) "其弗信矣乎！(Are these words believable?) 其末也，莊周以其荒唐之辭鳴。(At the end of the Chou dynasty, 莊子 used his capacious words to express himself) 楚，大國也，(The Chu nation was a big one.) 其亡也，以屈原鳴。(When it declined, Chuyun expressed the times.) 臧孫辰、孟軻、荀卿以道鳴者也。(臧孫辰、孟軻、荀卿 used doctrines to express their times.) 楊朱、墨翟、管夷吾、晏嬰、老聃、申不害、韓非、慎到、田駢、鄒衍、尸佼、孫武、張儀、蘇秦之屬，皆以其術鳴。(楊朱、墨翟、管夷吾、晏嬰、老聃、申不害、韓非、慎到、田駢、鄒衍、尸佼、孫武、張儀、蘇秦 used strategies to express their times.) 之興，李斯鳴之。漢之時，司馬遷、相如、揚雄，最其善鳴者也。其下魏、晉氏，(Down to the age of Weichin,) 鳴者不及於古，(those who "cried out" were less compentent than the ancients.) 然亦未嘗絕也；(But the tradition was ceaseless.) 就其善者：(Among the best,) 其聲清以浮，(their voices were fresh and light.) 其節數

以急，(Their rhythms were tense yet delicate.) 其辭淫以哀，(Their expressions were wanton and sad,) 其志弛以肆；(their will relaxed and unrestrained.) 其為言也，亂雜而無章。(Their compositions were disorderly.) 將天醜其德莫之顧邪？(It was likely that heaven so hated their vices that He ignored them.) 何為乎不鳴其善鳴者也？(Why not use those good at crying out to engage in utterance?)

唐之有天下，(With the downfall of the Tang dynasty)陳子昂、蘇源明、元結、李白、杜甫、李觀，皆以其所能鳴。(陳子昂、蘇源明、元結、李白、杜甫、李觀，Those who used their talents to express their times.) 其存而在下者，(For those who existed in low levels,) 孟郊東野始以其詩鳴。(孟郊東野 used their poems to express the times.) 其高出魏、晉(Their poetry was higher than those of the 魏晉 ages)，不懈而及於古，(Their sincerity, to some extent, had reached the standards of the ancients.) 其他浸淫乎漢氏矣。(Other works also gradually reached the standards of the Han dynasty.) 從吾遊者，(Among the persons learning from me,) 李翱、張籍，其尤也。(李翱、張籍 were the most outstanding.) 三子者之鳴信善矣，(The crying out of these three persons was excellent.) 抑不知天將和其聲，(Perhaps heaven would echo their voices,) 而使鳴國家之盛邪？(making them cry out for the prosperity of their nation.) 抑將窮餓其身，(Perhaps heaven would make their bodies hungry,) 思愁其心腸，(making their mind sad,) 而使自鳴其不幸邪？(making them cry for their misfortune.) 三子者之命，則懸乎天矣。(The fates of these three persons were up to heaven.) 其在上也，奚以喜？(What was worth happiness for those who possess high positions?) 其在下也，奚以悲？(What was worth sadness for those who are stuck in low positions?)

東野之役於江南也，(孟東野 went to 江南 to serve.) 有若不釋然者，(He seemed unhappy.)故吾道其命於天者以解之。(Therefore, I comforted him with these words—"an individual's fate is in the hands of heaven.")

This work in the form of a preface serves as a gift. The author used the line--"heaven uses those who are good at voicing"--to pacify 孟郊 who at that time were sent out to serve as a county officer. The whole work can be divided into two major parts-- "commentary" and "narration."

First let's take a look at the role of commentary. This part begins with the first line, ending in 「奚以悲」(what worth sadness). The structure is framed by "first generalization and then, detail."

1. The role of generalization: the first line--「大凡物不得其平則鳴」(Creatures will cry if not in balance)--is the topic sentence. According to Lin Sichun, "「不平」(not in balance) is a connecting line for the whole work. All kinds of voices are for crying out."[46]

2. The role of detail: this part can be further divided into 「鳴」 (cry out) and 「善鳴」(good at crying out).

As for the role of 「鳴」 (cry out), it begins with the second line of the first paragraph, ending in the last paragraph. Grass, wood, water, etc., are used in turn as examples to explain 「物不得其平則鳴」(Creatures will cry out if not in balance.)

In addition, as for the role of 「善鳴」(being good at crying out), it includes the second, third, and fourth paragraphs. At first, the author uses eight voices of various musical instruments to describe the state of being good at voicing. And then, the voices of four seasons are used as a kind of description. Furthermore, those good at composition and expression are introduced. After displaying a long list of big names of diverse eras, the author holds that either in crying out for the prosperity of their nation or in crying out for their

....

46 See Lin Yun-ming, *Collection of Analysis of Ancient Prose.* 《古文析義合編》
   Vol. 4 (Taipei: Kuanwen Bookstore, Oct. 1965) p.219.

misfortune, these were not worthy of happiness or sadness. This shows immense ease and comfort with tremendous awe.

Of these two sections of commentaries, Lin Si-chun said, "from voices of objects to human words, from human words to expressions, and then from different eras to the Tang dynasty, the author consistently uses the line--「天假善鳴」(Heaven chose those who were good at giving voice)--as a backbone to emphasize the importance of literary men in different eras. And then, the author mentions 東野, who, in his eyes, was so good at poetry that heaven was supposed to have given him the mission of giving voice to his era. Moreover, based on 「從吾遊」(those learning from me), he even indirectly praises himself, who considered all things in the mundane world trivial. How awesome his words are!"[47] Indeed, his opinion was full of deep insight.

In addition, let's take a look at the role of narration--the final paragraph. First, the line--「東野之役於江南也」(東野 went to 江南 to serve)--describes his trip. And then, the line--「有若不釋然者」(He seemed unhappy.)--points out 「不平」(not in balance). Furthermore, the final line wraps up the whole work. In this way, the author's intention is clearly stated.

In this work, the author intends to express that "Meng Chiao cried out by his poems." However, besides himself, he mentioned many people and events. Indeed, all of these serve to underscore Meny Chiao's crying by poems. Therefore, the description of his crying by poems functions as "master," while many other events and people that will cry if not in balance serve as "guest". Just as Wang Wen-ju put it: "All people and events, strange and complicated, tend to underscore Meng Chiads crying by poems."[48] The structure analysis

....

47 See *Collection of Analysis of Ancient Prose* Vol.4. 《古文析義合編》卷四 pp.220-221.

48 See *Collection of Annotated Ancient Prose*. 《精校評注古文觀止》Vol.7

diagram is as follows:

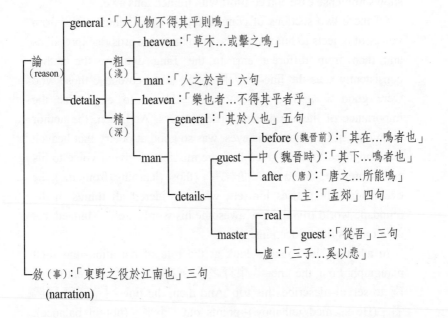

```
         ┌general：「大凡物不得其平則鳴」
         │              ┌heaven：「草木…或擊之鳴」
         │          ┌粗─┤
         │          │(淺)└man：「人之於言」六句
論 ──────┤          │      ┌heaven：「樂也者…不得其平者乎」
(reason) │          │      │      ┌general：「其於人也」五句
         │          │      │      │              ┌before（魏晉前）：「其在…鳴者也」
         └details───┤      │      │          ┌guest┼中（魏晉時）：「其下…鳴者也」
                    │精────┤      │          │     └after（唐）：「唐之…所能鳴」
                    │(深)  └man───┤          │     ┌主：「孟郊」四句
                    │             └details───┤  ┌real┤
                    │                         └master┤   └guest：「從吾」三句
                    │                             └虛：「三子…奚以悲」
         └敘（事）：「東野之役於江南也」三句
           (narration)
```

According to the diagram above, the author uses such compositional types as "narration and comments," "general and detail," "shallow and deep," "heaven and man," "guest and master," "present and past" to organized its textual materials, forming its compositional structure.

As to the structure of "reason, event, reason," we can see Peng Duansh's article.

天下事有難易乎？(What's the difference between easy things and difficult things in this world?) 為之，(If we are determined to do them,) 則難者亦易矣；(the difficult things will turn out to be easy.) 不為，(If we are not determined to do them,) 則易者

(Taipei: Taiwan Chunhua Bookstore, Nov. 1972) p.33.

亦難矣。(the easy things will turn out to be difficult.) 人之為學有難易乎？(What's the difference between hard to learn and easy to learn?) 學之，(If we learn it,) 則難者亦易矣；(the difficult learning will become easy.) 不學，(If we don't learn it,) 則易者亦難矣。(the easy learning will become difficult.)

吾資之昏，(My intelligence is poor.) 不逮人也；(I am less intelligent than other people.) 材之庸，(My talent is poor.) 不逮人也。(I am less competent than other people.) 旦旦而學之，(I learn everything day by day.) 久而不怠焉；(I persisted long in learning.) 迄乎成，(After I achieved something,) 而亦不知其昏與庸也。(my intelligence and talent appeared as good as other people's.) 吾資之聰，(My intelligence is excellent.) 倍人也；(I am far more intelligent than other people.)吾材之敏，(My mind is smart.) 倍人也。(I am far smarter than other people.) 屏棄而不用，(I neglect my intelligence and talent, making them fall into disuse.) 其昏與庸無以異也。(In this way, I am not smarter and more intelligent than others.) 然則昏庸聰敏之用，(The function of talent and intelligence) 豈有常哉？(Is not forever fixed and stable.)

蜀之鄙有二僧，(There were two monks in a remote area of China.) 其一貧，(One monk was poor,) 其一富。(the other was rich.) 貧者語於富者曰：(The poor monk said to the rich monk,)「吾欲之南海，何如？」("I want to go to the south sea; how do you feel about that?") 富者曰：(The rich monk said,)「子何恃而往？」("By what means will you get there?") 曰 (Tthe poor monk said,)：「吾一瓶一缽足矣。」("I will use only one bowl and one bottle.") 富者曰：(The rich monk said,)「吾數年來欲買舟而下，("for several years, I have intended to travel by boat to the south sea.) 猶未能也。(But I was never able to do that.)子何恃而往？」(How will you get there?") 越明年，(After two years) 貧者自南海還，(the poor monk returned from the South Sea.) 以告富者，(He told the rich monk about it.) 富者有慚色。(The rich monk felt ashamed.) 西蜀之去南海，(The distance between the two locations) 不知幾千里也；(is thousands of miles.) 僧之富者不能至，(The rich monk was not able to get there.) 而貧者至焉。(The poor monk could get there.) 人之立志，(In terms of man's determination) 顧不如蜀鄙之僧哉？(We need to learn a lesson from the two monks.)

是故聰與敏，(As for intelligence and talent,) 可恃而不可恃也。(they are always interdependable.) 自恃其聰與敏而不學，(Being too proud of one's talent and intelligence to learn) 自敗者也。(will lead to failure.) 昏與庸，(As for stupidity and incompetence,) 可限而不可限也。(They are not always limitations.) 不自限其昏與庸而力學不倦，(By breaking through limitations and persisting in learning,) 自立者也。(A person will become self-established.)

In this article, the author intends to encourage his descendants to work harder. It can be divided into three major parts--general introduction, examples, and conclusion. In addition, it uses a form of binary opposition.

First, take a look at the role of the general introduction: This part includes the first and second paragraphs. In the first paragraph, the author begins with doing things, and then mentions academic learning. It is pointed out that success in doing things and academic learning depends on action rather than learning or things per se. This paves the way for the further argument in the next paragraph. And then, in the second paragraph the author holds that despite a difference in intelligence, through diligence a less intelligent person can become as smart as an intelligent person. On the other hand, in case of tardiness, an intelligent person will get nowhere. And then, the two lines,「然則昏庸聰敏之用」, he points out that intelligence and stupidity are both unreliable. In this way, the conclusion of the final paragraph is introduced.

Second, we will discuss the role of the examples:

This part includes only the third paragraph in which the example of the monk's trip to the South Sea proves that hard work will produce success, and that laziness leads to failure. In this part, the author uses the first three lines to mention a rich monk as well as a poor monk. Next, by asking and answering questions, the author explains that the poor monk was willing to go to South Sea, and that the rich monk was not willing. And then, the expression「越明年」(after next year) is used to connect time, introducing three lines, from「貧者自南海還」(the poor returned from South Sea), which show the result: the poor monk found success but the rich monk failed. Furthermore, six lines, from「西蜀之去南海」(from West Su to South Sea), make a comparison between the rich monk and the poor monk in order to teach a moral lesson--men should learn from these monks, making up their own mind.

Finally, the part of conclusion will be discussed. This part includes only the last paragraph. Here, following the above,「不為」(without action),「不學」(without learning),「聰」(smart),「敏」(active),「屏棄不用」(give up and no use) and「富者不能至」(the rich can not reach), the author uses four lines, from「是故聰與敏」, to indirectly reveal that if an individual is too proud to learn he will fail. And then, following the above「為之」(do it),「學之」(learn it),「昏」(daisy),「庸」(useless),「且旦而學之」(learn it daily), and「貧者至」(the poor reached it), the author uses four lines, from「昏與庸」, to directly point out that despite his poor talent an individual can achieve success by hard work. In this way, the topic is manifested, bringing the whole to an end.

In terms of the outer form, this writing is excellent. The linguistic effect comes from a comparative approach and material selection. Generally speaking in employing positive and negative materials, most authors like to use sections as individual units to separate the positive and negative materials.

Su Shih's "Writing on Supreme Platform" can illustrate this kind of linguistic phenomenon. However, the author here uses the methodology of contrast and alternative to arrange the positive and negative materials to make the whole work consistent, creating a contrastive effect. This is worth our attention and worth learning.

In conclusion, this writing can be divided into four paragraphs. The first and second paragraphs serve the role of argument. It is pointed out that learning focuses on persistence rather than easiness or difficulty. Besides, the quality of talent is used for further explanation. And then, the third paragraph in the role of narration uses the example of the two monks to reaffirm the truth that efforts lead to success and laziness results in failure. Furthermore, the last paragraph serves the role of argument. Here, following the above 「不為」(without action)、「聰」(smart)、「敏」(active)、「屏棄不用」(give up and no use) and 「富者不能至」(the rich can not reach)，the author uses four lines, from 「是故聰與敏」, to indirectly point out that despite intelligence man will fall due to slovenry. In addition, following the above 「為之」(do it)、「學之」(learn it)、「昏」(daisy)、「庸」(useless)、「旦旦學之」(learn it daily) and 「貧者至」(the poor reached it)，the author uses four lines, from 「昏與庸」, to reveal the truth that despite poor talent, a man can strive and gain success. In this way, the topic is manifested.[49]   The structure analysis diagram can be shown as follows:

....

49 Chen Man-ming, *Analysis of Compositional Structures—As in the Textbooks for the Middle Schools.* (Taipei: Wanchunlo Publishing Company, May, 1999) pp.59-61.

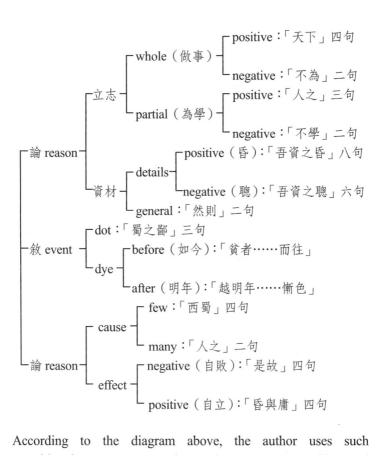

According to the diagram above, the author uses such compositional types as "narration and comment," "positive and negative," "general and details," "cause and effects," "partial and whole," "present and past," and "dot and dye" to organize its textual materials, forming its compositional structure.

As to the structure of "event, reason, and event," we can see Kue Yukung's work.

項脊軒，(At Hsiangchihsuan,) 舊南閤子也。(a small house to the south of my former house,) 室僅方丈，(the space was so limited) 可容一人居。(that only one person could live in it.) 百

年老屋，(An old house of one hundred years,)塵泥滲漉，(with ashes and mud leaking through the walls.) 雨澤下注，(Raindrops fell within.) 每移案，(Whenever I would move the table,) 顧視無可置者。(I looked around and could not find any place to put it.) 又北向，(The house faced north,) 不能得日；(so it could not get sunshine.) 日過午已昏。(In the afternoon the house got dark.) 余稍為修葺，(I repaired the house,) 使不上漏。(stopping the leakage.) 前闢四窗，(I opened the four windows)垣牆周庭，(Llow walls surrounded the yard,) 以當南日。(fencing off the sunshine from the south.) 日影反照，(As the sunshine was reflected itself,) 室始洞然。(the house turned bright.) 又雜植蘭、桂、竹、木於庭，(And I planted several kinds of plants in the garden.) 舊時欄楯，(The railings of olden time)亦遂增勝。(did brighten things up.) 借書滿架，(Tthe house was full of a collection of books.) 偃仰嘯歌，(I recited the some poems.) 冥然兀坐，(Then I sat quietly.) 萬籟有聲。(All kinds of sounds existed here.) 而庭階寂寂，(The yard was quiet.) 小鳥時來啄食，(Little birds came here to grab a meal.) 人至不去。(They stayed there even when some men came by.) 三五之夜，(On the fifteenth day of every month,) 明月半牆，(the bright moon shone on the walls.) 桂影斑駁，(The shades of trees were spread everywhere,) 風移影動，(moving with the winds.) 珊珊可愛。(How lovely it was!)

然余居此，(Yes, here I lived.) 多可喜，(There were many things to be happy about;) 亦多可悲。(also, there were many things I could be sad about.)先是，(First,) 庭中通南北為一，(the garden was linked from south to north.)迨諸父異爨，(After my uncles separated,) 內外多置小門牆，(Inside and outside the house there were many small doors and fences.) 往往而是。(They were everywhere.) 東犬西吠，(Dogs in the eastern wings barked at dogs in the western wings.) 客踰庖而宴，(Guests shuttled to kitchens in the front house to eat.) 雞棲於廳。

(Chickens squatted in the living room.) 庭中始為籬，(First, the garden was separated by the fence.) 已為牆，(And then the walls were built up.) 凡再變矣。(This was changed twice.) 家有老嫗，(There was an old woman)嘗居於此。(who had lived here.) 嫗，(This old woman) 先大母婢也，(had been the servant of my now deceased grandmother.) 乳二世，(She had nourished two generations.) 先妣撫之甚厚。(My deceased mother had treated her well.) 室西連於中閨，(The western part of the house was linked to a chamber.) 先妣嘗一至。(My deceased mother had lived here.) 嫗每謂余曰：(The old woman frequently told me,) 「某所，("here!) 而母立於茲。(your mother had stood here.") 」嫗又曰 (The old woman also said,) ：「汝姊在吾懷，("your elder sister was at my bosom.) 呱呱而泣；(She cried.) 娘以指扣門扉曰：(Your mother used her fingers to knock on the door.) 『兒寒乎？(Did the child feel cold?) 欲食乎？』(Did she want something to eat?) 吾從板外相為應答。」(I answered her from outside the door.") 語未畢，(Her words had not yet ended.) 余泣，(I cried.) 嫗亦泣。(The old woman cried, too.) 余自束髮讀書軒中，(I had read books in this house since the age of fifteen.) 一日，(One day) 大母過余曰：(my grandmother came to me,) 「吾兒，("my child,) 久不見若影，(I have not seen you for a long time.) 何竟日默默在此，(Why do you keep silent here all day long?) 大類女郎也？」(You are so like a girl.") 比去，(After leaving,) 以手闔門，(she closed the door.) 自語曰 (She murmured to herself,) ：「吾家讀書久不效，("the children of this family have not gained official posts for a long time.) 兒之成，(The success of this child) 則可待乎！」(was to be expected.") 頃之 (Soon after that) 持一象笏至，(she picked up a small ivory plate,) 曰：(saying,) 「此吾祖太常公宣德間執此以朝，("My grandfather has used it in the past.) 他日汝當用之。」(You could use it someday.") 瞻顧遺跡，(As I reflect on these things,)

如在昨日，(They seem to have happened yesterday.) 令人長號
不自禁。(I cannot help but cry.)
軒東故嘗為廚，(There was a kitchen in the eastern side of the
house.) 人往，(Anyone that went there) 從軒前過。(had to
pass by the front of the house.) 余扃牖而居，(I closed the
windows when inside.) 久之，(Yet, as time passed,) 能以足音
辨人。(I could recognize people by the sounds of their footsteps.)
軒四遭火，(There had been four fires in this house.) 得不焚，
(but it has not been burned down.) 殆有神護者。(It seems that
God has protected this house.)
項脊生曰：(Hsiangchishen said,) 「蜀清守丹穴，("A widow in
Szuchuan kept mineral mines of her ancestors.) 利甲天下，(She
gained a lot of profit.) 其後秦皇帝築女懷清臺。(And then, the
emperor of the Ching nation built a tower in memory of her.") 劉
玄德與曹操爭天下，(Liu Pei battled with Tsao Chao in order to
conquer the world.) 諸葛孔明起隴中。(ChuKeliang rose after
being recruited from amid farms.) 方二人之昧昧於一隅也，
(When the two men were obscure in their own corners of the
world,) 世何足以知之？(how could the world know of them?)
余區區處敗屋中，(I lived in this humble house.) 方揚眉瞬
目，(I raised up my eyebrows feeling so proud.) 謂有奇景。(I
thought these were special landscapes.) 人知之者，(If someone
knew this,) 其謂與坎井之蛙何異？」(He would say this was
no different from a frog in a shallow well.)
余既為此志，(I wrote this composition) 後五年，(five years
later.) 吾妻來歸，(My wife had married me.) 時至軒中，(She
often came to this house) 從余問古事，(and asked me things
about ancient times.) 或憑几學書。(Sometimes she sat at the
table to learn how to write characters.) 吾妻歸寧，(My wife
then went back to her parents' home.) 述諸小妹語曰：(Her
younger sisters said,) 「聞姊家有閣子，("we heard that our
elder sister had an attic,) 且何謂閣子也？」(but what does an

attic mean?") 其後六年，(Six years later,) 吾妻死，(my wife died.)室壞不修。(The room had fallen into decay and needed repair.) 其後二年，(For two years)余久臥病無聊，(I had been sick and had nothing to do.) 乃使人修葺南閣子，(I asked some men to repair the attic.) 其制稍異於前。(Its interior design is somewhat different from the previous one.) 然自後余多在外，(After that I had long stayed elsewhere.) 不常居。(I would not live here.)

庭有枇杷樹，(There was a tree in the garden.) 吾妻死之年所手植也，(My wife planted this in the year she died.) 今已亭亭如蓋矣。(Now it flourishes.)

This writing can be divided into six paragraphs.

Among these, the first, second and third paragraphs combine to serve in the role of narration, which includes present events and past ones. The narration of present events is evidenced by the first paragraph, which focuses on 「可喜」，describing the interior and outer spaces of the house. And the narration of past events belongs to the second and third paragraphs, which focus on 「可悲」，tracing certain historical facts about the house. This prepares us for the next part, that of argument. And in the fourth paragraph, which serves the role of argumentation, the author mimics the comments of Shihchi，comparing himself to Suchin，Kungmin，to disclose his ambition of rescuing the world.[50] As to the fifth and sixth paragraphs, they serve as another part of narration, which includes his deceased wife's life, the historical changes in the house, and the flourishing trees planted by his wife. Accordingly, 「可喜」serves as "guest, " while 「可悲」serves as "master."[51] The sequential

50 See Chang Yuan-fen's analysis. *Dictionary of Appreciation of Ancient Prose.* 《古文鑑賞辭典》p.1237.

51 See Lin Yu's *On Topics.* 《畏廬論文‧述旨》(Taipei: Wenching Publishing

arrangement is remarkably appealing.　The structure analysis diagram can be shown as follows:

```
       ┌ 敘（event）┬─ detail 一（可喜）:「項脊軒……可愛」
       │           ├─ general :「然余居此」三句
       │           └─ detail 二（可悲）:「先是……不自禁」
       │           ┌─ past（引古事－可喜）:「項脊……知之」
  ┌────┤ 論（reason）┤
       │           └─ present（述己懷－可悲）:「余區區……何異」
       │           ┌─ guest（可喜）:「余既……閣子也」
       └ 敘（event）┤
                   └─ master（可悲）:「其後……如蓋矣」
```

According to the above diagram, the author uses such compositional types as the narration-commentary type, the general-specific type, the guest-master type, and the present-past type, to arrange the textual materials, forming the compositional structure. In addition, the cases of narration and commentary, which are interwoven, can be seen in Tseng Kung's work, which is framed by the structure of "narration, commentary, narration, commentary."[52]

2.3 Other types

These types can make up several kinds of combination— landscape and reason, event and feeling, event and landscape and feeling, or landscape and event.　The first three types, in terms of compositional art, can be categorized as the general-specific mode,

....

Company, July 1987) pp.3-4.

[52] See Chou Hsiao-ping, *Types of Compositional Structures*, 《篇章結構類型論》 p.284.

while the last type belongs to the wholly real mode.[53] The compound type of landscape and reason can be illustrated by Chu Si's poem.

半畝方塘一鑑開，(There is an open pond.) 天光雲影共徘徊。
(Celestial light and cloud shadows are wandering together.)
問渠那得清如許？(How come the pond is so clean and fresh.)
為有源頭活水來。(There are living fwaters flow.)

The first two lines depict a pond with celestial light and cloud shadows, all of which can "make human mind clear and hearts open."[54] Thereafter, the third and fourth lines naturally follow. And the author skillfully uses the compositional type of "ask and answer" to describe the poem, which is thus inspiring.[55] The structure analysis diagram is as follows:

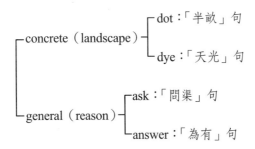

53 Also see Chen Chiao-chun, *Analysis of Real and Unreal Compositional Types.* 《虛實章法析論》(Taipei: Wenching Publishing Company, Nov. 2002) pp.256-260.

54 See Huo Sung-lin, *Major Sung Dynasty Poems.* 《宋詩大觀》 (Hong Kong, The Commercial Press Ltd., May 1988) p. 1119.

55 See Huo Sung-lin, *Major Sung Dynasty Poems.* 《宋詩大觀》 (Hong Kong, The Commercial Press Ltd., May 1988) p. 1118.

According to the diagram above, the author uses such compositional types as "general and concrete," "dot and dye," "ask and answer" to organize its textual materials, forming its compositional structure.

The compound type of "event" and "feeling" can be illustrated by Li Chihyi's poem entitled〈卜算子〉("Pusuanchih")

我住長江頭 (I live along the upstream part of Yangtze River) 君住長江尾 (You live along the downstream part of Yangtze River) 日日思君不見君 (I think of you every day; however, I cannot see you.) 共飲長江水 (We commonly drink the water of the same river)　此水幾時休 (When can the flow of waters stop?) 此恨何時已 (When can hatred cease?) 只願君心似我心 (Hopefully, your heart can be like mine) 定不負相思意 (I will definitely love you in return)

This poem is framed by the structure of "first event and then feelings." The author uses the first two lines to describe the far-apart distance. This belongs to the part of narration. And then, the following two lines describe the feelings of missing friends. In addition, the first two lines of the second half describe endless hatred. Finally, the last two lines describe the fidelity of feelings. The above six lines belong to the part of expressing feelings. Accordingly, Yangtze River is used as a means to an end, while「不見」(cannot see), a root of causes. The "unreal" materials, instead of any sentence of depicting landscapes, are employed to describe sincere, genuine and profound feelings. Therefore, in terms of diction and sense, it is very like ancient songs. Just as Tang Kuei-chang put it,"with fresh meanings and sophisticated diction, it is very like ancient songs."[56] Thus, the structure analysis diagram is as

....

56 See *Brief Interpretations of Tang Sung Dynasty Tzu.*《唐宋詞簡釋》(Taipei:

follows:

```
                          ┌─master（己）:「我住」句
        ┌─concrete（landscape）─┤
        │                 └─guest（彼）:「君住」句
        │                      ┌─cause（相思久）:「日日」二句
        │             ┌─ real ─┤
        └─general（feeling）─┤        └─effect（恨無已）:「此水」二句
                      └─ unreal :「只顧」二句
```

According to the above diagram, this Tzu uses such compositional types as "general (feeling)and concrete(landscape)," "guest and master" "unreal and real" and "cause and effect" to organize its texual materials, forming its compositional structure.

The compound type of "landscape" and "event" can be illustrated by Wang Wei's poem entitled "Wanchuan's Easy Life for Pei Di."

寒山轉蒼翠，(The chilly mountains turn emerald green,)秋水日 潺湲。(The autumn waters are daily murmuring.) 倚杖柴門 外，(Outside my thatch-door on my staff I lean,) 臨風聽暮蟬。 (Heeding evening winds, cicadas shrilling.) 渡頭餘落日， (Beyond the ford the sun nearly sunk;) 墟里上孤煙。(from the village a wisp of smoke floats free.) 復值接輿醉，(You are just like that jolly Jie-yu, drunk,) 狂歌五柳前。(Wildly warbling below my willow tree.)

This poem was created as a gift to please each other. Through the description of landscapes and characters, the easiness and pleasure of the author was disclosed. In the first two lines, the author used the structures of "first high and then low," and "first vision and then

Muto Publishing Company. March 1982) p.115.

acoustics" to describe the autumn scenery and evening scenery around Wanchuan. This emerged as a harmonious picture of colors and sounds. And then, the author used the structures of "first far and then near" and "first vision and then acoustics" to insert the scene of his listening to cicadas shrilling and Pei Di's chanting to a landscape of easiness. All of these created an artistic world of a union of objects and self, which might substantially express the fun of his living.[57] The structure analysis is as follows:

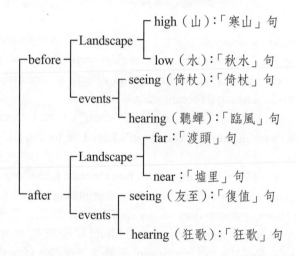

According to the above diagram, it can be seen that this poem used such compositional types as " landscape and thing," "present and past," "high and low," "far and near," and "consciousness shifting" to organize its contents and materials, forming its compositional structure.

The compound type of "thing," "landscape," and "feelings" can be illustrated by Hsi Chi-chi's poem entitled "Moyuerh."

....

57 See Chao Ching-pei's analysis, *Collection of Tang Dynasty Poems,* 《唐詩大觀》 p.149.

更能消、幾番風雨，(How can we resist these winds and raindrops?) 匆匆春又歸去。(Spring will soon go off.) 惜春長怕花開早，(Treasuring the springtime, I hope the flowers will take their time blossoming.) 何況落紅無數。(Before me the fallen flowers seem countless.) 春且住，(Spring, please wait!) 見說道、(Have you ever heard that?) 天涯芳草無歸路。(Grass wildly growing everywhere blocks your path.) 怨春不語。(I hate a silent spring.) 算只有殷勤，畫簷蛛網，盡日惹飛絮。(The spiders have been diligently using their webs to catch the flying willow leaves.) 長門事，(In this place, hoping for good days to come,) 準擬佳期又誤，(which will no doubt be missed,) 蛾眉曾有人妒。(they are jealous of my good looks.) 千金縱買相如賦，(Even though I can pay a tremendous amount of money for 相如's composition,) 脈脈此情誰訴。(to whom can I disclose my profound feelings?) 君莫舞，(Please don't dance!) 君不見、(Have you ever noted) 玉環飛燕皆塵土。(two well-known ladies in the imperial court were dashed to the dirt?) 閒愁最苦。(Sorrow tortures men most.) 休去倚危闌，(Don't lean against the terraces of the high rises!) 斜陽正在，煙柳斷腸處。(Sunset has been growing dimmer on the smoky willows, a place of extreme sadness.)

This poem is intended to express hatred and anger. The beginning two lines following「更能消」(How can we resist?) Generally point out that spring will soon be gone. In addition to the four lines following「惜春」(treasuring spring time) and four lines following「怨春」(hating spring) use a series of scenes including countless fallen flowers, wildly grown grass, and spiders' webs to describe a fading spring, serving as a prelude for the following story. In the following five lines, the author uses the analogy in which a queen of the Han Dynasty was deposed and she asked a poet Szuma Hsiangju to write a poem to inspire and move the emperor to express his own anger and hatred for his frustration in careers. In addition, two lines following「君莫舞」(Please don't dance.) use the analogies of Chao Feiyen and Yang Yu-huan to reveal that mean persons will sooner or later be ruined.　In this way, the feelings of hatred and anger are further depicted. Furthermore, the line of「閒愁」 (feelings of hatred and anger) serves as a topic sentence to unify the whole work. The final three lines use sunset as a metaphor to signify the decline of the nation. The scene of sunset is employed to project the extremely sad feelings.[58]　Thus, the structure of "concrete (landscape, events), generalization (feelings), concrete (landscape)" is used to depict the sentiments in an extremely marvelous way. The structure analysis diagram is as follows:

According to the diagram above, the author uses such compositional types as "general and concrete," "general and details" "guest and master" to organize its compositional structure. All of these stated compositional types are derived from experiences and common sense. The application of binary oppositions dialectically

<hr />

[58]　Chang Kuo-wu, "the sad scenes before eyes highlighted extreme sad emotion." And Chen Tin-chao comments, "the work ends in sadness and sorrow."　See *Anthology of Tzus,*《詞林觀止》p.518.

could reach the universal truth approximately. Among these, in expressing feelings, reasoning, depicting landscapes, narrating events, the most commonly used compositional types are "cause and effect" "present and past" "real and unreal" "general and details" and "positive and negative" "for they are most proper for integrating images and logical thinking.

Chapter **3**

Logical Contents of Structures of Composition and Paragraphs

The contents of the structure of Chinese composition found expressions not only in "image thinking" but also in "logical thinking." This chapter puts emphasis on its logical contents—the art of composition, making a study of its types, rules and other related problems.

I. Types of composition art

The art of composition deals with the logical relations of the contents of the composition.[1] To date about forty types of logical relations in compositions are found. These types are stated as follows: present-past method, long-transient method, far-near method, inside-outside method, left-right method, high-low method, big-small method, angle-shifting method, space-and-time blending method, state-changing method, consciousness-shifting method, root-end method, shallow-deep method, cause-effect method, many-few method, parallel method, feeling-landscape method, commentary-narration method, general-specific method, spatially unreal-real method, temporally real-unreal method, assumption-

....

[1] See Chen Man-ming's "On the Art of Composition," *A Collection of Essays in the Fourth International Conference on Chinese Rhetoric.* 《第四屆中國修辭學國際學術研討會論文集》 (Taipei: Chinese Rhetoric Association, Fu-jen Catholic University Chinese Department, May 2002).pp. 1-32.

factual method, generalization-details method, details-rough method, guest-master method, positive-negative method, establishing-breaking method, down-up method, asking-answering method, flat-side method, release-catch method, tense-relax method, inserting-narration method, supplementary-narration method, partial-whole method, dot-dye method, heaven-man method, picture-background method, and knocking-striking method.[2] Each of the composition arts will be introduced in terms of its "definition," "aesthetics," and "features."

1. Present-past method

Definition: a method by which present (now) and past (then) are properly arranged.

Aesthetics and features: A narration in which the events are described from past to present is the most common type of narration, one that most fits the laws in accordance with which the events or things develop. And the thing which develops according to the laws is the most beautiful of all. On the other hand, the narration of which the events are described from present to past aims to put forth the events most emotionally, beautifully and impressively. In addition, the sequential structure of "present, past and present" serves to repeat the strongest aesthetic emotion, forming echoes. Second to the narration from past to present, this is the next most

....

2 See Chen, Man-ming's *On the Major Contents of the Arts of Expressions and Composition; The New Design of the Arts of Composition.*《章法學新裁》(Taipei: Wanchuanlou Publishing Company, January 2001, first edition).pp. 319-360. Also see *On Several Special Kinds of Composition Art.* (Taipei: Taiwan Normal University, *Chinese Journal, June, 2002*).pp. 193-222. Also see Chou Hsiao-ping, *The Theory of Composition Art,* 《文章章法論》 (Taipei, Wanchuanlou Publishing Company, November, 1998, first edition) pp. 1-510; *The Types of Structures of Compositions*, (I) and (II) 《篇章結構類型論》上下, (Taipei, Wanchuanlou Publishing Company, February, 2000, first edition). pp. 1-620.

commonly used structure type.   There are also other narrative ways repeating both present and past, which form strong, repeating echoes between present and past.   In this way, an aesthetic sense is produced.[3]

2. Long-transient method

Definition: a method which properly makes time long or transient (short) in literary works.

Aesthetics and features: The arrangements of time as long or transient makes a comparison, in accordance with the ups and downs of emotion, between a long time and a short time.   When the literary work portrays the time span "from transient to long," transience will accordingly stress a long time, which itself will produce an aesthetic sense, and which will result in a historical sense. On the other hand, the time design, "from long to transient," aims to emphasize "transience," which is chosen for the greatest emotion.[4]

3. Far-near method

Definition: a method which makes a record of a spatial change.

Aesthetics and features: In the spatial change from near to far, the distance has been stretched from near to far, and then the sights and things attached to the space will be presented to the reader gradually, creating an effect on diverse levels. In addition, if the space is indefinitely expanded to a faraway place, man, more often than not, will embrace a sublime feeling, and his intrinsic emotion will be

....

3 See Chou Hsiao-ping, *The Types of Structures of Compositions*, 《篇章結構類型論》 pp. 40-42.   Also see *The Aesthetic Design of Time and Space in Classic Works* 《古典詩詞時空設計美學》(Taipei: Wengchin Publishing Company, November, 2002, first edition.) pp. 169-183.

4 See Chou Hsiao-ping, *The Types of Structures of Compositions*, 《篇章結構類型論》 pp. 50-51. Also see *The Aesthetic Design of Time and Space in Classic Works,* 《古典詩詞時空設計美學》 pp. 183-190.

greatly augmented.   On the other hand, a presentation from far to near will shorten the distance, putting near sights and things in the limelight. In addition, a few spatial structures with which spaces near and far are interwoven serve to satisfy the curiosity of those who love maverick aesthetics, and are in line with the traditional Chinese way of travel.[5]

4. Inside-outside method

Definition: a method designed to express the spatial change of a building in a literary work; the space may shift from inside to outside.

Aesthetics and features: Because buildings (being inclusive of doors, windows, walls, etc.) have certain things to separate   space, the spatial change will create an effect on various levels as well as an aesthetic feeling of depth, which is most instrumental in creating a world of depth and profundity.[6]

5. Left-right method

Definition: a method making a record of the spatial change between left and right.

Aesthetics and features: The space stretching to both left and right might well express an aesthetic feeling of balance, and can easily create a spacious feeling, making man feel calm, peace, and awe. In addition, this space can easily feature the characters or things that are balanced between left and right.[7]

......

5   See Chou Hsiao-ping, *The Types of Structures of Compositions*, pp. 67-69.　《篇章結構類型論》上 Also see *The Aesthetic Design of Time and Space in Classic Works*, 《古典詩詞時空設計美學》 pp. 54-66.

6   See Chou Hsiao-ping, *The Types of Structures of Compositions*, 《篇章結構類型論》上 pp. 82-83. Also see *The Aesthetic Design of Time and Space in Classic Works*, 《古典詩詞時空設計美學》 pp. 66-74.

7   See Chou Hsiao-ping, *The Types of Structures of Compositions*, 《篇章結構類

6. High-low method

Definition: a method which makes a record of the spatial change between high and low in a literary work.

Aesthetics and features: In the space from low to high, the direction goes upwards, giving man a sense of freedom and relaxation.   In addition, when it creates a space of height and sublimity, the aesthetic subject can be fused via objective views, finally creating a world of sublimity.   On the other hand, in the spatial change from high to low, the direction goes downwards, creating an amazing power, which is heavy, condensed, and bundled.   And the space of which high and low are interwoven can swiftly absorb the things up or down to help express the author's subjective feelings.[8]

7. Big-small method

Definition: a method describing changes such as expansion and condensation between a big space and small space.

Aesthetics and features: Spaces big and small demonstrate the beauty of a plane surface.   If the space is transformed by shrinking from a big space to a small space, it will be finally concentrated on a small spot, embracing the greatest effect of concentration.   On the other hand, if the space is formed by expanding itself from a small space to a big space, it will create an effect of augmentation and expansion, which is the uttermost beauty of a plane.   In addition, if the spaces are interwoven with big spaces and small ones, it will create an effect in which a big space can be much more expanded,

....

型論》上 pp. 89-90.   Also see *The Aesthetic Design of Time and Space in Classic Works*, 《古典詩詞時空設計美學》 pp. 77-83

[8]   See Chou Hsiao-ping, *The Types of Structures of Compositions*, 《篇章結構類 型論》上 pp. 102-103.   Also see *The Aesthetic Design of Time and Space in Classic Works*, 《古典詩詞時空設計美學》 pp. 83-91.

and in which a small space can be further condensed.[9]

8. Angle-shifting method

Definition: Instead of describing landscapes from a single angle, the author combines three elements of space—length, width, and height—to create the movement of angles, (perspectives) and thus expresses such changes in literary works.

Aesthetics and features: The traditional Chinese way of observation is looking upwards and downwards and observing near and far, which might easily create a space with the change of viewpoints. This kind of spatial structural method can not only freely gather diverse landscapes with diverse spaces, but create the beauty of leaping spaces.[10]

9. Space-and-time blending method

Definition: a literary method in which both the passage of time and the demonstration of space are taken into consideration in order to carve out the wholeness of the composition as well as the multiple aesthetic senses.

Aesthetics and features: Aware of spatial consciousness and temporal consciousness, the author presents them as forming a beautiful blending space and time, which can grasp both flowing time and expanding space. Man, standing on an extremely tiny spot in the universe, thus expresses his feelings about his own

....

9 See Chou Hsiao-ping, *The Types of Structures of Compositions*, 《篇章結構類型論》 pp. 120-121. Also see *The Aesthetic Design of Time and Space in Classic Works*, *The Aesthetic Design of Time and Space in Classic Works* pp. 91-97.

10 See Chou Hsiao-ping, *The Types of Structures of Compositions*, 《篇章結構類型論》上 pp. 133-134. Also see *The Aesthetic Design of Time and Space in Classic Works*, 《古典詩詞時空設計美學》 pp. 100-104.

microcosm in an impersonal universe.[11]

10. State-changing method

Definition: a method by which a certain change in all things in the outside world is expressed.

Aesthetics and features: If a person pays much attention to a certain characteristic of an object, this will intensely stimulate the chemical functions of his brain. With this kind of help, people can obtain very effective observation. If the author can observe the beauty in his observations of the state, he will accurately express it with words. Thus, a description of the change in the state comes to mind. However, this is indeed not an imitation of the shapes of things, but an imitation of the changing state of aesthetic emotion.[12]

11. Consciousness-shifting method

Definition: a method by which the author expresses his multiple consciousnesses of the sophisticated world.

Aesthetics and features: Man's conscious activities can not be separated from his feelings; his senses receive messages from the objective world, and then via the operation of aesthetic psychology, conscious beauties are produced.[13] Furthermore, the sense of seeing and the sense of listening are activated most frequently, and these two senses are also most intimately associated with beauty. Thus, these two senses are called the senses of beauty. However, both of these senses are inter-dependent, and included in the consciousness

....

11 See Chou Hsiao-ping, *The Types of Structures of Compositions*, 《篇章結構類型論》上 pp. 145-146. Also see *The Aesthetic Design of Time and Space in Classic Works*, 《古典詩詞時空設計美學》pp. 237-255.

12 See Chou Hsiao-ping, *The Types of Structures of Compositions*, 《篇章結構類型論》 pp. 179-180.

13 See Chou Hsiao-ping, *The Types of Structures of Compositions*, 《篇章結構類型論》 pp. 160-161..

of heart, which makes these senses unified.   This is its ultimate goal.

12. Cause-effect method

Definition: a method including one cause and one effect.   In Chinese, the sentence pattern—because..., so...--is commonly seen. As well, the sentence pattern—so..., because—is also seen in Chinese composition.   In addition, "so" and "because" frequently appear reciprocally.   Therefore, when this kind of thinking method is applied to Chinese composition, the cause-effect method is formed.

Aesthetics and features: Because the logic of cause and effect is widely used, the cause-effect method is frequently seen in literary works.   And the sequential development of cause and effect can produce beauty of regularity.   On the other hand, the logical sequence in the presentation of effect and then cause, more often than not, will stir the reader's curiosity. Moreover, other kinds of logical development can not only create beauty, but also deepen the context due to the repeated appearance of causes and effects.[14]

13. Many-few method

Definition: a method by which many and few are interwoven.

Aesthetics and features: The structure developing from many to few will create a focus, that is, "few." In addition, the structure developing from few to many will create the effect of augmentation. And the changes between many and few can break the inertia, creating a sense of freshness.[15]

....

14   13. See Chen Man-ming's "On the Mother Nature of the Art of Composition of Cause And Effect." (Taipei: *The World of Chinese Language and Monthly Literature* Vol. 18 (7), Dec., 2002) pp. 94-101.   Also see Chou Hsiao-ping, *The Types of Structures of Compositions*, 《篇章結構類型論》上 pp. 223-224..

15   See Chou Hsiao-ping, *The Types of Structures of Compositions* 《篇章結構類

14. Feeling-landscape method

Definition: a method by which an emphasis on concrete landscape can show forth the unsubstantially abstract feelings, strengthening those feelings and readers taste for literary works.

Aesthetics and features: In the relation between a subject and an object, the subject occupies a dominant position. The subject, according to some special feeling, chooses a proper image. This is, in a sense, feeling-determined. Therefore, landscapes and feelings are inter-dependent, producing an aesthetically harmonious feeling, which brings to the reader appreciation and understanding rather than reasoning and moral lessons.[16]

15. Commentary-narration method

Definition: a method which combines abstract teachings and concrete events, making them inter-dependent.

Aesthetics and features: The author, according to his particular need, chooses suitable events to express subjective feelings. Therefore, narration and commentary are concurrent, and the concrete events can reveal abstract theories and objective truths. These process are able to produce an aesthetic effect.[17]

型論》, pp. 234...

[16] See Chou Hsiao-ping, *The Types of Structures of Compositions*, 《篇章結構類型論》上 pp. 261-264. Also see Chen Chia-chun, *An Analysis of Substantial and Unsubstantial Art of Composition.* 《虛實章法析論》 pp.47-67. (Taipei: Wen-ching Publishing Company, November 2002, first edition.)

[17] See Chou Hsiao-ping, *The Types of Structures of Compositions*, 《篇章結構類型論》上 pp. 285-286. Also see Chen Chia-chun, *An Analysis of Substantial and Unsubstantial Art of Composition.* 《虛實章法析論》 pp.68-90.

16. General-specific method

Definition: a method in which general descriptions and specific ones are combined together.   Originally, it was so all-inclusive that it included other arts of compositions such as the feeling-landscape method, the narration-commentary method, the all-details method, and the unsubstantial-substantial method.   However, these four methods were so commonly seen that they were to be separated in order to set off their own features.   Thus, only two types remained—the thing-and-feeling type, and the landscape-and-logic type.

Aesthetics and features: Through this method, abstract and concrete images will form their own aesthetic beauty, while on the other hand, they will be put together to form an aesthetically harmonious beauty.[18]

17. Spatially unreal-real method

Definition: a method by which real space in sight and unreal space in imagination are combined together.   In this way, the space arrangement will become more flexible.

Aesthetics and features: With the help of exuberant imagination, real and unreal spaces are so inter-changeable that they can fully express the beauty of spatial shifts. In addition, real things and unreal things are co-existent, producing a vivid and mixed beauty for literary works.[19]

....

18 See Chou Hsiao-ping, *The Types of Structures of Compositions*, 《篇章結構類型論》上 p. 295. Also see Chen Chia-chun, *An Analysis of Substantial and Unsubstantial Art of Composition.* 《虛實章法析論》 pp.34-46..

19 See Chou Hsiao-ping, *The Types of Structures of Compositions*, 《篇章結構類型論》上 p. 318. Also see Chen Chia-chun, *An Analysis of Substantial and Unsubstantial Art of Composition.* 《古典詩詞時空設計美學》 pp.154-162. Also see Chen Chia-chun, *Analysis of Real and Unreal Compositional Art,* 《虛

18. Temporally real-unreal method

Definition: a most effective method by which real temporality (past or present) and unreal temporality (future) can be combined together to narrate events (describing landscapes), and to express feelings (arguments).

Aesthetics and features: this method can grasp the past, the present, and the future, so it has a unique advantage. In addition, real temporality and unreal temporality can be linked, saturated, and transformed reciprocally. Partial communication between the two sides can produce spiritual beauty, then developing into consistently harmonious beauty.[20]

19. Assumption-factual method

Definition: a method by which assumptions and facts are properly arranged together. Here, "assumption" refers to fictional things, while "reality," to what has already happened in the real world. These two things echo each other, constructing and organizing literary works.

Aesthetics and features: The so-called "facts" mean the reality extracted from the real world. While "assumption" occupies a special position in literary works, serving as a direct reflection of human psychology. It is indeed derived from reality and at the same time goes beyond reality, so it is more real than reality. When the two features echo each other in literary works, this expresses the reality that the objective world and the subjective world commonly manifest.[21]

實章法析論》pp.159-174.

[20] See Chou Hsiao-ping, *The Types of Structures of Compositions*, 《篇章結構類型論》上 p. 318. Also see Chen Chia-chun, *An Analysis of Substantial and Unsubstantial Art of Composition.* 《虛實章法析論》 pp.145-158.

[21] See Chou Hsiao-ping, *The Types of Structures of Compositions*, 《篇章結構類

20. Generalization-details method

Definition: a method using "generalization" and "details" to organize a composition describing the same kinds of things, landscapes, feelings, and logic.

Aesthetics and features: The formation of the generalization-detail method is based on the thinking logic of inducting and deducing. In other words, the inductive type of thinking can form a structure of "first detail, and then generalization," while the deductive type, a structure of "first generalization, and then detail." In addition, the structure of "generalization, detail, generalization," and the structure of "details, generalization, details" combine the inductive and deductive types of thinking. Therefore, "generalization" has the power to include all things, while "details," a beauty of order. Moreover, these two structures commonly possess a beauty of symmetry and unity.[22]

21. Detailed-rough method

Definition: a method by which detailed writings and rough writings are mixed to express various topics.

Aesthetics and features: Aesthetics comes in part from ratio, which means that the distribution into two halves is appropriate or

....

型論》下 pp. 331-332. Also see Chen Chia-chun, *An Analysis of Substantial and Unsubstantial Art of Composition.* 《虛實章法析論》 pp.189-205.

22 See Chen Man-ming's "On the General-Detailed Structure in Poetry." (Taipei: Papers in the First Chinese Rhetoric Conference), Chinese Rhetoric Association, National Taiwan Normal University Chinese Department, June, 1999. Also see Chou Hsiao-ping, *The Types of Structures of Compositions*, 《篇章結構類型論》下 pp. 355-356. Also see Chen Chia-chun, *An Analysis of Substantial and Unsubstantial Art of Composition.* 《虛實章法析論》 pp.91-118. Also see Tu Pi-hsia, *Analysis of Generalization-Detail Composition Method.* 《凡目章法析論》 (Taipei: National Taiwan Normal University Chinese Graduate Institute, MA thesis, July, 2003.)

inappropriate. Detailed writings and rough writings must put expressions of the topics before everything. This is related to whether or not the ratio between the parts and the whole body is appropriate. In addition, when the ratio between the parts and the whole or between parts and parts is appropriate, plenty of aesthetic enjoyment will be produced.[23]

22. Guest-master method

Definition: a method by which supplementary materials (guest) are employed to highlight the main materials (master) in order to powerfully express the topics.

Aesthetics and features: According to the association of similarity, the "guests" are sought to highlight the "master," thus producing a beauty of harmony. Both supplementary materials and main subject matter are designed to highlight the topics, creating a multiple unity and a beauty of harmony.[24]

23. Positive-negative method

Definition: Two or more than two kinds of extremely different materials are put together, making a strong contrast. The negative-natured materials are used to highlight the positive meanings, strengthening the persuasive and influential power of the topics.

Aesthetics and features: The positive-negative method is produced in accordance with the principle of "contrast," which requires vivid, fresh, and strong feelings for its great existing differences. In

....

23 See Chou Hsiao-ping, *The Types of Structures of Compositions*, 《篇章結構類型論》下 pp. 371-372. Also see Chen Chia-chun, *An Analysis of Substantial and Unsubstantial Art of Composition.* 《虛實章法析論》 pp.119-144.

24 See Chou Hsiao-ping, *The Types of Structures of Compositions*, 《篇章結構類型論》下 pp. 398-401. Also see Hsia Wei-wei, *Analysis of the Guest-Master Composition Method.* 《賓主章法析論》 (Taipei: Wen-ching Publishing Company, November 2002, first edition.)

addition, with the appearance of "a contrasting posture," the features of the subject are thus highlighted, and its posture becomes more beautiful. Moreover, the topics can become more influential by means of this method. These binary oppositions re-affirm the aesthetic principle of a multiple unity.[25]

24. Establishing-breaking method

Definition: "Establishing" and "breaking" form an opposition to vividly highlight the topic being discussed.

Aesthetics and features: The establishing-breaking method is formed by the principle of contrast. However, the emphasis on opposition makes the effect more powerful. In addition, "establishment," more often than not, is a prejudice generated from long-term misjudgments, that is, psychological laziness. Therefore, when the existing establishment is broken, this will make the reader's understanding much deeper, and the effect more profound.[26]

25. Asking-answering method

Definition: a method using "asking" and "answering" to compose a composition. However, a series of questions without answers have an organizing effect, and "dialogue" is also included in this method.

Aesthetics and features: Language has the dual nature of "stimulus" and "reaction." The former will perform the act of asking, while the latter, answering. In addition, common dialogue will also form the relation of "stimulus-reaction." In addition, "asking" has the effect of suspense, while "answering," a sense of

....

25 See Chou Hsiao-ping, *The Types of Structures of Compositions*, 《篇章結構類型論》下 pp. 432-434.

26 See Chou Hsiao-ping, *The Types of Structures of Compositions*, 《篇章結構類型論》下 pp. 455-456.

relaxation. Moreover, a series of questions without any answer could be linked for semantic consistency, and in case of no answer, the special effect of suspense will be created.[27]

26. Flat-side method

Definition: a method flatly mentioning several items, and then inserted annotating one or two of these items.

Aesthetics and features: The biggest advantage of the flat-side method is to use annotations to highlight the main points.   In addition, the parts flatly mentioned also have the functions of closing and opening, thus producing an aesthetic effect.[28]

27. Release-catch method

Definition: a method mixed by means of "sidetracking from the axis," and "coming back to the axis."

Aesthetics and feature: to "release" is to let it go, while to "catch" is to pull back. When aesthetic emotion flows outside, the expression is a form of releasing.   And then, the aesthetic emotion will be pulled back and concentrated on a point, which is an act of "catching." Owing to the interaction between releasing and catching, the ensuing power can deepen the emotion of literary works and strengthen aesthetic emotion.[29]

....

[27] See Chou Hsiao-ping, *The Types of the Structures of Compositions*, 《篇章結構類型論》下 p. 501.

[28] See Chen Man-ming's "On Chen Man-ming's On the Composition Structure of Flatly Mentioning and Sideways Closing". (Kaohsiung: *A Collection of Papers Published in the Second Chinese Rhetoric Academic Conference*. June, 2000.) pp. 193-214.   See Chou Hsiao-ping, *The Types of Structures of Compositions*, 《篇章結構類型論》下 pp. 527-528. Also see Kao Ming-hsing's *Analysis of Flat And Sideways Chinese Composition*. 〈平側章法析論〉   (Taipei: National Taiwan Normal University, MA thesis, May, 2004.) pp.1-172.

[29] See Fu Keng-shen's *Appreciation of Chinese Literature* 《中國文學欣賞舉隅》 (Taipei: Wanchunlo Publishing Company, November, 2002, first edition) pp. 80-

28. Tense-relaxed method

Definition: a method producing rhythms between tense and relaxed and then mixing them together.

Aesthetics and features: When the aesthetic emotion rises high, a tense rhythm is thus produced. And while the aesthetic emotion slows, a relaxed rhythm follows. The former gives man a feeling of nervousness, while the latter, a feeling of relaxation. The tense rhythms and the relaxed rhythms can coordinate together, echoing each other and making the sense of rhythm stronger.[30]

29. Partial-whole method

Definition: a method mixing parts or special examples with the whole body or general principles.

Aesthetics and features: When an author creates poetry and articles, he or she frequently uses both "parts" and "wholeness"/ special examples and general rules to organize materials. This method can take care of not only "wholeness" and "general rules" but "parts" and special examples, which might well express deeper and enduring feelings.[31]

30. Heaven-man method

Definition: a method of describing "nature" and "humans." The so-called "heaven" refers to "nature," while "human," to human affairs.

Aesthetics and features: In terms of depicting landscape, "heaven"

....

88.   Also see See Chou Hsiao-ping, *The Types of Structures of Compositions*, 《篇章結構類型論》下 pp. 547-548.

30 Also see See Chou Hsiao-ping, *The Types of Structures of Compositions*, 《篇章結構類型論》下 pp. 566-567.

31 Chen Man-ming's *On A Few Special Composition Methods.* 〈論幾種特殊的章法〉 pp. 176-181.

refers to the landscape of nature, while "humans," to the landscape of human affairs. In addition, in terms of doctrines, "heaven" refers to the Word/Logos, while "humans," to the way of humans. When "heaven" and "humans" simultaneously appear in the same work, an inter-flow may thus be produced—feelings are grafted onto Nature, and human affairs are developed, as well. The aesthetics of warmth and freedom is produced.[32]

31. Picture-bottom method

Definition: a method mixing focuses and background. Of the materials used in compositions, some are pictures where focuses are located, while others are bottoms serving as background. These two kinds of materials combine to form hierarchical logical levels.

Aesthetics and features: Compared to the "pictures," a "bottom" serves to embellish the picture. On the other hand, compared to "bottoms," "pictures" can serve as a focus. Thus, with embellishments and focuses, the composition will turn rich and multi-leveled, while at the same time its focus will become evident.[33]

32. Knocking-striking method

Definition: a method combining straightforward writing and roundabout writing. "Knocking" refers to roundabout writing, while "striking," to straightforward writing.

Aesthetics and features: When straightforward writing and roundabout writing are combined together, an effect of "roundabout

....

32 Chen Man-ming's *On A Few Special Composition Methods.* 〈論幾種特殊的章 法〉 pp. 187-191.

33 Chen Man-ming's *On A Few Special Composition Methods.* 〈論幾種特殊的章 法〉 pp. 191-196. Also see See Chou Hsiao-ping, "On the Spatial Structure of Picture -Background Method—as in A Few Tang-Dynasty Poems." (Taipei: The World of Chinese Language and Literature Vol.17 (5), October, 2001).

knocking and straightforward striking" will be created. Therefore, roundabout writing can embrace a flowing aesthetic beauty, and straightforward writing can bring about a feeling of sharp conclusion. No wonder this method offers much beauty.[34]

These thirty-two compositional methods are most frequently used. Each composition method can meanwhile be divided into four variants (for example, the generalization-detail method can be in the form of "first generalization, then detail," "first detail, then generalization," "generalization, detail, generalization," and "detail, generalization, detail.") In other words, based on the already discovered forty compositional methods, we can have about 160 structures. And such kinds of compositional methods and structures will be increasing.[35] Because the so-called compositional method is an objective one, the author can uncover and gain new methods and structures whenever he or she applies the already existing methods to creative writing. In other words, in deductive fashion, more plentiful compositional methods and structures will be discovered.

Indeed, there are some connections among these compositional methods. So, based on the general rules, a family tree of compositional methods can be shown as follows:[36]

....

34 Chen Man-ming's *On A Few Special Composition Methods.* 〈論幾種特殊的章法〉 pp. 196-202.

35 Wang His-chieh, "Prof. Chen's compositional method system is open, but not closed or exhaustive,or limited. First, there are compositional method problems not yet discovered. Second, with the evolving of compositions, new articles will bring about fresh compositional methods." See "A Small Talk Outside the Gate of Composition Methods" 〈章法學門外閒談〉 (Taipei, *The World of Chinese Language and Literature*, Vol. 18 (5), October, 2002.)

36 See Chen Chia-chun, "On the Nature of Composition Methods." *Fuchou Collection of Articles.* 《修辭論叢》(Fuchou, Sea Tide Photo Art Publishing Company, Dec. 2002). pp.145-163.

family	composition method		aesthetics
diagram family	I temporal	1. present-past method 2. long-transient method 3. asking-answering method	three-dimensional beauty
	II spatial	1. far-near method 2. big-small method 3. inside-outside method 4. high-low method 5. angle-shifting method 6. consciousness-shifting method 7. state-changing method	
cause-effect family	1. root-end method 2. shallow-deep method 3. cause-effect method 4. release-catch method		level beauty
unreal-real family	I concrete and abstract	1. general-specific method 2.dot-dye method 3. generalization-detail method 4. feeling-landscape method 5. commentary-narration method 6. detail-rough method	transformational beauty
	II temporal-and-spatial	1. temporally real-unreal method 2. spatially unreal-real method 3. space-and-time blending unreal, real method	

family	composition method		aesthetics
	Ⅲ. real and unreal	1. assumption-factual unreal, real method 2. desire-fact unreal, real method 3. dream-reality unreal, real method 4. fiction-reality unreal, real method	
contrary-embellishing method	I contrary	1. positive-negative method 2. establishing-breaking method 3. down-up method 4. many-few method 5. tense-relaxed method	contrary-embellishing beauty
	Ⅱ embellishing	1. guest-master method 2. flat-side method 3. heaven-man method 4. partial-whole method 5. knocking-striking method 6. parallel method	

The four families of composition art all include types of blending and contrasting. Judging from this, the nearly forty methods of art composition might well be unified by the principles of "blending" and "contrasting." That is, in the logical principle of "(zero) one, two, many," the structure of art compositions is in a binary form, which puts emphasis on "blending" and "contrasting," both of which can serve to unify the structure of composition art.

Indeed, the binary opposition structure of about forty composition arts indeed can be unified by the principles of "contrasting" and "blending"[37] Here the so-called binary form is not a kind of binary oppositions, but in essence a kind of binary blending. Therefore, if we can use the "two" ("blending" and "contrasting") to group the composition arts, we can unify the "many" of the composition arts, and trace them back to the origin of the "one (zero)," while exploring the aesthetic effects.

Furthermore, the composition arts can also be divided into three types: the contrasting type, the blending type, and the neutral type. When employing the contrasting type and the blending type, the beauty of contrasting and blending can be displayed by the selection of materials. In terms of the source of materials, three conditions exist, that is, the same thing, different things, and others. As to the third composition art, the neutral type, the binary form can be either contrasting or blending. The neutral type is inclusive of many kinds of composition art, most of which use a "bottom" to highlight a "picture."[38] It should be noted that the insert-narration method and the supplementary method can not be listed among these three types, for these two methods are difficult to categoriz in terms of contrasting and blending.

The detailed grouping of the composition arts can be seen as following classification:[39]

....

37 See Hsia-fan, *Aesthetics: Troubled Pursuit.* 《美學：苦惱的追求》 (Fuchou: Strait Literature Publishing Company, May, 1988, first Edition) p. 108.

38 The picture-bottom type is different from the picture-bottom method. Actually, the picture-bottom type is a big group, while the picture-bottom method is a small group. The picture-bottom method is a sub-group of the picture-bottom type. Both are similar for they use a "bottom" to highlight a "picture." However, if a "bottom" and a "picture" can be analyzed by the present-past method, long-transient method, far-near method, etc., they can be named after an analytical method. If not, they belong to the picture-bottom method.

39 Such grouping lists are offered by Chou Hsiao-ping, assistant professor of the Chinese department of National Cheng Kung University.

contrast	1. the same things：establishing-breaking method, down-up method, release-catch method 2. different things：positive-negative method 3. both：tense-relaxed method
blending	1. the same things：root-end method, shallow-deep method, cause-effect method, general-specific method, generalization-detail method, flat-side method, dot-dye method, partial-whole method 2. different things：guest-master method, parallel method, feeling-landscape method, commentary-narration method, knocking-breaking method 3. both ：consciousness-shifting method
neutral	1. picture-bottom： （1）temporal-spatial：present-past method, long transient method, far-near method, inside-outside method, left-right method, high-low method, big-small method , angle-shifting method, space-and-time blending method （2）unreal-real：spatially unreal-real method, temporally real-unreal method, assumption-factual method （3）other kinds：detail-rough method, heaven-man method, many-few method , diagram method 2. other kinds：state-changing method, asking-answering method

The above-mentioned two groupings have their own unique perspectives, which are instrumental in helping readers to gain a better understanding of the composition art.　In addition, comparison is a way to deepen understanding of the composition art and its inner logic, which can help in the study and application of the composition arts.

II. Laws of composition arts

The so-called composition arts aim to research the logical structures of compositions, analyzing how sentences are linked to form paragraphs, and how paragraphs are linked to form a composition. In the early years, the study of composition arts had aroused scholars' interests. In recent years, its scope, contents, and principles have been organized into a system, developing into a discipline.[40] To date, there are about forty methods of composition that can be clearly depicted. These methods all originated from humans' common rules formed by thinking and logic.[41] All of them

....

[40] Cheng Yi-shou, "Taiwan has established the new research field, the composition art, which is remarkably fruitful, and among which the representative works are Prof. Chen Man-ming's *New Design of Composition Art* and a series of works by his students such as Chou Hsiao-ping and Chen Chia-chun. The system of the study is so comprehensive that it can be called a discipline." See "Chinese Cultural Rich Soil, Genius of Composition Art: Reading Chen Man-ming's *New Design of Composition Art and Others*," *Conference Paper Collection: Chinese Traditional Culture and Modernization across the Two Sides of the Taiwan Strait.* 《海峽兩岸中華傳統文化與現代化研討會文集》(Soochow: Conference on Chinese Traditional Culture and Modernization across the Two Sides of the Taiwan Strait, May, 2002) pp. 131-139. Also see Wang His-chieh "Composition art" has many definitions. The composition art entails the rules of composition. On the one hand, it is objective, and simultaneously exists with compositions. Compositions depend on rules, either good or bad. On the other hand, composition art entails researchers' knowledge and theories according to their analyses of the existing compositions. ······For the latter type of composition art, the ancient Chinese made a lot of studies. However, the forming of the discipline of composition art has been on track in recent years. It is Prof. Chen Man-ming who initiated the establishment of the discipline." See *Small Talks Outside the Door of Composition Arts.* 〈章法學門外閒談〉 pp.92-95.

[41] 41See Wu Ying-tien, *A Study of the Structure of Compositions.* 《文章結構學》 (Beijing: Chinese People University Publishing Company, Aug. 1989, first edition.)

have the function of creating order, change, unity and producing consistency. Thus "order," "change," "unity," and "consistency" are the four major rules of composition art. The first three rules serve to use materials focusing on analysis. In addition, consistency serves to express feelings and meanings, emphasizing oneness. Therefore, the scope of the composition methods includes not only partial analyses (materials) but the consistency of wholeness (feelings and meanings).

1. Law of order

By "order" is meant placing materials into suitable positions. This law can be used by all composition methods to place materials into a suitable sequence. Take the more than ten composition methods listed below, for example. Their sequential structures are as follows:

1. present-past method: "first present, and then past," "first past, and then present"
2. far-near method: "first near, and then far," "first far, and then near"
3. big-small method: "first big, and then small," "first small, and then big"
4. beginning-end method: "first beginning, and then end," "first end, and then beginning"
5. real-unreal method: "first unreal, and then real," "first real, and then unreal"
6. guest-master method: "first guest, and than master," "first master, and then guest"
7. positive-negative method: "first positive, and then negative," "first negative, and then positive"
8. knocking-striking method: "first knocking, and then striking," "first striking, and then knocking"
9. establishing-breaking method: "first establishing, and then

breaking," "first breaking, and then establishing"

10. flat-side method: "first flat, and then to the side," "first to the side, and then flat"

11. generalization-detail method: "first generalization, and then detail," "first detail, and then generalization"

12. cause-effect method: "first cause, and then effect," "first effect, and then cause"

13. feeling-landscape method: "first feeling, and then landscape," "first landscape, and then feeling"

14. commentary-narration method: "first commentary, and then narration," "first narration, and then commentary"

15. picture-background method: "first background, and then picture," "first picture, and then background"

The sequential placing either from the beginning to the end or from the end to the beginning can be seen everywhere.   Take Meng Hao-jan's "To My Old Friend in Yangzhou from a Boat Moored at Night on Tonglu River," for example.

山暝聽猿愁，滄江急夜流。風鳴兩岸葉，月照一孤舟。建德非吾土，維揚憶舊遊。還將兩行淚，遙寄海西頭。

From murky mountains the monkeys' howls grieve my heart;
The dark blue waters ever nightly rush and dart.
Wind through foliage on either strand whispers and whines;
Upon my solitary boat the pale moon shines.
Jiande where I sojourn is not my native plot;
My old friend in Yangzhou miss I still and a lot.
Trickling tears will engrave each cheek with one lean line;
I'll send them far West to my home across the brine!

According to the title of the poem, the poem was written when the author moored his boat on Tonglu River, it was designed to express his feelings to an old friend in Yangzhou, and to manifest his sorrow over his life story.[42] This poem was based on the structure of "first background, and then picture." The background is portrayed in the first three lines. On the one hand, the vision of space is widened so that murky mountains, river waters, and riverside trees are showcased. On the other hand, the reader can likely hear the acoustic sounds in the author's depiction of the monkeys' whines, rushing waters, and treess blown by the winds. Thus, the space the author devotes the boat is filled with sorrow. In this way, the background before which the author expresses his feelings is fully presented. As for the "picture (focus)," in the line about the "solitary boat," through the shining of the moon the focus is upon the author in the solitary boat; in this way, he expresses his feelings, which acts as a focal "dot." The two lines about "Jian-de" mention that Tonglu is not his hometown (a guest) in order to pinpoint his memory of Yangzhou (his master). In Wan Chan's "Climbing Upstairs," "The land, despite its beauty is not my hometown, so how can I stay longer?" The feeling of sorrow was thus further condensed. In addition, the last two lines have been expanded from generalization to specification. Through meditation, he seems to send his tears far off to Yangzhou, which greatly deepens his sorrow over an old friend. This is the portion given to "dyeing." The sequences of the structure are as follows: "first background, and then picture;" "first dotting, and then dyeing;" "first guest, and then master;" "first generalization, and then specification." From this sequential order, it can be seen that the travel brings loneliness, and the feelings are sincere and deep.[43] The structural analysis table is presented below:

....

---

42 See Yu Shou-chen, *Comprehensive Analysis of Three Hundred Tang Dynasty Poems.* 《唐詩三百首詳析》 (Taipei: Taiwan Chunhua Bookstore, April, 1996, third edition) p. 161.

43 See Kao Pu-ying, *Tang and Sung Dynasties' Major Poems.* 《唐宋詩舉要》 (Taipei: Hsuehhai Publishing Company, February, 1973, first edition) pp.438-439.

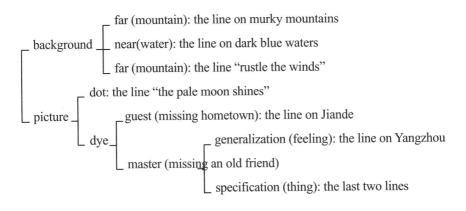

far (mountain): the line on murky mountains
background — near(water): the line on dark blue waters
far (mountain): the line "rustle the winds"

dot: the line "the pale moon shines"
picture — guest (missing hometown): the line on Jiande
dye — generalization (feeling): the line on Yangzhou
master (missing an old friend)
specification (thing): the last two lines

Therefore, it can be seen that in this poem a spatial shift of "far, near, far" was created.[44] In addition, the sequential order is as follows: "first background, and then picture," "first dot, and then dye," "first guest, and then master," "first generalization, and then specification." In other words, "order" (position change) is changed (position transformation), but the "order" is still the main part. And the structure is a blending one, which can deepen the feelings of missing old friends. The levels can be shown in the diagram:

Top   The 2nd level   The 3rd level   Bottom

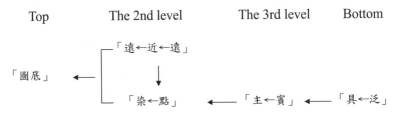

44 Chou Hsiao-ping, "On the Position Change, Position Transformation, and Aesthetics of Composition Art," *Paper Collection of Composition Art.* 《辭章學論文集》上(Fuchou: Sea Tide Photography Art Publishing Company, Dec. 2002, first edition.) pp. 98-122.

Corresponding to the structure of "many, two, one (zero)," "many" can refer to the structure and rhythm of "generalization and specification," "far and near," "guest and master," and "dot and dye." In addition, "two" can refer to the structure of "picture and background," which is the core structure.[45] And the key theme of missing one's hometown can form a unique rhythm, which is "one (zero.)

Moreover, take Wang Wei's "Retirement at Wangchuan—To Pei Di, for example.

寒山轉蒼翠，秋水日潺湲。倚杖柴門外，臨風聽暮蟬。渡頭餘落日，墟里上孤煙。復值接輿醉，狂歌五柳前。

The chilly mountains turn emerald green,
The autumn waters daily murmuring.
Outside my thatch-door on my staff I lean,
Heeding evening winds, cicadas shrilling.
Beyond the ford the sun has nearly sunk;
From the village a wisp of smoke floats free.
You are just like that jolly Jie-yu, drunk,
Wildly warbling before my willow tree.

Here, the author enjoyed himself with Pei Di in a specific setting. In describing the landscape and characters, he depicts his feeling of ease and relaxation. In the first two lines, he substantially describes water, land, the autumn scenery, and evenings around Wangchuan, which combined to form a harmonious picture of colors and sounds. And then, in a picturesque landscape of easiness and relaxation, the author describes his leaning on a staff to listen to the cicadas and Pei

....

45 See Sheng Chiachuang, *A Collection of Canonical Works.* 《歷代名篇賞析集成》 I (Beijing, Chinese Wenlien Publishing Company, Dec. 1988 first edition, p.618.

Di's wild chanting. Thus, an artistic world of oneness of object and self was formed. Li Hao said, "In terms of setting, time refers to the sunken sun, while space refers to a thatch door, a ford, a village, and a willow tree." It shoud be understood that the scenes are impressive and inter-dependent, forming part of a harmonious picture. While reading this poem, standing in for a moment, the reader is supposed to have an understanding of the space, and then can grasp the transient impression the poet creates skillfully and artistically.[46] The structural analysis table is listed below:

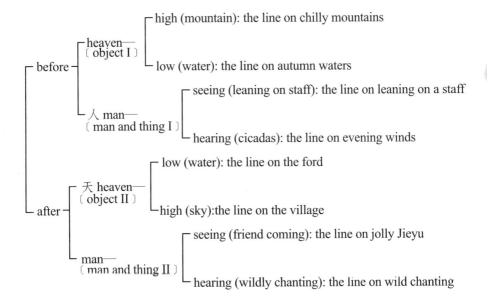

Therefore, it can be seen that the author used a few composition arts, that is, "present (after), past (before)," "heaven (object), man (personnel), "far and near," "high and low," "sense (seeing, listening)

....

46 See *Aesthetic Interpretation of Tang Dynasty Poetry.* 《唐詩的美學闡釋》 (Hofei: Anhei University Publishing Company, April, 2000, first edition.) p.255.

transformation," to form the structure of position shifting in order to "blend" the whole poem. Besides "present and past," the author uses "heaven and man," "high and low," "sense transformation," to carve out a double form, increasing the beauty of the rhythmical flow. Note that heaven and man form a contrast, expanding the space and horizon. These reinforce the author's enjoyment of ease. The diagram of the levels is as follows:

top level   second level   bottom level

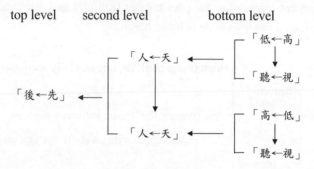

In terms of "many, two, one (zero)," "many" refers to the position shift and rhythm formed by the composition arts, as in "far and near," "high and low," and "sense (seeing, hearing) shift." "Two" refers to the position shift and rhythm formed by Ying and Yang; these composition arts are "heaven and man," (including present/after and past/before). Furthermore, "one" (zero) refers to the topic of "enjoyment of ease" and the elegant rhythm and style. As Kao Pu-ying put it, this poem "is natural and smooth, and the horizon is unimaginably enlarged and expanded."[47]

Such kind of "position change structures," which are in accordance with "order," are due to the human psychological need for "order," for which the author logically arranged the writing content. According to Sungshanchengyi's *Methods Teachers Use to*

....

[47] See Kao Pu-ying's *Major Poems of Tang and Sung Dynasties*. 《唐宋詩舉要》 p.422.

Inspire Pupils' Thinking Abilities translated by Ouyang Chungjen, the following principles are really related to "order"—"inspiring students' thinking in an orderly way," "inspiring students' thinking by analysis," "inspiring students' thinking by cause and effect," "inspiring students' thinking by knowledge," etc.[48] In addition, in To Hu-hui's *The Multidimensional Ways of Thinking,* he emphasized "reverse thinking," holding that we can engage in thinking in a reverse way.[49] Accordingly, the two-directional ways of thinking can be reflected in students' writing.

In the writing of sixth-grade students, orderly narration accounts for 87.61%; inserting narration, 3.54%; and reverse narration, 8.85%. Basically speaking, pupils can use only orderly narration. According to Huang Jengfa and others, the third grade students can use only orderly narration; 2.28% of the fifth grade students can use inserting narration. Some individual students can explain the things happening later in the opening sentences.[50]

Judging from this, we can see that for the author (student), "orderly thinking" is much easier than "reverse thinking."

However, in terms of "picture and background," "far and near," "dot and dye," "guest and master," and "generalization and specification," all of which are in the form of Ying and Yang, both "orderly" and "reverse" are combined in the form of "repetition,"

....

48 See *Methods Teachers Use to Inspire Pupils' Thinking Abilities*《教師啟發學童思考能力的方法》(Taipei, Youth Culture Business Company, July, 1989, 7th edition).pp.15-19, 85-88, 104-107, 126-129.

49 See *The Mulit-dimenional Ways of Thinking Ways*《全方位思考法》(Taipei, Wanhsiang Publishing Company, July, 1994, first edition. pp. 101-106.

50 50See Chu Chojen, Chu hsinghua, *A Psychological Introduction to Elementary Schools' Language Teaching.* 《小學語文教學心理學導論》(Shanghai: Shanghai Education Publishing Company, May, 2001, first edition) p. 195.

that is, "uniformity." Chen Hsueh-fan said,

The simplest form is repetition, which repeats the same thing. In terms of its constituent materials, it is uniformity. Therefore, the rule of repetition is one of uniformity. This kind of rule is essentially an extremely simple form, which can be used anywhere to induce the enjoyment of simplicity.[51]

The so-called "form" refers to "the combined relations among things."[52] For example, the so-called "first A, and then B" refers to the orderly combination of A and B. Judging from this, we can see that the "order" of composition arts, in a way, is "repetition" and "uniformity." This kind of "repetition" or "uniformity," Ouyang Chou, Ku Chenhua, and Sung Fanshen's *New Editing of Aesthetics* called "a law of uniformity," which is combined with "rhythm and order."

It is also called sameness of simplicity, sameness of uniformity, which is the most commonly seen and simplest form of beauty. It possesses oneness, purity, cleanness, and repetition, all of which exclude differences or oppositions. So, it gives man a sense of order. The sameness or repetition of colors, forms, or sounds will create a beauty of sameness and uniformity. Farmers plant seeds in fixed distances; buildings are designed in fixed sizes; In military parades, warriors are placed in conformity to their height, weight, clothes, steps, and saluting gestures. The frequently seen serial flowery designs also have a constant rhythmical sense, a kind of beauty of conformity, which gives man a sense of

....

51 See *An Introduction to Aesthetics.* 《美學概論》 (Taipei: Wenchin Culture Business Company, Dec. 1984, first edition.) pp.61-62.
52 See *An Introduction to Aesthetics*, 《美學概論》 p.60.

simplicity, cleanness, and freshness.[53]

It can be seen that "uniformity" and "repetition" will form "rhythm," bringing about a sense of order, which is instrumental in logical thinking. So, the law of order in composition art has a linear relation with logical thinking; both are closely related.

2. Law of change

So-called "change" refers to the sequential placement of materials. According to this law, each composition art can have an "orderly" and "reversed" effect in terms of its sequential arrangement. Based on this, we can see the sequential structure of the following composition methods.

1. present-past method: "present, past, present," "past, present, past."
2. far-near method: "far, near, far," "near, far, near."
3. big-small method: "big, small, big," "small, big, small."
4. root-end method: "root, end, root," "end, root, end."
5. unreal-real method: "unreal, real, unreal," "real, unreal, real."
6. guest-master method: "guest, master, guest," "master, guest, master."
7. positive-negative method: "positive, negative, positive," "negative, positive, negative."
8. down-up method: "down, up, down," "up, down, up."
9. establishing-breaking method: "establishing, breaking, establishing," "breaking, establishing, breaking."
10. flat-side method: "flat, side, flat," "side, flat, side."
11. generalization-detail method: "generalization, detail,

....

53 See *New Editing of Aesthetics.* 《美學新編》(Hangchou: Chechiang University Publishing Company, March, 1993, first edition.) p.76.

generalization," "detail, generalization, detail."
12. cause-effect method: "cause, effect, cause," "effect, cause, effect."
13. feeling-landscape method: "feeling, landscape, feeling," "landscape, feeling, landscape."
14. commentary-narration method: "commentary, narration, commentary," "narration, commentary, narration."
15. picture-background method: "background, picture, background," "picture, background, picture."

These structures of "place changes" consisting of "orderly placement," and "reversed placement" can be seen everywhere. Take Li Bai's "On Phoenix Terrace at Jinling," for example.

鳳凰臺上鳳凰遊，鳳去臺空江自流。吳宮花草埋幽徑，晉代衣冠成古丘。三山半落青天外，二水中分白鷺洲。總為浮雲能蔽日，長安不見使人愁。

On Phoenix Terrace the phoenix once came to play,
Terrace now vacant still roll on the river's waves.
Wu palace garden's buried by the wasted byway;
Ancient sages in noble gowns all lie in graves.
The three-peak'd mountain's half lost in the azure sky;
The two-fork'd stream by Egret Isle's split apart.
As floating clouds can at all times the sun defy,
Imperial Court, now out of sight, aggrieves my heart.

This poem describes the forlornness of life and grievances of a nation, expressing the feeling the author had while climbing a terrace.[54] According to the first line, the starting point was Phoenix

---

[54] See Yuan Hsing-pei, *A Synopsis of Tang Dynasty Poems.* 《唐詩大觀》 (Hong Kong: Commercial Press Publishing Company, Hong Kong branch, Jan. 1986, first edition) p. 329

Terrace where the author "came" and "went," which, in a sense, signifies the rise and fall of a nation.   This seems to be a "picture," presented by a contrastive structure.   In the third and fourth lines, "ruined palace" and "graves" were reminiscent of the fall of a nation, while "weeds in spring" and "ancient sages," the rise of a nation. Here, we get a strong contrast. And then, the three-peaked mountain and two-forked stream serve as a background to highlight the meaning and blend the structure.   Moreover, just as the bright sun is veiled by floating clouds, so the author is blackmailed by evil officials.   Expelled from the imperial court, he is deeply worried that his nation will perish.   This seems to be a "picture."   The structure diagram is depicted below:

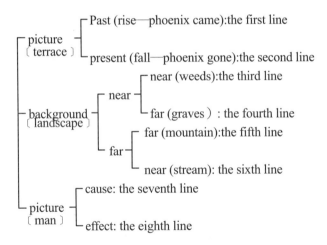

Through logical thinking, this poem was created with a blending structure of "picture, background, picture."   In addition, this poem was composed with both a contrastive and blending "position shifting structure"—"first past, and then present," "first near, and then far," "first far, and then near," and "first cause, and then effect." In addition, the combination of "orderly" and "reversed" marks change, producing "picture, background, and picture," as well as "near, far, near," which highlights the contrast. In this way, there is blending and uniformity in contrast and change; on the other hand, there is contrast and change in blending and uniformity. The delicate logical thinking deserves to be valued. The diagram of various levels is listed below:

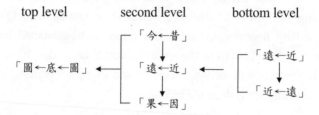

Therefore, in terms of "many, two, one (zero)," "many" refers to "present, past," "far, near," and "cause, effect," all of which consist of a two-level place-shifting blending structure and rhythm. "Two" refers to "picture and background," which contains transformational core structures and rhythms based on Ying and Yang. Furthermore, "one (zero)" refers to the unique style and rhythm, soft yet strong, expressing the "sadness of life story, and pains for his nation." The style and rhythm is the same as those of Li Bai's poem.[55]

Take Tu Fu's "Recapture of the Regions North and South of the Yellow River," for example.

劍外忽傳收薊北，初聞涕淚滿衣裳。卻看妻子愁何在，漫卷
詩書喜欲狂。白日放歌須縱酒，青春作伴好還鄉。即從巴峽
穿巫峽，便下襄陽向洛陽。

News broke from Jian the North Gate was recovered of late,

When these tidings reach my ears, my gown grows wet with tears.

....

[55] See Chou Chenfu, *On Literary Style* 《文學風格例話》 (Shanhai: Shanhai Education Publishing Company, July, 1989, first edition). p.103.

Reading my wife and son's face, of grief I find no trace;
Rolling up my poetry books, my joy like madness looks.
Though it is broad daylight still, I sing and drink my fill.
With verdure the spring's aglow, it's time we homeward go!
From Ba Gorge we'll sail our way through Wu Gorge in a day,
Advancing south to Xiangyang, we'll soon wind up at Luoyang.

This poem aims to describe the "mad joy" of recapturing the regions north and south of the Yellow River. And it was written in the frame of "first dotting and then dyeing." As to the feature of "dyeing," the inner structure is "details, generalization, and details." At the beginning, he bursts into tears while hearing of "the recapture of the regions north and north of the Yellow River." The news was so surprising that "my gown grows wet with tears." And then, depicting his wife's mad joy, he used "rolling up my poetry books" to engage in a substantial description, which belongs to the category of "details (I) ." Furthermore, the "mad joy" emerges as the topic of this poem, which belongs to the category of "generalization." And then, he sang and drank before sailing to his hometown. Finally, in the last line, he mentions his trip. All of these are designed to describe the "mad joy," which belongs to the "details (II)" Starting from "hearing the news," he reads his "wife and son's faces," rolling up his verse book, and then sailing downward off to go back to his hometown.[56] The "mad joy" of the family is vividly described.[57] In this way, the feeling of the whole poem is described consistently. The structure analysis is listed below:

....

56　See Chao Shan-lin, *The Theory of the Art of Poetic Works*.《詩詞曲藝術論》(Hangchou: Chechiang Education Publishing Company, June, 1998, first edition) p.124.

57　See Chen Man-ming's *The New Design of the Art of Composition*《章法學新裁》 p.383.

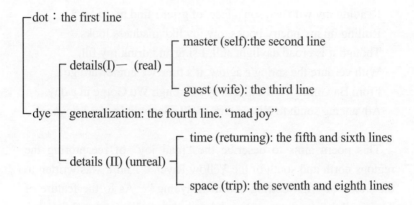

Therefore, it can be seen that the structure of this poem falls within the frame of position change—"detail (real), generalization, detail (unreal). In addition, the structures of position change— "first dot and then dye," "first master and then guest," "first time and then space"—make the poem consistent. In other words, "detail" (real) and "detail" (unreal), "cause" and "effect," "guest" and "master," "time" and "space" partially form an echo. Furthermore, "generalization" (mad joy) controls two "details," real and unreal, to make the feeling of the poem consistent. A diagram of the levels is depicted below:

top level   third level   bottom level

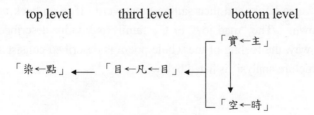

In terms of "many, two, one (zero)," many refers to the position-shifting blending structure and rhythm, which are formed by "dot and dye," "time and space," and "guest and master." Two refers to the position-shifting structure and rhythm, which are formed by "detail" and "generalization." And "one(zero) " refers to the unique style and rhythm, which express the topic of mad joy.[58]

Here, on the one hand, the person who "rolled up the verse books" is commonly considered to be Tu fu himself.[59] Indeed, on the other hand, the person can be "the wife (guest)," who showed no grief on her face. Besides, combined with the picture in which the poet's (master) was wet with tears, the family demonstrated their mad joy. Therefore, it seems that the second interpretation in which the wife is guest, while the poet is master, is more logically consistent.

The combination of "orderly" and "reversed" is more complicated than merely "orderly" or merely "reversed." This kind of change originates from the human psychology of seeking variety. In *An Introduction to Aesthetics*, Chen Hsuehfan said,

Human psychology more often than not needs various kinds of stimuli, which can keep consciousness awake. If the stimuli are changeless, consciousness will tend to have little or no response to them. Fundamentally speaking, a form of repetition is a weakness. For repetition is various kinds of sameness. Too many repetitions will dampen their power of stimulating our consciousness, which is indeed in favor of change and excitement.[60]

....

[58] See Chao Shan-lin, *The Theory of the Art of Poetic Works.* 《詩詞曲藝術論》 p.241.

[59] See Shih Shuang-yuan, *Appraisal Dictionary of Ancient Prose and Poetry for the Middle School.* 《中學古詩文鑑賞辭典》(Nanking: Chiangsu ancient book publishing company, July 1988) p.68. Also see Ho Sung-lin, *Anthology of Tang Dynasty Poetry.* 《唐詩大觀》, p.543.

[60] See *An Introduction to Aesthetics* 《美學概論》 pp.63-64.

Therefore, variety of structure can befits logical thinking and psychology. The mind of seeking variety has been reflected in the composition of the elementary school students. According to a survey,

> Chang Hungsi and others found that for different materials students will arrange diverse structure levels. When describing one thing, 21.6% of students love to use the structure of "one detail, one rough" to express it. And 58.9% love to use various structures to express different kinds of materials. The reason for students' favor of various structures is that the method is freely used without any unique opening or skillful ending. In short, the structural levels of students' compositions have been changed from a fixed model to various models.[61]

The common human rule is that based on "uniformity" man seeks "variety," which can promote man's thinking ability, keeping the mind alert. In the preface to his "Well-Rounded Thinking Method," Tohuhui in terms of life experiences held that,

> How to eliminate the dumbness of life is the problem of everyman. We can improve that by "changing the space of life," "changing the time of life," and "changing the habits of life." Observing things from whatever perspective, and subverting dogmatic thinking will develop into the habit of brainstorming. This kind of self discipline will keep you thinking smoothly, and your mind constantly creative.[62]

....

61　See *Teachers' Ways of Stimulating Pupils' Thinking Abilities.* 《教師啟發學童思考能力的方法》See note 48.

62　See "Well-Round Thinking Way; Prelude." 《全方位思考方法・序》 p.2.

Compared with "order," "variety" can form "rhythm," which is more complex. In *New Editing of Aesthetics*, Ouyang Chou, Ku Chienhua, and Sung Fanshen, explained "rhythm" derived from "variety" in this way,

Rhythm is a form of continuous and regular movement. As Kuo Mojo noticed, "It is well said that the beating of the heart and the breathing of the lungs are the origin of rhythm." There is nothing without rhythm in the world. Sunrise and sunset, full moon and nascent moon, winter and summer, the rotation of the four seasons, are rhythms of time changes. Working in the daytime and sleeping at night, regularly laboring and resting, are the rhythms of people's everyday life. Human bodies' breathing, pulse, emotion and thinking like a biological clock form a rhythmical life process. When the rhythm of the outside surroundings is harmonious with that of the human body, a man will feel physically comfortable and psychologically pleased.[63]

It can be seen that change in space, time and life, and change in the life process can cause "rhythm," which is in harmony with the human body's movement, leading to "psychological pleasure," which might well be an aesthetic effect, and which has a positive effect on logical thinking. In this way, we can see that changeable logical thinking has an immense impact on human life. Now, we are using composition art to grasp its rhythm in order to well understand logical thinking.

3. Law of consistence

The connecting law refers to the connection of the materials. For each composition art, partial "blending" and "contrast" can form

---

[63] See *New Editing of Aesthetics*. 《美學新編》 pp. 78-79.

links or echoes to achieve the effect of connection. In more than thirty composition arts, the contrastive types include "noble vs. mean," "close vs. strange," "positive vs. negative," "down vs. up," "establishing vs. breaking," "many vs. few," "detail vs. rough," "tense vs. relaxed," etc. Furthermore, the types in a "blending" relation are as follows: "present and past," "far and near," "big and small," "high and low," "shallow and deep," "guest and master," "unreal and real," "flat and side," "generalization and detail," "release and catch," "cause and effect," etc.[64] Generally speaking, for the composition arts, the downright "contrastive types" are few. More often than not, the contrastive types (master) are accompanied by the blending types (guest).   And the downright "blending" types are more commonly seen.   Moreover, less frequently seen are the "blending" types (master) accompanied by the "contrastive" types (guest).   This principle can especially apply to classic poetry. However, these above-mentioned combined ways can all provide a "connecting" effect.[65]   Take Hsin Chi-chi's "Hosinlang," a poem of irregular rhythm, for example.

綠樹聽鵜鴃，(Cuckoos were heard singing in the green tree.) 更那堪、鷓鴣聲住，(The voices of partridges ceased.) 杜鵑聲 切！(The cuckoos cried even louder!) 啼到春歸無尋處，(They cried until the end of spring.) 苦恨芳菲都歇。(It was hateful that all the flowers were gone.) 算未抵人間離別：(This was not as good as departure from the mundane world.) 馬上琵琶關塞

---

64 See Chen Man-ming, "On Four Major Laws of Compositional Art," *Paper Collection of Compositional Art.* 《辭章學論文集》 I pp.68-77.

65 Besides this effect, "contrast" and "blending" might influence the style of a composition.   More often than not, "contrast" would make a composition more stiff, while "blending" would make a composition softer.   See Chou Hsiao-ping, *Spatial and Temporal Design Aesthetics of Classic Poetry and Tzu.* 《古典詩詞 時空設計美學》 pp.323-331.

黑，(Wang Chaochun played the pi-pa on a horse, and the sky of the frontier turned dark.) 更長門翠輦辭金闕。(The carts of the palace had departed.) 看燕燕，(Swallows flew through the sky.) 送歸妾。(The woman was escorted back.) 將軍百戰身名裂，(After many wars, the general had gotten nowhere.) 向河梁、回頭萬里，(At the place of departure, I looked back.)故人長絕。(Friends were deceased.) 易水蕭蕭西風冷，(The waters and west winds were cold and crisp.) 滿座衣冠似雪。(The costumes of the guests were as white as snow.) 正壯士、悲歌未徹。(The sad songs of heroes were endless.) 啼鳥還知如許恨，(If the crying bird had known such hatred,) 料不啼清淚長啼血。(it would have cried blood instead of tears.) 誰共我，醉明月。(Who could accompany me drinking wine in the moonlight?)

This Tzu [poem of irregular rhythm] was composed in the order of "first guest and then master." In terms of "guest," we can see that from the line containing 「綠樹」 (green tree) to the line with 「苦恨」 (hatred), the spring birds' crying is used to describe 「苦恨」 (hatred). This is the first part of "knocking." And then, from the line with 「算未抵」 (this was not as good as) to the line with 「正壯士」 (heroes), the emphasis is shifted to "men." This indeed uses the technique of "first a flat beginning and then a sideways ending."[66] The example of two ancient women and two ancient men are used to describe 「苦恨」 (hatred) of departure from the mundane world. This indeed hints that at that time the treason of certain subjects and the sacrifice of heroes made a vivid contrast. In this way, the hatred of homes and the country finds

---

[66] See Chen Man-ming, "On the Compositional Structure of Flat Beginning and Then Sideways Ending." *Essays on Rhetoric*《章法學新裁》 (Taipei: Hungye Publishing Company, June 2000, first edition), pp. 435-459.

expression.[67]　This marks the feature of "striking."　Finally, the two lines with 「啼鳥」(crying birds) returns to the "sideways" feature, using imaginative writing to further describe the 「苦恨」 (hatred) of crying birds.　This marks the next feature, that of "knocking."　And in terms of "master," the two lines with 「誰共我」(who could accompany me) to express his feelings of departure, putting the whole ending to an end.　In this way, the endless hatred is wholly depicted.　Thus, the structure analysis diagram can be shown as follows.

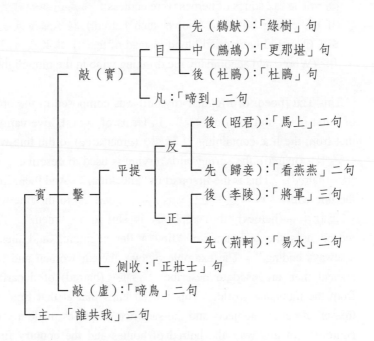

67 Kung Pen-tung, *Commentary Biography of Sinchichi*, 《辛棄疾評傳》 (Nanking: Nanking University Publishing, Dec. 1998) pp.400-401.　Also see Chen Man-ming "Tang Sung Tzu Collection—Sinchichi's Hosinlan" (*The World of Chinese Language and Literature,* June, 1996) pp.66-69.

Thus, the "blending" was performed by the position changing structures, such as "guest and master," "knocking and striking," "unreal and real," "general and detail," "flat beginning and sideways ending," "before/past, and after/present." In addition, the "contras" were formed by "positive and negative," with "change" being performed by "knocking" and "striking." That is, there was "contrast" in the "blending," while "change" was acheived by "sequential narration." For the feature of "change" occupied almost the whole work, with "contrast" appearing in the middle of the work to form a core structure. And "striking" was used for manifestation, while within "change," "contrast" was employed to highlight the core contents. In this way, the other parts of "blending" also served this purpose. With these arrangements, the style of this poem is "deep, crisp, leaping and volatile."[68] So, the 5-levelstructure analysis diagram can be shown as follows.

上層　　　次層　　　　三層　　　四層　　　底層

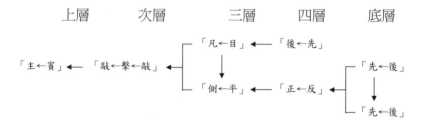

By grasping this diagram, we can clearly see the structure of "many, two, one/zero" of this Tzu. Many features refer to "flat-side," "general-detailed," "positive-negative," and "before-after (present-past,"—all these position changing structures and rhythms. In addition, two refer to "knocking-striking" (including guest-

68 Chen Tinchao, *Paiyuchai Tzu*, 《白雨齋詞話》卷一 Vol.1, Tang Kueichang, *Anthology of Tzus*《詞話叢編》4 (Taipei: Sinwenfan Publishing Company, Feb., 1988) p.3791.

master"), which make up the yin-yang core structure and rhythm. And one/zero refers to the topic of "hatred for home and country," and the style of "deep, crisp, leaping and volatile."

Also, take Lee Wen-shao's "Doctrine of Frugality," for instance.

儉 (Frugality)，美德也 (is a fine virtue,)，而流俗顧薄之。 (but has been ignored by the world.)
貧者見富者而羨之，(Poor men admire rich men.) 富者見尤富者而羨之。(The rich men admire even richer men.) 一飯十金，(One meal costs ten pounds.) 一衣百金，(A piece of clothing costs hundreds of pounds.) 一室千金，(A room costs hundreds of thousands of pounds.) 奈何不至貧且匱也？(In this way, all one's belongings get squandered and men become poor.) 每見閭閻之中，(It's frequently seen that in one's hometown) 其父兄古樸質實，(one's father and elder brothers live a simple and frugal life.)足以自給，(A man could live a life of self-sufficiency.) 而其子弟羞向者之為鄙陋，(But one man despised their frugality,) 盡舉其規模而變之(intending to live a luxurious life.) 於是累世之藏，(Thus, the belongings of several generations) 盡費於一人之手。(will be wasted by one man.) 況乎用之奢者，(In order to live a luxurious life,) 取之不得不貪，(he has to be greedy) 算及錙銖，(in everything.) 欲深谿壑；(His desire must be extremely deep.) 其究也，(In fact,) 諂求詐騙，(cozening and deceiving men,) 寡廉鮮恥，(being shameless) 無所不至；(in everything,) 則何若量入為出，(this kind of man cannot make ends meet.) 享恆足之利乎？(nor enjoy a life of self sufficiency.)
且吾所謂儉者，(So-called frugality) 豈必一切捐之？(is not necessarily to be mean in everything.) 養生送死之具，(Common life expenses,)吉凶慶弔之需，(necessary expenses for weddings and funerals,) 人道之所不能廢，(are important to live an ordinary human life.) 稱情以施焉，(By handling all of

these in a reasonable way,) 庶乎其不至於固耳。(expenses can be flexible.)

This passage aims to encourage individuals to develop the virtue of frugality, and avoid a luxurious life, which more often than not leads to shamelessness. The structure of the composition is "first generalization, and then detail." The initial part is "generalization," which directly pointed out that frugality, as a virtue (positive), is often neglected by the world (negative). This is the topic sentence which controls the whole composition. As to the feature of "detail," the author made comments from the negative side-- 「流俗顧薄之」 ("which has been ignored by the world"). And then, he came back to the positive side, making the comment 「儉美德也」 ("frugality is a fine virtue"). Following 「流俗顧薄之」 ("which has been ignored by the world"), he uses the five lines following 「貧者見富者」 ("poor men admire rich men") to generally explain the doctrine that luxury and waste will result in 「貧且匱」 (they would become poor). Second, the seven lines following 「每見閭閻之中」 ("it's frequently seen that in the hometown") use examples to explain that luxury and waste will cause the ruin of a family. Finally, the four lines following 「況乎用之」 (in order to live a luxurious life) point out the insatiable desire of 「奢者」 (luxurious persons). And then, the four lines following 「其究也」 ("in fact") point out the fruits of a luxurious life-- 「寡廉鮮恥，無所不至」 ("being shameless in everything"). The two lines following 「則何若」 ("this kind of man cannot make ends meet") turn from the negative side to the positive side, persuading men to live a life of frugality in order to enjoy self sufficiency. As to the ending section, the author uses especially the two lines following 「且吾所謂」 (the so-called frugality) to launch the four lines following 「養生送死」 ("common life expenses") so as to point out that frugality does not necessarily mean forsaking all belongings, and that common people need to 「稱情以施」("handle all of this in a reasonable way") in 「人道」("ordinary human life"), and to be flexible in expenses. The structure analysis diagram is as follows.

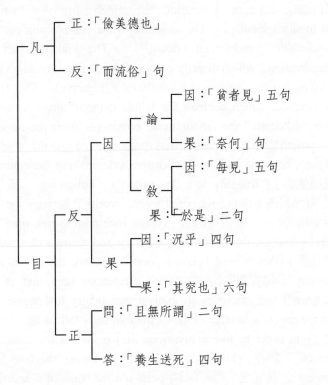

On the one hand, the author uses "positive" and "negative" to make a vivid "contrast" in order to link "generalization" and "detail." On the other hand, he combines "cause" and "effect", "narration" and "comments," "asking" and "answering" so as to achieve "blending." In this way, the passage mingles "contrast" and "blending." Thus, as a whole, it can successfully explicate the doctrine that 「儉美德也」("frugality is a fine virtue"). The diagram of levels is as follows.

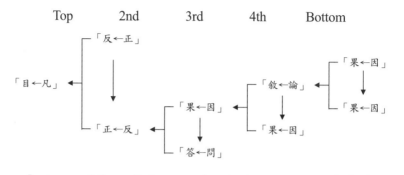

In terms of "many" (two, one/zero), the structure and rhythm formed by "cause and effect," "narration and comments," "asking and answering," and "positive and negative" belong to the category of "many." The structure and rhythm formed by "generalization and detail," as in 陰陽 (Yin and Yang), belong to the category of "two." The topic of 「儉美德也」 ("frugality is a fine virtue") and the strict, decent style belong to the category of "one/zero." And the topic is manifested by unifying image thinking and logical thinking.

To make paragraph or a composition "contrastive" and "blended," in terms of the organization of a paragraph, its theoretical basis is almost the same as "order" or "variety." However, to make a composition coherent and unified, the method turns out to be more complex. This can be observed from the development of thinking in elementary school students. In *Psychology of Elementary School Students,* Wang Yun, Yeh Chungken, and Lin Chungte noted,

In the elementary school students' development of the dialectical thinking process...there exists an order—from simple to complex, and from low to high. ...Their judgments of the different dialectical contents varied. The ratios of correct judgment from high to low are as follows: "intrinsic cause and extrinsic cause," "phenomenon and essence," "part and whole," and "opposition and unification."[69]

The categories including "major and minor," "intrinsic cause and extrinsic cause," and "phenomenon and essence" are associated with these composition arts, that is, "root and end," "deep and shallow," and "inner and outside." And "part and whole" is related to the composition arts including "generalization and detail," and "partial and whole." In addition, "opposition and unification" is associated with "blending" and "contrast." Sequentially speaking, they develop "from simple to complex." Namely, they are mostly based on "order" and develop into "variety" and finally become "unified and coherent."

In fact, "blending" and "contrast" are not necessarily permanently defined. The so-called "blending," in a sense, refers to a "unification" before "contrast." In addition, the so-called "contrast" or "opposition," more often than not, forms a state of "blending" or "unification," both of which further interact to form "a spiral structure."[70] In *Aesthetic Psychology*, Chiu Ming-chen said,

The principle of opposition penetrates the whole psychological movement of aesthetics and the creation of beauty. However, the psychological movement of aesthetics has its contradictory aspects of opposition and unification. Man, through conscious or unconscious self- discipline, coordinates all kinds of contradictions in
order that contradiction and opposition can be transformed into a unification of subjective aesthetic psychology. For example, the

....

69   See *Psychology of Elementary School Students*. 《小學生心理學》
       (Taipei: Wunan Bookstore, October, 1998, first edition) p. 168.
70   Two opposite things often interacts with each other and further form a spiral
       structure.   See Chen Man-ming, "Spiral Structure in Confucius Thinking."
       (Taipei: Taiwan Normal University, Chinese Journal, June, 2006) pp.1-34.

adaptation of subject to object is a process of turning contradiction into unification. Even if subject can be adapted to object or be opposed to the object, the psychology of the subject is still in a harmonious state. The principle of opposition and unification, which both exist, demonstrates that the contradictory parties, despite being opposed to and excluding each other, transform and unify each other. This is a universal law of opposition reflected in the aesthetic psychology.[71]

Aesthetics is an activity of reversal, which can be traced from end (composition and paragraph) to beginning (psychology—thinking). In addition, creative writing derived from "beginning" (psychology—thinking) develops into "end" (composition and paragraph). A literary work can be analyzed in order to discover its aesthetics and logical thinking based on "order" and "variety," and thus we can create "coherent" "blending" and "contrast."

Indeed, the formation of "blending" and "contrast" can be interpreted in terms of a literary skill, that is, "embellishing." In *Literary Writing And Aesthetic Psychology*, Tung Hsiao-yu noted,

Embellishing was originally a skill of Chinese painting, which dips ink or colors at the outskirts of the objects in order to highlight them. When this skill applies to literary writing, it refers to using one thing to embellish another thing to make the subject more vivid and impressive. In real life, many things serve to embellish others. So, as a reflection of life, literature can not isolate itself; that is, it needs embellishing.[72]

....

71 See *Aesthetic Psychology*. 《審美心理學》 (Shanhai: Futan University Press, April, 1993, first edition.) pp. 94-95.

72 See *Literary Writing And Aesthetic Psychology*. 《文學創作與審美心理》 (Chentu· Szuchuan Education Publishing Company, December, 1992, first edition.) p.338.

Since "in real life, many things serve to embellish others," the roles of "guest" and "master" in the process of "embellishing" do show the phenomenon of binary opposition, that is, Ying and Yang. Direct embellishing and overall embellishing form the phenomenon of "blending," while opposite blending forms the phenomenon of "contrast." In *Literary Writing And Aesthetic Psychology*, Tung Hsiao-yu said,

> Embellishing can be divided into "direct embellishing," "opposite embellishing," and "overall embellishing."
> Direct embellishing is when things of the same nature   embellish each other to make them more vivid and influential.   In other words, beautiful scenery is used to embellish joyful feelings; painful   scenery   is   used   to   embellish   feelings   of sadness. …opposite embellishing is to use objects of the opposite nature to embellish subjects in order to serve these subjects. That is, painful scenery is used to embellish joyful feelings; beautiful scenery is used to embellish feelings of sadness. …overall embellishing is to make all preparations for highlighting the main plot and climax.[73]

Accordingly, three types of embellishing, that is, "blending" or "contrast," can form "beauty," which can further combine "variety" and "uniformity."   The three types of embellishing can serve as a bridge for the formation of "order," "variety," and "uniformity."

4. Law of unification

The so-called "unifying" refers to the coherence of the feelings and meanings of materials. Here, "unifying" is concerned with

....
[73] See *Literary Writing and Aesthetic Psychology*, 《文學創作與審美心理》   as in note 72, pp. 339-341.

contents (including inner feelings and meanings and external materials), while the first three principles, forms (logic). That is, "unifying" is different from "uniformity," which results from the "blending" of the connecting law. Therefore, in order to "unify" contents, we have to resort to topics (feelings and meanings) and outlines (mostly the unification of materials.) Moreover, outlines can be divided into "single track," "double track" and multiple tracks," while different topics can be placed at the beginning of the composition, in the middle of the composition, at the end of the composition, or even outside of the composition.[74] The unifying rule can apply to all kinds of compositions. Take Wang Anshih's "Reading Mengchangchun's Biography," for example:

世皆稱孟嘗君能得士，(People said that Mengchangchun could gain good able men,) 士以故歸之，(, and thus so many good men came to work for him.) 而卒賴其力，(Relying on his abilities)，以脫於虎豹之秦。(they escaped from Chin, a nation as ferocious as a tiger or leopard.)

嗟呼！(Ah!) 孟嘗君特雞鳴狗盜之雄耳，(Indeed, Mengchangchun appeared to be the head of rogues, who could only play tricks like screeching cocks and thieving dogs.) 豈足以言得士！(How can we say that he could gain good able men?) 不然，(No,) 擅齊之強，(given the Chi nation's strength,) 得一士焉，(if she can gain a good able men,) 宜可以南面而制秦，(she will be able to face south conquering Chin, and become a hegemony.) 尚何取雞鳴狗盜之力哉！(There's no need to use the power of such rogues, who tackled the skills of screeching cocks and thieving dogs.)

雞鳴狗盜之出其門，(With such persons among his residents),

....

74 See Chen Man-ming's *On the Major Contents of the Art of Expression and Composition; The New Design of the Art of Composition.* 《章法學新裁》 same as note 2, pp. 351-359.

此士之所以不至也。(good able men won't be willing to come.)

The first four lines of this article point out the logic of "cause and effect." People's comments are used to praise the fact that Mengchangchun can "gain good able men." And then, it follows that by "relying on his abilities," they could escape from Chin, which is "as ferocious as a tiger or leopard," which contrasts with the people, who "play tricks like screeching cocks and thieving dogs." Accordingly, the semantic structure is framed by "real, unreal, real." As for the feature of "establishment," the phrase "screeching cocks and thieving dogs" follows "relying on his abilities they escaped from Chin" which is "as ferocious as a tiger or leopard." This article of less than one hundred words is to the point and extremely persuasive. The structural analysis table is as follows:

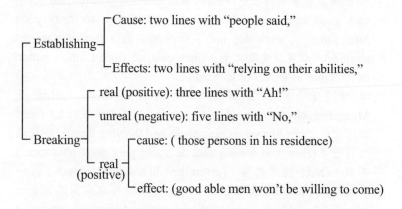

Accordingly, in terms of "paragraph," this article uses a core structure of position shifting to engage in "first establishing and then breaking" to form a contrast. However, there exists "blending" in the contrast. For in terms of "composition," in the feature of "establishing," the position shifting structure of "first cause and then effect" is used to form "blending." In addition, in the feature of "breaking," the position transformation structure of "real (positive),"

unreal (negative), real (positive)" is used to form a contrast. And then, the position shifting structure of "first cause and then effect" is used to form "blending." So, the major structure is "contrast" and "position shifting," and the minor structure is "blending" and "position shifting." In this way, the rhythm and style naturally become strong and intense. The diagram of levels is listed below:

top level   second level   bottom level

Therefore, from bottom level to top level, two "cause and effect," and one "unreal (negative), real (positive)" support one "establishing and breaking." Despite having only four structures, the composition, as a whole, is very complete. In terms of "many, two, one (zero)," "many" refers to two position shifting structures of "first cause and then effect" and a position transforming structure and rhythm of "real, unreal, real." In addition, two, a ying-yang opposition, refers to the core position shifting structure and rhythm of "first establishing and breaking." And "one (zero)" refers to the topic, that is, "good able men won't be willing to come."[75] This logical structure does make the short article condensed and persuasive.

Also see Yuan Hung-tao's "Night Travel on Six Bridge, waiting for the Moon" 〈晚遊六橋待月記〉.

西湖最盛，(The most beautiful scenery of West Lake)為春為月。(is in the spring on moonlit nights.) 一日之盛，(The most

....

75 See Kuo Yu-hen, *History of Chinese Prose.* 《中國散文史》中(Shanghai: Shanghai Ancient Book Publishing Company, March 2000) p.485.

beautiful scenery of a single day) 為朝煙，(is smoke in the morning) 為夕嵐。(and fog in the evening.)

今歲春雪甚盛，(This year there was so much spring snow) 梅花為寒所勒，(that the plums, restricted by the cold,) 與杏桃相次開發，(blossomed gradually with the apricots and peaches.) 尤為奇觀。(This was a spectacle.) 石簣數為余言：(ShihKuei said to me several times,)「傅金吾園中梅，(the plums of the garden of Fu Chinwu) 張功甫玉照堂故物也，(are all that remain of Chang Kungfu's Yuchaotang.)」急往觀之。」(We went hastily to enjoy the spectacle.) 余時為桃花所戀，(Fascinated by peaches at that time,) 竟不忍去湖上。(I did not go to the lake.)

由斷橋至蘇隄一帶，(from Tuanchiao to Suti) 綠煙紅霧，(green willows were like smoke and read peaches were like fog) 瀰漫二十餘里。(smoke and fog stretched more than twenty miles) 歌吹為風，(songs spread with winds) 粉汗為雨，(perspirations in cosmetics fell like rains) 羅紈之盛，(people dressed in silk and satins) 多於隄畔之草，(were more than grass beside the bank) 艷冶極矣。(how showy this was)

然杭人遊湖，(however, travelers in Hanchou) 止午、未、申三時。(used to travel at three watches) 其實湖光染翠之工，(the artistic value of the lake light and mountainous scenery) 山嵐設色之妙，(the wonder of the air in mountains) 皆在朝日始出，(all depended on the sunrise) 夕舂未下，(or the time before the sunset) 始極其濃媚。(trees and flowers were so beautiful at that time) 月景尤不可言，(scenery under the moon night was incredible) 花態柳情，(the posture of flowers and the shape of willows) 山容水意，(the countenance of mountains and the air of waters) 別是一種趣味。(served as special fun) 此樂留與山僧遊客受用，(the fun was for travelers and monks) 安可為俗士道哉！(not for ordinary people)

This passage aims to use the beautiful scenery of 西湖六橋 (West Lake Six Bridges) to depict the joy before the expected moonlight. First, the author directly points out that the most beautiful scenery is in the spring scenes and moon scenes (long) and that the best parts of the day are the morning smoke and evening fog (transient). This belongs to the feature of "generalization." And then, the plums, peaches, and apricots「相次開發」(blossoming gradually,) 「歌吹」(songs sung) and「羅紈」(white silk clothes) combine to depict the spring scene. This is「目一」(detail one). In addition, the seven lines following 「然杭人遊湖」(however, Hungchou people traveled on the lake) use mountain light and mountainous scenery to highlight the morning smoke and evening fog. This is「目二」(detail two). Furthermore, the six lines following「月景尤不可言」(the scenery in the moonlight was unimaginable) use flowers, willows, mountains and rivers as decorations to concretely depict the moonlit scenes and thus point out the「樂」(joy). This is「目三」(detail three). Accordingly, spring is used as track one; the moon, track two; morning smoke and evening fog, track three. The outline was thus written according to the structure of "first generalization and then detail." While the levels are very distinctive, the whole composition is very consistent. The structure analysis diagram is as follows.

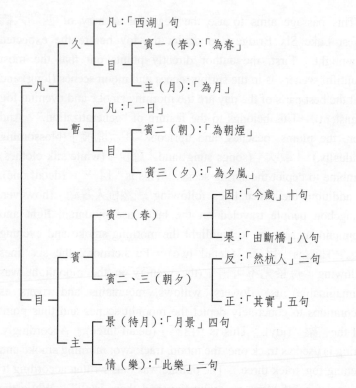

Therefore, it can be seen that the rhythms of the passage were constructed by the following structures—"first generalization and then detail," "first long and then transient," "first guest and then master," "first landscape and then feeling," "first cause and then effect," and "first negative and then positive." Among these, except for the structure of "first negative and then positive," which contains the feature of contrast, all of them belong to the place changing structure with the feature of blending. This leads to a style of "clarity, beauty, sublimity, and swiftness."[76] The diagram of four levels can be shown as follows.

....

76 See Wang Yinche, *Dictionary of Appreciation of Ancient Prose.* 《古文鑑賞辭典》下冊(Shanghai: Shanghai Tzesu Publishing Company, April 1997) p.1705.

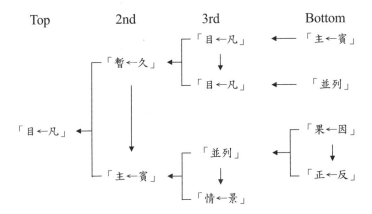

In terms of "many, two, one/zero," the top level of "generalization and detail," as a core structure, serves as the vital "two." The second, third, and bottom levels—the structures of "long and transient," "guest and master," "generalization and detail," "parallel," "landscape and feelings," "cause and effect," and "negative and positive"—function as "many."   And the topic of "the joy before the expected moonlight," and the style and rhythm of "clarity, beauty, sublimity and swiftness" turn out to be "one/zero."

A composition is supposed to use core feeling and reasoning (topic) or unified materials (outlines) to unify the whole body,

forming a semantic consistency to highlight the focal contents and to show its style, forming a rhythm. This is the key point in the success of a composition. In *Methods Teachers Use to Inspire Pupils' Thinking Abilities*, written by Sungshanchenyi and translated by Ouyang Chungjeng, "emphasizing consistent thinking" is considered to be one of the thinking methods.[77]   So, in *A Psychological Introduction to Elementary Schools Language Teaching,* Chu Chojen and Chu Hsinhua held that,

....

77 See *Methods Teachers Use to Inspire Pupils' Thinking Abilities*, 《教師啟發學童思考能力的方法》 as in note 47, pp. 145-150.

According to analyses, the point of disclosing the topic is closely associated with the composition's contents, structures, and writing methods.[78]

The so-called "disclosing the topic" means to establish topics or outlines to unify the whole composition. This surely is closely associated with "contents, structure and writing methods." In *A Study of the Structures of Compositions,* after commenting on "the unification and harmony of the whole structure," Wu Yingtien says,

In addition, there is a unification of perspectives, materials, and points of view. These are problems of logic and thinking. And the psychological factor of harmony is also to be taken into consideration.[79]

Just as this applies to the argument of compositions, so it can apply to other types of compositions. And the so-called "the unification of view points and materials," in a broader sense, refers to the unification of topics/outlines and whole materials. This is like the unification of composition structures, making the composition as a whole achieve uttermost harmony. What makes contents and forms unified and harmonious is the application of synthetic logical thinking. Therefore, Wu Yingtien said,

Aggressively and actively engaging in synthetic thinking can make the contents and structure of the work highly unified, fulfilling the purpose of "mastering normality and change."[80]

....

[78] *A Psychological Introduction to Elementary Schools Language Teaching,* 《小學語文教學心理學導論》 The same as note 50.

[79] See *A Study of the Structure of Compositions,* 《文章結構學》 same as note 42, p.359.

[80] See *A Study o fthe Structure of Compositions,* 《文章結構學》 as in note 40,

It can be seen that the unification law of composition art and synthetically logical thinking is closely related.

This kind of "unification" or "harmony" can be explored in terms of "form and principles." In *An Introduction to Aesthetics*, Chen Hsuehfan says,

The so-called form principle refers to multiple unification. Suppose the form of beauty is immensely disorderly, we will feel this cannot match the mood in which we judge beauty. Therefore, "unification" is remarkably essential. In addition, the things unified to one or two components, which would become boring although unification is easy to achieve. Therefore, variety is also essential. We feel that on the one hand, the object of beauty needs impressive unification, and that on the other hand, the components of the object of beauty need enormous various variety. Indeed, unification and variety are co-existent. This is the so-called organic unification. It is expected that "unification is in variety, and variety is derived from unification." In this way, unification will not be boring or monotonous, and variety won't follow the disorderly and confused. Therefore, the form principle will be "unity in variety."[81]

The fact that "unification is in variety, and variety is derived from unification." well explains the inseparable connection between "order," "variety," and "unification," all of which use "connection" (blending and contrast) as a bridge. In the New Editing of Aesthetics, the authors addressing "multiple unification," as compared with "blending" and "contrast," pointed out,

....
p.353.
[81] See *An Introduction to Aesthetics*, 《美學概論》 same as note 51, pp.77-78.

So-called unification refers to the fact that each individual part has some common features of form, and the fact there is some connection, echoing, embellishing and coordinating relations among these individual parts. That is, each part has to comply to the demands of the whole body, to serve for the harmony and consistency of the whole body. Varity without unification will make men feel that a work is fragmentary, confused, lacking a sense of completion. On the other hand, unification without variety will make men feel that it is boring and dry, lacking an enduring aesthetics. However, the relation between variety and unification should be sameness in difference, difference in sameness, oneness in many, many in oneness, properly complex and innovative. In addition, "one" and "many" are co-existent. The opposite parties are organically unified. Thus, variety and unification are interwoven, achieving a perfect form of beauty. Variety and unification frequently find expression in two basic types—contrast and blending. ...Both contrast and blending aim to combine unification and variety to demonstrate their beauty.[82]

It can be seen that "unification" and "variety" form a "binary opposition;" both are organically united. In other words, the beauty of "unification" should be based on "variety," while "variety" has to rely on "unification" for integration. Here, most important, Ouyang Chou and others use "binary opposition" (two)—"blending" (Ying) and "contrast" (Yang)-- to unite "
Variety" (many) and "unification" (one/zero) in order to highlight the connecting functions of "blending" (Ying) and "contrast" (Yang). This is vital for logical thinking, and is greatly instrumental for the structure of composition arts and its aesthetic effect.

....
82 See *New Editing of Aesthetics*, 《美學新編》 same as note 53, pp. 80-81.

When each author engages in writing, he/she would consciously or unconsciously use logical thinking based on common feelings and reasoning to organize diverse kinds of materials

Expressive of feelings. Especially in organizing the composition, the author more often than not would employ analysis and synthetic logical thinking, which compared with natural law will achieve "order," "variety" (many), "connection" (two) and "unification" (one/zero), as well as the compositional structure of "many, two, one/zero." Wu Yingtien pointed out, "The rules of composition structures, as the essence of the composition, can correspond to logical human thinking, which is a reflection of the essence of objective things."[83] Of the four major laws, the first three emphasize analytically logical thinking, while the last one, synthetically logical thinking. In creative writing, the employment of these two kinds of thinking are surely equally important. Therefore, in the composition arts, we ought to have a good command of these four laws—"order," "change," "connection," and "unification"—and the compositional structure of "many, two, one/zero." This is the most direct and effective method, and well proves the "objective existence" of composition arts.[84]

III. Perspectives of composition arts

Nowadays, there are no absolute structures for composition arts analyses. We have to use different angles to see which angle can best present the features of the contents and forms of compositions. Therefore, using a proper perspective is vital to composition art analysis. The several compositions below will be used to make a

....

83 See *A Study of the Structure of Compositions,* 《文章結構學》 as in note 40, p.9.
84 See "A Small Talk Outside the Gate of Composition Methods," 〈章法學門外閑談〉 as in note 34, pp.92-95.

brief explanation.

First, Liu Yuhsi's "Proverbs of A Humble House" will be used as an example.

山不在高，(A mountain need not be high:) 有仙則名；(If a fairy lives there, it will become famous.) 水不在深，(Water need not be deep:)有龍則靈；(If dragons are hidden therein, it will be vital.) 斯是陋室，(This is only a humble house.) 惟吾德馨。(My virtues like an aroma will be known nationwide.) 苔痕上階綠，(Green moss reaches my steps.) 草色入簾青。(Green grass can be seen outside my window curtains.) 談笑有鴻儒，(Great scholars talk and laugh here.) 往來無白丁。(No vulgar men shuttle around here.) 可以調素琴，(I can play an ancient Chinese string instrument.)閱金經。(I can read the Buddhist Scriptures.) 無絲竹之亂耳，(There are no strident sounds to disturb my ears.) 無案牘之勞形。(There are no official documents to consume my physical health.) 南陽諸葛廬，(The house is just like the Chuku residence in Nanyang)西蜀子雲亭。(This house is also like the Tzuyun garden house in Hsishu)孔子云：「何陋之有？」(Confucius said, "It is not humble, is it?")

In terms of "narration and commentary," all sentences before and including "There are no official documents to consume my physical health" combine to form the function of "narration."   And then, the remaining four sentences serve as "commentary."   Below is the table of structure analysis.

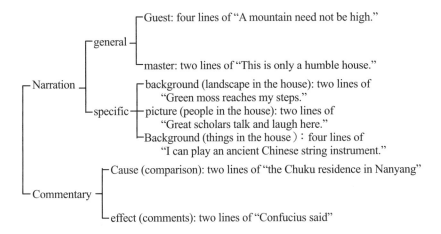

From this perspective, the meaning of "it is not humble" is highlighted all right, but the topic of "My virtues like an aroma will be known nationwide" is not well manifested. Therefore, if we interpret this composition from this perspective, there is still room for improvement in the interpretation. However, if we use the perspective of "generalization and detail," we can make up for this. The first six lines belong to the first "generalization" catalog, using the structures of "first guest, and then master," and "first negative and then positive." Starting from "mountain" and "water," the author then mentions "house," skillfully quoting "my virtues like an aroma will be known nationwide" from *Chochuan* (左傳). He highlights "virtue," using the word to penetrate the whole text. In addition, the eight lines following "Green moss reaches my steps" belong to the feature of "detail." Next, according to the list, we can see that there are two lines describing the landscape of the house, and two lines describing people in the house, and four lines describing things in the house. In this way, his joy and comfort in his humble house are fully expressed. Then, the remaining four lines belong to another catalog of "generalization," using the structure of "first cause and then effect" and antcccdents to praise his house echoing "virtue" in the first category of "generalization."   Below is the structure analysis list:

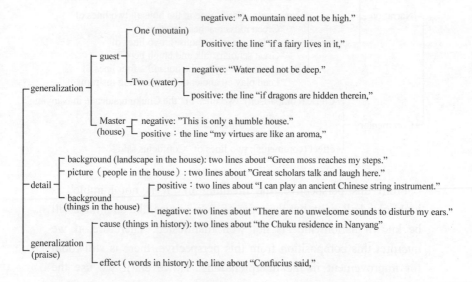

negative: "A mountain need not be high."
One (moutain)
                              Positive: the line "if a fairy lives in it,"
guest
                    negative: "Water need not be deep."
Two (water)
                    positive: the line "if dragons are hidden therein,"

Master   negative: "This is only a humble house."
(house)   positive：the line "my virtues are like an aroma,"

generalization

background (landscape in the house): two lines about "Green moss reaches my steps."
picture（people in the house）: two lines about "Great scholars talk and laugh here."
detail   positive：two lines about "I can play an ancient Chinese string instrument."
background
(things in the house)   negative: two lines about "There are no unwelcome sounds to disturb my ears."

cause (things in history): two lines about "the Chuku residence in Nanyang"
generalization
(praise)
effect (words in history): the line about "Confucius said,"

Thus, the first and second catalog of "generalization" and the second catalog of "generalization" combine to from the entire unit.[85]， This perspective is surely better than that of "narration and commentary."

And then, let's take a look at "Manchianghung" by Yuehfei.

怒髮衝冠，(My angry hair rushed through my hat.) 憑闌處、(I lean against railings) 瀟瀟雨歇。(The thunderstorm has just ceased.) 抬望眼、(My eyes look up.) 仰天長嘯，(I look up into the sky crying out unceasingly.) 壯懷激烈。(The hot blood of passion seems to soak my bosom.) 三十功名塵與土，(I am

....

85 See Chen Man-ming, *Composition Structure Analysis*, 《文章結構分析》 (Taipei: Wanchulou publishing company, 1999, May, first edition) p.65

not thirty years old, and my achievements are as trivial as dust and soil.) 八千里路雲和月。(I went eight thousand miles day and night.) 莫等閒、(Don't take life lightly.) 白了少年頭，(When your hair turns white,) 空悲切。(you will be sad.) 靖康恥，(The shame of national destruction) 猶未雪。(has not been washed away.) 臣子恨，(Hatred in the heart of subjects) 何時滅。(can not vanish.) 駕長車、(I will ride a chariot,) 踏破賀蘭山缺。(stepping on Holan Mountain and destroying it.) 壯志饑餐胡虜肉，(I am so ambitious that I will eat the flesh of the enemy.) 笑談渴飲匈奴血。(I laugh and talk drinking the blood of the enemy.) 待從頭、(I will start again) 收拾舊山河，(recovering the mountains and rivers of my former nation.) 朝天闕。(Then, I will proclaim the victory to the palace of the emperor.)

Considering the place where the topic "hatred in the heart of subjects can not vanish" appears, we can use the perspective of "generalization and detail" to analyze this composition, which is considered to have been written with the structure of "detail, generalization, detail."   Below is the structure analysis list:

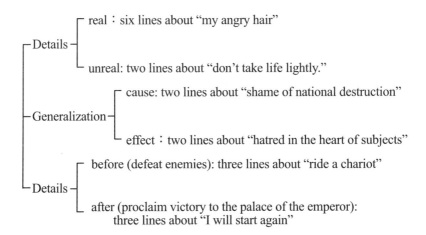

If we analyze the composition in this way, the topic can be well surveyed. However, assumption and fact can not be clearly separated. The part extending into the future via assumption includes 「莫等閒」 two lines as well as 「駕長車」 five lines.   In addition, the seven lines are cut apart by the feature of "generalization", so we cannot see through to their close relation.   Therefore, this perspective of analysis is not considered to be the best.

If we intend to see through this relation, we have to adopt the perspective of "unreal and real" (time), using the structure of "first real and then unreal" to present it.   In the first four lines, the outside scenery of "the thunderstorm has just ceased" and his own emotional state—"My angry hair rushed through my hat" and "I look up into the sky crying out unceasingly"—combine to describe his passion and hot blood.   And 「三十」 two lines start from effect and end with cause, pointing to the past to state that the reason for the hot blood and passion is failure in wars.   「莫等閒」 The two lines following the above two lines pointing to the future to state that another reason for the passion and hot blood is the brevity of time. For he is deeply sad, being afraid that his hair will soon turn white. All of these are designed to describe his hatred and explain the topic, exhaustively exposing his heart and ambition.   The three lines following 「駕長車」 (I will ride a chariot) serve to turn reality into fiction—through his imagination, the author depicts how he would drive a chariot to kill his enemies, washing away the shame of his nation.   As someone put it, "His soaring spirit seemed to mount to the clouds, and his voice would break rocks."   And the final two sentences still use the imagination to describe how the author would go and report to the emperor after washing away their shame.   Thus, the composition ends by highlighting the topic.   Reading these lines could enlighten and encourage us, just as Chen Tien-chou put it, "In reading these lines thousands of years later, the reader is filled with a lively spirit." (*Pai Yu-chai's Words on Tzu*) This is an excellent literary work showing strength and beauty.[86] The structure analysis diagram can be shown as follows.

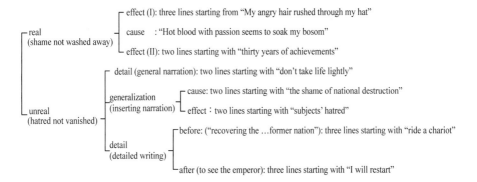

In this way, "unreal" and "real" form a contrast, using the method of inserting narration to manifest the topic. This analysis is imperfect all right, but it can highlight the features of the Tzu.

And now let's take a look at "On Releasing Prisoners" by Ouyang Hsiu.

信義行於君子，(Honesty and righteousness are the privilege of good men.) 而刑戮施於小人。(Punishment and killing are designed for rogues.) 刑入於死者，(The death penalty)乃罪大惡極，(is for a serious crime and extreme evil.) 此又小人之尤甚者也。(This is for the worst rogues.)寧以義死，(Whoever would die for righteousness) 不苟幸生，(rather than live in shame)而視死如歸，(seeing death as a coming home)此又君子之尤難者也。(These are the best persons.)

方唐太宗之六年，(In the sixth year of Tangtaitsung's imperial reign) 錄大辟囚三百餘人，(there were more than three

86 See Chen Man-ming, *A Walk in Tzu Forest—Structure Analysis of Tang Sung Tzu* 《詞林散步－唐宋詞結構分析》(Taipei, Wanchuanlou Publishing Company, Jan. 2000, first edition) pp. 269-270.

hundred persons listed for the death penalty in the prison catalogue) 縱使還家，(The emperor released them to go back home)約其自歸以就死；(the commitment was that they would come back to face the death penalty.)是以君子之難能，(it would be extremely difficult for a good person to fulfill this promise)期小人之尤者以必能也。(however, now these rogues were expected to fulfill the promise)其囚及期，(on the day they promised to come back, the prisoners) 而卒自歸，(eventually came back to the prison) 無後者；(None of them were late)是君子之所難，(This would have been difficult for good men to do it) 而小人之所易也。(but it seemed easy for rogues to do)此豈近於人情？(Didn't it go against human nature)

或曰：(some people said)「罪大惡極，(big crimes and extreme evil) 誠小人矣。(were indeed committed by rogues)及施恩德以臨之，(If they were treated with grace and virtue)可使變而為君子；(they could be transformed into good persons)蓋恩德入人之深，(perhaps grace and virtue could deeply influence people) 而移人之速，(they can change men rapidly)有如是者矣。」(This is the case)曰：(I said)「太宗之為此，(the reason the emperor did this) 所以求此名也。(was to gain fame)然安知夫縱之去也，(maybe when he released them) 不意其必來以冀免，(he expected that they would come back to be pardoned)所以縱之乎？(was this the reason for him to release them)又安知夫被縱而去也，(perhaps when they were released)不意其自歸而必獲免，(they expected that if they came back on their own, they would be pardoned)所以復來乎？(for this reason, they came back)夫意其必來而縱之，(it was said that because the emperor expected the prisoners to come back, he released them)是上賊下之情也；(the emperor like a thief imagined the situation)意其必免而復來，(the prisoners expected that they would be pardoned, so they came back)是下賊上之心也。(they like thieves explored the heart of the emperor)吾見上下交相

賊，(so it could be seen that both parties like thieves guessed each other's heart) 以成此名也，(such kind of reasoning made the case well-known) 烏有所謂施恩德，(was this real grace and virtue) 與夫知信義者哉？(was this real honesty and virtue) 不然，(If not) 太宗施德於天下，(the emperor nicely treated the nation)於茲六年矣，(it had been six years) 不能使小人不為極惡大罪；(he still could not keep rogues from committing serious crime and doing extreme evil) 而一日之恩，(however, one day's grace)能使視死如歸，(could make the prisoners see death as coming home) 而存信義；(in order to preserve honesty and righteousness) 此又不通之論也。」(this was not logical)
「然則，何為而可？」(however, what could we do) 曰：(I said)「縱而來歸，(when they came back after being released) 殺之無赦；(the emperor should have killed them instead of pardoning them) 而又縱之，(And then, the emperor once more released the prisoners) 而又來，(if they came back) 則可知為恩德之致爾。」(this was out of grace and virtue) 然此必無之事也。(But, this would be unlikely to happen)
若夫縱而來歸而赦之，(Since the emperor released them, he would pardon them after they came back) 可偶一為之爾。(the emperor should do this accidentally) 若屢為之，(if he often did this) 則殺人者皆不死，(killers could always survive the death penalty) 是可為天下之常法乎？(Was this a norm of the world) 不可為常者，(if this was a not a norm) 其聖人之法乎？(it could not become the saints' rule) 是以堯舜三王之治，(the three ancient holy kings ruled their people) 必本於人情；(in accordance with human nature) 不立異以為高，(they would'nt uphold strangeness) 不逆情以干譽。(Never　act against nature to chase fame)

This passage can be analyzed in a traditional way.　That is, the first and second paragraphs serve as an introduction.　The third paragraph and the first half of the fourth paragraph, especially the part asking and answering, combine to serve as the "development" of this essay.　And the second half of the fourth paragraph serves as the "conclusion."　The structure analysis diagram is as follows.

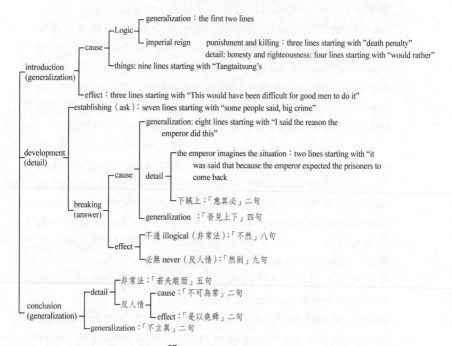

This kind of analysis[87] is acceptable; however, in an attempt to highlight its purpose of re-interpreting this essay, it　is advisable for us to use the perspective of "establishing, breaking" to analyze the article.　For, indeed, the structure of "breaking, establishing, breaking" was formed.　As to the first "breaking," all the lines from 信義行於君子(Honesty and righteousness is a privilege to good men.) to 此豈近於人情 (Isn't it against human

87　See Chen Man-ming, *Composition Structure Analysis*, 《文章結構分析》　as in note 85, pp. 248-249.

nature?) use "first detail and then generalization" as a scheme. At the outset, regarding "detail," the contrasting method was used to separate "reasoning" and "thing." It is pointed out that「大辟囚」(those facing the death penalty)「視死如歸」(seeing death as a coming home) are more valuable than「君子」(good men). Indeed, this could be considered unreasonable. In this way, "breaking" brought about "establishing." In addition, on the part of "establishing," the seven lines from「或曰罪大惡極」(some people said, big crime and extreme evil) established a case for explaining how Tangtaisung granted grace to people by releasing prisoners. This explains the causes of the "breaking." And the lines from「曰太宗為此」(I said, the reason the emperor did this) to the end of this article belongs to the next feature of "breaking," which was organized by the structure of "first cause and then effect." The "cause" adopted the logic of "first real and then unreal" to explain that it was unreal that「恩德入人」(grace and virtue could deeply influence people). In fact, this resulted from the fact that "both parties like thieves guessed each other's heart"「上下交相賊」. Accordingly, it could be considered that "this was not logical"「不通之論」and "it would be unlikely to happen"「必無之事」. It was severely criticized that the prisoners, seemingly seeing death as coming home, could be deeply influenced by grace and virtue. As to "effect," it was pointed out in the conclusion that releasing prisoners was abnormal and against human nature. The structure analysis diagram is as follows.

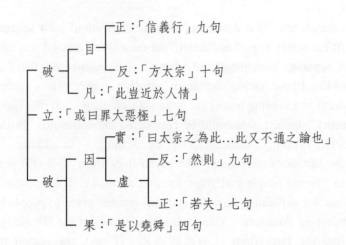

In this way, the structure of "breaking, establishing, breaking" severely criticizes the hypocrisy of releasing prisoners.   And it can be clearly seen that the beginning echoes the ending.

Now let's take a look at "A Reading of the Biography of Mengchangchun" by Wang Anshih.

世皆稱孟嘗君能得士，(People said that Mengchangchun could gain good able men,) 士以故歸之，(and thus so many good men came to work for him.) 而卒賴其力，(Relying on their abilities)，以脫於虎豹之秦。(They escaped from Chin, a nation as ferocious as a tiger and leopard.) 嗟呼！(Ah!) 孟嘗君特雞鳴狗盜之雄耳，(Indeed, Mengchangchun appeared to be the head of rogues, who could only play tricks like screeching cocks and thieving dogs.) 豈足以言得士！(How can we say that he could gain good able men?) 不然，(No,) 擅齊之強，(the Chi nation's strength,) 得一士焉，(if she can gain good able men,) 宜可以南面而制秦，(she will be able to face south conquering Chin, and become a hegemony.) 尚何取雞鳴狗盜之力哉！(There's no need to use the power of such rogues, who tackled the skills of screeching cocks and thieving dogs.) 雞鳴狗盜之出其

門，(With such persons among his residents), 此士之所以不至
也。(good able men won't be willing to come.)

In terms of "down-up," or "rising-falling" this short essay was
formed by the structure of "first up and then down." The feature of
"up" refers to the four lines from 「世皆稱」(people said that),
while the feature of "down," to all the lines following 「嗟呼」
(Ah). The structure analysis diagram is as follows.

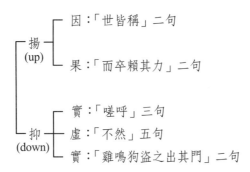

Since "up and down" suggests that both directions are equally
important, or only one direction is more important, this method
cannot demonstrate the features of the essay. Therefore, the "up
and down" perspective is questionable. However, in terms of
"unreal-real," this essay is formed by the structure of "real, unreal,
real." The structure analysis diagram is as follows.

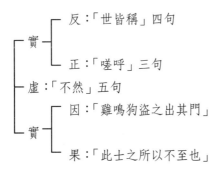

In terms of this angle, the five lines from 「不然」(No) show the nature of assumption.　However, this analysis is still imperfect, for it cannot manifest the nature of straightforwardness and sharpness. Furthermore, in terms of "positive, negative," this essay seems to be formed by the structure of "first negative and then positive."　The structure analysis diagram is presented below.

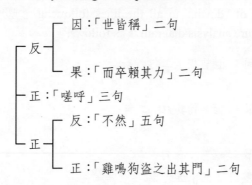

In this way, Mengchanchun considered 「能得士」(he could gain good able men) to be negative, and 「特雞鳴狗盜之雄」 (appeared to be the head of rogues, who could only play tricks like screeching cocks and thieving dogs) to be positive.　Thus, from the perspective of "negative, positive," certain features of this essay can be well demonstrated.　So, this perspective is better than "down-up" and "unreal-real," but it still cannot show the nature of "straightforwardness and sharpness."　Finally, from the perspective of "establishing, breaking," this essay can be formed by the structure of "first establishing and then breaking."　First, this essay employs the four lines from 「世皆稱」(people said that) to establish an individual case, adopting the linear logic of "first cause and then effect."　Through the mouths of other people, Mengchangchun was praised because "he could gain good able men."　And then, comes the sentence 「卒賴其力，以脫於虎豹之秦」(relying on their abilities, he escaped from the Chin, a nation as ferocious as a tiger or leopard), which overshadows the meaning of 「雞鳴狗盜」(such rogues, who tackled the skills of screeching cocks and thieving dogs) in order to introduce the following topic sentence.   And then, the author uses all the lines following 「嗟呼」(Ah), which in accordance with the logic of "real, unreal, real" serves to break the feature of "establishing." 「雞鳴狗盜」(screeching cocks and thieving dogs) closely follows 「卒賴其力，以脫於虎豹之秦」 (relying on their abilities he escaped from the Chin, a nation as ferocious as a tiger or leopard).   Despite the less than one hundred words of this essay, it is extremely sharp and convincing.   The structure analysis is listed below.

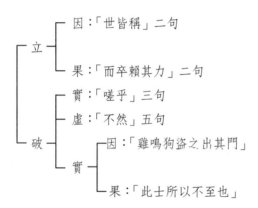

Apparently, this perspective is more convincing than "positive, negative."   It is so sharp and convincing despite its brevity.

Finally, let's take a look at *Niennuchiao Tzu* by Su Shih.

大江東去，(Eastward runs the Great River)浪淘盡，(Whose waves have washed away)千古風流人物。(All the talented and courteous men in history)故壘西邊，(West of the old fort)人道是三國周郎赤壁。(they say, there lies Chou's (the young general in the times of the Three Kingdoms) Red Cliff. 亂石崩

雲，(Broken rocks shatter the clouds)驚濤裂岸，(Thundering billows dash on the shore)捲起千堆雪。(Rolling up thousands of flakes of snow)江山如畫，(What a picture of rivers and mountains) 一時多少豪傑。(How many heroes there were at that time.)　遙想公瑾當年，(I cannot help thinking of the day when Kung-chin)小喬初嫁了，(first married Hsiao Chiao) 雄姿英發。(with a bright warlike air)羽扇綸巾，(a feather fan in his hand, a blue turban on his head)談笑間，(in the midst of his talk and laughter) 檣櫓灰飛煙滅。(annihilated the strong enemy who vanished like smoke and dust)故國神遊，(traveling through the former country in my imagination)多情應笑我，(I should be laughed at for such sentiments)早生華髮。(Turning my hair grey so early)人生如夢，(life is a dream)一尊還酹江月。(I sprinkle this bottle of wine to the river and the moon)

In terms of "present, past," the Tzu (poem with irregular rhythms) is constructed based on the structure of "present, past, present." The diagram of the structure analysis can be shown as follows--

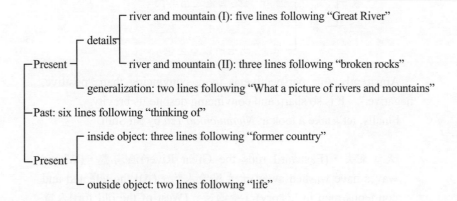

Indeed, the second half of the Tzu can be well analyzed from the perspective of time. However, in the first half, despite its mainly describing the scenery, historical figures are also included. Therefore, it seems vague to consider "present" as a conceptual generalization. More important, the main idea probably cannot be manifested based on this analysis. Furthermore, in terms of "unreal and real/feelings, landscape," this Tzu is constructed by the structure of "real, unreal, real." The structure analysis diagram can be shown below—

```
                  ┌─ landscape: ten lines from "Great River"
        ┌─ real ─┤
        │         └─ things: six lines from "thinking of"
        │
        ├─unreal ： three lines from "traveling through the former country
        │            in my imagination"
        └─ real ： two lines from "life is a dream"
```

This Tzu first aims to depict scenery and narrate events, and then ends by "employing scenery to include feelings." Actually, by means of analyzing feelings and landscape (events), certain features of the Tzu can be divulged. Besides, in this way, the topic of 「多情」 (sentiments) can catch the eye of the reader.[88] However, this analysis cannot serve to uncover the hidden meaning—the author intends to compare himself to General Chou. Therefore, this angle of analysis cannot be considered the best. In addition, in terms of "positive, negative," it forms the structure of "first negative and then positive." The structure analysis diagram is shown as follows.

....

[88] See Chen Man-ming, *Composition Structure Analysis*, 《文章結構分析》 same as note 85, pp. 258-259.

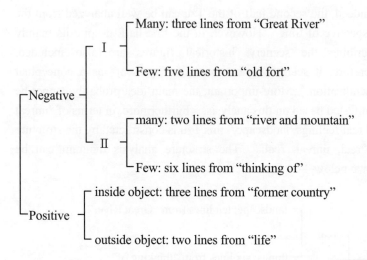

Here, 「眾」 (many) refers to many people, that is, 「千古風流人物」 (all the talented and courteous men in history) and 「多少豪傑」 (many heroes). In addition, 「寡」 refers to 「周郎」 (Chou), 「公瑾」 (Kung-chin). If this Tzu is analyzed from the perspective of the figures who appeared on Red Cliff, it will be adequate, for despite depicting scenery, the focal point of the Tzu is really a man, that is, General Chou. At that time, as a young general, he made great accomplishments. This works in contrast to the sadness of the author, who had felt frustrated in his own career. However, this kind of analysis completely neglects the relation between feelings and landscape. So, this perspective is inadequate. Finally, in terms of "heaven and man," the first two lines are "heaven" (outside things); the lines from 「故壘」 (the old fort) to 「早生華髮」 (turning my hair grey so early) serve as "man" (inside things); the last two lines function as "heaven" (outside things). In other words, the Tzu is based on the structure of "heaven, man, heaven."

Concisely speaking, the Tzu entitled "Meditation at Red Cliff" was written when the author was removed from his post and thus went to Huangchou. The initial feature of "heaven" made up the first two lines. Beginning with 「大江」 (the Great River) running eastward, the 「浪」、「淘」 (waves) are used as a medium. The meditation is tremendously expanded from "space" to "time." Flashing back to 「千古」 (history), the author points to 「風流人物」 (the talented and courteous men), who were washed away by waves. In this way, the universal philosophy of life manifests the sentiments aroused by the rise and fall of nations.[89] The limitations of life (inside things) are expanded to the unlimited universe (outside things). This leads to the enormous force of the Tzu, with the next "heaven" (outside things) being transformed into "man" (inside things). The feelings of the Tzu are fully manifested.

As for the feature of "man" (inside things), from 「故壘西邊」 (west of the old fort) to 「早生華髮」 (turning my hair grey so early), in terms of the past war of Red Cliff to the present self in remembrance of the old days, the order of "first bottom (background) and then picture (focus)" is used to describe the passing of time. The "bottom (background)" successfully employed the beautiful scenery of Red Cliff to further mention a few heroes who won battles in the war of Red Cliff. In addition, the focus is the young General Chou whose great achievements make a vivid contrast to the author's aging and triviality. Here, the author uses the sequence of "picture (General Chou), bottom (heroes), picture (General Chou)" to organize his materials. That is, he uses two lines from 「故壘」 (old fort) to explain his nostalgia over 「三國」 (the three kingdoms). Furthermore, he uses 「人道是」 (they say), a tone of doubt, to point out where Red Cliff might be located. Accordingly,

---

89 See Hsu Chung-yu, *An Introduction to Su Tung-po's Works*《蘇東坡文集導讀》 (Chentu: Pasu Bookstore, June 1990, first edition), p. 246. Also see the analysis of Ku Yi-sheng. See *Anthology of Tzu*《詞林觀止》上(Shanghai: Shanghai Ancient Books Publishing Company, April 1994, first edition), p. 276.

General Chou is introduced, serving as a point of departure for the author to expose his own feelings. The empty room for meditation actually increases the feeling and artistic value of the literary work. This is the first part of "picture" (General Chou). In addition, the lines from 「亂石」 (broken rocks) are used to delineate the landscape of Red Cliff. More important, the roughness of cliffs and waving of billows are highlighted to depict the awe and fear of that battlefield. The background is so astounding that it can highlight the heroic icon and everlasting achievements of General Chou. And then, the lines from 「江山」 (rivers and mountains) combine to tell about the beautiful scenery of the rivers and mountains and the talented, courteous man, serving as the best background for the "picture" of "General Chou."[90] This kind of linkage is really sophisticated. This is the feature of "bottom" (*Red Cliff*).

And then, the five lines from 「遙想」 (I cannot help thinking) follow the "picture" (General Chou) to put the focus on General Chou (Kung-chin). This was written in the sequence of "first dot (introduction) and then dye (contents)." The line 「遙想」 (I cannot help thinking) uses the memory of old days to introduce the following writings—this is the feature of "dot" (introduction). In addition, the lines from 「小喬」 (Hsiao Chiao) are used to substantially depict the substance of his memory of ancient times— this is the feature of "dye" (contents). Among the four lines of "dye," the line about "Hsiao Chiao" was inserted to describe the triumph of young General Chou. Moreover, two lines from 「雄姿」 (warlike air) successfully forge an amiable but strong image of General Chou. On the one hand, the author here pours out his admiration for and feelings about General Chou. On the other hand,

---

90 See Muchai, *Change in Tang, Sung Tzu.* 《唐宋詞流變》 (Beijing, Chinghua Publishing Company, November 1997, first edition) p.150.

he makes a vivid contrast with his 「早生華髮」(turning my hair grey so early) and nothingness.[91]   The 「反襯」(opposite highlighting) produced by contrast is very impressive.   Finally, the line「談笑間」(in the midst of talk and laughing) follows the previous lines to depict the heroic General Chou, who easily defeated the army of Tsaochao.   More important, the lines from 「檣櫓灰飛煙滅」(annihilated the strong enemy who vanished like smoke and dust) is employed to describe the irreversible defeat of Tsaochao and the great accomplishments of General Chou.   This is the last part of "picture" (General Chou).

Therefore, the structure of "picture (General Chou), bottom (heroes), picture (General Chou)" presents a big "bottom" (background).   And by the way, the three lines from 「故國神遊」(traveling through the former country in my imagination) are introduced to depict the big core "picture" (the author) of this Tzu.   Here, the author comes back to the present reality from 「三國」(three kingdoms), "teasing himself about his own aging, triviality, sentiments, and grey hair."[92]   The so-called "sentiments," some critics have pointed out, refer to General Chou or the author's deceased wife.   However, actually the "sentiments" are to be associated with the author himself, for 「多情應笑我」(I should be laughed at for such sentiments).   The author uses "sentiments" to describe his intense feelings about life's realities.   In contrast to General Chou's youth and achievements, the author's grey hair reflects his disappointment, anger, and sadness.   In addition, 「笑」(laughing) carries a tone of sarcastic helplessness to construct a bridge for 「人生如夢」(life is a dream) to connect

91 See Chanag Kuo-wu, *New Three Hundred Sung Tzu*《新選宋詞三百首》(Beijing: Beijing People Literature Publishing Company, January 2000, first edition), p. 89.

92 See Hsu Chung-yu, *An Introduction to Su Tung-po's Works.*《蘇東坡文集導讀》(Chentu: Pasu Bookstore, June 1990, first edition) p. 246.

「物內」(inside things/man) and 「物外」(outside things/heaven). Such interpretations seem more reasonable.

　　The later feature of 「天（物外）」(heaven/outside things) refers to the two lines from 「人生」(life). The line 「人生如夢」(Life is a dream), following the word "laughing" used in the previous line, develops reality into fiction, transforming limitation into infinity. It is held that life in the world is a dream. The elevation of 「如夢」(is a dream) sets the author free from 「多情」(sentiments), bringing him to a sublime world. And thus, there follows 「一尊還酹江月」(I sprinkle this bottle of wine to the river and the moon). Through this movement, echoing the initial feature of 「天（物外）」(heaven/ outside things), these lines do unify heaven and earth.[93]

　　Judging from this, it can be seen that the author expresses his sadness over his unfortunate fate. However, the sadness is also conceived in sublimity. In terms of composition art, this is largely connected with the structure of 「天（物外）、人（物內）、天（物外）」"heaven/ outside things, man/ inside things, heaven/ outside things." The structure analysis diagram is as follows.

---

93 See Yeh Chia-ying, *Linghsi Tzu*, 《靈谿詞說》(Taipei: The World of Chinese Language and Literature Magazine, December 1989, first edition) p.212.

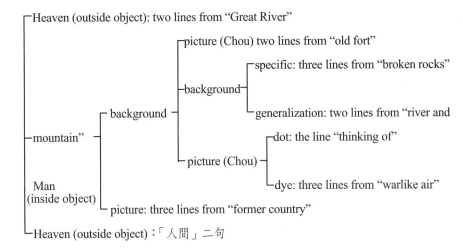

Although this perspective, if combined with others such as the picture-background method, the general-specific method, and the dot-dye method, still cannot manifest the feature of "many and few," the "dream" brought the author out of 「多情」(sentiments) inside things into the union between things and self. This kind of interpretation tends to be more comprehensive.

Therefore, an analysis of the structure of a composition should be made from all kinds of perspectives. In addition, a proper use of perspective requires a good understanding of the text and literary theories. And the employment of diverse literary perspectives still needs to be compared in case of any entangled relations.

IV. Several kinds of special composition arts

Composition art is the logic of making a composition. Because it was derived from common rules of human beings, this was noticed by specialists of composition art at a very early stage. But their studies still lack a comprehensive view. In recent years, due to much effort, the principles, scope and main contents of the composition art have been secured, forming a system. Although more than thirty kinds of composition art have already been discovered, we still do not have a comprehensive or thorough view. Therefore, we cannot apply an appropriate perspective in analyzing certain compositions. In this section, a few special "logics" in analyzing compositions will be introduced—the "partial-whole" method, "dot-dye" method, "heaven/nature-man/personnel" method, "picture-bottom" method, and "knocking-striking" method. Some classic poetry and prose may serve as examples. Furthermore, structure analysis diagrams are used for illustration.

1. Partial-whole method

Here, "partial" refers to parts or exceptions, while "whole," a whole body or general rules. When authors create compositions, they usually use "parts" and the "whole," "exceptional cases" and "general rules" that correspond to each other in order to organize their materials around feelings and meanings. This method is somewhat similar to the "root-end" method and "big-small" method. However, the "root-end" method puts more emphasis on the linear logic of events and reasoning. In addition, the "big-small" method stresses the importance of the size of space, and the consciousness of the senses. Actually, contrastively speaking, the "partial-whole" method emphasizes "part" vs. "whole," "exception" vs. "generalization," in reasoning, time, and space. Like other kinds of composition art, this method can also produce certain structures with the functions of order, change, and consistency/echoing. These structures are as follows: "first partial and then whole," "first whole and then partial," "partial, whole, partial," and "whole, partial, whole." Here, I will use Chang Chiu-lin's poem, "Hearty Encounter," as an example to illustrate the structure of "first partial and then whole."

孤鴻海上來，(A lone swan from the sea does fly,) 池潢不敢顧。(to settle on puddles it does not deign,) 側見雙翠鳥，(but espies and questions green birds twain) 巢在三株樹。(nesting in the poplar pearly:) 矯矯珍木巔，(perched on top of boughs so high,) 得無金丸懼。(don't you fear the threat of slingers?) 美服患人指，(Smart dress invites pointing fingers,) 高明逼神惡。(high climbers who tempt the gods defy.) 今我遊冥冥，(Bowmen now crave me in vain,) 弋者何所慕？(as I cruise the carefree sky.)

In this poem, the author compares himself to a lone swan, and the green birds twain to Li lin-fu and Niu Hsien-ke.[94] In this way, he expresses his feelings about his own life story. First, the four lines about "a lone swan" make of the lone swan (master) a contrast with the green birds twain (guest). It is pointed out that the lone swan from the sea did not dare to alight on puddles, and that the green birds twain risked their life to nest in the pearly poplar. This serves as narration. And then, the four lines from 「矯矯」 (so high) follow the presence of the 「雙翠鳥」 (green birds twain), turning from special examples (partial) to general rules (whole) for the purpose of advising his political foes. Furthermore, the final two lines turn to the lone swan (master) to explain why "it does not deign." This belongs to the feature of reasoning and expressing feelings. In terms of "guest-master," the structure analysis diagram can be as follows.

....

94 Chen Hang said, "After he was removed from office, he showed no intention of competing with others in one of his poems. So, he compared himself to a lone swan, while he compared the green birds twain to Lin-fu and Hsien-ke." See *Major Tang, Sung Poems,* 《唐宋詩舉要》 p. 8.

The four lines from 「矯矯」 (so high) are based on the structure of "first partial and then whole."

Conversely, the structure of "first whole and then partial" can be seen in Tufu's poem, "Military Strategy."

功蓋三分國，(In the era of the three kingdoms Chukeliang's achievements exceeded all.) 名成八陣圖。(He became famous for his military strategy.)江流石不轉，(Despite the flow of rivers stones do not move.) 遺恨失吞吳。(What is to be regretted is his defeat after attacking the Wu nation.)

This poem was created in 776 (Tang dynasty) when Tufu first arrived in Bienchou. And it aimed to laud Chukeliang. In the first two lines, through 「三分國」 (the three kingdoms) and 「八陣圖」 (military strategy), Chukeliang's achievements as a whole and his military contributions (partial) are brought up to praise him. This paves the way for the following memorable words. All of these belongs to the feature of 「揚」 (up). And the line about "the flow of rivers" on the one hand was written as a link to "military strategy," wherein stones stick despite the running rivers. This aims to express the author's feelings towards the ever-changing world. On the other hand, Chukeliang's unchangeable devotion shines forth. By this, the author expressed his regard and regret for

Chukeliang's life-long ambition, which was not eventually fulfilled. In this regret, his despondent feelings are manifested.   These belong to the feature of 「抑」(down).   The structure of "first up and then down" can be shown as follows.

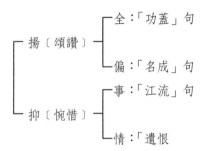

The two lines from 「功蓋」 (achievements exceeded all) form the structure of "first whole and then partial."

As to the structure of "partial, whole, partial," we can look at Hsin Chichi's poem entitled "Chingpingla."

連雲松竹，(The bamboos and pines on the mountains seem to be linked to the clouds.) 萬事從今足。(Everything is enough for my life.) 拄杖東家分社肉，(With a cane I went to my eastern home to share the sacrificial meat.)白酒床頭初熟。(The white wine beside the bed was newly made.)
西風梨棗山園，(With the west wind blowing, the fruit in the mountains became ripe.)兒童偷把長竿。(Children took long sticks to get at the fruit.) 莫遣旁人驚去，(Don't scare them away!) 老夫靜處閑看。(Let me calmly and peacefully observe everything.)

This poem aims to "express the author's view of mountains and gardens."   It was created in the first three years when he lived as a recluse nearby a lake.   In 「萬事從今足」(everything is enough for my life), he claims that everything as a whole is satisfactory for him. This belongs to the feature of "whole." And in 「連雲松竹」 (the bamboos and pines on the mountains seem to be linked to the clouds), he expresses "his view of mountains and gardens." By this, one of his pleasures, i.e., in everything (the first example of his satisfaction), is shown forth. This belongs to the feature of 「偏一」 (partial one). And then, in the two lines from 「拄杖」 (with a cane), he expresses another of his pleasures, that of sharing sacrificial meat and the making of white wine (the second example of his satisfaction). This belongs to the feature of 「偏二」 (partial two). As to the four lines from "the west wind," he again expresses his pleasure in everything when observing children taking long sticks to get at the fruit (the third example of his satisfaction). This belongs to 「偏三」 (partial three). Therefore, the structure analysis diagram can be shown as follows.

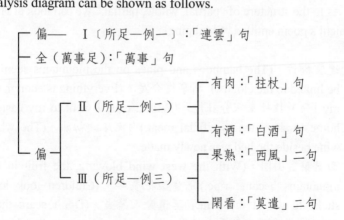

It can be seen that this Tzu as a composition is framed by the structure of "partial, whole, partial."

As to the structure of "whole, partial, whole," we can look at Wen Tien-hsiang's "Song of Breath of Righteousness."

天地有正氣，(There exists the breath of righteousness in the universe.)雜然賦流形；(It has spread in various forms.) 下則為河嶽，(On the earth it spread to rivers and mountains) 上則為日星，(In the sky it spread to the sun and stars.) 於人曰浩然，(In man there is an abundant breath of righteousness.) 沛乎塞蒼冥。(It abundantly saturates the universe.) 皇路當清夷，(When the world was at peace,) 含和吐明庭；(subjects breathed its peaceful breath and served the emperor.) 時窮節乃見，(In difficult times the integrity and honesty of subjects would be manifested.) 一一垂丹青。(and was recorded in history.)

在齊太史簡，(In the Chi nation, there was *Shihchi.)* 在晉董狐筆，(In the Chin nation, there were Tunghu's words.) 在秦張良椎，(In the Chin nation, there was Chang Liang's iron hammer.) 在漢蘇武節；(In the Han nation, there was Su Wu's staff.) 為嚴將軍頭，(General Yen, as head, had no fear of death.) 為嵇侍中血，(The Chi's blood was on the emperor's clothes.) 為張睢陽齒，(Chang Chui-yang's teeth were pulled out by rebels.) 為顏常山舌；(Yen Chang-shan's tongue was cut out by rebels.) 或為遼東帽，(Kuan ling acted as a recluse in Liaotung.) 清操厲冰雪；(His integrity was as clean as the ice and snow.) 或為出師表，(After Chukeliang's letter on behalf of an expedition,) 鬼神泣壯烈；(the ghosts and gods were all moved by his devotion.) 或為渡江楫，(Chu Ti plied paddles to cross the river,)慷慨吞胡羯；(vowing in high spirits to kill his enemies.) 或為擊賊笏，(Upon Tuan Hsiushih striking the thieves,) 逆豎頭破裂。(the rogues' heads were thus broken.)

是氣所磅礴，(Tthe breath of righteousness iwas unlimited.)凜烈萬古存。(Iit solemnly existsed in thise universe.) 當其貫日月，(Wwhen it penetratesd the sun and the moon,)生死安足論？(an individual willould ignore his own life.) 地維賴以立，(Tthe frame of the earth iwas sustained by this earth.) 天柱賴以尊。(Tthe pillars of heaven awere honored by it.) 三綱實繫命，

(The relations between subjects and the emperor, fathers and sons, husbands and wives, are also sustained.) 道義為之根。 (Righteousness and morality are the foundation of this breath.)

The first three paragraphs of this hymn point out that the breath of righteousness sustains ethics and a universal life. The first paragraph uses two lines of "the universe" to introduce the "breath of righteousness," which serves as a generalization to introduce the following arguments. This belongs to the feature of "generalization." And eight lines from "on the earth" flatly mention heaven, earth, and man to pinpoint the omnipresence of the breath of righteousness. Furthermore, in association with "man," the breath of righteousness is the origin of humans' upright character. So it is enormously influential. This belongs to the first "whole." In addition, in the second paragraph, twelve examples of ancient saints' faith and righteousness are stated to illustrate the breath of righteousness. This belongs to the feature of "partial." The third paragraph uses four lines from "this breath" to expand the twelve saints' breath of righteousness to all human beings. In these three paragraphs, consisting of eight lines, first, the four lines from 「是氣」 (the breath of righteousness) expand the twelve ancient saints' breath of righteousness to human beings. The now-and-here time and space is stretched to infinity. This still focuses on "man," asserting the existence and function of the breath of righteousness. In addition, the four lines from 「地維」 ("the frame of the earth") are stretched to "earth" and "heaven." Finally, the two lines from 「三綱」 (the three human relations) conclude the above six lines, pointing out that "the breath of righteousness" is the power sustaining heaven, earth, and the life of man. This is the feature of the next "whole." Therefore, it can be seen that the structure analysis diagram of this work can be shown as follows.

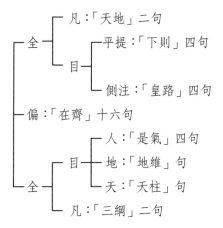

In terms of these three paragraphs, these passages were formed by the structure of "whole, partial, whole."

2. Dot-dye method

"Dot-dye" was originally referred to as one of the basic skills of painting.[95] However, Liu Hsi-chai of the chin dynasty applied this term to composition art.[96] His so-called "dot-dye" referred to "feelings (dot) and landscape (dye)," which duplicated the "unreal, real" method, a "feelings, landscape" method in the big family of composition art. Therefore, "dot-dye" was peculiarly borrowed to describe a kind of composition art. "Dot" refers to a certain point of time and space, used for an introduction, bridge or ending of a narration, description of landscape, feelings, or reasoning. In other

....

95 《See *Family Doctrine of the Yens*》, 顏氏家訓 "the prince is good at portraying. He uses the method of dotting and dying for the guests as real as themselves. So kids can know the persons from the portraits." (Taipie: Sanming Bookstore, Sep. 1993) p.386.

96 See Liu Sidai, *General Introduction to Tzu and Songs, Paper Collection of Liu Sidai.* 《劉熙載文集》 (Nanking: Chiasu Ancient Book Publishing Company, Dec. 2000) p.147.

words, "dot" is only a point of departure or perspective, while "dye" refers to all kinds of contents. This kind of composition art is frequently seen, and can form the following structures—"first dot and then dye," "first dye and then dot," "dot, dye, dot," and "dye, dot, dye." All of these consist of the functions of order, change, and consistency/echo. As to "first dot and then dye," we can look at *Mengtzu, Lilo*, as an example.

齊人有一妻一妾而處室者，(In the Chin nation, a man supported a wife and a concubine under one roof.) 其良人出，(Whenever this husband went out,) 則必厭酒肉而後反。(he would come back home after a lot of eating and drinking.)其妻問所與飲食者，(His wife asked him with whom he ate and drank.) 則盡富貴也。(He said that all of them were rich and powerful.) 其妻告其妾曰：(His wife told the concubine:) 「良人出，(whenever our husband goes out,) 則必厭酒肉而後反。(he will come back home after eating and drinking a lot.) 問其與飲食者，(We have asked him with whom he ate and drank.) 盡富貴也，(He has said that all of them were rich and powerful.) 而未嘗有顯者來。(However, we never see any celebrities coming here.) 吾將瞷良人之所之也。」(I will quietly follow him in order to see where he goes.)

蚤起，(In the morning of the following day,) 施從良人之所之，(she followed in her husband's footsteps.) 遍國中無與立談者。(Nobody stopped to talk to her husband.) 卒之東墦間，(She saw her husband go to the graveyards outside the city) 之祭者乞其餘；(where he begged for the remaining offerings.) 不足，(But he did not eat his fill.) 又顧而之他。(So he went to other places to beg for food.) 此其為厭足之道也。(This was the way he satisfied his stomach.)

其妻歸，(His wife came back home) 告其妾曰：(snf told his concubine,) 「良人者，(our so-called husband) 所仰望而終身

也；(is a person his wife can depend on all her life?!) 今若此！」(How disappointed we must be in our husband!)與其妻訕其良人，(The two women cursed their husband) 而相泣於中庭。(and started crying.) 而良人未之知也，(But their husband did not know the truth.) 施施從外來，(He confidently returned home,) 驕其妻妾。(being proud of himself before these two women.)

由此觀之，(Judging from this,) 則人之所以求富貴利達者，(the ways by which people seek fame and wealth) 其妻妾不羞也而不相泣者，(more often than not bring to couples tears of shame.) 幾希矣。(Righteous ways are so few.)

This essay consists of four paragraphs, which can be divided into two parts—"narration" and "comments." The first three paragraphs are "narration," and the final one "comments." As to the feature of "narration," the three lines from 齊人有一妻一妾而處室者，(In the Chin nation, a man supported a wife and a concubine under one roof), as an introduction, generally depict the fact that 則必饜酒肉而後反。(he would come back home after a lot of eating and drinking) and that 驕其妻妾(he was proud of himself before these two women). These belong to the feature of "dot." And then, the lines from 其妻問所與飲食者，(his wife asked him with whom he ate and drank) to 驕其妻妾(He was proud of himself before these two women) concretely describe the process by which his wife and concubine begin doubting, tracing and then find and cry over the truth without his awareness. These belong to the feature of "dye." As to the "comments," that is, the four sentences of the final paragraph, the author thus feels that in pursuing success, everyman is seemingly as shameless as this man. In this way, the satirical topic is fully expressed. The structure analysis diagram can be shown as follows.

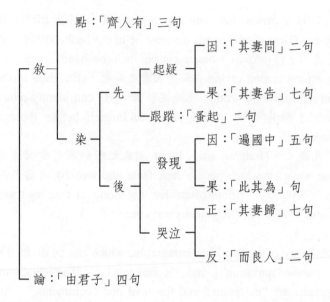

The feature of "narration" forms the structure of "first dot and then dye."

As to the structure of "first dye and then dot," we can look at Pai Chu-yi's Tzu, "Long Memory."

> 汴水流，(The Pien river flows;) 泗水流，(The Ssu river flows.) 流到瓜州古渡頭。(Flowing on to Guachou harbor it goes.) 吳山點點愁。(My sorrow is as spacious as the mountains.)
> 思悠悠，(Thoughts are immensely long.) 恨悠悠，(Hatred is immensely deep.) 恨到歸時方始休。(Hatred will not end until I go back home.) 月明人倚樓。(I look forward to my hometown under the moonlight.)

In this Tzu, the author describes his feelings (dye) at a time when he "looks forward to his hometown under the moonlight" 「月明人倚樓」 at Guachou harbor (dot). The first four lines describe what he sees. Indeed, in the first three lines, "water" is depicted. The two rivers are constantly flowing, which highlights a hatred of departure.   And then, in the line about 「吳山」 (mountains), the 「點點」 of the mountains also highlights a hatred of departure.   In this way, feelings are conceived in terms of landscapes, which pave the way for the following four lines which serve to express feelings. The three lines from 「思悠悠」 (thoughts are immensely long) concretely point out the topic of 「悠悠」之「恨」 (hatred is immensely deep) (referring to contemporary times), and then the line with 「恨到」 (hatred) aims to exaggerate "hatred" in an imaginative way (referring to the future).   Based on the above two parts of "dye," the concluding line 「月明人倚樓」 (I look forward to my hometown under the moonlight) naturally emerges, serving as "dot" to express the author's feelings under the moon light.   So, the structure analysis diagram can be shown below.

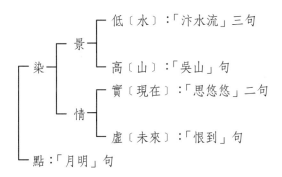

Thus, in terms of composition, this Tzu is formed by the structure of "first dye and then dot."

As to the structure of "dot, dye, dot," we can look at "Stupid Old Man Removes Mountains" in *Liehtzu*.

太形、王屋二山, (Taihsing Mountain and Wangwu Mountain) 方七百里, (with a girth of seven hundred kilometers) 高萬仞 (were extremely high) 本在冀州之南、 (and originally located in the south of Chichou.)河陽之北。(In the north of Hoyang)北山愚公者,(there was a stupid old man at the northern mountain.)年且九十,(His age was ninety years.) 面山而居。(He lived at the face of the two mountains) 懲北山之塞,(hindered by a portion of the northern mountain.) 出入之迂也,(Travel was not efficient.) 聚室而謀曰:(He gathered together his family members, saying:)「吾與汝畢力平險,("You and I will do our best to eliminate the barrier of the mountains,)指通豫南,(and then, we can directly go south to Yuchou,)達於漢陰,(to the south of Han river.) 可乎?」(Can we not do that?") 雜然相許。(They unanimously agreed.) 其妻獻疑曰:(But his wife still doubted,)「以君之力,("your strength) 曾不能損魁父之丘,(cannot reduce a small mountain like Kueifu.)如太形、王屋何?(How could you level these two huge mountains,) 且焉置土石?」(and where to put the mud and stones?") 雜曰:(They all said,)「投諸渤海之尾("let's toss the mud and stones at the end of the Pohai) 隱土之北。(north of Yintu.")」遂率子孫荷擔者三夫,(Thus, he led forth his family members; three of them bore the gear for carrying the mud and stones,) 叩石墾壤,(after breaking up the stones and dig the mud,) 箕畚運於渤海之尾;(to carry them to the end of the Pohai.) 鄰人京城氏之孀妻有遺男,(A son of the widow living next door,) 始齔,(who was just seven or eight years old,) 跳往助之;(earnestly wanted to help him.) 寒暑易節,(Come summer and winter) 始一反焉。(he would go back home to rest for a while.)

河曲智叟笑而止之曰:(A wise old man in Hochu laughed, intending to stop him:) 「甚矣,("you go too far,) 汝之不慧!(you are so unwise!) 以殘年遺力,(Your longevity and strength are limited.) 曾不能毀山之一毛,(You cannot destroy even the grass of these mountains.) 其如土石何?」(How can you deal with the mud and stones?") 北山愚公長息曰:(The stupid old man of the northern mountain sighed and said,) 「汝心之固,

("your heart is so stubborn) 固不可徹，(and so unreasonable.) 曾不若孀妻弱子。(You are less reasonable than a widow and an orphan.) 雖我之死，(If I die,)有子存焉；(my descendants will still live on.) 子又生孫，(My sons will have children,) 孫又生子；(these grandchildren will have children,)子又有子，(their sons will have sons)子又有孫；(and their sons will have children.)子子孫孫，(Of sons and grandchildren) 無窮匱也。(there is no end.) 而山不增，(The height of the mountains won't increase.) 何苦而不平？」(How can the mountains not be leveled?") 河曲智叟亡以應。(The wise man had nothing more to say.)

操蛇之神聞之，(The snake-handler god heard of this,) 懼其不已也，(fearing that he wouldn't stop.)告之於帝，(The god reported it to the Supreme God.) 帝感其誠，(Moved by the stupid old man's sincerity,) 命夸娥氏二子負二山，(he ordered his two sons in Kuaerhshih to bear off the two mountains,) 一厝朔東，(putting one in the east of Shuofan,) 一厝雍南。(the other in the south of Yungnan,) 自此冀之北、(from north of the Chichou) 漢之陰，(to the south of the Han river,) 無隴斷焉。(where there were no high lands or stones.)

This allegory aims to explain the doctrines—"Where there is a will, there is a way," and "God helps those who help themselves." The first four lines are used to explain the setting and reasons for this story. They are an introduction to the essay. In addition, the final two lines serve as the ending of this story. These both belong to the feature of "dot." And then, the lines from 北山愚公者(there was a stupid old man at the northern mountain) to 一厝雍南 ([putting] the other in the south of Yungnan) formally use a concrete plot to describe this story. This is the feature of "dye." In this part, the author uses the order of "first cause and then effect" to make a combination. The lines from 北山愚公者，(there was a stupid old man at the northern mountain) to 河曲智叟亡以應 (the wise man had nothing more to say) tell the story: Ignoring the wise man's laughter, the stupid old man is so determined to remove the mountain that he wins the loyalty and help of his family and neighbors. This serves as "cause." In addition, the lines from 操蛇之神聞之， (the snake-handler god heard of this) to 一厝雍南 ([putting] the other in the south of Yungnan) describe how the stupid old man's efforts move the heavenly God, Who thus tells the gods to use their power to help remove the mountain. This is "effect." In terms of this perspective,[97] the structure analysis of this article can be shown as follows.

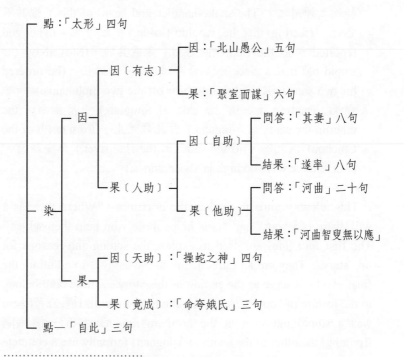

....

97 We can also use the cause-effect perspective to form the structure of "first cause and then effect." See Chen Man-ming's *Structural Analysis of Compositions*. 《文章結構分析》 pp.129-133.

In terms of "composition," this article is framed by the structure of "dot, dye, dot."

Take the 〈石州慢〉詞 ("Shihchouman" Tzu) by Hochu, for instance.

薄雨收寒，(The thin rain ceased and the cold air was dispersed.) 斜照弄晴，(The sunshine shone down and the weather turned fine)春意空闊。(The the sense of spring was immense.) 長亭柳色纔黃，(Beside the pavilion appeared the yellow willow.) 倚馬何人先折？(Someone leaning against a horse broke branches.) 煙橫水漫，(Smoke saturated the wilderness, and spring water spread everywhere.) 映帶幾點歸鴻，(A few wild geese flew over the horizon.) 平沙銷盡龍荒雪。(Ice and snow melted on the plain.) 猶記出關來，恰如今時節。(I remember that the scene was like this when I left.)　將發。(When I set off,) 畫樓芳酒，(in the house she had prepared wine and food,) 紅淚清歌，(shedding tears and singing a song for me.) 便成輕別。(Since then, we have bid farewell.) 回首經年，(Flashing back to past years...) 杳杳音塵都絕。(we lived far apart from each other.) 欲知方寸，(To see such hearts...) 共有幾許新愁？(were there so many fresh sorrows?) 芭蕉不展丁香結。(Like rolled leaves and unblossoming flowers,) 憔悴一天涯，(we were apart and melancholy.) 兩厭厭風月。(Facing wind and the bright moon, we remembered each other.)

This poem aims to describe feelings aroused by departure. From the line with 「薄雨」(thin rain) to the line with 「平沙」(the plain), the author describes a scene of early spring after rain by means of concrete images such as rain, yellow willow, wild geese, and melting snow. In addition, he uses the story of his breaking willow branches as a gift to friends to highlight his feelings of departure. This is the first part of "dye." And then, he uses six lines from 「猶記」 (it was remembered), adopting the narration of "first present and then past" to reveal that after he bade farewell to a beautiful woman at the end of last year (inside the Great Wall), he arrived here (outside the Great Wall).   In this way, his observations and feelings are seen to be set in a conspicuous location.   This is the feature of "dot."   And then, the seven lines from 「回首」 (flashing back), in the order of "first feelings and then landscape," first mention 「新愁」 (fresh sorrows), using leaves and followers as metaphors and then uniting fiction and the reality of space to eventually express feelings through landscape.[98]   This is the next part of "dye."   According to this analysis, the structure diagram can be shown as follows.

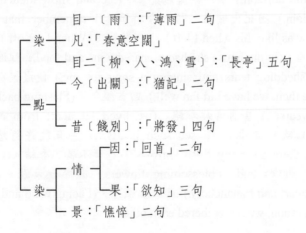

Therefore, in terms of "composition," it is framed by the structure of "dye, dot, dye."

....

98 Tang Kuei-chang, "The two lines from 『憔悴』 (melancholy) ended in the landscape, pinpointing a romance frustrated by long distance.   From this, our horizon is accordingly widened."   See *Concise Interpretation of Tang, Sung Poems* 《唐宋詞簡釋》 (Taipei: Muto Publishing Company, March 1982, first edition) p. 119.

3. Heaven-man method

The so-called "heaven" refers to "nature," while "man," to "personnel." Generally speaking, while describing landscape or engaging in reasoning, the author frequently mentions "heaven" and "man." In terms of describing landscape, "heaven" refers to natural scenery, while "man," to scenes with personnel. In addition, in terms of reasoning, "heaven" refers to the way of God, while "man," to the ways of man. Although it's not so adequate to apply the term "heaven-man" to composition art, I still have to use this term since no other terms can better fit. Moreover, the method can form the following four structures as well: "first heaven, and then man," "first man and then heaven," "heaven, man, heaven," and "man, heaven, man." Now I will state examples to explain the category, "describing scenery." As to the structure of "first heaven and then man," we can look at one of Wang Wei's poems.

寒山轉蒼翠，(The chilly mountains turn emerald green,)
秋水日潺湲。(the autumn waters daily murmuring.)
倚杖柴門外，(Outside my thatch-door on my staff I lean,)
臨風聽暮蟬。(heeding evening winds, cicadas shrilling.)
渡頭餘落日，(Beyond the ford the sun has nearly sunk;)
墟里上孤煙。(from the village a wisp of smoke floats free.)
復值接輿醉，(You are just like that crazy Jie-yu, drunk,)
狂歌五柳前。(wildly warbling before my willow tree.)

This poem was designed to describe the author's joy over his companion, Peiti. In a certain setting, the author reveals his sense of ease by describing the natural scenery and the characters' traits. In the first two lines, he depicts the autumn and evening scenery nearby Wangchuang. A harmonious picture consisting of colors and sounds is thus formed. Further, in the final two lines, through the pictures of natural ease, we see how the author leans on his staff, listening to the cicadas shrilling, and Peiti wildly warbling.　An artistic world of the union between self and other beings is carved out.[99]　And the happiness of the author's life is substantially expressed.　The structure analysis diagram can be shown as follows.

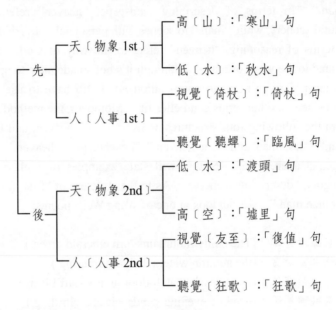

Thus, it can be seen that the structure of "first heaven and then man" is formed.

As to the structure of "first man and then heaven" we can take a look at Lee Ching-chao's Tzu "Shenshenman."

尋尋覓覓，(Looking but in vain.)冷冷清清，(Cold and crisp,) 悽悽慘慘戚戚。(melancholy,)乍暖還寒時候，(the weather was so capricious.)最難將息。(It was difficult for me to take a rest.)

....

99　See Lee Hou, "Aesthetic Interpretation of Tang Dynasty Poems,"　《唐詩的美學 闡釋》　as in note 46, p. 255.

三杯兩盞淡酒，(Though drinking two or three cups of wine,)怎敵他、晚來風急。(how could resist the strong sweeping wind?) 雁過也，(Wild geese flew over.)最傷心，(I was sad then.)卻是舊時相識。(They seemed like old friends from the north.) 滿地黃花堆積。(Fallen chrysanthemums covered the ground.) 憔悴損、(I was thin and sick.)如今有誰堪摘。(Now, who would pick up the flowers?)守著窗兒，(I leaned against the window.)獨自怎生得黑。(How could I wait from dawn to dusk?) 梧桐更兼細雨，(Trees and slim rain) 到黃昏、(till dusk.)點點滴滴。(The rain drops dripped.) 這次第，(At present,) 怎一箇愁字了得。(how could the word "sadness" describe the situation?)

This Tzu aims to express sorrow. In terms of composition, it is framed by the structure of "first cause and then effect." As to the feature of "cause," from the beginning line to the line with 「到黃昏」 (to dusk), these lines were written in the order of "generalization, detail, generalization." The first "detail" refers to the three lines following 「尋尋」 (looking). In the cold fall, the author could not help but feel sad about seeing the change of faces in looking for old trails. In terms of logic, this lays a bridge to the line, 「最難將息」 (it was difficult for me to take a rest). In addition, "generalization" refers to the two lines following 「乍暖」 (the weather was so capricious), which being a generalization serves as a link. The sorrow and melancholy are naturally exposed. As to the next "detail," it begins with the line from 「三杯」 (three cups) and ends in 「到黃昏」 (till dusk). First, the line with 「三杯」 (three cups) is used to describe the change to someone tasting wine (man). And then, from the line 「怎敵他」 (how could I resist) to 「如今」 (now), the natural scene is depicted—sweeping wind, flying wild geese, and fallen flowers (heaven). Furthermore, two lines from 「守著」 (leaned against) are used to describe a personal scene of the person leaning against the window (man). Moreover, two lines from 「梧桐」are employed to describe the natural scene of trees soaked by raindrops (heaven). This is a detailed description of 「最難將息」(it was difficult for me to take a rest), serving as a prelude to the final two lines. As to the feature of "effect," 「這次第」(at present) concludes the feature of "cause" in the above. And then, 「愁」(sadness) appears to manifest the topic. The structure analysis diagram can be shown as follows.

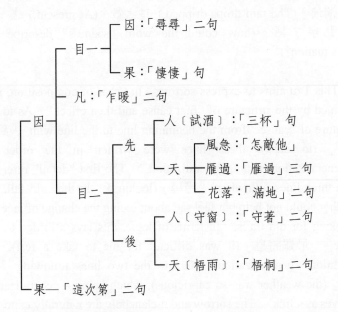

As to the feature of "detail two," apparently the structure of "first man and then heaven" is formed.

As to the structure of "heaven, man, heaven," we can look at Wu Wen-yin's Tzu "Wansisha."

門隔花深夢舊遊，(With bunches of flowers blooming in front of my door, a past dream came upon me.) 夕陽無語雁歸愁。

(Sunset found no words and birds flew over in sorrow.) 玉纖香動小簾鉤。 (My hands moved aside the curtains.)　落絮無聲春墮淚，(Flowers fell in silence and spring wept.) 行雲有影月含羞。(Shadows of clouds flew over, and the moon grew shy.) 東風臨夜冷於秋。(The east wind was colder than autumn.)

This Tzu aims to describe the nostalgia after a dream by means of "first unreal (in a dream) and then real (after a dream)." The line from 「夕陽」 (sunset) to the ending line, being a "real", serve to describe a dream. 「門隔花深」 (bunches of flowers blooming in front of my door) directly points to travel in the dream, disclosing the place in a profound way.[100] And then, in the second and third lines, the author describes his rolling aside the curtain after the dream (personnel/man) to watch the silent sunset and birds coming home (nature/heaven). In this way, nostalgia (sorrow) is highlighted. And then, in the final three lines, the fallen flowers, shy moon, east wind observed after the dream are depicted (nature/heaven). Especially noteworthy, 「絮落」 (the fallen flowers) are compared to 「春墮淚」 (spring wept). 「行雲有影」 (shadows of clouds) is compared to 「月含羞」 (the shy moon). Furthermore, 「冷於秋」 (colder than autumn) is used to reinforce the melancholy in the night and thus to deepen the feelings of nostalgia. Accordingly, nostalgia (sorrow) saturates the whole Tzu. Therefore, the structure analysis diagram can be shown as follows.

....

100 Wu Hweijun, "『門隔花深』 refers to the dreamy old land, pointing out the depth of the dreamy land." See *Aesthetic Perspectives of Tang Sun Tzu.*. 《唐宋詞審美觀照》 (Shanghai: Sheilin Publishing Company, Aug. 1999.) p.14.

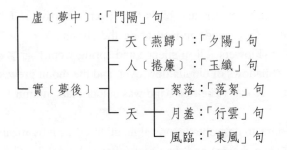

As to the feature of "real" (after the dream), the structure of "heaven, man, heaven" is formed.

The structure of "man, heaven, man" can be seen in 〈慶東原〉 (Chingtunyuan) by Ma Chihyuan.

暖日宜乘轎，(Warm days suit riding on a sedan chair)春風堪信馬，(and springtime, a tame horse.) 恰寒食有二百處秋千架。(just by our humble fare are two hundred swings.) 向人嬌杏花，(Toward us waft the delicate apricot flowers;) 撲人衣柳花，(alighting on our clothes fall the willow flowers,) 迎人笑桃花。(welcoming us, the laughing peach flowers.) 來往畫船遊，(To and fro travel the painted boats,) 招颭青旗掛。(pure-blue banners hang beckoning in the wind.)

This Tzu was designed to describe the spring scenery, consisting of human scenes such as a sedan chair, horse, swings, painted boats, pure-blue, (man) and natural scenes such as apricot flowers, willow flowers and peach flowers (heaven).   The spring scenery is vividly presented, highlighting the author's happy mood at that moment. In view of the narrative order, the structure analysis diagram can be shown below.

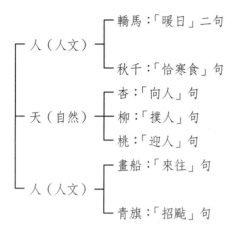

In terms of "composition," it was framed by the structure of "man, heaven, man."

4. Picture-background method

Generally speaking, the author uses such temporal and spatial materials as "background" as well as "focus." Like a painting, the "background," as a "bottom," can highlight the "focus." In addition, the "focus" can bring the effect of concentration to the "background." This is a so-called "picture."[101] While being applied to the composition art, this logic can produce the effects of "order," "change," and "unification," meanwhile forming the following structures—"first picture and then bottom," "first bottom and then picture," "picture bottom picture," "bottom picture bottom." The structure of "first picture and then bottom" can be seen in Wangwei's poem entitled "Chulikuan."

....

101 Wan Shosiung, "In terms of visionary psychology, the visionary objects appearing from the background are called "figure.""...and the neighboring background is called "ground." See *Psychology of Painting Art.* 《美術心理學》 (Taipei: Shansin Publishing Company, 1975)

獨坐幽篁裏，(Sitting among bamboo alone,) 彈琴復長嘯。(I play my lute and croon carefree) 深林人不知，(in the deep woods where I'm unknown.) 明月來相照。(Only the bright moon peeps at me.)

The description of lonely men and solitary scenes in the poem highlight the author's enjoyment of solitude. The first two lines use 「獨坐」(sitting alone) 、「彈琴」(playing lute) 、「長嘯」 (croon carefree) to describe a person alone. This emerges as the focus of this poem, playing the part of "picture." In addition, the final two lines describe solitary scenes. The empty 「深林」 (deep woods) and the shining 「明月」(bright moon) serve to highlight a solitary landscape. This is the background of this poem, highlighting the previous two lines and thus serving as "bottom." The structure analysis diagram can be shown as follows.

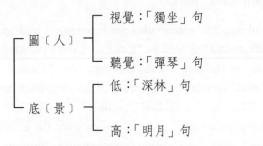

In terms of "composition," this poem was composed in the structure of "first picture and then background." As to the structure of "first background and then picture," we can take a look at Liu Chung-yuan's "River Snow."

千山鳥飛絕，(From hill to hill no bird in flight.)
萬徑人蹤滅。(From path to path no man in sight.)
孤舟蓑笠翁，(Straw-cloak'd man in a lone boat, lo!)
獨釣寒江雪。(Sole fisher on a course clad in snow.)

This poem uses the silence, solitude and cold of men and things to describe the author's pride and loneliness, reflecting his unique character.　In the first two lines, four things-- 『山』 (hill) 、『鳥』 (bird) 、『徑』 (path) 、『人』 (man)—are used to describe its background.　On the one hand, 『千』 (thousand) 、『萬』 (ten thousand) are employed to widen the space.　On the other hand, 『絕』 (no)、『滅』 (no) are used to highlight the calm scenery. This serves as "bottom."　The final two lines uses 『舟』 (boat)、 『雪』 (snow) to highlight the 『蓑笠翁』 (straw-cloak'd man). And 『孤』 and 『獨』 are used to depict the loneliness of the straw-cloak'd man.　This plays the part of "picture."[102]Therefore, the structure analysis diagram can be shown below.

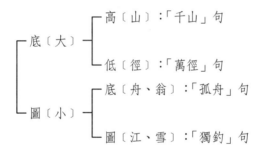

The composition was indeed framed by the structure of "first background and then picture."

As to the structure of "picture, background, picture," we can look at Li Pai's "On Phoenix Terrace at Jinling."

鳳凰臺上鳳凰遊，(On Phoenix Terrace the phoenix once came to play.) 鳳去臺空江自流。(Terrace now vacant, still roll on the

102 See Chen Man-ming, "Composition Forms with Topics Outside: as in Poems And Tzu." *Papers of the Third Chinese Rhetoric Conference* 《第三屆中國修辭學學術研討會論文集》 (Taipei: Chinese Rhetoric Association, Graduate Institute of Chinese at Minchuan University, June 2001), p. 1119.

river's waves.) 吳宮花草埋幽徑，(Wu palace garden's buried by the wasted byway;) 晉代衣冠成古丘。(ancient sages in noble gowns all lie in graves.) 三山半落青天外，(The three-peak'd mountain's half lost in the azure sky;) 二水中分白鷺洲。(the two-fork'd stream by Egret Isle's split apart.) 總為浮雲能蔽日，(As floating clouds can at all times the sun defy,) 長安不見使人愁。(Imperial court, now out of sight, aggrieves my heart.)

On Phoenix Terrace at Jinling

The author expresses his pain and sadness over his own life and country through his travel to Phoenix Terrace.　In the first line, he points out the location of Phoenix Terrance at Jinling. He uses 「遊」(play) 「去」(vacant) to signify the rise and fall of the country.　This is the first part of "picture."　And then, the two lines from 「吳宮」(Wu palace) use 「幽徑」(wasted byway) and 「古丘」(graves) to describe the fall of the country.　In addition, 「吳宮花草」(Wu palace garden) and 「晉代衣冠」(ancient sages in noble gowns) are used to describe the peak of the old days. These two sides make a vivid contrast.　And then, there are the two lines following 「三山」(the three-peak'd mountain) and 「二水」 (the two-fork'd stream), and 「長安」(the imperial court). For 「臺」(terrace) and 「人」 (man/the author), this serves as "bottom/background" to highlight both of them.　Finally, through 「浮雲」「蔽日」(floating clouds can veil the bright sun), the author signifies that evil subjects outshine the good ones. Furthermore, in 「長安」「不見」(imperial court now out of sight), he reveals his anger at being forced out of the imperial court.　And he also shows his concern about the Tang dynasty, which at that time might perish like the six dynasties.　The is the next part of "picture."　The structure analysis diagram can be shown as follows.

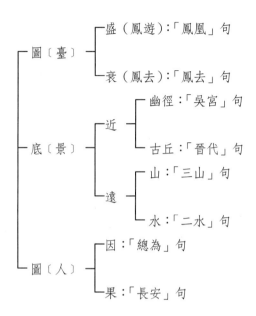

Accordingly, this composition was framed by the structure of "picture, background/bottom, picture."

As to the structure of "bottom, picture, bottom," we can take a look at Wen Ting-yu's Tzu "Keng lotzu."

玉爐香，(A fine urn spread ash and smoke.) 紅蠟淚。(Red candles seemed to shed tears.) 偏照畫堂秋思。(Light projected on a person sorrowful over autumn.) 眉翠薄，(Decorated eyebrows became thinner.) 鬢雲殘，(Hair disheveled...)夜長衾枕寒。(night so long that the bed turned cold.) 梧桐樹，(The Wu-tung trees...) 三更雨，(It rained at midnight.) 不道離情正苦。(The sadness over departure was untold.) 一葉葉，(Leaves fell.) 一聲聲，(Raindrops made sounds.) 空階滴到明。(Raindrops dropped on the empty steps until dawn.)

This Tzu aims to describe the feelings of departure. First, the author uses the initial two lines to describe a drawing room with the ash and smoke of a fine urn, as well as the tears of red candles. This serves as the beginning of the narration, and the first part of "bottom." And then, the four lines from 「偏照」 (light projected) focus on a beauty in the drawing room, that is, the protagonist of this Tzu. This is written in the order of "first generalization and then specification." The 「偏照」 (light projected) of the red candles was used as a bridge to generally describe a beauty sitting in a drawing room and mourning over autumn. Furthermore, her eyebrows, hair, and bed are specifically depicted in an attempt to visualize the sadness of autumn. This is the feature of "picture." And then, the next six lines, following the line 「夜長衾枕寒」 (night so long that the bed turned cold) describe the trees and rain outside the drawing room. Combined with the urn smoke and candles' tears, these lines highlight and magnify the focus in a both inward and extraneous way. In this way, the work appears so impressive. This is the next part of "bottom." The structure analysis diagram can be shown as follows.

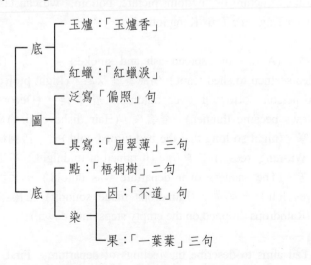

此就「篇」而言，所形成的是「底、圖、底」的結構。

5. Knocking-striking method

"Knocking-striking," in a sense, both refer to the action of "striking." But, strictly speaking, in Chinese "knock" and "strike" slightly differ in meaning. According to *Explaining Words*, " 'strike' means to strike an object from its two sides." This explanation can be echoed by Hsu Kai's *Hsichuan.* Judging from this, the difference in the two words lies in the fact that "knock" in Chinese refers to "striking from two sides of an object or a person." Therefore, in terms of composition art, "knock" refers to indirect writing, while "strike," direct writing. This definition can differentiate the "knocking-striking" method from other methods of composition art, such as "positive-negative," " flat-side," and "guest and master."[103] And the method can also be transformed into the following structures—"first knock and then strike," "first strike and then knock," "knock, strike, knock," and "strike, knock, strike." In this way, the "echoing effects" such as "ordering," "changing," and "unifying" can be produced. Indeed, the structure of "first knock and then strike" can be seen in Suche's "A Note on Hungcho's Happy Pavilion."

昔楚襄王從宋玉、景差於蘭臺之宮，(In the past, King Chuhsiang took Sungyu and Chingchai to Nantai Palace.) 有風颯然而至者，(There a wind came up.)王披襟當之曰：(The king unbuttoned his overcoat to receive the wind, saying:) 「快哉此風！("how pleasant it is!) 寡人所與庶人共者耶？」(Is

---

103 "strike-knock" mainly uses different things to express similar feelings. The use of "knock" is used to echo the part of "strike." This is different from such compositional types as "positive, negative," "guest, master," and "flat, side." And these compositional types can be seen in Chen Man-ming's *New Design of Compositional Types.* 《章法學新裁》 pp. 345-360.

this a pleasure I share with my subjects?") 宋玉曰：(Sungyu said,) 「此獨大王之雄風耳，("this 'virile' wind is only for a great king.) 庶人安得共之！」(Your subjects cannot share it.") 玉之言蓋有諷焉。(His words suggested sarcasm) 夫風無雌雄之異，(Indeed, wind was neither male nor female.) 而人有遇不遇之變。(However, men had either good fortune or misfortune.) 楚王之所以為樂，(The reason for the king's happiness) 與庶人之所以為憂，(and the reason for the subjects' sadness) 此則人之變也，(were the vicissitudes of human life.) 而風何與焉？(Did this have any relation with the wind?) 士生於世，(Man lives in the world.) 使其中不自得，(If he is not happy in his heart,) 將何往而非病？(wherever he goes, he will feel sad.) 使其中坦然，(If he feels peaceful in his heart,) 不以物傷性，(his nature is not hurt by the outside world;) 將何適而非快？(wherever he goes, he will feel happy.) 今張君不以謫為患，(At present Mr. Chang does not feel sad about his removal from his previous post,) 竊會計之餘功，(but is taking advantage of his leisure time,) 而自放山水之間，(relaxing among mountains and rivers.) 此其中宜有以過人者。(This is because he has certain good points which exceed other people's.) 將蓬戶甕牖無所不快，(Even in a grass door or broken brick window could he find happiness.) 而況乎濯長江之清流，(The clear current of the Yangtze River will wash away pollution in the heart.) 揖西山之白雲，(with inviting white clouds in the western mountains as friends) 窮耳目之勝以自適也哉？(and the extremely abundant landscape beauty as a delight for ears and eyes.) 不然，(If not for) 連山絕壑，(high mountains and deep valleys,) 長林古木，(ancient forests and woods,) 振之以清風，(blown by the wind,) 照之以明月，(shining under the bright moon,) 此皆騷人思士之所以悲傷憔悴而不能勝者，(sad poets and sentimental people would feel deeply sad.) 烏睹其為快也哉？(Where would we see happiness?)

In terms of composition, these words belong to the feature of "comment" within the structure of "first narration and then comment." In the dialogue between King Chuhsiang and Sungyu, (「昔楚襄王 (in the past, King Chuhsiang) ……安得共之 (cannot share it)」), 「快哉」(how pleasant) was disclosed and led these lines (「玉之言 (his words) ……而風何與焉」(did this have any relation with the wind?)) to make an indirect comment, which also served as a bridge for the following direct comments.[104] This is the feature of "knocking." In addition, in terms of "whole" (「士生於世 (man lives in the world) ……物傷性」(his nature is not hurt by the outside world)), these lines illuminate the topic of 「快哉」(how pleasant). In addition, in terms of "partial," (「今張君 (at present Mr. Chang……為快也哉」(where we could see happiness)), the post removal of Chang Men-te was used to directly depict the topic of「快哉」(how pleasant).[105] This is the feature of "striking." Accordingly, the structure analysis diagram can be shown below.

---

104 Wang Wen-ju commented on 「而風何與焉」(was there any relation with the wind): "For 『快哉』(how pleasant), the comments refer to Chang Men-te. This was paradoxically both continuous and discontinuous." See *Comments on Anthology of Ancient Prose*《精校評注古文觀止》 (Taipei: Taiwan Chunhua Bookstore, Oct. 1998.), p. 38.

105 Wang Wen-ju commented on「以自適也哉」(as enjoyment). "Decently describing 『快哉』(how enjoyable). This is very sweet." As as in note 104.

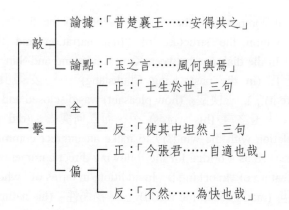

So, this work is framed in the structure of "first knocking and then striking."

As to the structure of "first striking and then knocking," we can look at Hanyu's "Preface to see Tung Shao-nan off to Hopei."

燕趙古稱多感慨悲歌之士。(Yen and Chao used to be places full of heroes, who often sighed and sang sad songs.) 董生舉進士,(Tungsheng was attending the public exams for recruiting officers.) 連不得志於有司,(But he could not be allowed entry by the examiners so many times,) 懷抱利器,(though he was highly talented.) 鬱鬱適茲土,(When he sadly went to this place,) 吾知其必有合也。(I knew he would meet people that would suit him.) 董生勉夫哉!(Go ahead, Tungshen!)
夫以子之不遇時,(You have not had good fortune.) 苟慕義彊仁者,(People who love righteousness and honor love) 皆愛惜焉。(will love and value you.) 矧燕趙之士,(People in Yen and Chao) 出於其性者哉!(find love and righteousness natural.) 然吾嘗聞風俗與化移易,(I heard before that customs are changed by cultivation.) 吾惡知其今不異於古所云邪?(How can I know whether the current situation is different from ancient times?) 聊以吾子之行卜之也。(I will know the reality by your

visit of them.)

吾因子有所感矣。(I have some ideas about your trip.)為我弔望
諸君之墓,(Please visit the tomb of Yuehyi.)而觀於其市,
(Take a tour of the city.) 復有昔時屠狗者乎?(Did some heroes
make a living by killing dogs?) 為我謝曰:(Please thank them
for me.)「明天子在上,可以出而仕矣。」(Nowadays, we
have a bright emperor, so we can do our best by serving as
officers.)

This preface as a gift aims to see Tung Shao-nan off in his travel
to Hopei.   At that time, the political situation was unstable there.
So the author "had no reasons to encourage him to go there, but if
the author directly discouraged him, he'd better refrain from seeing
him off."[106]

Taking this into consideration, the author avoided the "present" of
Hopei, and started the work from the perspective of the "past."
First, from the beginning line to 「出乎其性者哉」(find love and
righteousness natural), in the order of "cause, effect, cause," the
author tells us that in ancient times there were many 「慕義彊仁」
(people who love righteousness and honor love) in Yen and Chao
(Hopei).   He predicted that Tungshen would be 「愛惜」(loved
and valued) and 「有合」(meet suitable people) on this trip.
Therefore, he should be psychologically prepared for this trip.   And
then, from 「然吾嘗聞」(I heard before) to 「董生勉乎哉」(go
ahead, Tungshen), he mentions that the current customs of Yen and
Chao might be different from those of ancient times.   Thus, from a
contrary perspective, he encourages Tungshen, making a prediction
as to whether Tungshen would get along with people in Hopei.
This further affirms that Tungshen should take this trip.   The above

....
106 See Lin Yun-min, *Collections of Ancient Prose Analysis,* Volume 4 《古文析義
    合編》卷四 (Taipei: Kungwen Bookstore, Oct. 1965), p. 216.

two paragraphs, as the feature of "striking," serve the purpose of encouraging Tungshen to travel to Hopei.   Furthermore, in the final paragraph, he advises Tungshen to say that "nowadays, we have a bright emperor, so we can do our best to serve as officers." 「明天子在上」 This serves as the feature of "striking," hinting that Tungshen had better not go there.   Accordingly, the structure analysis diagram can be shown as follows.

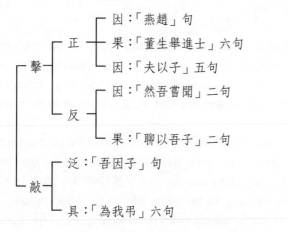

In terms of "composition," this forms the structure of "first striking and then knocking."

As to the structure of "knocking, striking, knocking," we can look at Hsing Chi-chi's "Hohsinglang."

綠樹聽鵜鴃，(Cuckoos were heard singing in the green tree.) 更那堪、鷓鴣聲住，(The voices of partridges ceased.) 杜鵑聲切！(The cuckoos cried even louder.) 啼到春歸無尋處，(They cried until the end of spring.) 苦恨芳菲都歇。(It was hateful that all the flowers were gone.) 算未抵人間離別：(This was not as good as departure from the mundane world.) 馬上琵琶關塞黑，(Wang Chaochun played the pi-pa on a horse, and the sky of the frontier turned dark.) 更長門翠輦辭金闕。(The carts of the palace had departed.) 看燕燕, (Swallows flew through the sky.) 送歸妾。(The woman was escorted back.) 將將將軍百戰身名裂, (After many wars, the general had gotten nowhere.) 向河梁、回頭萬里, (At the place of departure, I looked back.)故人長絕。(Friends were deceased.) 易水蕭蕭西風冷, (The waters and west winds were cold and crisp.) 滿座衣冠似雪。(The costumes of the guests were as white as snow.) 正壯士、悲歌未徹。(The sad songs of heroes were endless.) 啼鳥還知如許恨, (If the crying bird had known such hatred,) 料不啼清淚長啼血。(it would have cried blood instead of tears.) 誰共我, 醉明月。(Who could accompany me drinking wine in the moonlight?)

This Tzu was composed in the order of "first guest and then master."   In terms of "guest," we can see that from the line containing 「綠樹」 (green tree) to the line with 「苦恨」 (hatred), the spring birds' crying is used to describe 「苦恨」 (hatred).   This is the first part of "knocking."   And then, from the line with 「算未抵」 (this was not as good as) to the line with 「正壯士」 (heroes), the emphasis is shifted to "men."   This indeed uses the technique of "first a flat beginning and then a sideways ending."[107]
The example of two ancient women and two ancient men are used to describe 「苦恨」 (hatred) of departure from the mundane world. This indeed hints that at that time the treason of certain subjects and the sacrifice of heroes made a vivid contrast.   In this way, the hatred of homes and the country finds expression.   This marks the feature of "striking."   Finally, the two lines with 「啼鳥」 (crying birds) returns to the "sideways" feature, using imaginative writing to

....

107 See Chen Man-ming, "On the Compositional Structure of Flat Beginning and Then Sideways Ending." *Essays on Rhetoric* 《修辭論叢》二輯(Taipei: Hungye Publishing Company, June 2000, first edition), pp. 193-214.

further describe the 「苦恨」 (hatred) of crying birds.　This marks the next feature, that of "knocking."　And in terms of "master," the two lines with 「誰共我」 (who could accompany me) to express his feelings of departure, putting the whole ending to an end. In this way, the endless hatred is wholly depicted.　Thus, the structure analysis diagram can be shown as follows.

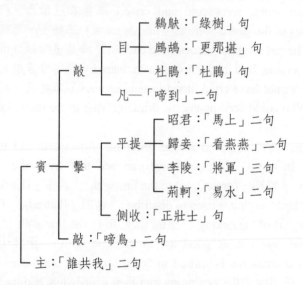

On the part of "guest," the composition is framed by the structure of "knock, strike, knock."

Take Chia yi's article, for example.

孝公既沒，(After Hsiaokung passed away,) 惠文、武、昭襄，蒙故業，(the kings—Huiwen, Wu, and Chaohsiang inherited what was his.) 因遺策，(Following his previous policies,) 南取漢中，(going south to take Hanchung,) 西舉巴蜀，(going west to conquer the two nations in Pashu,) 東割膏腴之地，(going east to occupy fertile lands,) 北收要害之郡。(going north to occupy areas of importance,) 諸侯恐懼，(the dukes, being afraid,)會盟而謀弱秦，(met together and planned how to sack the Chin nation.) 不愛珍器重寶肥饒之地，(Not loving valuable and precious things as well as fertile lands,) 以致天下之士，(using these to appeal to men of talent around the world,) 合縱締交，(they united to resist the Chin nation,) 相與為一。(forming a union.) 當此之時，(At that time) 齊有孟嘗，(in the Chi nation, there was Mengchangchun;) 趙有平原，(in the Chao nation, Pingyuanchun;) 楚有春申，(in the Chun nation, Chungshengchun;) 魏有信陵；(in the Wei nation, Hsinglinchun.) 此四君者，(These four persons)皆明智而忠信，(were wise and trustworthy,) 寬厚而愛人，(generous and affectionate,) 尊賢重士，(respecting good men and valuing talent,) 約從離橫，(and committed to resist the Chin's ambition to conquer all nations) 兼韓、魏、燕、趙、齊、楚、宋、衛、中山之眾。(by uniting the armies of the Han, Wei, Yen, Chao, Chi, Chu, Sung, Wei, Chungshan.) 於是六國之士，(Therefore, among the wise men of six nations) 有甯越、徐尚、蘇秦、杜赫之屬為之謀；(there were Ningyueh, Husshang, Suchin, Tuho, all of whom made plans;) 齊明、周最、陳軫、召滑、樓緩、翟景、蘇屬、樂毅之徒通其意；(Chiming, Chouchui, Chenchen, Chaohua, Louhuan, Tiching, Suli, Yuehyi, all of whom engaged in communication;) 吳起、孫臏、帶佗、兒良、王廖、田忌、廉頗、趙奢之倫制其兵。(Wuchi, Sunpin, Taito, Erhliang, Wangliao, Tienchi, Lienpo, Chaoshe, all of whom could lead armies.) 嘗以十倍之地，(Ten times the land of the Chin nation,) 百萬之眾，(millions of soldiers) 叩關而攻秦。(marched to Hankukuan to attack the Chin nation.) 秦人開關延敵，(When the people of the Chin nation opened Hankukuan to face their enemies,) 九國之師，(the armies of the nine nations) 逡巡遁逃而不敢進。(were so afraid, they fled.) 秦無亡矢遺鏃之費，(The Chin nations did not have to use any weapons) 而天下諸侯已困矣。(to frustrate the dukes of all the nations.) 於是從散約

解，(In this way, the coalition collapsed.) 爭割地而賂秦。(The dukes wasted no time in giving the Chin pieces of land as a bribe.) 秦有餘力而制其敝，(The Chin nation had maintained the strength to conquer its enemies.) 追亡逐北，(By its pursuit of the defeated armies,) 伏尸百萬，(millions of corpses piled up.) 流血漂櫓；(Bloodshed emerged in streams.) 因力乘便，(The Chin nation used an advantageous situation and timing.) 宰割天下，(Controlling the whole world,) 分裂河山，(separating the lands of all nations,) 強國請服，(strong nations were conquered.) 弱國入朝。(Weak nations became subjects) 施及孝文王、莊襄王，(until King Hsiaowen, King Chuanghsiang.) 享國日淺，(The days of these two kings were short.) 國家無事。(No major events took place throughout the nation.)

Following the first paragraph, this paragraph further depicts how powerful the Chin nation was.   From 「孝公既沒」(after Hsiaokung passed away) to 「北收要害」(going north to occupy areas of importance), the author directly depicts three kings of the Chin nation (King Huiwen, King Wu, and King Chaohsiang). After the death of Hsiaokung, thanks to 「蒙故業」(inherited what was his) and 「因遺策」(following his previous policies), the Chin nation achieved a lot by bullying the six nations.   This is the first part of "striking."   Second, from 「諸侯恐懼」(the dukes, being afraid) to 「叩關而攻秦」(marched to Hankukuan to attack the Chin nation), the author spared no efforts to describe how the six nations struggled to counter-attack the Chin nation.   First, two lines--「諸侯恐懼」(the dukes, being afraid) and 會盟而謀弱秦，(they met together and planned how to sack the Chin nation)—are used as a topic sentence.   And then from 「不愛珍器」(not loving valuable and precious things) to 「制其兵」(lead armies), strategies (unification), manpower (good prime minister, soldiers, advisers, envoys and generals), and real actions (attacking the Chin nation) are combined to manifest the unified power of the six nations. In this way, the author uses "indirect writing" rather than 「反襯」 (contrastive highlighting) to describe powerful Chin nation.[108] This is the feature of "knocking." And then, from 「秦人開關」 (when the people of the Chin nation opened Hankukuan) to 「弱國入朝」 (weak nations became subjects), the author changes his way of writing from the previous indirect writing to direct writing, strenuously depicting how the strength of the Chin nation led to her final victory. This is the feature of "striking."

....

108　Commonly speaking, critics saw this as "opposite highlighting." Wang Wen-ju, for example, makes comments on 「相與為一」 (becoming a union). "While intending to describe powerful Chin nation, the author points to dukes. This serves as an opposite highlighting." In addition, he made comments on 「尊賢而重士」 (respecting good men and valuing talents)—"The author highly appraises four prime ministers in order to indirectly highlight the strength of Chin nation." Furthermore, he made comments on 「趙奢之倫制其兵」 (Chaoshe all of whom could lead the armies)—"The author strenuously describes how dukes attained talents in order to reversely highlight the strength of Chin nation. Same as note 24, vol. 6, pp. 6-7. While making comments on the features of this article, Wang Keng-lin highlights "opposite highlighting."— "In the previous article, the author describes how the predecessors of Chinshihhuang occupied Kuangchung, overlooking the nations in Shangdung. The article starts by depicting the strength of the nations in Shangdung. " Judging from 『當是時....中山之眾』 ('uniting the armies..., Chungshan'), it can be seen that a lot of excellent politicians, diplomats, strategists offered advice and fought on the battlefield—"ten times the land of Chin nation, millions of soldiers, marched to Hankukuan attacking Chin nation." Despite their spacious land, many soldiers and talents, "when people of Chin nation opened Hankukuan to face their enemies, the armies of the nine nations were afraid and scared away." In this way, the writing gets more forceful than what is depicted directly. Likewise, when it comes to describing Chin nation, which was disintegrated overnight, the author also uses the skill of opposite highlighting." See *Evaluation and Appreciation of Ancient Literary Works*. 《古代文學作品鑑賞》 (Shanghai: Shanghai Ancient Books Publishing Company, March 1988, first edition), pp. 48-49.

Finally, the last three sentences serve to mention the rule of King Hsiaowen and King Chuangsiang in order to initiate the third paragraph connected with Chinshihhuang. In this way, it plays a role in connecting the different paragraphs. The semantic structure can be shown as follows.

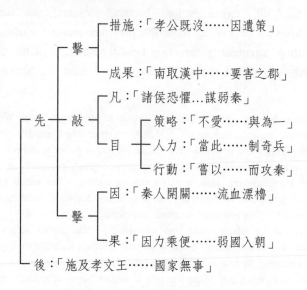

As for the feature of "before" in this paragraph, it forms the structure of "striking, knocking, striking."

The above-mentioned five methods of composition concern the logic of arranging paragraphs and constructing a composition. These rules, like those of other composition methods, exist not only in creatures and events but in universal psychologies, forming a long, invisible chain penetrating humans and things. Accordingly, the function of ordering, changing, linking and unifying makes of "psychology," phenomenon/works," and "aesthetics" a union. [109]

....
[109] According to the Binding Theory, a masterpiece could combine "Truth, Goodness, Beauty" and the "Author, Readers, and the Works" Various MA theises and Ph. D. dissertations deal with these topics. Seealso Chen, Manming's

The author, works, and readers are naturally unified. However, ordinary people (including authors) more often than not take it for granted. They usually mistake "composition art" for "man-made" bondage and neglect it. Therefore, it's urgent to make a comprehensive study of composition art in order to clear up these misunderstandings.

On theMajor Contents of the Arts of Expressions and composition: The New Design of the Arts of Composition.《章法學新裁》(Taipei: Wanchuanlou, 2001), pp.100-105.

Chapter **4**

Synthetic Contents of Structures of Lexical Composition

In terms of comprehensiveness, a 「辭章」 ci-zang's (lexical composition: expressions and composition) section structure mainly follows a section's topics and guidelines. In this chapter, the following issues will be discussed respectively in order: "topics and guidelines", "a topic's manifestation", and "the basic formats of arranging topics and guidelines".

I. Topics and guidelines

Many people tend to confuse a ci-zang's motif, creed, and contents due to the close relationships among them. Once in a Chinese Education seminar for high school teachers in the southern region, one attendee made such a mistake when discussing Fang Bao's article "The anecdotes of Zuo Zhong Yi Gong". The teacher thought the motif was about teacher-student relationships rather than "zhong yi". This is an example of mistaking partial content for the motif. In another discussion about "Compliments on Confucius Family", an attendee thought the motif was "Longing". This is an example of confusing creeds with the motif. Hereafter, we use the two abovementioned articles as examples, supplemented with a few other ci-zhang to illustrate the relationships among motifs, creeds, and content.

1. In terms of prose

First, we see "The anecdotes of Zuo Zhong Yi Gong".

My father once told me the story about Zuo Guang Dou visiting the capital city. That day, the weather was freezing with strong winds and snow. Zuo in plain clothes went out to do a tour of inspection, accompanied by a few escorts. They entered an ancient temple. There was a man lying prone on the desk. An article just written was on the desk. After Zuo read the article, he took off his coat and put it on the man. Zuo closed the door for him. After asking a monk in the temple, that man was Shi Ke Fa. At the exam, when calling Shi's name, Zuo gazed at Shi and when Shi turned in his exam, Zuo announced Shi the very best on the spot. Later when Shi was summoned to visit Zuo's wife, Zuo told his wife "Our sons all lack talents. This man is the only person who can assume my ambitions."

After Zuo was framed and sent to prison, Shi was lurking outside the prison everyday, but he could not gain access owing to the tight security. Even the servants could not get in. After a while, Shi heard Zuo was tortured and might die anytime. He brought gold and cried in front of the guards. The guards were moved so they let Shi enter the prison under disguise. Shi pretended to be a cleaner. After leading Shi into the prison, the guard pointed at Zuo's direction. Zuo was sitting on the ground. His face had been deformed beyond recognition. In his left leg, from knee down, it was all broken. Shi kneeled down and could not help crying. Zuo recognized his voice but could not open his eyes. Zuo strenuously lifted his arm and used fingers to prop open his eye. His eyes were filled with furious flames. He angrily chastised Shi, "Fool! You are not supposed to be here. The state is suffering from corruption and I am done. You are the only hope now. How can you take such risks and jeopardize your chance to contribute to the state? If you do not get out of here immediately, there will be no need for villains to frame you, for I will kill you right here right now!" While speaking, Zuo picked up a torture gadget on the ground and pretended to throw at Shi. She quited down and ran out. Afterwards, every time when Shi talked about this, he would shed tears and say, "My teacher's heart was made of stone."

In the last few years of chong zhen, an outlaw named Zhang Xian Zhong led his confederates and appeared in the areas of Gi, Huang, Gian, and Tong. Shi was defending at Fong Lu Dao. Everytime there was an alarm, Shi would give up sleep for months but have his soldiers take turns to get some rest. He would stay outside the tent. He only rest by leaning on two stronger soldiers' back. The soldiers could take turns. In cold nights, when he stood up, the ice on his armor would fall and make loud noise. Some people advised him to have some rest. He replied, "I do not want to fail my country, nor do I want to fail my teacher."

When Shi passed Zuo's home, he would definitely pay a visit to greet Zuo's parents and commemorate Zuo's wife.

According to Zuo's nephew, the words Zuo said to Shi in prison were from Shi's personal recount.

先以〈左忠毅公軼事〉一文來說：

先君子嘗言：鄉先輩左忠毅公視學京畿。一日，風雪嚴寒，從數騎出，微行，入古寺。廡下一生伏案臥，文方成草。公閱畢，即解貂覆生，為掩戶，叩之寺僧，則史公可法也。及試，吏呼名，至史公，公瞿然注視。呈卷，即面署第一。召入，使拜夫人，曰：「吾諸兒碌碌，他日繼吾志事，惟此生耳！」

及左公下廠獄，史朝夕窺獄門外。逆閹防伺甚嚴，雖家僕不得近。久之，聞左公被炮烙，旦夕且死，持五十金，涕泣謀於禁卒，卒感焉！一日，使史公更敝衣草屨，背筐，手長鑱，為除不潔者。引入，微指左公處，則席地倚牆而坐，面額焦爛不可辨，左膝以下，筋骨盡脫矣！史前跪，抱公膝而嗚咽。公辨其聲，而目不可開，乃奮臂以指撥眥，目光如炬，怒曰：「庸奴！此何地也，而汝來前！國家之事，糜爛至此，老夫已矣！汝復輕身而昧大義，天下事誰可支拄者？不速去，無俟姦人構陷，吾今即撲殺汝！」因摸地上刑械，作投擊勢。史噤不敢發聲，趨而出。後常流涕述其事以語人曰：「吾師肺肝，皆鐵石所鑄造也！」

崇禎末，流賊張獻忠出沒蘄、黃、潛、桐間，史公以鳳廬道奉檄守禦。每有警，輒數月不就寢，使將士更休，而自坐幄幕外，擇健卒十人，令二人蹲踞，而背倚之，漏鼓移則番代。每寒夜起立，振衣裳，甲上冰霜迸落，鏗然有聲。或勸以少休，公曰：「吾上恐負朝廷，下恐愧吾師也。」

史公治兵，往來桐城，必躬造左公第，候太公、太母起居，拜夫人於堂上。

余宗老塗山，左公甥也，與先君子善，謂獄中語，乃親得之於史公云。

This article was describing an anecdote about Zuo Guang Dou's "zhong yi" 「忠毅」. The text can be divided into three main components, including a prelude, main body, and aftermath.

In the prelude (i.e., the beginning), the story is mainly about how Zuo Guang Dou met and promoted Shi Ke Fa. The author spoke from his father's tone and pointed out it was when Zuo Guang Dou visited the capital city that he met Shi Ke Fa, which served as the onset of the following narrative. Then, the author used "one day" and "when the exam was over" to connect the timeline based on which the narrative described how Zuo Guang Dou met Shi Ke Fa and named him number one right on the spot at the exam, when he was doing a tour of inspection in plain clothes. The author stressed the weather was freezing with strong wind and snow, which implied Zuo Guang Dou's perseverance and fortitude, because normally officials would not do a tour of inspection in a weather like that. This was followed by "summoned" to lead to the parts about paying a formal visit to Zuo Guang Dou's wife. In this context, Zuo Guang Dou told Shi Ke Fa "all my sons lack talent", which betokened Zuo Guang Dou's high hopes on Shi Ke Fa, for he believed only Shi Ke Fa could assume his patriotism. This description vividly presented Zuo Guang Dou's aspiration for recognizing talents for the state.

The main body is in the next paragraph. This part is about Shi Ke Fa visiting Zuo Guang Dou, who had been framed and sent to prison. Because what happened could only be known to Shi alone, this anecdote therefore had to involve Shi in the story. In part, Sh was in the story due to his own "zhong yi" which could fortify Zuo Guang Dou's "zhong yi", but it is also because this anecdote could not have been witnessed by anyone other than Shi. The word "ji" served as a transition in the context. The first four sentences illuminate the facts that Zou was imprisoned and denied any contact with the outside world. Then, "jiou zhi" and "yi ri" described in an orderly manner the timeline where Zou was tortured to near death, Shi risked his life to bribe the prison guards, and then when Shi met Zou in prison, Zou was angry and chased away Shi. This is the main plot in this anecdote and it was portrayed impressively. With only a few words, the reader could already feel Zou's "zhong yi", and be touched by it. The last "hou" brought out Shi's emotional comments on Zou's worries about the state and fortitude.

In the aftermath, including the third, fourth, and fifth paragraphs, the author talked about in the third paragraph how Shi was affected by Zou and followed Zou's aspirations by defending outlaws with "zhong yi". In the following paragraph, it described how much respect Shi showed to his teacher's family to show Shi's virtues regarding "do his best" and "do what he is supposed to do". In the last paragraph it offered credibility to this story by stressing the source of the story, which corresponded to the beginning where it said "my father once told me". It provided a coherent ending.

In this article, the author used Zou's promoting Shi, Shi's risky visit in prison, and Zou's influence on Shi in terms of "zhong yi" as the content. The content was based on the creed "zhong yi", which was also the motif. In the context, the part describing Zou's "zhong yi" was primary, while Shi's "zhong yi" was secondary. This is to say when describing Shi's "zhong yi", the author was actually describing Zou's "zhong yi". This indirect complimenting was indeed superb finesse in writing.

Next, we move on to the article, "Compliments on Confucius Family".

According to Tai Shi Gong, in the book "Shi" it says, "people lift their head when seeing a tall mountain; people walk in it when there is a wide street." Although we could not get there, in our hearts, we are still admiring. I read Confucius' books and imagined his integrity. When I was in Lu, I went to visit Confucius' temple, vehicles, costumes, and music instruments. Students practiced social manners on time. See these, I did not want to leave. In the history, we have had quite a few monarchs and people of virtue. The glory they had while alive ended when they perished. However, Confucius was only a commoner, but he passed on his legacy to his offspring and it lasted for more than ten generations. All scholars respect him. From aristocrats to anyone who teaches "liou yi", they all rely on Confucius's moral standard to determine right and wrong. In this sense, Confucius should be considered a saint.

再看〈孔子世家贊〉一文：

太史公曰：《詩》有之：「高山仰止，景行行止。」雖不能
至，然心鄉往之。余讀孔氏書，想見其為人。適魯，觀仲
尼廟堂，車服、禮器，諸生以時習禮其家，余低回留之，
不能去云。天下君王至於賢人眾矣，當時則榮，沒則已
焉。孔子布衣，傳十餘世，學者宗之。自天子王侯，中國
言六藝者，折中於夫子，可謂至聖矣！[1]

This commentary adopted a structure including "fan" (overview),
"mu" (listing), and "fan" (overview). The first "fan" started from the
beginning of the article and ended at "we are still longing". It used
*"people lift their head when seeing a tall mountain; people walk in
it when there is a wide street."* to lead to "admiring" as the creed
which dictate the following text. The "mu" started from *"I read
Confucius' books"* and ended at *"rely on Confucius's moral standard
to determine right and wrong"*. In the three sections, it began with a
micro view and escalated into a macro perspective. First, it
mentioned *"I read Confucius' books"* and *"visit Confucius' temple"*
and these expressed his personal view on Confucius. Second,
"imagined his integrity" and *"I did not want to leave "* showed the
author's admiration toward Confucius, and it implied why
Confucius was listed as "shi jia". Finally, in the third section *"rely
on Confucius's moral standard to determine right and wrong"*
depicted how the intellects all rely on Confucius' standard. The last
"fan" included the last sentence *"In this sense, Confucius should be
considered a saint"* pointed out the motif and ended with coherence.

From the above discussion, it can be known that Tai Shi Gong's
this article was based on "admiring" as the creed. The content
contained the admiration toward Confucius from the author,

....

1 Wang Wen Ru's comments: See *Comments on Anthology of Ancient Prose.*《精
校評注古文觀止》 Volume 5 (Taipei: Taiwan Zhong Hua Publications 6th
edition, November 1972), p.8.

Confucian pupils, and the intellects. It set up a gradual escalation and consummated the admiration in terms of saint, which is the motif. Although the article is not long, it entails profound meanings. Therefore, the reader could not help admiring Confucius as well.

Li Si's "Jian Zhu Ke Shu" was also written based on a "fan" "mu" "fan" structure. The motif was illuminating the disadvantage of expulsion in an attempt to dissuade Qin Wang from expelling foreign guests.

I heard about officials were suggesting expelling all foreign guests in Qin, and I believe this will be a mistake.

When Qin Mu Gong searched for talents, he found You Yu in Xi Rong, redeemed Bai Li Xi from Dong Wan, invited Jian Shu from Song, and recruited Pi Bao and Gong Sun Zhi from Jin. All these five people were not born in Qin, but Qin Mu Gong valued them and put them in the right place. As a result, Qin Mu Gong was able to annex more than twenty countries and dominated Xi Rong. Qin Xiao Gong adopted Shang Yang's legal reform and changed Qin's customs. Qin people thus became more diligent and willing to work for the state's collective good because the state had been wealthier and stronger. Vassals all submitted to Qin. He also captured the troops of Chu Wei and occupied acres of land. Qin has remained a super power ever since. Qin Hii Wang used Zhang Yi's strategy and annexed San Chuan. In the west, they absorbed Ba Shu; in the north, they took over Shang Jun; in the south, they acquired Han zhong in the conquest of many savage tribes. They also controlled Yang Ying and the fort of Cheng Gao. They profited from productive lands and dismissed the six-nation-alliance. All vassals came from west to ingratiate Qin, and the merit is long-lasting until today. Qin Zhao Wang had Fan Suei as the prime minister. He abolished Rang Hou and exile Hua Yiang Juen. He expanded his sovereignty and prevented other factions to grow. The vassals' power was gradually being minimized. Hence, Qin established its kingdom. The aforementioned four monarchs all utilized help from outside Qin and achieved greatness. In light of this view, foreign guests did not do anything that hurt Qin. Had the four monarchs not denied foreign talents, Qin would have had no prosperity and reputation as it has now.

Now your majesty owns all kinds of treasure that did not originate from Qin but your majesty still cherish them. Why is that? If it must come from Qin to be useful, then all those treasures and gems should not have been displayed in the palace. Those beautiful women should not have been married. The foreign steeds should not have been raised in the staples. If all the decorations, clothes, and music must be Qin's, they should not have been allowed. Why did people listen to foreign music? It is only because it was fun and enjoyable. If that is the case with music, then how come when it comes to talents, we need to apply a different standard? Regardless of the qualifications and abilities, as long as you are not Qin, you should be expelled. If this is true, it means your majesty values beauty, music, gems, and treasures more than human talents. This is not the way to lead the world and gain control over vassals.

I heard that if the land is extensive, crops will be abundant. If a country is huge, there will be more people living in it. If a military force is formidable, the soldiers will be brave. Tai Shan is tall because it does not exclude any soil. A river is long because it does not choose streams. A king does not pick and choose his people and that is how his virtue can manifest. Therefore, no land should be excluded due to location, and no people should be left out due to nationality. When four seasons are all wonderful blessing will naturally ensue. This is how our ancestors could be invincible. Now, Qin seems to want to abandon its people and force them to assist the enemies. This will discourage talents from all places to come west to Qin. You might as well lend weapons to your rivals and send foods to opponents.

Many goods do not originate from Qin but they are still valuable. Likewise, many talents were not born in Qin but they are still loyal to Qin. It will be naïve to pray for safety when Qin is about to chase away foreign guests and have them enter the enemy's countries. This will only do harm to Qin's people. Inwardly, this is debilitating Qin; outwardly, this is antagonizing vassals.

他如李斯的〈諫逐客書〉一文：

> 臣聞吏議逐客，竊以為過矣。
> 昔繆公求士，西取由余於戎，東得百里奚於宛，迎蹇叔於宋，來丕豹、公孫支於晉。此五子者，不產於秦，繆公用之，并國二十，遂霸西戎。孝公用商鞅之法，移風易俗，民以殷盛，國以富彊，百姓樂用，諸侯親服，獲楚魏之師，舉地千里，至今治彊。惠王用張儀之計，拔三川之地，西并巴蜀，北收上郡，南取漢中，包九夷，制鄢郢，東據成皋之險，割膏腴之壤，遂散六國之從，使之西面事秦，功施到今。昭王得范雎，廢穰侯，逐華陽，彊公室，杜私門，蠶食諸侯，使秦成帝業。此四君者，皆以客之功。由此觀之，客何負於秦哉？向使四君卻客而不內，疏士而不用，是使國無富利之實，而秦無彊大之名也。
> 今陛下致昆山之玉，有隨和之寶，垂明月之珠，服太阿之劍，乘纖離之馬，建翠鳳之旗，樹靈鼉之鼓。此數寶者，秦不生一焉，而陛下說之，何也？必秦國之所生然後可，則是夜光之璧，不飾朝廷；犀象之器，不為玩好；鄭衛之女，不充後宮；而駿良駃騠，不實外廄；江南金錫不為用；西蜀丹青不為采。所以飾後宮，充下陳，娛心意，說耳目者，必出於秦然後可，則是宛珠之簪，傅璣之珥，阿縞之衣，錦繡之飾，不進於前；而隨俗雅化，佳冶窈窕，趙女不立於側也。夫擊甕叩缶，彈箏搏髀，而歌呼嗚嗚快耳者，真秦之聲也。鄭、衛、桑間，韶虞、武象者，異國之

樂也。今棄擊甕叩缶而就鄭衛，退彈箏而取韶虞，若是者
何也？快意當前，適觀而已矣！今取人則不然，不問可
否，不論曲直，非秦者去，為客者逐。然則是所重者在乎
色樂珠玉，而所輕者在乎民人也！此非所以跨海內，制諸
侯之術也！

臣聞地廣者粟多，國大者人眾，兵彊者則士勇。是以泰山
不讓土壤，故能成其大；河海不擇細流，故能就其深；王
者不卻眾庶，故能明其德。是以地無四方，民無異國，四
時充美，鬼神降福。此五帝三王之所以無敵也。今乃棄黔
首以資敵國，卻賓客以業諸侯，使天下之士，退而不敢西
向，裹足不入秦，此所謂藉寇兵而齎盜糧者也。

夫物不產於秦，可寶者多；士不產於秦，而願忠者眾。今
逐客以資敵國，損民以益讎，內自虛而外樹怨於諸侯，求
國無危，不可得也。

The first "fan" is the first paragraph. The author openly specified the motif so as to connect the following "mu" and "fan". [2]

The "mu" included the second, third, and fourth paragraphs. There were two angles in the second paragraph. First, starting from *"Qin Mu Gong searched for talents "* to *" foreign guests did not do anything that hurt Qin"*, it used counterproof to illustrate the success in the past when the monarchs, including Mu Gong, Xiao Gong, Hui Wang, and Zhao Wang, embraced foreign talents. It followed a chronological order. It used these successful examples to support the conclusion that foreign guests did not hurt Qin. In another section, a direct view opposing expulsion was proposed. It started from *"Had the four monarchs not denied foreign talents"* to *"Qin would have had no prosperity and reputation as it has now"*. In this section, the

2   Wang Wen Ru's comments: See *Comments on Anthology of Ancient Prose.*《精
    校評注古文觀止》Volume 4 (Taipei: Taiwan Zhong Hua Publications 6th edition,
    November 1972), p.43.

author used the subjunctive mood to specify the fault of expelling foreign guests. In the third paragraph, there was two sections: "tiao fen" started from "*Now your majesty owns all kinds of treasure*" to "*It is only because it was fun and enjoyable.*" In this section, he used Qin Wang's preference for exotic gems, instruments, beauty, and music as examples to illustrate his point that either goods or people they do not have to originate from Qin to be useful. Another section was "zong gua", starting from "*how come when it comes to talents, we need to apply a different standard?*" to "*This is not the way to lead the world and gain control over vassals.*" This section summarized the section "tiao fen" to further accentuate the fault of expulsion by emphasizing that appreciating treasures more than talents is not the way to dominate the world. In the fourth paragraph, again it included two sections containing opposite perspectives. In the indirect section, starting from "*I heard that if the land is extensive, crops will be abundant*" to "*This is how our ancestors could be invincible*", it pointed out the benefits of being inclusive and therefore implied the fault of expulsion. In the direct section, starting from "*Now, Qin seems to want to abandon its people and force them to assist the enemies*" to "*You might as well lend weapons to your rivals and send foods to opponents*", it pointed out when guests are expelled they will definitely turn to rival countries and become assets to fight against Qin. This is a direct argument asserting the fault of expulsion.

The last "fan" was the last paragraph. In this part, it concluded the third paragraph with "*Many goods do not originate from Qin but they are still valuable*" and then concluded the second paragraph with "*Likewise, many talents were not born in Qin but they are still loyal to Qin*". Finally, it concluded the fourth paragraph with the rest of the text to perfectly induce the motif of this article.

From the above analysis it is obvious this article's content was mainly about Qin Wang's favorite talents and treasures. It used both a direct and an indirect approach to illuminate the creed and motif, which resided in *"about officials were suggesting expelling all foreign guests in Qin, and I believe this will be a mistake"*. It provided pertinent evidence and the argument was reasonable. The wording was especially convincing enough to appease "officials" suggestions. Consequently, Qin Wang rescinded the ordinance of expulsion. This is a vivid example of how writing can be powerfully influential.

2. In terms of poetry

The following are three poems or ci「詞」.

獨有宦遊人，偏驚物候新。(Only the people traveling away from home would be so sensitive to the natural changes in the surroundings.) 雲霞出海曙，(The rosy clouds above the sea are glorious, which signifies the Sun is about to emerge.) 梅柳渡江春。(In Jiang Nan the flowers are already red and trees are green, but in Jiang Bei, spring has just arrived.) 淑氣催黃鳥，(The climate prompts orioles to sing), 晴光轉綠蘋。(and the warm sunshine turns apples greener.) 忽聞歌古調，歸思欲霑巾。(The old song sung by you triggers my nostalgic tears soaking my shirt.)

風乍起，吹皺一池春水。(Suddenly a pond of spring That is crinkled by wind)閒引鴛鴦芳徑裏，(Mandarin ducks are in a fragrant path leisurely playing)手挼紅杏蕊。(Rubbing the red apricot pistils in her hand)　鬥鴨闌干遍倚，(A fight between ducks after she alone leans on a railing) 碧玉搔頭斜墜。(Obliquely the jade hairpin is hanging)終日望君君不至，(Yet her husband's still no back though she misses him daylong)舉頭聞鵲喜。(Then she upholds her head to express joy when magpies singing)

明月別枝驚鵲，(Magpies are startled by the bright moonlight) 清風半夜鳴蟬。(Breezes bring over cicadas' cries)稻花香裏說豐年，(The fragrance of rice speaks for a bumper harvest)聽取蛙聲一片。(While frogs are singing along)　七八個星天外，(A few starts were up in the sky a moment ago)兩三點雨山前。(Suddenly rains are falling before the mountain)舊時茅店社林邊，(The old inn is still there by the woods)路轉溪橋忽見。(Walking past the creek, it shows up in sight)

The first poem is Du Shen Yan's "He Jin Ling Lu Cheng Zao Chuen You Uang". This poem's structure is "first fan then mu". The "fan" started from *"Only the people traveling away from home"* to lead to *"would be so sensitive to the natural changes in the surroundings"*, which was the creed of the entire poem. The creed organized three "lian". There were two parts in the "fan": "han" and "Jing" were the first part. These two "lian" described what was seen in the trip, which was in response to *"natural changes in the surroundings"* in the creed. The second part was "wei lian". *"The old song sung by you"* consisted with title which implies the author went on this trip with someone else. Then, *"triggers my nostalgic tears"* echoed with *"so sensitive"*, which was the motif of the poem—nostalgia. *"Soaking my shirt"* served as embellishment to paint a picture that is in contrast to *"the natural changes in the surroundings"*.[3] This is an excellent portrayal that will have people ponder.

The second article above is Feng Yan Si's "Ye Jin Men". This ci adopted a "first mu then fan" structure. The "mu" started from the beginning and ended at *"A fight between ducks after she alone leans on a railing"*. This was composed of three layers. The first layer

---

3   See Gao Bu Ing   *Major Tung Sung Poetry.* 《唐宋詩舉要》 (Taipei: Xue Hai Publications, 1st edition, Feb 1973), p.412.

contained the first two sentences. It described what "Wang Jun" saw before the pond. *"That is crinkled by wind"* accented the sorrow of *"Yet her husband's still no back"*. The next layer included *"Mandarin ducks are in a fragrant path leisurely playing"* and *"Rubbing the red apricot pistils in her hand"*, which depicted the situation when "Wang Jun" was in the path. *"Mandarin ducks"* was in contrast to loneliness. *"Rubbing the red apricot pistils in her hand"* further conveyed the sorrow of *"Yet her husband's still no back"*. The last two sentences were the "fan". *"Yet her husband's still no back though she misses him daylong"* concluded the "mu", and *"Then she upholds her head to express joy when magpies singing"* was meant to force the sorrow to appear so as to conclude the entire text. This is a typical example in which the motif was placed on the outside. It made the meaning even more profound.[4]

The third article was Xin Qi Ji's "Xi Jiang yue", also entitled "Ye Xing Huang Sha Dao Zhong". In this ci, the "shang pian" was used to describe all kinds of sounds he heard when walking down the "Huang Sha Dao" at night. It started with magpies, and cicadas, and then frogs. This was following a crescendo order. The "xia pian" was used to depict what he saw. At first, there were scarce stars, raindrops before the mountain, and then it was the inn before the creek. This is from far to near. Accordingly, the author outlined a picture of a quiet night in rural town. From outside this picture served as a foil character for the author's peaceful mind, which was the motif. This is so-called implicit connotation.[5]

Given the abovementioned three articles, the first one's motif was "nostalgia", from inside; the creed was *"would be so sensitive to the*

....

4 See Chen Man Ming, *A Walk in Tzu Forest*《詞林散步》 (Taipei: Wuan Juan Lou Publications 1st edition, January 2000), pp.48-50.

5 See Chen Man Ming, *A Walk in Tzu Forest*《詞林散步》 (Taipei: Wuan Juan Lou Publications 1st edition, January 2000), pp.326-328.

natural changes in the surroundings", and the content was a trip in early spring. The second article's motif was "sorrow", from outside; the creed was "*Yet her husband's still no back though she misses him daylong*", and the content was about the perceptions and actions while waiting for her husband to come back. The third one' motif and creed was "peace of mind", from outside; the content was about what he saw while walking the Huang Sha Dao at night. They were all different but all were artful in a unique way.

From the above examples, we can see that the gist an author tries to express could be the motif, or creed, or neither. The content while intimately connected with motif and creed, is not appropriate to be seen as the motif or creed. There is a saying goes "a miss is as good as a mile", so it requires caution when distinguishing motif, creed, and content.

II. Manifestation and concealment of topics

Ci-zhang's motif supposedly is the easiest part to recognize, because it is the idea the author is trying to convey. It is supposed to be made apparent. However, sometimes for practical reasons or for skillfulness, the author might hide the underlying meaning or the real motif and result in difficulty in telling the motif. Hence, ci-zhang's motifs could be illustrious or latent. Some of them are seemingly illustrious but not really. There is quite a variation. The following are a few instances for illustration.

1. Fully manifested topics

There are quite a few ci-zhang whose motifs are clearly stated. Based on the location of the placement, there are three types: heading placement, middle placement, and ending placement.

An example of heading placement is Li Si's "Jian Zhu Ke Shu" (analyzed in part 1 of this chapter). The author in this article started directly with "*I heard about officials were suggesting expelling all foreign guests in Qin, and I believe this will be a mistake*", which openly pointed out the motif, and to make this motif more convincing the author purposefully used the text to substantiate his viewpoint. He first in the second paragraph cited the instances of Miou Gong, Xiao Gong, Hui Wang, and Zhao Wang to illustrate how success could be achieved by using foreign talents, which served as an indirect view on the fault of expulsion. In the third paragraph, he used the treasures, instruments, gems, and beauties for examples to provide a direct view on the fault of expulsion. Finally the last paragraph echoed with the previous text and summarized the motif "it is wrong to expel foreign guests". Thus, the motif was clearly and sufficiently being manifested.

An example for middle placement is Du Fu's poem, "Wen Guan Jun Shou He Bei He Nan".

劍外忽傳收薊北，(I suddenly heard about the recovery of Ji Bei by the troops while I was in Jian Wai.) 初聞涕淚滿衣裳。(Upon hearing the surprising news, my tears have soaked my clothes.) 卻看妻子愁何在？(I turned around to take a look at my wife and noticed the misery that had been haunting this family was gone.) 漫卷詩書喜欲狂。(I packed up the books in a hurry, and almost became ecstatic.) 白日放歌須縱酒，(In the daylight I sang and drank at free will.) 青春作伴好還鄉。(It was just about time to go back to hometown in spring.) 即從巴峽穿巫峽，(Immediately we took a boat from Ba Xia through Wu Xia.) 便下襄陽向洛陽。(Following the river we arrived at Xiang Yiang and then turned to Luo Yiang.)

The motif of this poem is describing the ecstasy when hearing about the news that the troops have recovered He Bei He Nan. The author first described how he shed tears of joy when learning about the recovery. He used "suddenly"[6] and "surprising" to emphasize the unexpectedness so as to enhance the joy. *"My tears have soaked my clothes"* depicted the strength of delight, which set up for the following *"almost became ecstatic"*. Then, he moved the focus onto his wife and described how happy his wife was. Following *"turned around to take a look"*, *"the misery that had been haunting this family was gone"* induced the motif "ecstasy". *"Packed up the books in a hurry"* provided a behavioral portrayal. In the middle part, the description went abstract. He used *"I sang and drank at free will"* to connect with *"almost became ecstatic"*, and *"about time to go back to hometown"* to connect with "wife", which implied the intention to go home in spring. At the ending part, to be coherent with *"go back to hometown"*, it described the itinerary all the way. This adequately played up *"almost became ecstatic"*. In this way, from *"suddenly"* *"surprising"* *"to take a look"* and *"packed up the books in a hurry"* *"Immediately"* to *"arrived at"*, the author vividly depicted the ecstasy of his and his wife's. Wang You Zhong thought "every word in this poem is full of joy" (Li Dai Shi Ping Jie). This comment exactly grasped the feature of this poem, and this ecstasy was manifestly stated in the text.

Hu Shi's "Mu Qin De Jiao Hui" is an example for ending placement.

Everyday at dawn, my mother would wake me up and ask me to put some clothes on and sit up. I never knew how long she had been up sitting there. She waited for me to clear my head and then started telling me what I did or said wrong the day before. She would ask me to recognize the mistakes and ask me to study hard. Sometimes she told me about my father's merits. She said, "You shall follow

----

6   See Gao Bu Ing ,*Major Tung Sung Poetry.*《唐宋詩舉要》 (Taipei: Xue Hai Publications, 1st edition, Feb 1973), p.569.

your father's steps. In my whole life I only knew one perfect person and that is your father. You need to emulate him and cannot shame his good name." She would weep over sad memories. After the daylight fully emerged, she would have me get dressed and go to morning school. The key to the school's gate was kept in the teacher's house, so after seeing the closed gate I ran to the teacher's house and knocked. Someone in the teacher's house would pass on the key underneath the door. I took the key and ran back to school, opened the gate, and sat down to start reading books. Eight or nine out of ten days I would be the first one opening the gate. After the teacher arrived, I memorized new content in the books and then went home for breakfast. My mother disciplined me strictly. She is not only a kind mother but also plays the role of a demanding father. However, she never scolded me or punished me in front of people. If I did something wrong, she would stare at me. I would be awed by her harsh stare. If the mistake was not serious, she would wait until the next morning to reprimand me. If the mistake was huge, she would wait until late night and close the door to scold me first and then punish me. Sometimes the punishment involves pinching me, or kneeling. No matter what the punishment was, I was not allowed to sob. She disciplined her son not in order to impress anyone else.

In an afternoon in early autumn, I was playing around at the door after dinner. I was wearing only a vast. That time my mother's sister, aunt U Ying, was living in our house. She thought I might be cold so she took a blouse and asked me to put it on. "Put it on! It's getting cold", she said. I recklessly replied with "Cold? (the pronunciation is similar to "moamg" (mother) in Mandarin Chinese) I have even no father!!" No sooner had I said this than I saw my mother walking out of the house. I put on the shirt quickly but she already heard my talking back. That night after it was quiet outside she had me get down on my knees. She harshly criticized me. She said, "Your father is dead and this is not something you should use for a wisecrack."

She was so furious that she could not stop shivering while sitting there. I was not allowed to go to sleep. I was weeping while kneeling and I used my hands to wipe off the tears. Some bacteria entered my eye from my hands and caused me to suffer an eye disease for more than one year. No doctor seemed to know the cure. My mother was so worried and blamed herself. She heard this eye disease could be cured by licking with a tongue. One night she woke me up and really used her tongue to lick my eye. This is my demanding mentor and also my kind mother.

I lived with my mother's discipline for nine years and was deeply affected. I left her when I was fourteen years old. I survived in the crowds for twenty some years without anyone's restraints. If I have learned a tad of good temperament, or if I have learned a little friendliness, or if I could forgive people and be considerate, it should be attributed to my mother.

> 每天，天剛亮時，我母親便把我喊醒，叫我披衣坐起。我從不知道她醒來坐了多久了。她看我清醒了，便對我說昨天我做錯了什麼事，說錯了什麼話，要我認錯，要我用功讀書。有時候，她對我說父親的種種好處。她說：「你總要踏上你老子的腳步，我一生只曉得這一個完全的人，你要學他，不要跌他的股。」（跌股就是丟臉、出醜。）她說到傷心處，往往掉下淚來。到天大明時，她才把我的衣服穿好，催我去上早學。學堂門上的鎖匙放在先生家裏，我先到學堂門口一望，便跑到先生家裏去敲門。先生家裏有人把鎖匙從門縫裏遞出來，我拿了跑回去，開了門，坐下唸生書。十天之中，總有八、九天我是第一個去開學堂門的。等到先生來了，我背了生書，才回家吃早飯。
>
> 我母親管束我最嚴，她是慈母兼任嚴父。但她從來不在別人面前罵我一句，打我一下。我做錯了事，她只對我一望，我看見了她的嚴厲眼光，便嚇住了。犯的事小，她等到第二天早晨我睡醒時才教訓我。犯的事大，她等到晚上

人靜時，關了房門，先責備我，然後行罰，或罰跪，或擰
我的肉。無論怎樣重罰，總不許我哭出聲音來。她教訓兒
子，不是借此出氣叫別人聽的。

有一個初秋的傍晚，我吃了晚飯，在門口玩，身上只穿著
一件單背心。這時候，我母親的妹子玉英姨母在我家住，
她怕我冷了，拿了一件小衫出來叫我穿上。我不肯穿，她
說：「穿上吧！涼了。」我隨口回答：「娘（涼）什麼！老
子都不老子呀。」我剛說了這句話，一抬頭，看見母親從
家裏走出，我趕快把小衫穿上。但她已聽見這句輕薄的話
了。晚上人靜後，她罰我跪下，重重地責罰了一頓。她
說：「你沒了老子，是多麼得意的事！好用來說嘴！」她
氣得坐著發抖，也不許我上床去睡。我跪著哭，用手擦眼
淚，不知擦進了什麼黴菌，後來足足害了一年多的眼翳
病，醫來醫去，總醫不好。我母親心裏又悔又急，聽說眼
翳可以用舌頭舔去，有一夜她把我叫醒，真用舌頭舔我的
病眼。這是我的嚴師，我的慈母。

我在我母親的教訓之下住了九年，受了極大極深的影響。
我十四歲（其實只有十二歲零兩三個月）便離開她了。在
這廣漠的人海裏，獨自混了二十多年，沒有一個人管束過
我。如果我學得了一絲一毫的好脾氣，如果我學得了一點
點待人接物的和氣，如果我能寬恕人，體諒人，──我都
得感謝我的慈母。

This article consisted of two main components in terms of its structure.

First, the listing portion included the first three paragraphs.

1st paragraph: It adopted a narrative style to describe his everyday routine and his mother's expectation on him.

2nd paragraph: It served as a bridge between the first and the third paragraphs.

3rd paragraph: It used a realistic style to recall one event regarding his frivolous talk back and how he was punished for it and how much his mother was worried about his health.

Second, a conclusion was in the last paragraph. In this paragraph, the author first mentioned "*I lived with my mother's discipline for nine years and was deeply affected. I left her when I was fourteen years old. I survived in the crowds for twenty some years without anyone's restraints*" to stress that in more than thirty years of his life the only person who had ever disciplined him was his mother. This shows how much he was influenced by his mother. Then he used three IF to specify the motif, "*it should be attributed to my mother*", which shows his mother's greatness.

In this article, there was "demanding" and also "kindness". Nonetheless, the primary point was about "kindness" and "demanding" was secondary. Moreover, practically speaking, the author when writing this article had already transferred the "demanding" into today's "kindness". Thereby, the motif was really just "kindness". The author purposefully used the first and the third paragraphs to concretize kindness. Since the first paragraph was about morning and minor mistakes while the third paragraph was about night and big mistakes, they seemed to be independent. Thus, a second paragraph was used to connect the context. We can see that from "*My mother disciplined me strictly*" to "*she would wait until the next morning to reprimand me*", this section was responding to the first paragraph. The rest was connected to the third paragraph. The first half was linked to the previous paragraph, and the second half was connected to the following paragraph. This served as a decent transition.[7] All of the above descriptions were prepared for the last sentence "*it should be attributed to my mother*", which is the motif. This is quite obvious.

....

7 See Chen Man Ming, *The New Design of the Arts of Composition.* 《章法學新裁》 (Taipei: Wuan Juan Lou Publications 1st edition, January 2001), pp.44-46.

2. Manifested topics accompanied by concealed ones

Sometimes authors would conceal the true meaning of the motif, although seemingly the motif is manifest. It takes some effort to tell when trying to grasp this type of motifs.

In the article "Huang He Jie Bing Ji" written by Liou E, the motif was in the fifth paragraph.

Facing the view where snow and moonlight reflect each other, Lao Can thought of Xie Ling yun's poem: "the bright moonlight illuminates the snows; the northerly winds are vigorous and mourning". But for the people who had experienced the bleakness of the north, who would have known how pertinently the "mourning" was used in such a context?

"Mourning" in this text was the motif. The author used it to particularly summarize the bleak scenes depicted in the first four paragraphs. It also induced the pity in the last paragraph and hence cohered with the context throughout the article. This "mourning" was adopted from Xie Ling yun's "Sui Mu Shi", which is composed of six sentences as follows:

殷憂不能寐，(I was feeling so sad that I could not fall asleep)
苦此良夜頹。(I was agonized by this long night.)
明月照積雪，(The bright moonlight was illuminating the snows.)
北風勁且哀。(The northerly winds were rigorous and mourning.)
運往無淹物，(Time has never stop passing by)
年逝覺已催。(My time also elapsed and never comes back)

The author only adopted two sentences from this poem, but already captured the conception of the entire poem. For example, when describing Lao Can's affection while looking at the Wain, didn't the description match *"Time has never stop passing by; My time also elapsed and never comes back"*? At the end it said "Lao Can went back to the inn in the mopes, and fell asleep." Did Lao Can really fall asleep? Of course not, why? The answer could be found in *"I was feeling so sad that I could not fall asleep; I was agonized by this long night"*. The sad feeling was the same as in the mopes, and also was the morning of *"The northerly winds were rigorous and mourning"*. This is the motif of this article. What exactly was the author feeling sad about? What was the mourning about? Was it true he was simply depressed by his aging? To answer this question, we need to take a look at the following text.

I again thought about what was said in "Sho Jin": "In the north is the Ladle, but it lades our no liquor." Now the nation is being through a lot, the courtiers are just afraid of penalty, so they would rather pretend there is nothing happening. As a result, nothing is functioning properly. How is this going to end? If the national affairs are like this, how do people maintain their families?

This passage was originally seen in the last paragraph of the article, after "how will this end?" and before "thinking of this". From these words, it was clear the author was sad not only about himself, but also about the nation. That is why the author would link his own frozen tears with the frozen Huang He, and transform the frozen river back to people's tears. In line with this, it became clear why the author would describe squeezing ice in the second paragraph and banging on ice in the third paragraph. The shame is the editor of the textbook thought this passage was redundant and crossed it out. Consequently, the deeper meaning of the author's mourning was undetectable.[8]

....

8 See Wang Guo Wuei,《人間詞話刪稿》, "Ci Hua Cong Bian" five 《詞話叢

Also, as in Cui Hao's "Huang He Lou":

昔人已乘黃鶴去，(People from the past have left riding yellow cranes)此地空餘黃鶴樓。(The only thing left here is the empty Huang He Lou)黃鶴一去不復返，(Yellow cranes were gone and never came back)白雲千載空悠悠。(In a thousand years, there was only clouds floating in the air)晴川歷歷漢陽樹，(Under the sunshine, Han Yang can be seen clearly)芳草萋萋鸚鵡洲。(Along with the Ying Wu Zhou surrounded by luxuriant grass)日暮鄉關何處是，(After the Sun went down, where is my home town?)煙波江上使人愁。(It saddens me on the river covered with fog)

This poem's motif was "nostalgia" as specified at the end. This is quite obvious but the author used Han Yang, located in the northwest of Huang He Lou, to bring out Ying Wu Zhou, located in southwest of Han Yang. It implied some regrets. This is because when seeing Ying Wu Zhou, normally people would think of that underappreciated cocky hermit Mi Heng. According to "Hou Han Shu: Wen Wan Zhuan", Mi Heng showed his talent when he was young, but was very arrogant. He was recommended by Kong Rong but could not get along with Cao Cao and Liou Biao. Finally he died in the hands of Huang Zu. After Mi Heng died he was buried on a sandbank, and this sandbank was Ying Wu Zhou. In light of this, the author was comparing himself with Mi Heng in relation to the underappreciated talent. Perhaps some people would think such emotion is not consistent with nostalgia, but this is not true because these two feelings are actually closely related. That is why Du Fu's "Lu Ye Shu Hui" said "A man's reputation is not solely based on publications; public servants should retire only when they are old

編》五(Taipei: Xin Wen Feng Publications 1st edition, February 1988), p.4257.

and sick (resentment of being underappreciated); what is it really like being alone without dependence? It is like the gulls flying in the immense sky alone (nostalgia)". Liu Yong's "Ba Sheng Gan Zhou" also said "I am reluctant to look for home town from a high place, for my home town is already far away. It will be hard to stop missing it (nostalgia). I lament the past years. Why did I stay there for so long? (resentment)". From these examples, it is very natural to talk about the resentment of being underappreciated and nostalgia. In this sense, Cui Hao in this "Huang He Lou", besides expressing his nostalgic affection, also secretly conveyed his resentment for being underappreciated.

Another example is Su Xun's "Liou Guo Luen" in which the seeming motif was clarified in the very first paragraph.

The six-nation-alliance failed not because the weapons were not enough or the tactics were not good. The failure was because we were trying to make peace with Qin by submitting our lands. By doing so, we were diminishing our strength, and thus we failed. Some asked "The six nations all collapsed one after another. Is it all because trying to make peace with Qin by surrendering lands? I said, "Even though some nations did not do that, they were still conquered because of those who did so. When they lost strong support, they could not remain independent. Therefore, the root cause was still trying to making peace with Qin."

六國破滅，非兵不利，戰不善，弊在賂秦。賂秦而力虧，破滅之道也。或曰：「六國互喪，率賂秦耶？」曰：「不賂者以賂者喪。蓋失強援，不能獨完。故曰，弊在賂秦也。」

Here, when it said *"The failure was because we were trying to make peace with Qin by submitting our lands"* and *"Even though some nations did not do that, they were still conquered because of those who did so*", it was talking about the motif, also the argument. This argument was convincing due to the support by the second and third paragraphs where substantiated evidence was provided. However, the author stated at the last paragraph:

The six nations and Qin were all vassal nations. The six nations were not as powerful as Qin, but still had a chance to defeat Qin instead of trying to bribe Qin. If Qin, a nation that owns the whole world, ends up failing like the six nations, then Qin is even inferior to the six nations.

夫六國與秦皆諸侯，其勢弱於秦，而猶有可以不賂而勝之
之勢；苟以天下之大，而從六國破亡之故事，是又在六國
下矣。

He pointed out "*still had a chance to defeat Qin without trying to bribe Qin*". This is a reverse conclusion that served to elicit the deeper motif to mock Bei Song's peacemaking policy by bribing Qi Dan in his time. Lin Xi Zhong said "The real target was criticizing Bei Song's policy."[9] This is a rather correct interpretation. As the two aforementioned examples, this article's motif was seemingly manifest but its deeper meaning was hidden.

3. Fully concealed topics

It has always been true that ci-zhang is usually meant to be implicit and hides its motif between the lines. Therefore, it is vary common to see a motif hidden outside the text. Generally speaking, the ones that narrate a story or describe scenery largely belong to

....

9 See "Gu Wen Xi Yi He Bian" Volume 7 《古文析議合編》卷七(Taipei: Guang Wen Publications, reprint, October 1965), p.765.

this category, such as Wue Fei's "Liang Ma Dui". It was recording Wue Fei's responses to Song Gao Zong's inquiries, and Wue Fei's responses are the main body of the article. In this main body, Wue Fei analyzed the differences between good horses and bad horses in terms of the amount of food they eat, character, and performance. He thought good horses are:

They can eat a lot but rather picky on the foods. They are strong but don't show off, so they can run a long way.

此其受大而不苟取，力裕而不求逞，致遠之材也。

On the other hand, the bad horses are:

They don't eat much but they practically eat anything fed to them. They like to run very fast but get tired easily, so they are not dependable.

此其寡取易盈，好逞易窮，駑鈍之材也。

From this it seems Wue Fei was implicitly suggesting Song Gao Zong need to recognize good talents, use them properly, trust them, and cherish them. This implication resided completely outside the text, and was very easy to be absorbed. Also an example is the previously discussed article, Fang Bao's "The anecdotes of zuo zhong yi gong". The first paragraph was the prelude pertaining to Zuo's promoting Shi Ke Fa. It was a vivid depiction of Zuo's enthusiasm and devotion in finding talents for the nation. The second paragraph was the main body describing Zuo's imprisonment and Sho Ke Fa's risky visit. It adequately portrayed Zuo's fortitude and loyalty to the nation. The following three paragraphs were the aftermath. It started with Shi Ke Fa's being inspired by Zuo and followed Zuo's steps spending tough time defending outlaws, and then it talked about Shi's respect for his teacher's family. Then, it emphasized that the anecdote mentioned was based on a true story to echo with the beginning when it said "my father once told me". This method may appear to be discursive but the gist "zhong yi" was connecting the whole text from outside the text. It described both Zuo and Shi's "zhong yi" but Zuo's "zhong-yi" was primary, while Shi's "zhong yi" was auxiliary. This is to say, when talking about Shi's "zhong yi" it was actually talking about Zuo's "zhong-yi". Therefore, the motif of this article was Zuo's "zhong yi" but it was hidden outside the text. It could be overlooked without circumspection.

'The above two articles both use narratives to imply the motif. Some others use describing scenery to imply the motif, such as Li Bai's "Huang He Lou Song Meng Hao Ran Zhi Guang Ling".

故人西辭黃鶴樓，(My old friend left Huang He Lou in the west.)煙花三月下揚州。(In the blossoming spring and the foggy March, he went downstream to Yang Zhou.)孤帆遠影碧空盡，(The sail of the boat gradually disappeared in the green mountains.)惟見長江天際流。(The only thing can be seen was the Chang Jiang's water flowing toward the sky.)

There were two components in this poem. The first one was the narrative part, the first two sentences. It narrated the fact that an old friend was leaving Wu Chang and headed to Yang Zhou. The second component was the scenery, the last two sentences. It described the scene when the friend's boat was moving away and disappeared at the edge where the water connected to the sky. The author used an event to induce scenery, and used the scenes to link Wu Chang and Yang Zhou from outside. This showed the reluctance to part with his friend. Tang Ru Xuen said, "*Huang He Lou, a place for part ways;*

Yang Zhou, a place people are headed to. Blossoming spring was the background of departure; March was the time of departure. When the sail has reached out of sight, the long river water symbolized how much missing was. The reluctance was nonverbal." The last sentence points out the prominent feature of this poem's hidden motif.

From the above discussion, we know ci-zhang's motifs could be manifest or concealed, so it has to be examined carefully. When teaching or interpreting ci-zhang, if we can understand the purpose of each paragraph combined with the understanding on the writing skills, it should not be too hard to grasp the in-depth meaning of ci-zhang.

III. Several basic types of arranging topics or guidelines

Every ci-zhang writer, either in the past or contemporary, would want to use words to vent when their thoughts and opinions have accumulated to the tipping point. When they are using words to vent their ideologies, the first problem they encounter is the arrangement of the motif and creed. The arrangements, although subjected to the author's idiosyncratic creativity, share some common types, in terms of location.

1. Placed in the beginning

This type of arrangement is placing the motif (creed) at the beginning of the article. It serves as an overview and then according to the motif (creed), divides the remaining part into several portions in order. This type, in terms of the structure, was called "wai liou" in the past, and called "yan yi" nowadays. It is very common in many written works, such as poems, ci, or essays, due to its straightforwardness.

Poems:
Zu yong's "Su Shi Bie Ye"

別業居幽處，(Su Shi's villa is located in a secluded place.)到來生隱心。(People after coming here usually would start considering isolation.)南山當戶牖，(Zhong Nan Shan is right outside the windows)灃水映園林。(Feng Shui surrounds the grove)竹覆經冬雪，(The snow that has not thawed yet is still on top of the bamboos.)庭昏未夕陰。(It's not yet twilight but it has got darker in the yard.)寥寥人境外，(Very few people are around here, so it is very quiet.)閑坐聽春禽。(We can soothingly sit here and listen to birds' chirping in spring.)

Li Bai's "Xie Gong Ting"

謝公離別處，(This is the place where Xie Gong left)風景每生愁。(Every time I see it, I miss the old times.)客散青天月，(The poets all left and the only thing left is the bright moon)山空碧水流。(In the mountains it is bleak and the water keeps flowing.)池花春映日，(The flowers blossom and then wither under the Sun)窗竹夜鳴秋。(The bamboos outside the windows are quietly making sounds.)今古一相接，(Imaging the past and today are connected)長歌懷舊遊。(As if Xie Gong's traces resonate with me)

Du Fu's "Deng Lou"

On the top of the tower, the view is picturesque, but after all these years in wartime, I only feel pity and the view only makes it more desolate. The water of Jin Jiang reflecting spring scenery makes the earth colorful. The clouds floating around U Lei Mountain symbolize the vicissitudes over time. Our dynasty is steadfast. Those outlaws from the west do not even think about invading us. Although Liou Chan was not a good monarch he still made his way into a memorial temple. Our monarch now is as incompetent as Liou Chan but we do not have someone like Zhu Ge Liang to help him. I can only chant "Liang Fu In" to entertain myself, even though I have Zhu Ge Liang's aspiration.

花近高樓傷客心，萬方多難此登臨。錦江春色來天地，玉壘浮雲變古今。北極朝廷終不改，西山寇盜莫相侵。可憐後主還祠廟，日暮聊為〈梁甫吟〉。

The first of the three poems was about "isolation". The author in shou lian specified the motif (creed) right away, "secluded place" and "isolation". Then in Han lian and jing lian following the first sentence of qi lian, he described Su Shi villa's secluded environment. Then the Wei lian connected to the second sentence in qi lian to concretely depict "isolation". The second poem is about missing the old times. As the first poem, this piece specified the motif *Every time I see it, I miss the old times* right at the beginning. The it used two sentences to describe the scene in the past, and another two sentences for the scene at present time. *"Imaging the past and today are connected"* connected the context and induced *"As if Xie Gong's traces resonate with me"* to echo with *"miss the old times"*. The third poem is about worrying about the current political situation. At the beginning the author laid out the motif by reversing the causality. The third and fourth sentences then depicted what he saw on the high ground. The fifth and sixth sentences described *"all these years in wartime"*. Finally he in wei lian expressed his worries about no talents being appreciated in the nation. The meaning was very profound. These poems obviously all point out the motif (creed) at the beginning, and then follow the organization to describe it. It is called "Gang Ju Mu Zhang" and it is highly organized.

Ci (A poem, e. g.):

Wei Zhuang's "Pu Sa Man"

The night I left her was hard to bear. I still remember the decorations in her room. When the moon started to fade, I departed. She said good bye with tears. The pipa decorated with feathers was there. The orioles were singing. She asked me to come home early. By the window, she looked like a flower.

> 紅樓別夜堪惆悵，香燈半掩流蘇帳。殘月出門時，美人和淚辭。　琵琶金翠羽，絃上黃鶯語。勸我早歸家，綠窗人似花。

Fong Yan Si's "Die Lian Hua"

Who says time heals everything? Every spring, I still feel disconsolate. It is hard not to drink alcohol because the short-lived flowers remind me of sadness. The person in the mirror is getting thinner and thinner, but I could not help it. On the riverbanks there is green meadow and the willow trees are flickering by the wind. The old worries have been discarded but new ones keep coming. How come this happens every year? I stand on the bridge alone, and the chilly winds are fluttering my sleeves. The crescent moon on top of the trees is moving toward and people have all gone home.

> 誰道閑情拋棄久，每到春來，惆悵還依舊。日日花前常病酒，不辭鏡裏朱顏瘦。　河畔青蕪堤上柳，為問新愁，何事年年有？獨立小橋風滿袖，平林新月人歸後。

Zhou Bang Yan's "Liou Chou. Qiang Wei Xie Hou Zuo"

It is time to change winter clothes, but pitifully I am not at home and see time passing by fast. I beg for spring to stay a little longer, but spring is disappearing quickly like a bird. Where are the roses now? The heavy rain and strong wind last night buried all the pretties. Petals scatter on the ground like a beauty's hairpin falling on the floor. The fragrance still lingers. They roughly embellish the small path and flying gently in the alley of yang liou. Are there any sentimental people taking pity on the fallen flowers? Only bees and butterflies occasionally knock on the windowsills to pass on the affection like a matchmaker.

It is extremely quiet in Dong Wan. The plants are gradually flourishing and create a shadow that blocks light and shines green. They embrace the precious roses and constantly sign. The roses stretch out their long twigs to hook passengers' clothes as if they are pulling the collar looking for messages. The view shows infinite parting feelings. I picked up a small flower and barely pin it to my hood. It is not at all like a fresh flower on a beauty's hairpin that flickers and leaning toward people. Roses, don't float away through the tides. Perhaps the broken petals still have missing written on them. How could we tell?

正單衣試酒，悵客裏、光陰虛擲。願春暫留，春歸如過翼，一去無跡。為問花何在？夜來風雨，葬楚宮傾國。釵鈿墮處遺香澤，亂點桃蹊，輕翻柳陌。多情為誰追惜，但蜂媒蝶使，時叩窗槅。東園岑寂，漸蒙籠暗碧。靜繞珍叢底，成嘆息。長條故惹行客，似牽衣待話，別情無極。殘英小、強簪巾幘，終不似、一朵釵頭顫裊，向人欹側。漂流處、莫趁潮汐。恐斷紅、尚有相思字，何由見得。

Xin Qi Ji's "Zhe Gu Tian: You Gan"

We were all born different. Chou Wen Wang found Jiang Tai

Gong and let him in the back seat of the cart. Therefore Chou's dynasty lasted for a long time. However at the same time, there were Buo Yi and Zhu Qi who hid in the mountain and would rather starve to death than be involved in politics.

People have different ambitions. Some strive for fame and wealth, while others freely live a casual life.

出處從來自不齊。後車方載太公歸；誰知寂寞空山裏，卻有高人賦采薇。　黃菊嫩，晚香枝，一般同是采花時。蜂兒辛苦多官府，蝴蝶花間自在飛。

The first ci is about the resentment of parting. Its motif *"The night I left her was hard to bear"* was made clear at the beginning. Then it described the place and the ambience. It used the beauty's words and pipa to induce the reluctance to leave, which makes the reader feel the same way.

The second ci was about the sentiment in spring. The author started with a rhetorical question, and relying on the answer to point out the motif *"I still feel disconsolate"*. The following sentences although seemed to be about drinking and getting thinner, also centered on "disconsolate", because drinking and getting thinner were exactly the result of feeling disconsolate. In the second half of the ci, it transformed views into sentiments. It was quite distinct that it was still about feeling disconsolate. It simply used a different perspective. In the last two sentences it further described the author's standing alone and being disconsolate under the moon. The meaning was profound by means of transforming the view into sentiments.

The third ci is using the fallen flowers as a metaphor for regretting wasting time. It was fairly lengthy but was divided into only two sections. In the first half, the author quickly pointed out the motif *"but pitifully I am not at home and see time passing by fast"*, followed by the description of the withering of the roses to infer *"spring is disappearing quickly like a bird"*. Then it used the bees and butterflies' *"occasionally knock on the windowsills"* to imply no one cares. It ended at the "pitifully". In the second half, it first used two sentences to connect the *"spring is disappearing quickly"*, describing the quiet phenomenon after roses fell. Then, the following sentences were connecting to *"Are there any sentimental people taking pity on the fallen flowers?"*. It was about a poet after seeing a view started becoming sentimental. At last, it likened flowers' falling to it's drifting. The author used this story to show his genuine concern about wasting time in a strange land. It is so touching.[10]

The last ci was about the fact that people were not born the same. In this ci, *"We were all born different"* revealed the creed, and then according to this creed, it cited three examples to back it up. In the first example, Tai Gong was entering politics, which is "out", whereas Buo Yi and Zhu Qi were hidden, which is "in". This is the difference in humans. In the second example, chrysanthemums started to blossom, which is "out", while wan xiang was withering, which is "in". This is the difference in plants. In the third example, bees worked hard, which is "out", while butterflies were carefree, which is "in". This is the difference in insects. In this organization where the overview comes first and then systematically listing the content, the motif would be especially recognizable, just as the other three ci mentioned above.

Prose:
    "Zuo Zhuan: Cao Gui Luen Zhan"

....
[10] See Chen Man Ming, *A Walk in Tzu Forest* 《詞林散步》 (Taipei: Wuan Juan Lou Publications 1st edition, January 2000), pp.234-236.

The spring in Lu Zhuang Gong's tenth year, Ci's army was invading Lu. Lu Zhuang Gong prepared to engage in the battle. Cao Gui asked for a meeting. His fellow townsmen said, "There are a bunch of people with high ranking and wealth, why do you want to be involved?" Cau Gui replied, "Powerful people tend to be nearsighted and lack knowledge. They cannot be discreet." So, he went on to visit Lu Zhuang Gong. Cao Gui asked, "What are you counting on to fight this war?" Zhuang Gong answered, "When I had clothes or foods, I did not keep them to myself. I always shared them with my subordinates." Cao Gui said, "These small favors never reached the general public, so they will not listen to you." Zhuang Gong said, "I never lied to the God I worship, I always honestly told God what I had" Cao Gui said, "This small amount of sincerity is not enough to earn God's blessing." Zhuang Gong said, "When investigating either big cares or insignificant ones, even if I had no specialty in it, I always follow the evidence." Cao Gui said, "This is about doing your job right. You may rely on this quality to fight this war. Please allow me to go with you when fighting the war."

Zhuang Gong sat in the same cart with Cao Gui. Lu's troops and Ci's troops met in Chang Shao. When Zhuang Gong was about to signal battle by drumming, Cao Gui said, "Not yet." After Ci's troops drummed three times, Cao Gui said, "Now it's the time." The outcome was Ci's troops were heavily defeated. Zhuang Gong planned on pursuing, Cao Gui said, "No!" He then left the cart to inspect the trail marks left by Ci's troops, and climbed high to survey Ci's troops. He now said, "Let's go!"

After triumphing over Ci, Zhuang Gong asked about why Cao Gui did what he did. Cao Gui replied, "Winning a battle depends on courage. The first time they drummed, the courage was full. The second time they drummed, the courage diminished, and the third time, it was gone. Their courage was gone, but ours was exuberant.

That is how we beat them. Ci was a powerful country, so it was hard
to predict. I was afraid they might have set up ambush. After I saw
their trails were messy and their flags were down, I knew it was
okay to pursue."

十年春，齊師伐我，公將戰。曹劌請見，其鄉人曰：「肉
食者謀之，又何間焉？」劌曰：「肉食者鄙，未能遠
謀。」遂入見。
問何以戰？公曰：「衣食所安，弗敢專也，必以分人。」
對曰：「小惠未遍，民弗從也。」公曰：「犧牲玉帛，弗敢
加也，必以信。」對曰：「小信未孚，神弗福也。」公
曰：「小大之獄，雖不能察，必以情。」對曰：「忠之屬
也，可以一戰。戰則請從。」
公與之乘，戰於長勺。公將鼓之，劌曰：「未可。」齊人
三鼓，劌曰：「可矣。」齊師敗績，公將馳之，劌曰：「未
可。」下視其轍，登軾而望之，劌曰：「可矣。」遂逐齊
師。
既克，公問其故，對曰：「夫戰，勇氣也。一鼓作氣，再
而衰，三而竭。彼竭我盈，故克之。夫大國難測也，懼有
伏焉；吾視其轍亂，望其旗靡，故逐之。」

This article was centered on one main gist, "providence". There
were four paragraphs in the article. The first paragraph described
Ci's troops invaded Lu and Cao Gui's meeting with Zhuang Gong.
The fellow townsmen's question led to the creed of this article,
"providence".[11] The second paragraph through the conversations
between Cao Gui and Zhuang Gong explained what could be

....

11 Wang Wen Ru's comments. See *Comments on Anthology of Ancient Prose*.《精
校評注古文觀止》(Taipei: Taiwan Zhong Hua Publications 6th edition,
November 1972), p.21.

counted on to win the war, which was "doing your job right", rather than "small favors" or "insignificant sincerity". This attested to Cao Gui's providence even before the war started. The third paragraph was about how Cao Gui commanded the troops. Through two instances (drumming after Ci had drummed three times and observing before pursuing), it showed his providence during the war. In the last paragraph, it supplemented the description with the inquiry from Zhuang Gong so as to explain the reasoning of Cao Gui's decisions. Apparently, "providence" was the key word throughout the text. The author used the actual history, such as "*The spring in Lu Zhuang Gong's tenth year*", "*troops met in Chang Shao*", and "*Ci's troops were heavily defeated*" to account for the temporal background. He wove in the dialogues between Cao Guei and his fellow townsmen and Zhuang Gong. Cao Gui was the center and others served as an inducer to illuminate that Lu was able to defeat Ci due to Cao Gui's providence. This is a very neat and efficient arrangement.

Another example would be Lu You's "Ba Li Zhuang Jian Gong Jia Shu"

When Li Guang was fired from his position as 'can zheng', I was twenty years old. He often visited my father at home, and two of them would discuss politics all day. When mentioning the treacherous Qin Kuai, they would use the demeaning term 'Xian Yiang' instead. The disgust and indignation were all reflected on their expressions.

One morning, he came to my home and had breakfast together. He told my father "I heard the prime minister Zhao Ding was framed by Qin Kuai and was exiled to Hai Nan. He was so sad and cried when passing Nan Ling. If I were him, I would not cry. If the government wanted to exile me, I would take off right away. How can I let my children see me cry?" When he was saying this, his eyes were sparkling and his voice was orotund. The fortitudinous attitude was inspiring. After forty years, when I read Li Guang's letters, I found his attitude had not changed at all, although he was exiled to a remote island. Every word he said to his family was lived up to and is worth passing onto the next generation as an exemplar. From his writing, I could imagine the scene where he put up shoes and got on road without hesitation.

又如陸游〈跋李莊簡公家書〉：

> 李丈參政罷政歸鄉里，時某年二十矣。時時來訪先君，劇
> 談終日，每言秦氏，必曰咸陽，憤切慨慷，形於色辭。
> 一日平旦來，共飯，謂先君曰：「聞趙相過嶺，悲憂出
> 涕；僕不然。謫命下，青鞋（鞋）布襪行矣，豈能作兒女
> 態耶！」方言此時，目如炬，聲如鐘，其英偉剛毅之氣，
> 使人興起。
> 後四十年，偶讀公家書，雖徙海表，氣不少衰，丁寧訓戒
> 之語，皆足垂範百世，猶想見其道「青鞋（鞋）布襪」時
> 也。

This article started with Li Guang's returning to home town and met with the author's father. It delicately brought up *"The disgust and indignation were all reflected on their expressions"* as the creed. Then he contrasted what he saw when he was twenty years old with what he read about Li Guang when he was sixty years old to illustrate Li Guang's integrity and fortitude that were exemplary. The section about *"heard the prime minister Zhao Ding was framed"* was to describe the indignation through words. The section about *"his eyes were sparkling"* was to describe the indignation through expressions. The "mu" followed "fan" and was connected by one motif. This was indeed a vivid description.[12]

2. Placed at the end

This type is describing the content first according to the motif (creed) and then at the end to specify the motif (creed). This is called "nei liou" (conduits) in the past and "induction" in contemporary. Because it has the advantage to entice the reader to read more, it is also commonly seen in poems, *ci,* or prose.

Poems:

Li Bai's "Deng Jin Ling Feng Huang Tai"

鳳凰臺上鳳凰遊，(There were once phoenixes staying in Feng Huang Tai.)鳳去臺空江自流。(Now phoenixes were gone and this empty platform is accompanied by the never-ending flow of the river.)吳宮花草埋幽徑，(The once magnificent palace and plants are all buried in this deserted path.)晉代衣冠成古丘。(Those officials in Jin dynasty are now merely dust and dirt under the tombstones, even though they all once owned eminent achievements.)三山半落青天外，(I stand on the platform looking at the three mountains from a distance. They are still standing tall.)二水中分白鷺洲。(Bai Lu Zhou divides Qin Huai He into two courses.)總為浮雲能蔽日，(The clouds in the sky sometimes block the Sun.)長安不見使人愁。(Hence I could not see Chang An, and it makes me worried.)

Du Fu's "Qu Jiang"

A petal is falling and it signifies spring is leaving. The petals flying by the wind induce sentiments. I can only watch the withering flowers being blown away. Stop being sentimental. Let's drink! The tomb has been deserted for a while and the stone qi lin is lying on the ground. If the changes in the surroundings are like this transient, we should have fun now. Why are we binding ourselves with some unpredictable fame?

> 一片花飛減卻春，風飄萬點正愁人。且看欲盡花經眼，莫
> 厭傷多酒入脣。江上小堂巢翡翠，苑邊高塚臥麒麟。細推
> 物理須行樂，何用浮榮絆此身？

Su Shi's "He Liou Dao Yuan Yong Shi"

Confucius traveled around many countries because he was worried for the people, while Jie Yu was a crazy manic. Cang and Gu were two very different individuals but they both had their goats killed. Lu Gi wrote "Hao Shi Fu" to promote his merit, while Ue Ren was misunderstood. Being famous and being unknown are not that different if no one could tell who is real. Good and bad are getting harder to tell, and there have been so many successes and failures in the history that are no longer being remembered.

> 仲尼憂世接輿狂，臧穀雖殊竟兩亡。吳客漫陳〈豪士
> 賦〉，桓侯初笑越人方。名高不朽終安用，日飲無何計亦
> 良。獨掩陳編弔興廢，窗前山雨夜浪浪。

    The first passage mentioned above was about reminiscence. Like the first article, it started with introducing Feng Huang Tai and "*Now phoenixes were gone and this empty platform*" implied grief which was connected to the "worry" at the end. In the following sentences it used *"once magnificent palace"* and *"officials in Jin dynasty"* to release the sentiment regarding reminiscing the ancients. At the end, *"Hence I could not see Chang An, and it makes me worried"* pointed out the motif "worry".

The second article was about living in the moment. The author first used the decay with respect to the flowers, the tomb, and the stone qi lin to insinuate nothing lasts forever, so we should seize the moment and have fun. Then, *"If the changes in the surroundings are like this transient, we should have fun now"* summarized the previous text, and came to the conclusion *"Why are we binding ourselves with some unpredictable fame"*. It precisely encompassed the gist of the whole article.[13]

The third article was about reminiscing the past and worrying about today. The author compared and contrasted several stories and expressed the motif at the end. Just like the other three articles, this ending added the finishing touch.

Ci:

Feng Yan Si's "Die Lian Hua"

The green trees lean on the railings. The breeze pulls up the willow twigs. Suddenly the zither's melody come through, and swallows flies out of the window.

Everywhere I see, I see the flowers and a shower falls. When I was asleep the warblers' chirping awakened me, and I could not find back my sweet dreams.

> 六曲闌干偎碧樹。楊柳風輕，展盡黃金縷。誰把鈿箏移玉柱，穿簾燕子雙飛去。　滿眼游絲兼落絮。紅杏開時，一霎清明雨。濃睡覺來鶯亂語，驚殘好夢無尋處。

----

13 See Gao Bu Ing, *Major Tung Sung Poetry.*《唐宋詩舉要》(Taipei: Xue Hai Publications, 1st edition, Feb. 1973), p.557.

Yan Shu's "Wan Xi Sha"

A swallow flies through the curtain. It is time for flowers to wither and fall on the grass in the yard. The reflection of the railings around the pond is in the cold water's ripples.

A breeze pulls the curtain and light rain falls on the lotus leaves. After sobering up and people are leaving, loneliness starts to come.

小閣重簾有燕過，晚花紅片落庭莎，曲闌干影入涼波。
一霎好風生翠幕，幾回疏雨滴圓荷，酒醒人散得愁多。

Zhou Bang Yan's "Rui Long Yin"

In the place where houses of ill fame gather, I see the wither pistils in plum trees, but the peach trees just blossom. It is still early so the houses of ill fame are still closed and quiet. Only some familiar swallows fly here to build a nest. I stand here sentimentally because I thought of the obsessed girl. She peeked at me from outside the door. In the morning she put on makeup and waving her long sleeves. She giggled.

I came back here and inquired about that girl from the neighbors, but the person dancing with her only remembered Qiou Niang's name and her price then. I pick up a pen to write ci. I still remember what I wrote to her back then. Who can keep me company now and have fun in the garden and walk in Dong Chan? Everything has changed. The past is gone with the lonely big bird. This trip only gives me sorrows. The willows outside are hanging like golden threads. In twilight I ride a horse to go back. It drizzles at the pond. I am in this yard that saddens me watching the rain through the curtain

章臺路，還見褪粉梅梢，試花桃樹。愔愔坊陌人家，定巢燕子，歸來舊處。　黯凝佇，因念箇人癡小，乍窺門戶。侵晨淺約宮黃，障風映袖，盈盈笑語。

前度劉郎重到，訪鄰尋里，同時歌舞，惟有舊家秋娘，聲價如故。吟箋賦筆，猶記〈燕臺〉句。知誰伴，名園露飲，東城閑步，事與孤鴻去。探春盡是、傷離意緒。官柳低金縷，歸騎晚，纖纖池塘飛雨。斷腸院落，一簾風絮。

Xin Qi Ji's "Qing Ping Yue: Ti Shang Lu Qiao"

清泉奔快，不管青山礙。(The stream water is running fast, despite the impediment of the mountains.)十里盤盤平世界，更著溪山襟帶。(It is a ten-mile long circuitous long road protected by the rivers and mountains.)　古今陵谷茫茫，(Since ancient time, life's ups and downs have been common.)市朝往往耕桑。(Very often those once important people ended up farming in country.)此地居然形勝，似曾小小興亡。(This place is at a vantage point but still seems to have failed stories.)

The first ci was about shocking decay. It talked about how the wind "shocked" the willows and the zither "shocked" the swallows. Then it described the scenery which implies decay. *"When I was asleep the warblers' chirping awakened me"* induced *"I could not find back my sweet dreams"*. It echoed with the precious description of decayed scenes. The view coupled with the feeling render the readers the sense of "shocking decay".

The second ci was about sentiments. The motif was in the last sentence *"After sobering up and people are leaving, loneliness starts to come"*. The sentiment described here is fairly abstract, so the author reflected it on what could be seen. First, it was the swallow and then is the fallen flowers, and the reflection of the railings, followed by the breeze. Finally, it was the drizzle fallen on the lotus leaves. From near to far, to the author who just got sober, every one of them added some sentiment. No wonder he had so many sentiments.

The third one was about the sadness about leaving. This piece consisted of three parts. In the first part the author used what he saw when coming back to his childhood place to specify the location and time. In the second part, he used *"I stand here sentimentally"* as a transition to induce *"I thought of"* to echo with *"I see"* in the first part. Also, it led to the following description of the first time when he met the girl. He described the girl's makeup, dress, and mannerism in detail, which prepared for the last part. The last part was the conclusion and the ci's gist. The author used *"I came back here"* to connect to the first part, comparing himself with Liou Lang and the sadness of not knowing where she went. Then he went on to describe the things about he and the girl's interaction and dating. Then he concluded with[14] *"This trip only gives me sorrows"*, which was the motif. The last four sentences were used to intensify the sadness with visual views. This is using visuals to produce emotions. Although Zhou Ji said this is old wine in a new bottle, artistically it still presents superb skills.[15]

The fourth ci was about the ups and downs in life. First, the author described the terrain's advantages and then *"Since ancient time, life's ups and downs have been common"* depicted the ups and downs. Finally, the last sentence concluded the whole ci with emotions. The above four ci are all different in content but in terms of the

....

14　Chen Fei Shi "Song Ci Ju" 《宋詞舉》 (Nan Jin: Jiang Su Antique Books Publications 1st edition 1st print, April 2002), p.104.

15　Chen Fei Shi "Song Ci Ju" 《宋詞舉》 (Nan Jin: Jiang Su Antique Books Publications 1st edition 1st print, April 2002), p.105.

arrangement of the motif and creed, they are well coordinated.

Prose:

"Li Ji: Tan Gong Xuan Yi Ze"

Jin Xian Gong wanted to kill his son, Shen Sheng. Gong Zi Zhong R told Sen Sheng, "Why didn't you tell your father what you think?" Shen Sheng said, "No, my father is only happy with Li Gi. I am afraid if I told him, him would be upset." Zhong R said, "Then why don't you run away?" Shen Sheng said, "No, my father would say I plot to murder him. There is no country without a father. Besides, where can I go?" Shen Sheng then went to say goodbye to Hu Tu and said, "I am guilty. I didn't listen to you, and now I can only die. I am not afraid to die. Our king is old and his favorite son is still young. This country is suffering. You refused to work for the king. If you would agree to work for the king I would be blessed by you and I am willing to die." Afterwards, Shen Sheng kowtowed and then killed himself. Therefore, people called him "Gong Shi Zi".

晉獻公將殺其世子申生。公子重耳謂之曰：「子蓋言子之志於公乎？」世子曰：「不可。君安驪姬，是我傷公之心也！」曰：「然則蓋行乎？」世子曰：「不可。君謂我欲弒君也。天下豈有無父之國哉？我何行如之？」使人辭於狐突曰：「申生有罪，不念伯氏之言也，以至於死；申生不敢愛其死？雖然，吾君老矣，子少，國家多難。伯氏不出而圖吾君；伯氏苟出而圖吾君，申生受賜而死！」再拜稽首，乃卒。是以為恭世子也。

This piece is all about "Gong", so the last sentence *"people called him "Gong Shi Zi""* was the motif. He was called "Gong" but not "Xiao" for a reason. Through Zhong R's questions, it showed Shen Sheng cared about his father, and did not want to upset his father. He was submissive to his father. Later he said goodbye to Hu Tu, which showed that he was worried about the country until he died. However he killed himself in Xing Cheng, which actually made Xian Gong look bad. That is why after his death, he was called "Gong" but not "Xiao". At the end of this article it pointed out this gist to conclude it. Another similar example is "Shi Ji: the Compliments on Confucius's Family", which was discussed in this chapter's part 1. It also pointed out the motif at the end, "Zhi Sheng". The inductive approach expressed the utmost admiration.

3. Placed in the middle

This is placing the motif (creed) in the middle of the article. This type usually adopts an interjectional approach. This is more often seen in lyrical poems, but not in prose.

Poems:

Wang Buo's "Song Du Shao Fu Zhi Ren Shu Zhou"

城闕輔三秦 (Guan Zhong San Qin protects Chang An's palaces and high walls.)風煙望五津。(Looking at Shu Chuan from a distance, the five harbors are immersed in mist.)與君離別意；(Parting from you, the feeling in heart is needless to say.)同是宦遊人。(You and I both left home to serve the government, being away from home.)海內存知己，(As long as we are true friends)天涯若比鄰。(Even if we are far away from each other, our heart should still be adjacent.)無為在歧路，(Therefore, when we get to the point where we have to part ways,)兒女共霑巾。(We shall not cry our eyes out and be too sentimental.)

Li Bai's "Song You Ren"

青山橫北郭，(A mountain range is lying outside Bei Cheng.)白

水繞東城。(The river water is surrounding Dong Cheng.)此地一為別，(Today after we say goodbye here)孤蓬萬里征。(You will be like a lonely straw drifting around.)浮雲遊子意，(The volatile clouds are sending the travelers' regrets.)落日故人情。(The sunset symbolizes our reluctance to bid farewell.)揮手自茲去，(After we say goodbye, we will be moving farther away.)蕭蕭班馬鳴。(The horses' neighing seems to be say they are unwilling to say goodbye, either.)

Li Bai's "Zi Yie Ge"

長安一片月，(Chang An under the moonlight seems peaceful.)萬戶搗衣聲。(But the beating sounds when washing clothes in the households suggest agony.)秋風吹不盡，(The autumn winds never stop)總是玉關情。(They carry the concern about the people fighting a war at U Men Guan.)何日平胡虜，良人罷遠征？(When will the enemy be defeated so that my husband can come back?)

Du Fu's "Chun Wang"

國破山河在，(The nation is being invaded, and only the mountains and rivers remain the same.)城春草木深。(Spring has come and in the empty Chang An grass and tress are especially dense.)感時花濺淚，(I am sad about the nation's misery and cannot help crying facing these pretty flowers.)恨別鳥驚心。(When the family is broken, the birds' chirping is somehow disturbing.)烽火連三月，(The war has continued for months.)家書抵萬金。(A message from family would worth tons of gold.)白頭搔更短，(Being bothered by all this, the grey hair is getting thinner.)

渾欲不勝簪。(It keeps shedding and it almost cannot hold a
hairpin.)

The first one of these four poems was about farewell. The author
first specified the departure place, Chang An, and the destination,
Wu Jin. This is to expand the space so as to create a magnificent
scene, which was prepared for the following lyrical description.
Then he described the sadness stemming from saying goodbye,
which was the motif. The last part was the words he said to the guest,
corresponding with "*Parting from you, the feeling in heart is
needless to say*".[16]

The second piece was also about farewell. It consisted of three
sections: qi lian, han jing lian, and wei lian. The qi lian and wei lian
were both used to describe the scenery. Qi lian was about the
departure location and the static scenes there, while wei lian was
about the dynamic views after the friend had left. These two sections
were supposed to be adjacent, but the author separated them on
purpose, away from the han jing lian, which was the lyrical part.
This section started with "*here*" and "*drifting around*" to connect to
the qi lian and led to wei lian. "Bie" and "Zheng" pointed out
farewell, and "*volatile clouds*" and "*sunset*" served to integrate the
views in qi lian and wei lian. This metaphor led to "*the travelers'
regrets*" and "*reluctance to bid farewell*", which clarified the sadness
of parting. Thus, the motif was made distinct.

The third piece was about a young woman missing her husband,
who was fighting in a war. The author began with the woman's
whereabouts, Chang An, and described the sounds from washing

....

16 See Gao Bu Ing, *Major Tung Sung Poetry.*《唐宋詩舉要》(Taipei: Xue Hai
Publications, 1st edition, Feb 1973), p.408.

clothes. This was naturally conducive to the concern about her husband. Thereby, he described the concern in the third and fourth sentences. It was successfully tied to the first two sentences. The "autumn" besides pointing out the season, also intensified the concern, which was the motif of this poem. Hence, the fifth and sixth sentences used an interrogative sentence to further stress the concern about the husband fighting at U Men Guan.

The last poem was about the sentiment of the contemporary and the upset of saying goodbye. There were four sections in this poem. Its motif was "the sentiment of the contemporary" and "the upset of being apart". The author placed the motif in the second section on purpose. The other three sections were supplementary. The first section described the lack of people and materials. This was mainly about the sentiment of the contemporary. The third section described the painfulness regarding the inability to hear from family during wartime. This was mainly about the upset of being apart. The fourth section was about both "the sentiment of the contemporary" and "the upset of being apart". So, the entire poem was just about these two subjects. It is not hard to imagine the poet's anxiety due to the multiplying of these two kinds of sadness.[17]

The above four poems all have their motif (creed) placed in the middle part of the text instead of the beginning or the end.

Ci:

Wei Zhuang's "Pu Sa Man"

勸君今夜須沈醉，(Tonight you must get drunk.)尊前莫話明朝事。(Before these wineglasses, don't talk about the future.)珍重主人心，(Since the host said so, I would respect his wishes.)酒

17 Yu Shou Zhen, *Comprehensive Analysis of Three Hundred Tang Dynasty Poems.* 《唐詩三百首詳析》(Taipei: Taiwan Zhong Hua Publications 3th edition 5th print, April 1996), p.176.

深情亦深。(Because the glass is full and the host's passion is also full-hearted.)　須愁春漏短，(My angst is about the transience of a fun night like tonight.)莫訴金盃滿。(I will stop complaining you pour too much wine in my glass.)遇酒且呵呵，(We should be happy while having a chance to drink.)人生能幾何！(A good time like this won't happen too often in life.)

Fan Zhong Yan's "Su Mu Zhe"

碧雲天，黃葉地。(Under the blue sky, the yellow withered tree leaves cover the ground.)秋色連波，(The autumn scenes are transposed on the water rings.)波上寒煙翠。(Above the water green mist pervades the air.)山映斜陽天接水，(The setting sun shines on the mountains and the sky and the water are united.)芳草無情，更在斜陽外。(Only that callous grass stretches over the Sun)　黯鄉魂，追旅思。(The people traveling on the road are haunted by the yearning for home.)夜夜除非，好夢留人睡。(Every night, unless there was a sweet dream, it was hard to sleep tight.)明月樓高休獨倚，(It is unwise to lean on the railings and gaze at the moon alone.)酒入愁腸，化作相思淚。(If that, all the alcohol you drank will turn into tears of yearning.)

Ou Yang Xiou's "Ta Sha Xing"

候館梅殘，(The plum blossoms in the courtyard have withered.)溪橋柳細。(The willows by the stream are waving their fine twigs like dancing.)草薰風暖搖征轡。(The breeze is blowing the straws and the reins on the horse.)離愁漸遠漸無窮，(The farther I am away from home the more my angst is accumulating.)迢迢不斷如春水。(It is like the nonstop water running through the river all the way)　寸寸柔腸，(The person yearning has a broken heart.)盈盈粉淚。(The tears slip down the face with makeup.)樓高莫近危闌倚。(The tower is too tall so don't lean on the railings.)平蕪盡處是春山，(The only thing in sight is the mountains.)行人更在春山外。(The person I miss is further than the mountains.)

Liou Yong's "Yu Lin Ling"

寒蟬淒切，(After autumn, the cicadas' cries sound plaintive.)對長亭晚，(Facing the kiosk, it is almost evening.)驟雨初歇。(A sudden shower just ceased.)都門帳飲無緒，(In the tent set up for a farewell party, I drink in a gloomy mood.)方留戀處，(Just when I am still reluctant to leave,)蘭舟催發。(The boat is about to leave.)執手相看淚眼，(Holding each other's hands, we have tears in the eyes.)竟無語凝咽。(We could not say a word, for everything is stuck in the throat.)念去去、千里煙波，(I figure this long trip will be an odyssey.)暮靄沈沈楚天闊。(That night, a clear sky was above the foggy land.)　多情自古傷離別，(Since always, the hardest thing for a sentimental person is parting.)更那堪、冷落清秋節。(It is especially unbearable when we part ways in such chilly and depressing autumn.)今宵酒醒何處，(Who knows where I will be when I wake up from the hangover.)楊柳岸、曉風殘月。(There are probably only willow-covered riverbanks, gusty winds in the dawn, and the disappearing moon.)此去經年，(It will be years before I come back.)應是良辰好景虛設。(Even if the weather is nice and the view is beautiful, I don't think that will make it better.)便縱有、千種風情，更與何人說。(Although I have all the affection in heart, there is no one I can talk to.)

The first ci cited above was about the host's zeal. The ci was composed of three parts. The first part was the first two sentences. The second part was the third and fourth sentences. The third part was the last four sentences. In the first and third parts, the author recounted the dialogues between the host and the guest in the evening. They were originally adjacent, but the author intentionally separated them, and interrupted with the second part to point out the motif which was the host's zeal. It was a rather special arrangement.

The second ci was about missing hometown in fall. The shang pian was about scenery and xia pian was lyrical. In shang pian, the author used the "Ding Zhen" method, step by step from near to far recording what he saw on the tower. This produced lingering sensations. Tang Gui Zhang said, "The first section described the sky connected to water connected to mountains connected to grass; the sky with clouds, the water with mist, and the mountain with setting sun. From top to bottom, from near to far, it was spiritual, which is hard to achieve even for a painting."[18] This comment is dead on. In the second half, the lyrical part consisted of two sections. The first section contained the first four sentences, pertaining to the yearning for home while traveling outside. In this section, the author skillfully used *"the yearning for home"* to induce the motif. The second section was the last three sentences. These three sentences were still lyrical but they also portrayed a view depicting the author's leaning and drinking while looking at the moon and missing home. This concretized the abstract yearning for home, which integrated the views described in shang pian. The view was intertwined with the sentiments. This method was superb, ad admirable.

The third one was about saying goodbye in spring. Like the first piece, it was composed of three parts: the first 3 sentences, the

....

[18] See "Tong Song Ci Jian Shi" 《唐宋詞簡釋》 (Taipei: Mu Duo Publications 1st edition, March 1982), p.48.

middle five sentences, and the last three sentences. In the first and third parts, the author from near to far described what he saw when seeing off the traveler. First, it was the withered plum blossoms, and then it was the willows. Then there was grass, followed by the mountains. Obviously, these views were connected to accentuate the reluctance to part, but the author purposefully interrupted it with the lyrical part. In the lyrical part, he pointed our the motif "sorrow for parting" first, and then in order used "*the nonstop water*", "*a broken heart*", "*The tears slip down the face*" to specify the sorrow. The first part was connected with "*The farther I am*", and "*lean on the railings*" led to the third part. This way, the text was connected as one entity. Through this connection, the second part's sentiments and the scenery in the first and third parts were able to promote each other. This punctilious arrangement was probably the reason why it can never get tired of reading this ci.

The fourth ci was about saying goodbye in fall. The author used a specific-then-abstract method. The ci consisted of two parts: specific and abstract. The specific part started from the beginning to "*for everything is stuck in the throat*". It described the scenes around the kiosk and the reluctance to say goodbye between the two persons. The abstract part started from "*I figure this long trip*" to the end. There were three sections to described "*Holding each other's hands, we have tears in the eyes.*

We could not say a word, for everything is stuck in the throat.", the night, and the day after in order. The motif (creed) resided in "*Since always, the hardest thing for a sentimental person is parting*" and it was placed in between the first and second sections to summarize the entire ci. This arrangement was smooth and the transition was seamless. This is indeed a masterpiece.[19]

....

19 See Chen Man Ming , *A Walk in Tzu Forest*《詞林散步》 (Taipei: Wuan Juan Lou Publications 1ˢᵗ edition, January 2000), pp.143-145.

Prose:

Li Mi's "Chen Qing Biao"

Mi speaking:

Due to fate, I encountered misery when I was little. I father passed away when I was six-month old. After four years, my uncle forced my mother to remarry. My grandmother, Liu Shi, pitied me having no father and weak, so she took care of me. When I was little, I was susceptible to illness. I could not walk when I was nine years old. Until I had my own family, I had no one to depend on. I have no uncles or siblings. The family was small and not blessed very much. I had a son until I was fairly old. Relatives were not close. At home, there were no servants. I practically lived alone with my own shadow. Liu Shi has been ill for a long time, and could often stay in bed. I fed her and prepared her medication, and I never left her.

When Jin Dynasty was established, I benefited from the prominent govern. Early, Tai Shou Kui recommended me for Xiao Lian, and then Ci Shi Rong recommended me for Xiou Chai. I turned down both of them due to the fact that no one could take care of my grandmother. I did not obey the order. The government particularly for me issued another summon to appoint me as Lang Zhong, and not long ago I was again appointed to be Xi Ma due to the country's mercy. An nobody like me should be honored to have such a chance to serve the prince. I could not return this favor even if I die. However, when I reported the same reason explaining why I could not accept the appointment, I was heavily criticized and accused of evading the government's duties intentionally. The mayors came and urged me to depart and the governor also came to rush me urgently. I really wanted to follow my lord's order and be contributive to the country, but my grandmother's illness is worsening. I want to be selfish and be my family, but my request was not granted, which has out me in a dilemma.

I believe your majesty is ruling this country with Xiao. Those homeless elders were being taken care of, not to mention my situation is even more compelling. I served as a public servant for Shu Han. I was Lang Zhong and Shang Shu Lang. I was pursuing fame and wealth, so I am not trying to play aloof from politics. I am just a humble subjugated person who is not worth mentioning. I have been lucky to be appreciated, so how could I dare to be manipulative? It is really because my grandmother does not have much time left in her life. I wouldn't have had today but for my grandmother's caring, and my grandmother cannot make it through her last days without me. We are codependent, and thus I am really reluctant to leave my grandmother at home alone. I am forty-four years old and my grandmother is ninety-six. I still have many chances to serve my majesty, but I don't have much time to serve my grandmother. Like cloaks feeding their parents when they are old, I would like to do the same for my grandmother. Please allow me to be selfish in this capacity and accompany my grandmother for these last days.

My hardship is witnessed by not only the locals but also gods. I hope my majesty would take pity on my silly but sincere heart, and grant me this favor so that Liou Shi can reserve the rest of her life. I will repay this favor with my life, and even if I die I will still do anything for you. Now I am with my terrified soul I am respectfully submitting this written plaint.

臣密言：

臣以險釁，夙遭閔凶。生孩六月，慈父見背。行年四歲，舅奪母志。祖母劉愍臣孤弱，躬親撫養。臣少多疾病，九歲不行；零丁孤苦，至於成立。既無叔伯，終鮮兄弟；門衰祚薄，晚有兒息；外無期功彊近之親，內無應門五尺之僮；煢煢獨立，形影相弔。而劉夙嬰疾病，常在床蓐；臣侍湯藥，未曾廢離。

逮奉聖朝，沐浴清化。前太守臣逵，察臣孝廉；後刺史臣榮，舉臣秀才；臣以供奉無主，辭不赴命。詔書特下，拜臣郎中。尋蒙國恩，除臣洗馬。猥以微賤，當侍東宮，非臣隕首，所能上報。臣具以表聞，辭不就職。詔書切峻，責臣逋慢。郡縣逼迫，催臣上道。州司臨門，急於星火。臣欲奉詔奔馳，則劉病日篤；欲苟順私情，則告訴不許；臣之進退，實為狼狽。

伏惟聖朝以孝治天下，凡在故老，猶蒙矜育；況臣孤苦，特為尤甚。且臣少仕偽朝，歷職郎署，本圖宦達，不矜名節。今臣亡國賤俘，至微至陋，過蒙拔擢，寵命優渥；豈敢盤桓，有所希冀！但以劉日薄西山，氣息奄奄，人命危淺，朝不慮夕。臣無祖母，無以至今日；祖母無臣，無以終餘年。母孫二人，更相為命；是以區區，不能廢遠。臣密今年四十有四，祖母劉今年九十有六，是臣盡節於陛下之日長，報劉之日短也。烏鳥私情，願乞終養！

臣之辛苦，非獨蜀之人士，及二州牧伯，所見明知；皇天后土，實所共鑒。願陛下矜愍愚誠，聽臣微志；庶劉僥倖，保卒餘年。臣生當隕首，死當結草。

臣不勝犬馬怖懼之情，謹拜表以聞。

This article contained four paragraphs. It was all about "xiao" admittedly. This xiao, as the creed, was specified at the beginning of the third paragraphs. On the other hand, in the fourth paragraph the motif was reinforced with "*I hope my majesty would take pity on my silly but sincere heart, and grant me this favor so that Liou Shi can reserve the rest of her life*". These words sufficiently accounted for the purpose of this writing. However, to serve this purpose and preserve "xiao" required solid reasoning to be convincing. This reasoning was based on the hardship that other people did not usually need to face, which led to "*My hardship is witnessed by not only the locals but also gods*". To substantiate this assertion, he in the first two paragraphs described the happenings in detail, and then in the third paragraph described his dilemma on account of personal feelings (xiao) and acceptance (zhong). From these descriptions his hardship could be seen and then he reasoned with the priority in terms of time. Therefore, he begged for permission to entertain personal feelings (xiao) and turn down acceptance (zhong). The author stuck to "xiao" throughout the text genuinely so there was no feigning in the article. No wonder it was so touching and consequently realized his wishes.[20]

Another example was Liou E's "Huang He Jie Bing Ji"

Lao Can washed his face and stored his luggage. He locked the door and went out to the riverbank. He saw the Yellow River came down from southwest and it happened to be a turn here and moved ahead to east. The river was not really wide, about 1 km from one side to the other. Given the volume of the water at the moment, at best it was about 300 meters wide. However, the ice, one on top of another, exceeded the surface by 24 cm.

He kept walking upstream about one or two hundred feet, and he saw the ice was still moving down until being blocked by the ice before it. The coming ice kept pressing and making squeaky sounds. Eventually the ice would be forced forward and to push down the preceding ice. The river was merely 300 meters wide and the mainstream was only 60 or 90 meters wide. The rest was frozen streams. The ice surface was level and covered with dust and dirt carried here by the winds. It looked like a beach. The mainstream in the middle, however, was still rampant and pushing the stuck ice to the sides. Some ice was broken due to pressure and projected to the

....

20 Wu Shu Cai comments: See *Comments on Anthology of Ancient Prose.*《精校評 注古文觀止》卷七 (Taipei: Taiwan Zhong Hua Publications 6th edition, November 1972), p.1.

bank. The ice could go as far as 180 cm. Many pieces of fragmented ice were standing like a small screen. After an hour or so, this section of ice was stuck as well.

Lao Can went downstream and passed the original place and kept walking down. He saw two boats with approximately 10 or more people onboard. They all held a wood stick, breaking the ice. They broke some in the front and then some in the back. On the other side of the river, there were two other boats doing the same thing.

The sky was getting dark, so he planned on going back to the inn. He took another look and found the shadows of the willows were already on the ground, gently wavering. The moon had been shedding moonlight. Back in the inn, after dinner, he again walked out to the riverbank. The north wind had stopped, but it was even chillier without the wind. Lifting his head a little, he looked at the mountains in the south. It was snow white reflecting the moonlight. It was very beautiful. The mountain ridges on the other hand were not distinguishable. A few clouds were caught in between them so it was not easy to tell them apart from the mountains. He paid some extra attention and finally recognized what were clouds and what were the mountains. Although both clouds and mountains were white and both of them were shimmering, the clouds were under the moon, so the light came from behind. In contrast, the mountains reflected the moonlight by means of the snow covered on them, so the light was different. But, that only applied to the near mountains. Further away, the sky was white, and the mountains were white, and the snow was white, so it remained undistinguishable.

In light of the scene involving snow and moon, Lao Can recalled Xie Ling Yun's poem: "the bright moonlight illuminates the snows; the northerly winds are vigorous and mourning." If you had not experienced the bleak weather in the north, how would you have known the art of using "mourning"?

The moon was lighting up the ground. He lifted his head and could not see any star in the sky. Only the Wain in the north, Kai Yang, and Yiao Guang, etc. could barely been seen. The Wain was leaning on the west of Zi Wei Xing Huan. The handle was up and the head was down. Lao Can was thinking: "Time lapses fast. The handle is about to point to east, and people are about to get one year older. How is this going to end after the roaming year after year?" When thinking of this, he could not help shedding tears and lost the mood for sightseeing. He walked back slowly. While waking, Lao Can felt something clinging to his face. He touched them with hands and they turned out to be ice. At first he did not understand why, later when he figured out he smiled. That was the tears he shed just now. The weather was too cold that they were frozen immediately. There were probably a few icy beads. Lao Can gloomily went back to the inn and went to bed.

又如劉鶚〈黃河結冰記〉：

老殘洗完了臉，把行李鋪好，把房門鎖上，他出來步到河
隄上看。只見那黃河從西南上下來，到此卻正是個灣子，
過此便向正東去了。河面不甚寬，兩岸相距不到二里。若
以此刻河水而論，也不過百把丈寬的光景。只是面前的
冰，插得重重疊疊的，高出水面有七、八寸厚。
再望上游走了一、二百步，只見那上游的冰，還一塊一塊
地慢慢價來，到此地被前頭的冰攔住，走不動，就站住
了。那後來的冰趕上他，只擠得嗤嗤價響。後冰被這溜水
逼得緊了，就竄到前冰上頭去。前冰被壓，就漸漸低下去
了。看那河身，不過百十丈寬，當中大溜，約莫不過二、
三十丈。兩邊俱是平水，這平水之上，早已有冰結滿。冰
面卻是平的，被吹來的塵土蓋住，卻像沙灘一般。中間的
大道大溜，卻仍然奔騰澎湃，有聲有勢，將那走不過去的
冰，擠得兩邊亂竄。那兩邊平水上的冰，被當中亂冰擠破

了，往岸上跑，那冰能擠到岸上有五、六尺遠。許多碎冰被擠得站起來，像個小插屏似的。看了有點把鐘工夫，這一截子的冰，又擠死不動了。

老殘復行望下游走去，過了原來的地方，再望下走。只見兩隻船，船上有十來個人，都拿著木杵打冰。望前打些時，又望後打。河的對岸，也有兩隻船，也是這們打。

看看天色漸漸昏了，打算回店，再看那隄上柳樹一棵一棵的影子，都已照在地下，一絲一絲地搖動，原來月光已經放出光亮來了。回到店中，吃過晚飯，又到隄上閒步。這時北風已息，誰知道冷氣逼人，比那有風的時候還屬害些。抬起頭來看那南面的山，一條雪白，映著月光，分外好看。一層一層的山嶺，卻不大分辨得出。又有幾片白雲，夾在裏面，所以看不出是雲是山。及至定神看去，方才看出那是雲，那是山來。雖然雲也是白的，山也是白的；雲也有亮光，山也有亮光，只因為月在雲上，雲在月下，所以雲的亮光，是從背面透過來的。那山卻不然，山上的亮光，是由月光照到山上，被那山上的雪反射過來，所以光是兩樣子的。然祇稍近的地方如此，那山往東去，越望越遠，漸漸地天也是白的，山也是白的，雲也是白的，就分辨不出甚麼來了。

老殘就著雪月交輝的景致，想起謝靈運的詩：「明月照積雪，北風勁且哀」兩句，若非經歷北方苦寒景象，那裏知道「北風勁且哀」的一個「哀」字下得好呢？

這時月光照得滿地灼亮，抬起頭來，天上的星，一個也看不見。只有北邊北斗七星、開陽、搖光……像幾個淡白點子一樣，還看得清楚。那北斗正斜倚紫微星垣的西邊上面，杓在上，魁在下。老殘心裏想道：「歲月如流，眼見斗杓又將東指了，人又要添一歲了！一年一年地這樣瞎混下去，如何是個了局呢？」想到此地，不覺滴下淚來，也就無心觀玩景致，慢慢走回店去。老殘一面走著，覺得臉上有樣物件附著似的，用手一摸，原來兩邊掛著了兩條滴滑的冰。起初不懂甚麼緣故，既而想起，自己也就笑了。

原來就是方才流的淚，天寒，立刻就凍住了。地下必定還
有幾多冰珠子呢。老殘悶悶的回到店裏，也就睡了。

This article had two main parts: scenery and lyrics. In the scenery
part, it could be further divided into two sections (i.e., twilight and
evening) based on the temporal order. The first section included the
first three paragraphs, describing the twilight view. The first
paragraph depicted the freeze in the Yellow River. The second
paragraph was about the view where ice was pressed and pushed
onto the riverbanks. It was from small to large.　The third
paragraph from near to far described the view of breaking ice from
one side of the river to the other side. The second section was the
fourth paragraph. It was about the view under moonlight. The author
depicted the mountains near him and the grounds, and then from
near to far utilized the chilly wind, the snow, and the moonlight to
describe the mountains farther away and the sky. His description of
the interaction of the snow and moonlight was purely esthetic. In the
lyrics part, there were two paragraphs, the fifth and the last ones. In
the fifth paragraph, the author cited Xie Lin Yun's poem "Sui Mu
Shi" to transform scenery into lyrics. This raised "mourning" to
conclude the scenes in the first four paragraphs and led to the last
paragraph. Thus, the text was linked through as one entity. Xie Lin
Yun's original poem was *"I was feeling so sad that I could not fall
asleep; I was agonized by this long night; The bright moonlight was
illuminating the snows; The northerly winds were rigorous and
mourning; Time has never stop passing by;*

My time also elapsed and never comes back". The author only
adopted the third and fourth sentences but was able to integrate the
gist into the article.　For example, in the first half when Lao Can
was looking at the Wain, the sentiment arising corresponded to
"Time has never stop passing by; My time also elapsed and never

comes back" And, when it said "*Lao Can gloomily went back to the inn and went to bed*", did Lao Can really fall asleep? Of course not, why? The answer could be found in "*I was feeling so sad that I could not fall asleep; I was agonized by this long night*". The "feeling sad " was "gloomily" and it was exactly the "mourning" in "*northerly winds were rigorous and mourning*", which was the creed. Given this creed, we can know that the descriptions of scenery in the first fourth paragraphs were abstract, serving as a contrast. The sentiment in the last paragraph was substantial, serving as the main body. The Xie's poem cited was placed here to serve as a transition to the creed. It played an crucial role in the context. The last paragraph integrated the Wain under the moon into the view of the interaction between the moon and the snow. It implied "*Time has never stop passing by*" so as to lead to the mourning. The mourning was concretized by the mention of tears and linked the iced tears to the ice on the Huang He to analogize the ice with people's tears. The author used the sorrowful views to induce the sorrowful sentiments. By means of the seamless connection he skillfully disclosed his worries for the nation. This is an advanced writing skill indeed.

4. Placed outside the texts

This type is hiding the motif and omitting it in the text. The reader has to interpret it outside the text. This is very implicit and achieved the so-called reading without text. It is the most common type in a variety of writings.

Poems:

Li Bai's "Yu Jie Yuan" 李白〈玉階怨〉:

玉階生白露，(Dews have emerged on the jade stairs.)夜久侵羅襪。(Standing there too long at night would have the socks soaked.)卻下水精簾，(I went in the house to pull down the crystal curtain.)玲瓏望秋月。(Through the drapes I admire the exquisite autumn moon alone.)

Liou Yu Xi's "Shi Tou Cheng" 劉禹錫〈石頭城〉：

山圍故國周遭在，(The mountains that used to surround the old capital city are still surrounding it.)潮打空城寂寞回。(The tides constantly hitting the empty city, and after the tides recede the empty city becomes more lonesome.)淮水東邊舊時月，(The old moon is on the east side of Qin Huai He.)夜深還過女牆來。(It still turns around to shed light on the walls.)

Yuan Zhen's "Xing Gong" 元稹〈行宮〉：

寥落古行宮，(In the hollow lonesome ancient imperial palace for short stays,)宮花寂寞紅。(Only the follows are still lively.)白頭宮女在，(Occasionally there would be one or two elderly maids,)閒坐說玄宗。(sitting there and talking about the Tang Xuan Zong.)

The first one of the three poems was a piece pertaining to some resentful sentiments. It was merely describing a beauty's action and the surroundings, but strong resentful sentiments could be sensed already. Xiao Cui Ke commented, "There was no one word about resentment but it could be sensed outside the text." The author arranged the motif outside the text, which made it more touching.

The second poem was about the rise and fall. Seemingly it was merely describing the tidal sounds and moonlight, but the author clandestinely used *"the old capital city"* and *"The old moon"* to manifest the prosperity of Liou Chao, in sharp contrast to the present *"the empty city"* and *"more lonesome"*. This sufficiently revealed the sentiments outside the text. Shen De Qian said, "The moon and the landscapes are still there but the prosperity of Liou Chao vanished. This caused some thinking between the lines."[21] Therefore, this poem albeit concise was connotative and worth pondering.

The third poem was also about the rise and fall. As the last one, the meaning of the text seemed very simple. It was just about the view inside a palace and some maids' chatting. However, the author used *"ancient"*, *"elderly"*, and *"Xuan Zong"* to contrast the Xuan Zong's prime time with the present *"hollow lonesome"* and *"sitting"*. This contrast denoted the rise and fall. Xu Wen Yu said, "This poem portrayed degradation and the elderly maids' reminiscence. The rise and fall were adequately presented in such a short poem." No wonder Shen De Qian would say, "These four sentences were enough to substitute for "Chang Hen Ge".

Ci:

Wen Ting Yun's "Pu Sa Man"

小山重疊金明滅，(The overlapping hills are flickering in the morning.)鬢雲欲度香腮雪。(The sideburns are snow white)懶起畫蛾眉，(Lazily get up to fix eyebrows)弄妝梳洗遲。(Slowly put on makeup and groom.)　　照花前後鏡，(Looking at the newly added flower in the mirrors in the front and in the back.)花面交相映。(The red flowers and the complexion glorify each other)新貼繡羅襦，(The dress I just put on)雙雙金鷓鴣。(Pairs of gold partridges are embroidered on the dress.)

---

21 See Gao Bu Ing, *Tang and Sung Dynasties' Major Poems.*《唐宋詩舉要》 (Taipei: Xue Hai Publications, 1st edition, Feb 1973), p.764.

Li Yu's "Yu Lou Chun"

晚妝初了明肌雪，(The maids after makeup at night have the skin white as snow.)春殿嬪娥魚貫列。(The concubines and maids stand in the hall in a straight line.)鳳簫聲斷水雲間，(The melodies coming from bamboo flutes and reed pipes are transmitted all over the place.)重按〈霓裳〉歌遍徹。(The double rendition of "Ni Shang Yu Yi Qu" aroused singing that resonates everywhere)　臨風誰更飄香屑，(Who is releasing the dust of sandalwood that oozes perfume?)醉拍闌干情未切。(After a few drinks I sing along at the railings, which makes it more fun.)歸時休放燭花紅，(When the singing and dancing stop, we should not light up those red candles.)待踏馬蹄清夜月。(Just follow the moonlight and the clop and leave leisurely.)

Yan Shu's "Wan Xi Sha"

一曲新詞酒一杯，(I am drinking while listening to the songs with new lyrics.)去年天氣舊池臺。(I remember the weather last year. There were the same building and kiosk.)夕陽西下幾時回？(When will the setting sun in the west come back here?)無可奈何花落去，(We have no choice but to watch the beautiful flowers fade.)似曾相識燕歸來。(The returning swallows seem familiar.)小園香徑獨徘徊。(In the small pathways surrounded by aroma, I am lingering alone.)

The first ci was about a woman's complaints. The author described the ambiance in the first sentence and specified the location and time to lead to the following description of the person. From the second to the last sentence, it followed the temporal order to describe the woman's every move. First, she woke up, then got up sluggishly, then washed up and put on makeup, and wore flowers and tried on clothes. Through these routines, the author compelled the woman's complaints outside the text. Tang Gui Zhang commented, "This piece depicted a woman's complaints by very subtle presentation and the gradation was very organized."[22] This is a very pertinent comment.

The second one was about the fun in a party. In the first half, the author described the joyful scenes in both visual and acoustic senses. In the second half, he then described the joy in olfaction, taste, and spirit. The whole ci did not mention the word 'joy' but the text conveys joy all along. Li Yu Lin said, "The first half was the happiness of going out, while the second half was about the happiness of coming back. (Cao Tang Shi Yu Jun)" He managed to find "joy" from outside the text to link the two halves. This is perceptive.

The third one was about old memories. The first half described the phenomena in sight. It connected *"the weather"*, *"the same building and kiosk"* with *"the setting sun"*, *"last year"* and hence induced the feelings of isolation. The second half described *"flowers fade"*, *"returning swallows"*, *"pathways"*, and *"lingering"*. Through the usage of *"no choice"*, *"seem familiar"*, and *"alone"* it revealed the gloominess. Tang Gui Zhang said, "This ci was harmonious but not cheesy. It was implicit but not irrelevant. It was obviously about thinking of someone but it did not mention anyone. Rather, it used the scenery to express the feelings."[23] Using scenery to express feelings can result in long-lasting implication.

....

22 See *Brief Interpretations of Tang Sung Dynasty Tzu.*《唐宋詞簡釋》(Taipei: Mu Duo Publications 1st edition, March 1982), p.3.

23 See *Brief Interpretations of Tang Sung Dynasty Tzu.*《唐宋詞簡釋》 (Taipei: Mu Duo Publications 1st edition, March 1982), p.54.

Prose:
Lie Zi's "Yu Gong Yi Shan"

Tai Xing and Wang Wu are two tall mountains. The measure of area is 350 km^2 and the height is over 2500 meters. They were originally located in the south of Ji Zhou and the north of He Yang. At the foot of Bei Shan, there was a man, named Yu Gong. He was almost 90 years old. His residence was facing the mountain. He had been agonized by the impediment of the mountains and had to meander to find a way out and to return to home. One day Yu Gong convened a meeting of his family. He suggested, "Let us shovel down the mountains so as to create a path straightly leading to southern Yu Zhou and reaching the south of Han Shui. What do you think?" People generally agreed. Yu Gong's wife raised a question, "Your strength is not even enough to shovel down a small hill like Kui Fu. What can you do about Tai Xing and Wang Wu? Besides, how are you going to dispose of the sandstone?" Collectively people replied, "We can put it on the edge of Buo Hai, north of In Tu. Yu Gong then led three stronger descendents to dig up the rocks and dirt, and carried them to the edge of Buo Hai. There is a widow, named "Jing Cheng", who had a son at the age of 7 or 8. The boy was also capering on the way to help. It took as long as the season changed for him to return from one trip.

A sage from He Qu teased Yu Gong and tried to talk him out of it, "You are so unwise. In the rest of your life, you can barely remove a straw, not to mention rocks and dirt." Yu Gong signed and responded, "Your mind is too obstinate to change. You are more closed-minded than a widow and a child. Even if I die, I have sons and they will have their sons who will have their sons. Generation after generation, it is endless. On the other hand, the mountains are not getting any bigger or taller. It's just a matter of time before they are wiped out." The sage was speechless.

The deity of mountains heard about this and was worried they would continue digging. He reported this to the Almighty, who was moved by U Gong's persistence. He then ordered Kua E Shi's two sons to move the two mountains, one of which was placed in the east of Shuo Fang, and the other in the south of Yong Zhou. Thereafter, there were no obstacles blocking the south of Ji Zhou and the south of Han Shui.

This is a well-known fable in China. In this story the author implied "Where there is a will, there is a way" outside the text. It is worth pondering. There were four paragraphs. In the first paragraph, the author narrated how Yu Gong was determined to remove the two mountains due to the blocked traffic routes and gained support from his family. In the second paragraph, it recorded where they disposed of the sandstone, and started to lead his descendents to embark on the task. In the third paragraph, it was the dialogue taking place when the sage made fun of Yu Gong and tried to dissuade him. However, Yu Gong did not budge, because he believed persistence will result in success eventually. The last paragraph described Yu Gong's perseverance moved the deities and they consequently granted him help and removed the mountains for him. Apparently, the first three paragraphs were about willpower and self-motivation, while the last paragraph was about the way it pans out. Through such a simple story, the reader can comprehend the implicit meaning while being entertained by the story itself. This is a common characteristic of all fables, and this is what other literary forms can not compare with. Nonetheless, sometimes a fable could still specify the motif in the text, such as Liou Zong Yuan's "Qian Zhi Lu", which expressed its intended sarcasm in the end by "Had the donkey not revealed his own weaknesses the tiger would have been intimidated by its own doubts and chosen not to attack. It is pathetic to end up like this." Thus, the motif was directly shown in the text, which is distinct from the traditional fables that tend to arrange the motif outside the text.

Another example is Liou Yi Qing's "Shi Shuo Xin Yu".

When Jin Ming Di was very little, one day he sat on Yuan Di's laps. Someone happened to come from Chang An, so Yuan Di asked him about Luo Yang and could not help shedding tears. Ming Di asked, "Why are you crying?" Yuan Di thus told Ming Di all about the matters regarding Jin Dynasty's moving east across Chang Jiang. Then he asked Ming Di, "Which one do you think is farther, the Sun or Chang An?" Ming Di replied, "The Sun. I never heard anyone coming from the Sun, so the Sun must be farther." Yuan Di was surprised by his response. The next day, Yuan Di convene a meeting with his courtiers and he told them about what Ming Di said the day before. He then asked Ming Di the same question again. This time unexpectedly Ming Di said, "the Sun is nearer". Yuan Di pulled his face and asked, "How come your answer is not the same as yesterday?" Ming Di said, "When I raise my head, I can only see the Sun but not Chang An."

晉明帝數歲，坐元帝膝上。有人從長安來，元帝問洛下消息，潸然流涕。明帝問：「何以致泣？」具以東渡意告之。因問明帝：「汝意謂長安何如日遠？」答曰：「日遠。不聞人從日邊來，居然可知。」元帝異之。明日，集群臣宴會，告以此意；更重問之。乃答曰：「日近。」元帝失色曰：「爾何故異昨日之言耶？」答曰：「舉目見日，不見長安。」

This was a story about the smartness of Jin Ming Di. The author started with the fact that Ming Di was very little sitting on Yuan Di's laps. This was followed by someone bringing news about Luo Yang's being occupied by the enemy. This caused Yuan Di's tears and induced Ming Di's question. This was prepared for the further dialogue. Then it described Yuan Di's one question and Ming Di's two answers. The question was *"Which one do you think is farther, the Sun or Chang An?"* The two answers were "the Sun is farther" and "the Sun is nearer". To the same question, only one day apart Ming Di responded differently. He reasons were in order *"I never heard anyone coming from the Sun"* and *"I can only see the Sun but not Chang An"*. From these two answers, the author pointed to Ming Di's smartness with ease. Although smartness was never in the text, it was obvious outside the text, which is especially impressive.

The aforementioned four types of arrangement of the motif can all easily be found in all forms of ci-zhang. Hence, when we are writing, reading, or teaching, if we can get a handle on these four types, the article's motif will become clear. Thereby, it helps distinguish the relationships between "fan" and "mu", abstract and concrete, primary and secondary, etc. All these will contribute to better writing, reading or teaching.

IV. The structural types concerning topics or guidelines placed in the middle

In the previous part we discussed the placement of the motif or creed. In terms of location, there are four types: at the beginning, in the middle, at the end, and outside the text. Except for the middle placement, the other three types are very common and have been appreciated greatly. As for the middle placement, it is rare and only few literary critics noticed it. For example, Li Mu Tang said in "Qiou Shan Luen Wen":

An article's spirit resides in its finish. Some moved it forward;

some kept it in the middle; some save it at the end.[24]

Also, Song Wen Wui said in "Ping Zhu Wen Fa Jin Liang":

When the focal point is determined, it is okay to reveal it at the beginning, or disclose it in the middle, or save it until the end.[25]

The "*some kept it in the middle*" and "*disclose it in the middle*" both referred to this middle placement. It is a shame that not many people paid enough attention to this. Therefore, in June 1985 I published an article entitled, "The Basic Formats of the Arrangement of the Motif in Ci-Zhang" in the fourteenth issue of the "Guo Wen Xue Bao" associated with National Taiwan Normal University. In this article, I used poems, ci, and prose as examples to discuss the features of these placements. In January 1988, in an attempt to point out the significance of this placement, I published another article entitled, "A Few Articles with Motifs Placed in the Middle" on the third volume eighth issue of the "Guo Wen Tian Di". However, I have never elaborated on the structure of "pian". Given the necessity, this part of text is dedicated to the typology of structure based on the method of "fan mu", the method of abstract and concrete, the method of primary and secondary, and the method of cause and effect. Su Shi and Xin Qi Ji's ci are used as examples to make up the deficiency.

1. General-details structures

"Fan" means a summary. "Mu" means details. Based on "fan" and "mu", there are four types of structure to constitute a "pian". They

----

24 See Wang Bao Xin "Gu Wen Ci Tong Yi" Volume 11 《古文辭通義》卷十一引 (Taipei: Taiwan Zhong Hua Publications 2nd edition, April 1984), p.2.

25 See "Pin Zhu Wen Fa Jin Liang" 《評注文法津梁》 (Taipei: Fu Wen Publications 2nd edition, February 1993), p.48.

are "first fan then mu", "first mu then fan", "fan mu fan", and "mu fan mu".[26] In general, in a "mu fan mu" structure, "fan" is in the middle of the text and that is where the motif or creed will surface.

For instance:

Su Shi's "Wang Jiang Nan"

春已老，春服幾時成。It is the end of spring. When will the spring clothes be finished?

The river is steady. Something is soft.

I am drinking happily.

A few rain drops just fell down.

曲水浪低蕉葉穩，舞雩風軟紵羅輕。酣詠樂昇平。微雨過。何處不催耕。百舌無言桃李盡，柘林深處鵓鴣鳴。春色屬蕪菁。（蘇軾〈望江南〉）

This ci was composed at the ninth year of Song Shen Zong Xi Ning (the year of 1076), before March 3rd. The motif was "Yue-sheng-ping (to celebrate peace)" in the middle. It served as "fan". The first two sentences regarding the spring clothes were derived from "Dian Chu, Luen Yu: Xian Jin". The two sentences about "Qu-shui lang-di" (the wave of Qu-shui is low) came from "Shi Jian, Hou Han Shu: Li Yi Zhi (zhong)". These four sentences were based on imagination to let "Yue-sheng-ping" stand out. This is mu one. The five sentences about "Wei-yu-kuo" (after the drizzle) were describing what he saw. "Wei-yu-ku" was visual; the three sentences about "where" were acoustic; "Chun-se" (spring scenery) was visual. The author utilized the visual and acoustic sensations to represent

....

26 See Chen Man Ming " An Application of General-Detail Method on Su Xin Tzu " 《凡目法在蘇辛詞裏的運用》(Taipei: Guo Wen Tian Di Volume 11, Issue 11 and 12, April and May 1996), pp. 36-44, pp. 56-65.

Nature's vitality so as to strengthen the motif "Yue-sheng-ping". This is "mu two". This was the structure of "mu fan mu". The following is a diagram of the structure.

```
                                                  ┌ Pan-cheng-chun-fu: "chun-yi-lao"
    ┌ Mu One (personnel matters: abstract) ┤
    │                                             └ Liou-shang-qu-shui: "qu-shui"
    │
    ├ Fan: Drinking happily
    │
    │                                     ┌ Visual: "Wei-yu-kuo" (after the drizzle)
    └ Mu Two (nature: concrete) ┼ Acoustic: "He-chu" (where)
                                          └ Visual: "chun-se" (spring scenery)
```

Another example is Su Shi's "Jian Zi Mu Lan Hua"

The summer wind is blowing and the afterglow is shining.

The shadows of bamboos on the eastern wall are in disorder but distinct.

Everybody in the full house feel nice and cool.

The chill of the cold spring makes its way into the sleeves but does not wet the clothes.

Suddenly sober up from the drunkenness

Seem to hear the splash in the deep well

In the sight it is the sprinkles of the cold spring falling onto the hostess's spotlessly white arm, like snow flakes.

This ci was made in May, Song Zhe Zong Wen You seventh year (the year of 1092). It was noted "On May the 24th, met at the study room; the master drew spring water in a big basin and steeped the white hibiscuses; the guests have found their inner peace; the summer heat is no longer a torment." According to this, the content and the intent of this ci could be known. The first two sentences formed a causal relationship. It described the scene at sunset and the environment. This was mu one. The third sentence was the fan. *"Nice and cool"* was the creed and the motif. It is noteworthy that although this placement seems to be in the front portion, it should be considered a middle placement as far as structure is concerned. This is crucial in analysis. The rest of the text was describing what happened when the subject (Zhao Bu Zhi) was "drew spring water and steeped hibiscuses". *"Makes its way into the sleeves"* specified the spring water and *"Suddenly sober up"* depicted the sound and the form of the spring water in the well. The two sentences about *"snow flakes"* were describing the spring water's sprinkling over the lotuses. The coolness was like snow. These five sentences described *"Nice and cool"* in detail, which was the mu two. The following is the diagram of the structure.

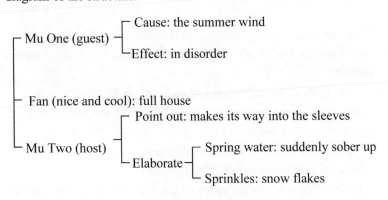

One more example is Xin Qi Ji's "Que Qiao Xian"

Going away for summer in the mountain full of pine trees. Taking shelter from rain under the eaves of the thatched cottage. I have come and gone leisurely like this several times. When I got drunk, I admired the splashed spring water while placing a hand on the grotesque rock. Suddenly I realized that was the same spot where I got drunk last time. The son from a household on the east side is getting married. The daughter from a household on the west side is also having a wedding. The lights were brightly lit in front of the boisterous houses filled with laughing and chatting. The acres of rice flowers are transpiring fragrance. It was cultivated by the wind and dews swaying every night.

> 松岡避暑，茆簷避雨，閒去閒來幾度。醉扶怪石看飛泉，
> 又卻是、前回醒處。　東家娶婦，西家歸女，燈火門前
> 笑語。釀成千頃稻花香，夜夜費、一天風露。（辛棄疾
> 〈鵲橋仙〉）

This ci was written in Song Xiao Zong Chun Xi sixteenth year (the year of 1189). It was noted, "Ji You Shan Xing Shu Suo Jian". The motif was leisure. It started with two sentences about a leisure activity, i.e., going away for summer in a mountain full of pine trees and taking shelter from rain under the eaves of the thatched cottage. This was mu one. Then *"I have come and gone leisurely like this several times"* pointed out the creed. This was fan. The following two sentences described a second leisure activity, which was admiring the splashed spring water. This was the first part of mu two. The two sentences about weddings were about the first leisure view, which was about the laughing and chatting. The last two sentences formed the second leisure view, which was about the acres of rice flowers blown by winds. The above four sentences constituted the second part of the mu two. The author used leisure to link the context and the leisure was vividly supported by what he did and saw.[27] The diagram of the structure is as follows:

----

27 Chang Guo Wu, See "Introduction to Xin Jia Xuan's Tzu" 《辛稼軒詞集導讀》 (Cheng Du: Ba Shu Publications: 1ˢᵗ edition 1ˢᵗ print, September 1988), p.229.

```
┌─ Mu One (leisure activity one): first two sentences
│
├─ Fan (leisure): I have come and gone leisurely like this several times
│
│              ┌─ Leisure activity two: the two sentences about getting drunk
└─ Mu Two ─┤
           │              ┌─ One: the two sentences about weddings
           └─ Leisure views ─┤
                          └─ Two: the last two sentences
```

One last example is Xin Qi Ji's "He Xin Lang"

I have been rather decrepit. I resent that all my friends and acquaintances are old and feeble. How many years do I have left? The long white hair is hanging down. On second thought, I decide to laugh it out. Is there anything that can please you? I see the green mountains and they appear to be lovely. I think this is the same way the mountains see me. Perhaps, this is because our emotions and appearances share some resemblance.

I scratch my head while drinking at the eastern facing window. A poem will be finished soon. This moment is worth relishing. In Jiang Zuo there are people who aggressively pursue fame and wealth in Jiang Zuo. They can never grasp the wonder of this thick wine. I turn my head to shout. The clouds and winds are flying in response. I don't regret that I could not meet the people in the past. I am sorry that the people in the past did not see my frenzy. There are too few people who understand me nowadays.

甚矣吾衰矣。悵平生、交遊零落，只今餘幾！白髮空垂三千丈。一笑人間萬事。問何物、能令公喜？我見青山多嫵媚，料青山、見我應如是。情與貌，略相似。　一尊搔首東窗裏。想淵明、〈停雲詩〉就，此時風味。江左沈酣

求名者，豈識濁醪妙理。回首叫，雲飛風起。不恨古人吾
不見，恨古人、不見吾狂耳。知我者，二三子。（辛棄疾
〈賀新郎〉）

This ci was produced in the first year of Song Ning Zong Qing Wen (the year of 1198). It was noted, "In the garden, one day, I sat alone in Ting-Yun. The sound of water and the mountain scenery were all amusedly. Then I made several sentences to voice my yearning to relatives and friends.". In light of this, this ci was written to commemorate friends. The author went from resentful to drunk to frenzy. This was similar to the situation where Tao Yuan Ming was writing "Ting Yun Shi". The author used the three sentences starting with "*I scratch my head while drinking at the eastern facing window*" to denote this connotation. The "relishing" was the creed linking to the context. From the beginning to "*share some resemblance*", it was about resentment. It first pointed out missing friends. From "*I have been rather decrepit*" to "*to laugh it out*", it depicted the disappointment, which was the cause. From "*Is there anything*" to "*share some resemblance*", it depicted the use of scenery as a token for his emotions, which was the effect. In the part about frenzy, it started with the two sentences about "*Jiang Zuo*" to describe the drunkenness, followed by "*I turn my head to shout*", which was the effect. From "*I don't regret*" to the end, it directly revealed the frenzy and ended with self-pity on having no one understanding him. This was the cause. This constituted a structure of "mu fan mu". A diagram is in the following.[28]

....

28 See Liou Si Fen "Xin Qi Ji's Tzu" 《辛棄疾詞選》 (Taipei: Wuan Liou Culture Company 1st edition, October 1982), p.109.

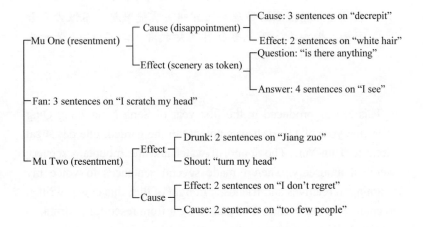

2. Abstract-concrete structures

The method of abstract and concrete encompasses a wide range of forms. Besides emotion and scenery, description and commentary, comprehensive and detail (emotions and matters, theory and scenery), conjecture (wishes, fantasies) and reality, it also involved time and space. In this text,[29] we only discuss emotion and scenery, comprehensive and detail (emotions and matters) as examples. As far as this method is concerned, placing the motif or creed in the middle inevitably constitutes the structure of "concrete, abstract, concrete".

For example, Su Shi's "Xing Xiang Zi" （蘇軾〈行香子〉）

一葉舟輕。(A small boat is lightweight.) 雙槳鴻驚。(With

-----

29 See Chen Man Ming, "On A Few Tactics of Employing Compositional Materials" 〈談運用辭章材料的幾種基本手段〉 (Taipei: Zhong Deng Jiao Yu Volume 36, Issue 5, October 1985), pp.5-23. Also see Qiou Xiao Pin, *On Compositional Art* 《文章章法論》 (Taipei: Wuan Juan Lou Publications 1st edition, November 1998), pp.222-278.

double paddles, it is fleeting like a startled goose.) 水天清、影湛波平。(The sky is blue and reflected in the lucid and clam water.)魚翻藻鑑，(The fish in the water are countable and frequently jump out of the water.)鷺點煙汀。(The egrets are like white dots casually scattering around.)過沙溪急，(The creek in the morning was rapid.)霜溪冷，(The creek at dawn was cold.) 月溪明。(The creek under the moon was crystal.)　重重似畫，(The overlapping mountains seem like a painting.)曲曲如屏。(They also look like a tortuous screen from a different angle.) 算當年、虛老嚴陵。(Many years ago, Ian Zi Ling wasted his time here.) 君 臣 一 夢 ，(Emperors and hermits all have disappeared like a dream)今古空名。(They only left behind a meaningless name.)但遠山長，雲山亂，曉山青。(Only the mountains, clouds, and the morning sunlight lasted until today.)

This ci was made in Song Shen Zong Xi Ning sixth year (the year of 1073). It was noted "passing by Qi Li Lai" The first five sentences at the beginning described the views before the boat arriving at Qi Li Lai. The next three sentences described the changes in the view in different times. "Rapid", "cold", and "crystal" implied the different moods according to the changes in the view. The two sentences about *"the overlapping mountains"* described the view on the shore when passing by Qi Li Lai. The views were thus orderly linked together, and it was the first concrete part so far. The three sentences about *"many years ago"* were using Ian Zi Ling's story to express his feelings about *"disappeared like a dream"*. (See Hou Han Shu: Yi Min Zhuan: Yan Guang) This was where the motif resided, and was the abstract part. The last sentence was concluded with the views, depicting the changes in the view when passing through Yan Ling Lai. It symbolized the author's mood changing from heavy to delightful. This was another concrete part. This was a structure in line with "concrete, abstract, concrete), where feelings and views were intertwined. A diagram is as follows.[30]

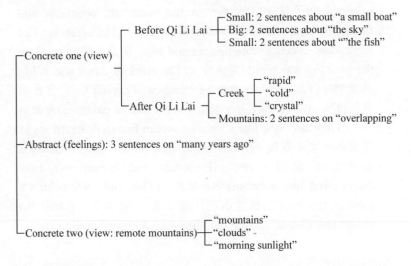

Another example is Su Shi's "Wan Xi Sha". （蘇軾〈浣溪沙〉）

雪裏餐氈例姓蘇。(Once again the person whose last name is Su is struggling to make a living in this freezing snow.)使君載酒為回車。(Xu Tai Shou carried wine to Lin Gao.)天寒酒色轉頭無。(Drinking in this cold weather will consume all the wine in no time.)   薦士已聞飛鶚表，(I have heard that Xu Tai Shou wrote a recommendation letter for me to the government.)報恩應不用蛇珠。(I don't think I need to repay this favor with expensive gifts.)醉中還許攬桓鬚。(I just need to show my gratitude by getting drunk and then stroke Tai Shou's beard.)

....

30 Long Mu Xun. See "Dong Po Wue Fu Qian Jiang Shu" Volume 1《東坡樂府箋講疏》卷一(Taipei: Gong Wen Publications 1st edition, September 1972), p.3.

This ci was the third one in a set, written in Song Shen Zong Wen Feng fourth year (the year of 1081). It was noted, "On December 2, it was snowing a little after the rain. Xu Tai Shou brought wine to visit me. I wrote the three ci, entitled Wan Xi Sha." It started with the three sentences about *"freezing snow"* to describe Xu Tai Shou's visit and they both got drunk. This was the first concrete part. The next two sentences about *"recommendation letter"* form causality to point out the creed. It meant to say Xu Tai Shou's done favor for him (cause) but he had nothing to return this favor with (effect). In the last sentence, he borrowed the story about Xie An stroking Huan In's beard (see "Jin Shu: Huan In Zhuan") to show his gratitude and appreciation toward Xu Tai Shou. This was the second concrete part.

```
┌─Concrete One (matter) ─┬─ First (visit): 2 sentences on "the freezing snow"
│                        └─ After (drunk): "cold weather"
│
├─Abstract (emotion) ─┬─ Cause (a favor): "recommendation letter"
│                     └─ Effect (nothing to return): "repay this favor"
│
└─Concrete Two (matter): "getting drunk"
```

Another example is Xin Qi Ji's "Qing Pin Wue". （辛棄疾〈清平樂〉）

遠床飢鼠，蝙蝠翻燈舞。(Rats are crawling around my bed. Bats are flying around the lamp.)屋上松風吹急雨，(Outside the pine tress are blowing in the strong wind and heavy rain.)破紙窗間自語。(The ragged paper windows are making sounds as if murmuring.)　平生塞北江南，(In my whole life, I have been toiling between Sai Bei and Jiang Nan.)歸來華髮蒼顏。(When I return, now my hair is all white and face is aged.)布被秋宵夢覺。(I wake up under the cloth blanket at the night in autumn.)眼前萬里江山。(My country's territory once again appears in front of me.)

This ci was written while the author isolated himself from the society around the year of 1186. It was noted, "living alone in Sage Wang's house". In the shang pian, the first two sentences provided a visual. The next two sentences offered acoustic sensation. They presented a bleak scene betokening the country was no longer the same. This was the first concrete part. In the xia pian, the first two sentences were lyrical, although it was not purely lyrical. They expressed his feelings about his situation, which was the motif. This was the abstract part. The last two sentences described the scenery after waking up from a dream, implying the fact that the country was still occupied by enemies. This was the second concrete part. This pian's structure was hence "concrete, abstract, concrete". The feelings and the views were successfully blending together and created a sorrowful sentiment.[31]

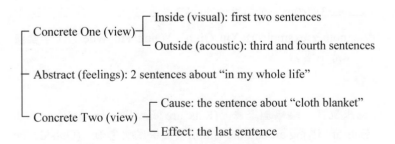

```
                          ┌ Inside (visual): first two sentences
      ┌ Concrete One (view)┤
      │                    └ Outside (acoustic): third and fourth sentences
      │
 ─────┤ Abstract (feelings): 2 sentences about "in my whole life"
      │
      │                     ┌ Cause: the sentence about "cloth blanket"
      └ Concrete Two (view) ┤
                            └ Effect: the last sentence
```

31 Chang Guo Wu. See "Introduction to Xin Jia Xuan 's Tzu" 《辛稼軒詞集導讀》 (Cheng Du: Ba Shu Publications: 1st edition 1st print, September 1988), p.182.

（辛棄疾〈八聲甘州〉）

故將軍飲罷夜歸來，After Li Guang was dismissed from his military position, one day he went home after few drinks. 長亭解雕鞍。He was stopped before Ba Ling, so he took down the saddle and spent the night in the open air. 恨灞陵醉尉，匆匆未識，桃李無言。That drunken guard at Ba Ling was so reckless that he did not recognize this hero. 射虎山橫一騎，Li Guang rode the horse to the mountain to hunt tigers. 裂石響驚弦。The bow made a huge sound and a rock was penetrated by the arrow. 落魄封侯事，He was never appreciated and was never appointed to a higher position. 歲晚田園。In his old age, he was removed from his post and could only hide in countryside.　誰向桑麻杜曲，No one wants to leave a comfortable and wealthy life. 要短衣匹馬，移住南山。And move to Nan Shan to support a living by hunting. 看風流慷慨，譚笑過殘年。Decided to open his mind Spending the rest of his life carefree 漢開邊、功名萬里，When Han Dynasty was expanding its territory, he was a main contributor. 甚當時、健者也曾閑。How come a man like Li Guang would be discarded by the authorities? 紗窗外、斜風細雨，一陣輕寒。Outside the window screen, there were light winds and rains. They brought chills.

This ci was also written when the author was living a hermitical life around the year of 1185. It was noted, "I was reading Li Guang Zhuan at night and could not sleep. I thought of pact between Zhao Chu Lao and Yiang Min Zhan, so I used Li Guang's story to express my thoughts." From the first sentence to *Spending the rest of his life carefree*", it was narrative. Here, it employed a "first mu then fan" structure to divide the text into two layers. In the shang pian, it described Li Guang's story. In the xia pian, it used Du Fu's Qu Jiang chapter three "My life if ends is not fate. Fortunately I still have some farms. I will move to live by Nan Shan. I will wear plain dress and ride horses like Li Guang. I will spend the rest of my life by watching hunting tigers." They shared the same commonality; that is, LI Guang. That was the first concrete part. The two sentences about "Han Dynasty" still relied on Li Guang's story to express his feelings. It was bemoaning Li Guang's being sidelined. This was the motif, which was the abstract part. The last two sentences were summarizing the feelings by describing the views. It secretly borrowed Su Shi's "Han Liou Dao Wuan Iong Shi": "Du yan chen bian diao xing fei, chuang qian shang yu ye lang lang.". He used this to conclude the text, which was the second "concrete" part.[32]

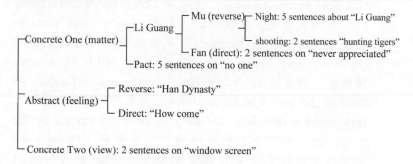

3. Secondary-primary method

"Primary" means the main point. "Secondary" means auxiliary. This type of structure consists of "secondary, primary", "primary, secondary", "secondary, primary, secondary", and "primary, secondary, primary". Among them, "secondary, primary, secondary"

....

32 See Liou Si Fen "Xin Qi Ji ' Tzu" 《辛棄疾詞選》(Taipei: Wuan Liou Culture Company 1st edition, October 1982), p.70.

is more likely to contain a motif or creed in the middle.
For example, Su Shi's "Jiang Cheng Zi":

鳳凰山下雨初晴。Under Feng Huang Shan, the rain just stopped. 水風清。晚霞明。The water is lucid. The afterglow is bright. 一朵芙蕖，開過尚盈盈。The woman who plays the zither is as pretty as the lotus. 何處飛來雙白鷺，如有意，慕娉婷。 Two egrets flew in as if they are also admiring the beauty of the woman.   忽聞江上弄哀箏。Suddenly the melody sounds sad. 苦含情。遣誰聽。This kind of sadness, who can be unaffected? 煙斂雲收，The mist and the clouds seem to fade due to the heartbroken melody. 依約是湘靈。This splendid but sorrowful music can only come from a goddess. 欲待曲終尋問取，Wanted to wait until the song is over to ask about it 人不見，But, the player has been gone 數峰青。Only the green mountains still stand tall. (蘇軾〈江城子〉)

This ci was produced in Song Shen Zong Xi Ning seventh year (the year of 1074). It was noted, "On the lake singing with Zhang Xian Tong, we heard zither playing". Its shang pian was used to describe the lake view. This was secondary in line with "secondary, primary, secondary". The first secondary part was the first three sentences, describing the view after rain. The primary part was the sentence regarding *The woman who plays the zither is as pretty as the lotus*". The last secondary part was about the *"Two egrets"*. In this order, he depicted the lake view from far to near beautifully. In the xia pian, the first four sentences first bring out the woman who was compared with a goddess, and her melody's sadness. This sadness was the motif. Therefore, this was the primary part. The following three sentences borrowed from Qian Qi (Sheng Shi Xiang Ling Gu Se) "when the song ends, the person has been gone. Only the green mountains can be seen from the river" to echo with Feng Huang Shan mentioned at the beginning. This was the last secondary part. The author used the clear view as the secondary force to contrast the primary sadness, which made the sadness more endless and more affective.[33]

```
                              ┌ Secondary: 3 sentences about "Feng Huang"
 ┌ Secondary One (view)─┤ Primary: 2 sentences about "a flower"
 │                            └ Secondary: 3 sentences about "two egrets"
 │
 ├ Primary (people)─┌ Acoustic: 3 sentences about "the melody sounds"
 │                       └ Visual: 2 sentences about "fade"
 │
 └ Secondary Two (view): 3 sentences about "wanted to wait"
```

Another example is Su Shi's "Jian Zi Mu Lan Hua".

雙龍對起。Two one trees stand tall opposite to each other as two dragons. 白甲蒼髯煙雨裏。They have white scales and green whiskers and fly in the misty rain. 疏影微香。In the sifting shadows I seem to smell some aroma. 下有幽人畫夢長。There is a monk asleep lying under it.   湖風清軟。The wind over the lake is soft and gossamer. 雙鵲飛來爭噪晚。A pair of magpies flies into the tree and chirping noisily. 翠颭紅輕。The breeze slightly blows the green trees and the red flowers are gently vibrating 時下凌霄百尺英。Occasionally the red flowers would fall down from the tree slowly. (蘇軾〈減字木蘭花〉)

This ci was written in Song Zhe Zong Wen You fourth year (the year of 1089). It was noted, "By Qian Tang Xi Hu, a monk named,

---

[33] Long Mu Xun, See "Dong Po Wue Fu Qian Jiang Shu" Volume 1《東坡樂府箋講疏》卷一(Taipei: Gong Wen Publications 1st edition, September 1972), p.14.

Qing Shuen living there, In front of his house, there were two old pine trees. They both had flowers that climb onto them. Shuen often lay under the trees. One day, I passed there and the pine trees were disturbed by the wind. Shuen asked me to write something about the fallen flowers. Therefore, I wrote this." It started with three sentences describing the two old pine trees. This was the first secondary part. It was followed by *"There is a monk asleep lying under it"*. This described the sleeping monk under the pine trees, who was Qing Shuen. This was the primary part. The last four sentences described the flowers falling down due to the magpies' tread. This was the last secondary part. Apparently, the author used the old pine trees and fallen flowers (secondary) to strengthen the monk's casualness.

```
                                   ┌ Trees: 2 sentences about "two dragons"
      ┌ Secondary One (pine trees) ┤
      │                            └ Shadow aroma: "in the sifting shadow"
      ├ Primary (casual monk): "there is a monk"
      │                                ┌ Cause: 3 sentences about "the wind"
      └ Secondary Two (fallen flowers) ┤
                                       └ Effect: "occasionally"
```

One more example is Xin Qi Ji's "Dong Xian Ge".

There are a few fellows at Jiang Tou. They were talking about politics. They all said this year is a peaceful year. When they saw your gorgeous clothing, accessories, and appearances, they said you are just like Bei Song's Si Ma Guang.

Remotely, when they knew the king wanted to see you in the prime minister's office where the lights are especially bright, they gave you Xian Shao right after Wen Xiao. I ask God how many springs we have. It is like in the corporal life. We often see you glow as if in a painting. I wish someday you can recover all the lands belonging to us and return them to our king. I wish to see both you and your son are successful. You can wait in the capital for our king to go back.

> 江頭父老，說新來朝野，都道今年太平也。見朱顏綠鬢，
> 玉帶金魚，相公是，舊日中朝司馬。　遙知宣勸處：東閣
> 華燈，別賜〈仙韶〉接元夜。問天上，幾多春，只似人
> 間，但長見、精神如畫。好都取山河獻君王；看父子貂
> 蟬，玉京迎駕。(辛棄疾〈洞仙歌〉)

　　This ci was produced in the first year of Song Xiao Zong Chuen Xi first year (the year of 1174). It was noted, "the prime minister's birthday". In shang pian, the first three sentences described the joy of having a peaceful year.　Then, the following four sentences pointed out Yeh Heng was the prime minister and offered compliments on his achievement, which led to the celebration of the birthday. This was the first secondary part. In xia pian, the first seven sentences were the birthday good wishes, which was the primary part. The three sentences about *"recover all the lands"* were anticipating Yeh Heng's success in taking back the lost lands, which was meant to reinforce the birthday good wishes. This was the last secondary part. To make the motif regarding the birthday more distinct, it used a peaceful year and Yeh Heng's present and future accomplishments as the reinforcer (secondary) to express birthday good wishes to Yeh Heng (primary).

```
┌ Secondary One (present)┌ Cause: 3 sentences about "Jiang Tou"
│                        └ Effect: 4 sentences about "when they saw you"
│
│ Primary ┌ King's blessing: 3 sentences about "the king wanted to see you"
│         └ Birthday wishes: 4 sentences about "I ask God"
│                            ┌ Cause: "recover all the lands"
└ Secondary Two (future) ┤
                           └ Effect: 2 sentences about "both you and your son"
```

One last example is Xin Qi Ji's "Qian Nian Diao".

A person's conduct should be like a wine pot. It is always nicely leaning toward people. Most importantly, it is obsequious. We should say yes to everything. The bigwigs are like "Hua Ji" talking nonsense nonstop. They favor people like Di Yi who always ingratiate them. They are like gan cao in herbal medicine. They could cure all illness. Hence win the name as Guo Lao.

When I was young, I liked to engage in a harangue after few drinks. I often offended someone everytime when I started talking. The art of getting along with people is profound. I only learned about it recently. However, I have not been adept in following others' opinions. I look at them. They are well-liked by their superiors. They are just like mynah birds that are good at mimicking people's talking.

> 卮酒向人時，和氣先傾倒。最要然然可可，萬事稱好。滑
> 稽坐上，更對鴟夷笑。寒與熱，總隨人，甘國老。　　少
> 年使酒，出口人嫌拗。此箇和合道理，近日方曉：學人言
> 語，未會十分巧。看他們，得人憐，秦吉了。（辛棄疾
> 〈千年調〉）

This ci was written in Song Xia Zong Chuen Xi thirteenth year (the year of 1186). It was noted, "laughing at flattering speeches". In the first nine sentences, it used some instruments and herbal medicine to sarcastically describe people who have no opinions and like to cater. This was the first secondary part. The following six sentences about "*When I was young*" were directly about the author's arrogant and gauche personality. This was the primary part. The last three sentences again sarcastically describe mynah birds are popular because of their ability to mimic speech. This was the last secondary part. The sarcasm was successfully conveyed.[34]

```
                          ┌─Wine pot: 4 sentences about "wine pot"
  ┌─Secondary One (sarcastic)─┼─Hua Ji and Di Yi: 2 sentences about "Hua Ji"
  │                        └─Gan cao: 2 sentences about "cure all illness"
  │                        ┌─Past: 2 sentences about "when I was young"
  ┼─Primary (the author)─┤
  │                        └─Present: 4 sentences about "the art"
  │
  └─Secondary Two (sarcastic: mynah birds): 3 sentences about "I look at them"
```

4. Cause-effect methods

This method is commonly used in ci-zhang. Its structure is composed of "cause, effect", "effect, cause", "cause, effect, cause", "effect, cause, effect". In "effect, cause, effect",[35] in terms of pian, the cause in the middle may contain the motif or creed.

For example: Su Shi's "Jiang Cheng Zi"

I wan bashful and timid to see others. I always furtively and covertly cried because I could not see my husband who was in the capital of the country. The road to the capital seemed to be endless. I sang and drank for our parting. It was easy for me to see the sky, but not my husband. I had my eyes filled with the spring scenery in this "Gu-shang-zhu-ge". However, when I sought to recollect the past, I got no answers.

....

34 See Xia Wuei Wuei, *Analysis of the Guest-Master Composition Method.*《賓主章法析論》 (Taipei: Wen Jin Publications 1st edition 1st print, December 2002), p.342.
35 See Chen Man Ming "Tan Pian Zhang Jie Gou" "Shang" "Xia" 《談篇章結構》（上）（下） (Taipei: Guo Wen Tian Di Volume 15, Issue 5 and 6, October and November 1999), pp. 65-71; pp. 57-66.

翠娥羞黛怯人看。掩霜紈。淚偷彈。且盡一尊，收淚聽
〈陽關〉。漫道帝城天樣遠，天易見，見君難。
畫堂新㰽近孤山。曲闌干。為誰安，飛絮落花，春色屬明
年。欲棹小舟尋舊事，無處問，水連天。（蘇軾〈江城
子〉）

```
                    ┌─ Earlier (cried covertly): 3 sentences about "the married woman"
      ┌─ Effect One ┤
      │             └─ Later (Sang and drank): 2 sentence about "the parting"
      │        ┌─ Effect: the sentence about "the capital"
 ─────┼─ Cause ┤
      │        └─ Cause: 2 sentences about "seeing her husband was difficult"
      │             ┌─ Concrete (present): 3 sentences about "the new studio"
      └─ Effect Two ┤
                    └─ Abstract (next year): 5 sentences about "the spring scenery"
```

Another examples is Su Shi's "Zui Luo Puo"

分攜如昨。It seems we said goodbye just yesterday. 人生到處
萍飄泊。Life is like duckweed floating around. 偶然相聚還離
索。We happened to meet but soon need to say goodbye again.
多病多愁，We suffer from not only illness but worries. 須信從
來錯。I should believe this is a mistake since beginning. 尊前
一笑休辭卻。Don't say no to the opportunities to happily
drink. 天涯同是傷淪落。We are the same kind of losers. 故山
猶負平生約。I violated the promise that I would retire early and
go home. 西望峨嵋，When I overlook the E Mei mountain in
the west, 長羨歸飛鶴。I often envy those cranes flying home.
（蘇軾〈醉落魄〉）

This ci was also written in Song Shen Zong Xi Ning seventh year
(the year of 1074). It was noted, "A dedication to Yang Yuan Su".

Yang Yuan Su, also Yang Hui, was Hang Shou at the time. He was an old friend to Su Shi and they were both underappreciated in their career. This time, Su Shi was about to leave Jin Kou to Mi Zhou. He had to leave Yang Yuan Su in a hurry.[36] Naturally, he started to become sentimental. Hence, Su Shi said in the middle *"We are the same kind of losers"*. This was the underlying motivation for his sentiments. From the beginning to *"I should believe"*, it was centered on the sentiment about parting. The sentences about "go home", were centered on the idea of retiring. Thus, the structure of this pian was "effect, cause, effect".

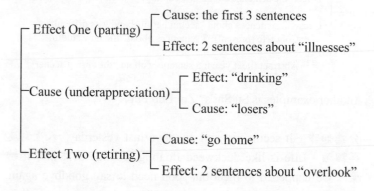

Another example is Xin Qi Ji's "Shui Long In".

楚天千里清秋，The sky above Chu area was clear in this autumn view. 水隨天去秋無際。The river is extending to the sky, so it seems endless. 遙岑遠目，I overlook the remote mountains 獻愁供恨，玉簪螺髻。. The views can only trigger my worries and resentment, although they look like women's pretty hairpins. 落日樓頭，(The sunset is hiding behind the

....

36　Chen Er Dong. See "Su Shi Ci Xuan" 《蘇軾詞選》 (Bei Jin: Ren Min Literate Publications 1st edition, 8th print, July 1986), pp.23-24.

buildings.) 斷鴻聲裏，江南遊子。(The lost goose is howling. I am like a vagabond in Jing Nan.) 把吳鉤（鉤）看了，欄干拍遍，無人會，登臨意。(I take a look at the useless sword. I pound on the railings repeatedly. No one appreciates me.) 休說鱸魚堪膾，儘西風，季鷹歸未？(Now the west wind is blowing, who does not want to go home?) 求田問舍，怕應羞見，劉郎才氣。(I am not like Zhang Han, who went home for foods. Nor am I like Xu Si, who was trying to buy a house.) 可惜流年，憂愁風雨，樹猶如此！(I am worried the time has past. The country is unstable. I am getting too old to serve my country.) 倩何人、喚取紅巾翠袖，搵英雄淚？(Who can I ask to wipe out my heroic tears?)（辛棄疾〈水龍吟〉）

This ci was written in the first year of Song Xiao Zong Chuen Xi first year(the year of 1174). It was noted, "Visiting Jian Kan Shang Xin Ting". The motif was about the depression of *"No one appreciates me"*. It started with four sentences about *"The sky above Chu Di"* to describe the views from Shang Xin Ting. In order, they were sky, river, and mountains. The depression was blended into these views. They were followed by the sentences about *"The sunset"*. He used sunset and lost goose as the inducer to introduce himself as a vagabond. Furthermore, he mentioned the useless sword and pounding the railings to show there is nothing he could do even with all his aspirations. This was the first effect. The motif could be seen at *"No one appreciates me"*. This was the primary part in the cause. He then used some stories about Zhang Han, Xu Si, and Huan Wen to strengthen the expression of his agony resulting from the failure to convince the government to fight a war. This was the concrete part of the cause. The last sentence turned into abstract and concluded the whole text implying his strong aspiration to retrieve his homeland by war. This was the last effect. The author successfully vented his accumulated rancor.[37]

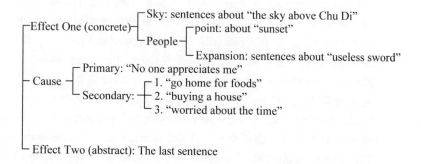

The last example is Xin Qi Ji's "Shui Diao Ge Tou"

我飲不須勸，I don't need to you to encourage me to drink. 正怕酒尊空。 I only fear the wine glass is empty. 別離亦復何恨，此別恨匆匆。 There is no need to be sad about parting. The only regret is that we could not spend more time together. 頭上貂蟬貴客， There were people who wear expensive clothes. 苑外麒麟高塚，They all ended up in the graves. 人世竟誰雄。 Who is the real hero? 一笑出門去，千里落花風。 To look at the bright side, we can all laugh it out and take off. The wind is shaking off those colorful flowers. 孫劉輩，能使我，不為公。 People like Sun Zi and Liu Fang are powerful, but at worst they can only prevent me from being promoted. 余髮種種如是， I am too old as my hair is falling. 此事付渠儂。 These matters are of no importance to me anymore. 但覺平生湖海，I only regret that all my life I am drifting around. 除了醉吟風月，此外百無功。 Except for drinking and writing poems, I did

<hr>

37 Liang Qi Chao. See "Xin Jia Xuan Xian Sheng Nian Pu" 《辛稼軒先生年譜》 "Zeng Ding Ben Jia Xuan Ci Bian Nian Qian Zhu" 《增訂本稼軒詞編年箋注》附(Taipei: Hua Zheng Publications, December 1978), p.8.

not have much accomplishment. 毫髮皆帝力，更乞鑑胡東。
Anyways, what we have is all owing to the king's mercy. Now,
I can only hope to spend the rest of my life peacefully in the east
of Jian Hu. (辛棄疾〈水調歌頭〉)

This ci was written in Song Xiao Zong Chuen Xi fifth year (the
year of 1178). It was noted, "Chuen Xi Ding You, since we were
displaced from Jiang Ling to Long Xing, we were summoned and
given a farewell dinner by Si Ma Jian, Zhao Qing and Wang Cao. Si
Ma Fu's "Shui Diao Ge Tou" had mentioned this." From this, we
can know Xin Qi Ji's this work not only expressed the resentment
for leaving (secondary), but also revealed his discontent with his life
(primary).[38] This discontent and resentment surfaced in the middle.
They could be found in the text from "*There is no need*" to "*from
being promoted*". The sentences about parting were related to the
resentment for leaving. The sentences about "*expensive clothes*"
implied the disparity in family status. The two sentences about
"*laugh it out*" were meant to reinforce it. All the above was the
secondary part. The sentences about "*People like Sun Zi and Liu
Fang*" were describing his being excluded from the authorities. This
was the primary part and the motif was here. If we grasped the cause
here, then the effects at the beginning and at the end would become
conspicuous. The first effect involved the first two sentences at the
beginning. They talked about drinking, which implied the
resentment for leaving and the discontent with his life. The second
effect started with "*I am too old as my hair is falling*" and "*These
matters are of no importance to me anymore*". They mentioned his
aging. Then in the sentences about "*I only regret*" he described his
doing nothing, and in the last two sentences he said he desired to

....

38 Chang Guo Wu, See "Xin Jia Xuan Ci Ji Dao Du" 《辛稼軒詞集導讀》 (Cheng
Du: Ba Shu Publications: 1st edition 1st print, September 1988), p.142.

live a peaceful life. Weren't these all the result of resenting being underappreciated?

```
┌─Effect One (drunk): the first two sentences
│
│                                              ┌─ Resentment for leaving: 2 sentences about "parting"
│                                    ┌─ Point ─┤
│              ┌─ Secondary ─┤              └─Discontent with life: 3 sentences on "expensive clothes"
├─Cause─┤              └─ Reinforce: 2 sentences about "laugh it out"
│              └─Primary (whining about life): 2 sentences on "Sun Zi and Liu Fang"
│
│                              ┌─Being old: 2 sentences on "I am too old"
│                   ┌─ Cause ─┤
└─Effect Two ─┤              └─No accomplishment: sentences on "I only regret"
                    └─ Effect (desire to life a secluded life): the last two sentences.
```

From the aforementioned discussions, it is salient that an article's motif or creed can be placed in the middle and there are many types of structure to form the lexical composition. Because they tend to play a role that connects the first half and the second half, they often achieve the stress on the motif or creed and symmetry. This is rather special. There are other structures which are also possible, and they need to be explored separately.

Chapter **5**

Logical Structures of
"Many, Two, One/Zero"

In the logical structure of 'multiplicity/duality/singularity/(naught)', *zhang* (the local text) refers mainly to 'multiplicity/duality' and *pian* (the global text) to 'singularity/(naught)'. It is required by this logic that *zhang* and *pian* be united in one entity, a logic that highlights the interrelationship between them. This chapter explores the logic of 'multiplicity /duality/singularity/(naught)' (Hereafter referred to as M/D/S(N)) manifested in the text (pian-zhang) by first reviewing the nature of the logic and second examining its aesthetic effects.

I. The structure of "many, two, one/zero"

1. the formation of the structure of "many/multiplicity, two/duality, one/singularity/zero/naught"

Undertaking the neverending knowledge-seeking cycle of 'having form' and 'devoid of form', the ancient sages sailed through layers of mist and came to identify the first cause of the cosmos, and its activities that bring about the whole creation on earth. The process of creation, from emptiness to being, is embodied in a progressive order of '(naught)/singularity/duality/multeity' (or (N)/S/D/M), as what is in the mean time established in its regression from multeity to naughtiness.

In *Zhouyi* (also called *I Ching*), or the *Book of Changes* of the Zhou Dynasty (including the *Yizhuan*, or the Commentaries), where our discussion begins, the arrangement of the sixty-four hexagrams implies the M/D/S/(N) structure. *The Treatise on the Order of the Hexagrams*, one of the Commentaries of *Zhouyi* describes the process of which such a structure comes into being. The hexagrams, notwithstanding the fact that their 'given significances are decided by their order'[1], can truthfully reflect the structure with their symbolic nature, or 象 *xiang*, emblematic concept that represents changes and varieties of the universe and human life[2], as is demonstrated in the following passages.

有天地，然後萬物生焉 (Where there were heaven and earth, there were generated all things.) 盈天地之間唯萬物，(Filling up between heaven and earth are all things.) 故受之以屯；(Hence after *Qien* (meaning heaven) and *Kun* (meaning earth), the hexagram of *Tuen* is given.) 屯者，盈也。(*Tuen* denotes filling up.) 屯者，物之始生也，(Tuen is what all things were at their beginning.) 物生必蒙，(Things at the beginning were necessarily ignorant.) 故受之以蒙；(Hence Hexagram of *Meng* is given.) 蒙者，物之稚也。(*Meng* means ignorance and the earliest stages of things.) 物稚不可不養也，(Things at their earliest stages must be provided with nourishment.) 故受之以需；(Hence the hexagram of *Xu* is given.) 需者，飲食之道也。(*Xu* means the way of eating and drinking.) (Section 1)……有天地然後有萬物，(Heaven and earth existing, all things were generated.) 有萬物然後有男女，(All things having existence, there came male and female.) 有男女然後有夫婦，(From the

1 Dai Lianzhang, *The Formation of Yizhuan and Its Thinking* (易傳之形成及其思想)(Taipei: Wenjing, 1989), pp. 186~7.

2 Xu Fuguan, *A History of Chinese Thinking about Humanity: The Pre-Qin Period*s (中國人性論史:先秦篇)(Taipei: The Commercial Press, 1978), p.202. See also Feng Yolan, *Anthology of Feng Yolan*(馮友蘭選集) (Beijin: The Beijing University Press, 2000), p.394.

existence of male and female there came afterwards husband and wife.) 有夫婦然後有父子，(From husband and wife there came father and son.) 有父子然後有君臣，(From father and son there came ruler and minister.) 有君臣然後有上下，(From ruler and minister there came high and low.) 有上下然後禮義有所錯。(When high and low had existence, afterwards came the arrangements of propriety and righteousness.) 夫婦之道不可以不久也，(The rule for the relation of husband and wife is that it should be long-enduring.) 故受之以恆；(Hence the hexagram of *Xian* is followed by that of *Heng*.) 恆者，久也。(*Heng* means long enduring.) 物不可以終久於其所，(Things cannot long abide in the same place;) 故受之以遯；(and hence *Heng* is followed by the hexagram of *Dun*.) 遯者，退也。(*Dun* denotes withdrawing.) 物不可以終遯，(Things cannot be for ever withdrawn;) 故受之以大壯。(and hence *Dun* is succeeded by the hexagram of *Dazhuang)* ……渙者，離也。(....*Huan* denotes separation and division.) 物不可以終離，(A state of division cannot continue forever,) 故受之以節。(and therefore *Huan* is followed by *Jieh*.) 節而信之，(Meaning the system of regulations, *Jieh* means trust by men,) 故受之以中孚。(and hence it is followed by *Zhong-fu*.) 有其信者必行之，(He who believes is sure to carry it into practice;) 故受之以小過。(and hence *Xiao-guo* follows.) 有過物者必濟，(Anything that surpasses others is sure to succeed;) 故受之以既濟。(and hence *Ji-jih* follows.) 物不可窮也，(The succession cannot exhaust itself;) 故受之以未濟終焉。(therefore it is followed by *Wei-jih*, which concludes the hexagrams.) (Section 2)

The passages highlight the changing processes of oppositions and correlations derived from the 64 hexagrams. The cosmological process, described here in the passage from Section 1 of the *Treatise on the Order*, and the process of humanity, as in the passage from

Section 2, are interrelated and explained correspondingly. Sze-Kwang Lao, when discussing the cosmological order in *Zhouyi*, says,

> The fact that the hexagrams are designed for divination means that they, in their symbolic representations, not only refer to the cosmological process but are also applicable to the process of human life. Out of this is revealed yet another traditional theory about the correspondence between the process of the cosmos and that of the human life.[3]

This correspondence is further contained within the ceaseless cycles of change and order. As Dai Lian-chang points out,

> Han Kang-bo mentioned in his commentary on *The Order of the Hexagram* that 'ancient scholars regarded the hexagrams from *Qian* to *Li* as upper canon, representing the heavenly, or cosmological, course, while *Xian* through *Wei Chi* as lower canon, representing the human affairs'. He refuted this interpretation since the hexagrams consist of six lines that absorb and synthesize all the Three Elements, i.e. the heaven, the earth and the mankind, in order to exhaust alterations. In this sense, 'how can be there an upper-lower separation of heavenly from human sections?' [I think] a mechanical dichotomy between heavenly rules, as upper, and human affairs, as lower, is not plausible; however, it is in *The Treatise on the Order* that the *Zhouyi* authors' attempt to 'synthesize the Heaven and the Mankind in order to exhaust alterations' can be best revealed.[4]

....

3 Lao Sze-Kwang, History of Chinese Philosophy: A New Compilation (新編中國哲學史), vol. 1（Taipei：San Min Bookstore, 1984）, pp.85-86.

4 Dai Lianzhang, The Formation of Yizhuan and Its Thinking, as in note 1 above.

Among the alterations that *Zhouyi* claims to exhaust, some proceed from the heaven through to the human and represent the (S)/D/M structure, while others the human to the heaven, representing, reversely, M/D/(S). (S) refers to Tai Chi, D to the coupling of heaven and earth, or yin and yang, hard and soft, whilst M stands for creation, including human affairs. Tai Chi and yin/yang, though not mentioned in the text, are always implied: without them, the Heaven and the Earth might never create the mundanity, nor can the authors be motivated to 'synthesize the heaven and the mankind in order to exhaust alterations.'

Tai Chi (Tao) and yin/yang (hard/soft) are described mainly in the *Treatise of the 'Tuan' Interpretations* and *Treatise of Appended Words*, in a way that represents the S/D/M structure.

大哉乾元，(Vast is *Qian* as the great and the original!) 萬物資始，(All things owe to it their beginning.) 乃統天。(It contains heaven) ……乾道變化，(.... The method of *Qian* is to change and transform,) 各正性命。(so that everything obtains its correct nature as appointed.) (〈乾象〉) ('Chien Tuan')

至哉坤元，(Limitlessness is *Kun* as the great and the original!) 萬物資生，(All things owe to it their beginning.) 乃順承天。(It supports and contains all things under heaven.) 坤厚載物，(Its comprehension is broad, and its brightness great.) 德合无疆。(All things obtain (by it) their full development.) (〈坤象〉) ('Kun Tuan')

一陰一陽之謂道，(One yin and one yang is called the Way, or Tao.) 繼之者善也，(What is tied to it is goodness;) 成之者性也。(what completes it is life.) (〈繫辭上〉) (*Appended Words* I)

是故易有太極，(Therefore in *Zhouyi* there is the 'grand terminus', or Tai Chi,) 是生兩儀，(which gives life to the two properties;) 兩儀生四象，(the two properties give life to the four emblematic symbols,) 四象生八卦。(which give life to the eight trigrams.) (〈繫辭上〉) (*Appended Words* I) 天地絪縕，萬物化醇；(The halitus of heaven and earth intermingles to give forms to the creation,) 男女構精，萬物化生。(while the seeds of male and female exchange to give life to the creation.) (〈繫辭下〉) (*Appended Words* II) 乾坤其易之門邪！(To *Yi* may *Qian* and *Kun* be the gate!) 乾，陽物也；(*Qian* denotes what is of the yang matter,) 坤，陰物也。(while *Kun* what is of the yin matter.) (〈繫辭下〉) (Appended Words II)

According to the 'Tuan' interpretations, on two things the generation of the world depends: *Qianyuan*, or *Qian* as the original, and *Kunyuan*, or *Kun* as the original. Since *yuan* means the beginning of halitus[5], and in relation to the theory of *Qian* denoting the yang matter and *Kun* the yin matter, *Qianyuan*, meaning the beginning of the masculine breath, is 'a generative capacity of strength', and, on the other hand, *Kunyuan*, meaning the beginning of the feminine breath, is 'that of suppleness'. It is out of these two capacities that the all beings form and transform. *Qianyuan* projects and *Kunyuan* receives, followed by all entities which unfold and realize themselves in due course of arriving at harmony[6]. What is embodied in this process is exactly the structure of 'singularity (*yuan*)/duality (*Qian* and *Kun*)/multeity (all beings)'.

The passages from *Treatise of Appended Words* correspond explicitly to the *Treatise of Tuan*. Special attention should be given

5 Li Dingzuo, *Annotated Zhouyi and Its Supplementary* (周易注疏及補正), in *Selected Interpretations of Zhouyi* (周易集解), vol.1 (Taipei: World Bookstore, 1963), p.4. Dai Lianzhang also points out, 'In the pre-Qin periods, *yuan* means 'head'. Extended uses include 'the first one', 'cardinal', 'beginning', and 'origin'.' In Dai, *op. cit.*, in note 1 above. p.92.

6 Dai, *op. cit.*, in note 1 above, p.93.

to those describing how *I* proceeds from *ying* and *yang* to contain its elemental emblems. Here, the authors of the Treatises use *Yi*, Tao, or Tai Chi to contain yin (*Kun*) and yang (*Qian*) as the seeds of the unending creation. This origin, in light of 'creation', is *Yi*, hence the saying 'Creation denotes Changes'. As a symbol of 'initiative', it is Tai Chi, as interpreted in the ancient Etymological Dictionary *Shuowen Jiezi*'s note on the word 'one': 'In the beginning as Tai Chi, alone stands Tao. Out of it heaven and earth are separated, and the creation of all things follows.'[7] From the perspective of the principle of yin/yang, it is Tao, hence the thesis 'yin and yang constitute Tao.' Distinctive as they might sound, all the three are integrated in one. Therefore, the S/D/M structure can be seen represented in the process, of which singularity denotes Tai Chi, Tao, or *Yi*; duality denotes yin/yang or *Qian/Kun* (heaven and earth); and multeity the creation of all things. All this explanation agrees with what the *Tuan* treatise has to teach us.

Let us take a look at the Taoist classic, *Lao Tzu*. Building his thinking mainly upon the structure of 'not-being/being/not-being'[8], Lao Tzu uses Tao as a median center for uniting 'being' and 'not-being' (or naught). Not-being refers to formlessness and shapelessness, as depicted in the passage 'The Tao is forever unnamed in its true nature' (Chapter 32 of *Lao Tzu*, hereafter as C32), whereas 'being' denotes existence in certain forms and shapes, as depicted in 'True nature broken and scattered. Next comes action as tools' (C.28). Lao Tzu believes living in the cosmos starts from

---

7 Huang Qintang, *Zouyi Interpreted*(周 易 縱 橫 談)(Taipei: Dongda, 1995), pp.33~34.

8 This coincides with the movement of '(N)/S/D/M' to 'M/D/S/(N)'. Applied to 'being', it can generate a spiral structure out of the cycling of 'S/D/M' and 'M/D/S'. See Chen Manming, 'Philosophical Deliberation on Textual Laws', in *Selected Papers on Theory of Texts* (辭章學論文集), vol.1 (Fuzhou: Haichao Publishing House, 2002), pp.40~67.

'true nature' (not-being, or naught) through 'action as tools'(being) and returns to 'true nature'(not-being, or naught). The first part of the process, from not-being to being, is illustrated with the following passages.

道可道，非常道；(The Tao that can be spoken of is not the true Tao) 名可名，非常名。(The Name that can be named is not the true Name.) 无，名天地之始；(From not-being were called heaven and earth.) 有，名萬物之母。(一章)
From being all things were born. (C.1)

道之為物，惟恍惟惚。惚兮恍兮，(The Tao is nothing but elusive and intangible. Oh, it is intangible and elusive,) 其中有象。(and yet within is image.) 恍兮惚兮，(Oh, it is elusive and intangible,) 其中有物。(and yet within is form.) 窈兮冥兮，(Oh, it is dim and dark,) 其中又精。(and yet within is essence.) 其精甚真，(This essence is genuine,) 其中有信。(二一章) (and therein lies faith.)(C.21)

有物混成，先天地生，(There is a thing formed in chaos existing before heaven and earth.) 寂兮寞兮，(Silent and solitary,) 獨立不改，(it stands alone, unchanging.) 周行而不殆，(It goes around without being frail.) 可以為天下母，(It may be the Mother of the world.) 吾不知其名，(Not knowing its name,) 字之曰道，(I can only style it Tao.) 強為之名曰大。(With reluctance, I would call it Great.) 大曰逝，(Great means out-passing,) 逝曰遠，(out-passing means far-reaching,) 遠曰反。(far-reaching means returning.)(C.25)
        (二五章)

道常无為，(Tao abides in non-action,) 而无不為。(三七章) yet nothing is left undone. (C.37)

天地萬物生於有，(All things are born of being.) 有生於无。(四十章) (Being is born of not being.) (C.40)

道生一，(Tao begets One,) 一生二，(One begets Two,) 二生

三，(Two begets Three,) 三生萬物。(Three begets all things.) 萬物負陰而抱陽，(All things carry the yin and embrace the yang.) 沖氣以為和。（四二章）(And by breathing together, they live in harmony.)(C.42)

Out of these passages a clear picture arises in relation to Lao Tzu's thesis of 'naught' developing into 'existence', or 'not-being' into 'being'. Passages such as 'the Tao that can be spoken of is not the true Tao', 'the Tao is nothing but elusive and intangible', 'Tao begets One, One begets Two, Two begets Three', 'being is born of not being', etc., all go in the same direction as 'not-being' develops into 'being'. As the force of generating the cosmic creation, the Tao in its entirety represents the unity of 'naught' and 'existence', or 'not-being' or 'being'. As the origin of such a creation, its nature is interpreted in the word 'naught' exactly because it 'can't be heard and seen' ('On Lao Tzu' in *Han Fei Tzu*) [9]. The process of leading 'not-being' into 'being' goes along with what is depicted in this chapter as that of the cosmic creation of all things and matters from 'singularity' to 'multeity'. That is why Zong Bai-hwa claims,

Tao functions as the force of the Mother Nature, not intervened by human agency and without aims and volitions. 'All things are born of being. Being is born of not being.' Tao forms into a body of chaotic vagueness, which in turn transforms into all beings. Therefore the sayings, 'The Great Tao flows everywhere. It cannot be controlled'(C.34), 'It goes around without being frail'(C.25), 'That which returns is Tao moving' (C.40), 'True nature broken and scattered. Next comes action as tools.' (C.28) The process of which Tao breaks into all beings is from oneness into plurality, from the formless into the formable. [10]

Hsu Fuguan similarly explains,

The process of the cosmic creation demonstrates that Tao resides in a process of leading what is shapeless and immaterial into what is shaped and materialized. However, the Tao is unity and is oneness. The creation from Tao takes the form of breaking up the wholeness, a process of scattering the one into many. [11]

Halfway between the single and the multiple stands Two, receiving the One and unfolding the Many at the same time. This Two, as found in 'Tao begets One, One begets Two, Two begets Three, Three begets all things', has been interpreted differently by scholars for centuries. Some, such as Jiang Xicang and Ren Jihan, believed it means nothing but a figure; some thought it stands for 'heaven and earth', such as Xi Tong and Gao Hen; yet others considered it as 'yin and yang', such like He Shanggong, Wu Chen, Zhu Qianzhi, and Oda Harunoki. The last seems to be closest to the original meaning. First, given that 'ends' can be traced back to their 'roots', the one, or the Tao, as 'roots' to the whole creation, should be of the same nature with its creation. This nature, to be sure, consists in the forces of yin/yang in that, in Lao Tzu's words, 'all things carry yin and embrace yang'. If so, then the Two as in 'One begets Two' is best seen as yin and yang, of which Lao Tzu somehow stops short of speaking. Huang Zhou goes further to say,

My view is that 'the One', after Zhu Qianzhi, refers to the

....

10 Zong Baihwa, *Collected Works of Zong Baihwa*(宗白華全集), vol.2 (Hefei: Anhui Education Publishing Ltd., 1996), p.810.
11 Xu Fuguan, *op. cit.*, in note 2 above, p.337.

original chi, 'the Two', after Oda Harunoki, to the chi of yin and yang, and 'the Three', as homonym to *san* 參, means actually 'to join', the last being an interpretation held by, among others, Ruo Mu in his 'Causerie in Jixia', where 陰陽三合, meaning literally yin and yang are joined by a third party, is realized as 陰陽參合, meaning yin and yang join together. Therefore, 'Three begets all things' in effect means yin and yang join together to create the world.[12]

That the force of yin and the force of yang constitute what Lao Tzu originally meant by 'Two' is a view held by many. Furthermore, the dichotomy of 'heaven and earth' belongs with that of 'yin and yang as two kind of force', as heaven is seen as yang and earth as yin. The difference: heaven and earth appear in the spatio-temporal form so as to cradle everything[13], while ying and yang appear in their 'virtuous capacity' (in the Ming Dynasty scholar Zhu Xi's words) for creating the world. Put this way, 'One' for Lao Tzu is equal to the Tai Chi in the treatises of *Zhouyi*, 'Two' to the two spontaneous forces, yin and yang, and from One and Two the creation of all things follows. *Lao Tzu* hence re-presents the same S/D/M structure as found in *Zhouyi* (and its commentaries).

However, it is worthwhile to make two further points here. (1) Even if the S/D/M structure found in *Lao Tzu* differs from that in Zhou I, the very existence of such structure remains intact. This very

....

12 For an overview of the interpretations and quotations mentioned above, see Huang Zhou, *Commentary on Annotations to the Silk-copy Lao Tzu* (帛書老子校注析) (Taipei: Students' Bookstore, 1991), p.231.

13 'In Chinese thinking, heaven and earth is of the spatiotemporal form for cradling all things. Therefore, heaven and earth should come into being prior to the creation, or the latter would be adrift in the void. 'One begets two', in this view, means one begets heaven and earth.' In Xu Fuguan, *op. cit.*, in note 2 above, p.335.

much depends on (2) our understanding of the Tao in 'Tao begets One' both as the fundamental force of cosmic creation and as embodiment of 'not-being' [14]. As commented upon by Wang Bi, to say Tao 'is non-existing seems to be wrong because from it things and matters are generated; to say Tao is existing seems nonetheless wrong because in it no shape could be found' [15]. Lao Tzu's Tao can be understood as nothingness, a hazy void, instead of real zero [16]. It precedes the 'one', therefore a truth in absentia [17], tentatively shown as naught in parentheses. Thus, a structure of '(N)/S/D/M' is created to complement the inadequacy of the 'S/D/M' structure of Zhou I and to depict a more completed compliant process of cosmic creation.

In relation to the progressive structure, a regressive process of 'M/D/S/(N)' [18] can now find its grounds in the structured text. First, any textures other than the core structure belong to 'Multeity'. Secondly, to 'Duality' belongs the core structure of the text that makes possible the binary operation of complementing and confronting at the same time the chi of yin and yang in order to procure its own reconciliation and contrast with other structures. Thirdly, the theme of the text and its style, aroma, atmosphere, realm, and other things based on the unity of it pertains to 'Singularity (Naught)'. Lastly, but not the least, it is logical to refer to the style

....

14 Lin Qiyen, History of Chinese Scholastic Thinking (中國學術思想史)(Hong Kong: Bookman, 1999), p.34.

15 *Wang Bi's Comments on Lao Tzu* (老子王弼注) (Taipei: Heluo Publishing, 1974), p.16.

16 Feng Yolan, *op. cit.*, in note 2 above, p.84.

17 Tang Junyi, *An Original Discourse on Chinese Philosophy: Introduction*(中國哲學原論: 導論篇)(Kowloon: Life Publishing, 1966), pp.350~351.

18 Chen Manming, 'On the Spiral Structure of Multeity, Duality, Sigularity (Naught): A look into *Zhouyi* and *Lao Tzu*'(論「多」、「二」、「一（0）」的螺旋結構—以《周易》與《老子》為考察重心), in *Journal of Taiwan Normal University*, vol.48, no.1(Taipei: Taiwan Normal University, 2003), pp.1~20.

and other abstract powers of the text by the part of (Naught).

The discussion presented here demonstrates the universality of the 'M/D/S/(N)' structure within the realm of literature as well as philosophy. Applied onto text and context, it first organizes multiple structures around a core structure of binary operation, which in turn is based on the (intangible) unity of coherent features. On the other hand, it can correspond readily to the four laws of textual construction: order (shifting) and changing (twisting) pertain to Multeity, coherence (harmonizing and contrasting through hardness and softness) pertains to Duality, and unity (theme, style, rhythm, atmosphere, realm, etc.) to Singularity (Naught). The binary operation of softness and hardness (yin and yang, virtuousness and righteousness)[19] extracted from the complex of them functions as a bridge for global cohering between multiplicity and unity, or a medium through which the text can proliferate and converge. Added to it is the concept of 'naught in brackets' representing the first cause of (con)textual construction. It can be argued that the theorization as a whole provides room for and has positive bearings on the scientific analysis of Chinese literature, esthetics, and philosophy.

2. A few examples of the structure of "many, two, one/zero"

In this section, examples of prose and poem are given to demonstrate how the (con)textual structure of M/D/S(N) is applied pervasively and unchangeably. First, 'Song Yu to the prince of Chu' from *Chu Ci*:

King Xiang of Chu asked Song Yu, "What have you done that should cause the officers and people of the State to abuse you so clamorously?"

Song Yu replied, "Abuse me indeed they do, but pardon my

....

19 See Li, *op. cit.*, in note 5 above, pp.404~405.

boldness, and I will explain.　A stranger was singing in one of our villages the other day, and this was the subject of his lay: There is the music of the masses; there is the music of a narrower circle; that of a narrower circle still; and lastly, the classical music of the cultured few. The classical music is too lofty, and too difficult of comprehension, for the masses.

"Among birds there is the phoenix; among fishes, the leviathan. The phoenix soars aloft, cleaving the red clouds, with the blue firmament above it, away into the uttermost realms of space. But what can the poor hedge quail know of the grandeur of heaven and earth? The leviathan rises in the morning in one ocean to go to rest at night in another. But what can the minnow of a puddle know of the depth of the sea?

"And there are phoenixes and leviathans, not only among birds and fishes, but among men. There is the great man, full of nervous thought and of unsullied fame, who dwells complacently alone. What can the vulgar herd know of me?"

> 楚襄王問於宋玉曰:「先生其有遺行與?何士民眾庶不
> 譽之甚也!」宋玉對曰:「唯,然,有之;願大王寬其
> 罪,使得畢其辭。客有歌於郢中者,其始曰下里巴人,
> 「國中屬而和者數千人;其為陽阿薤露,國中屬而和者
> 數百人;其為陽春白雪,國中屬而和者,不過數十人;
> 引商刻羽,雜以流徵,國中屬而和者,不過數人而已;
> 是其曲彌高,其和彌寡。故鳥有鳳而魚有鯤。鳳凰上擊
> 九千里,絕雲霓,負蒼天,翱翔乎杳冥之上;夫蕃籬之
> 鷃,豈能與之料天地之高哉?鯤魚朝發崑崙之墟,暴鬐
> 於碣石,暮宿於孟諸,夫尺澤之鯢,豈能與之量江海之
> 大哉?故非獨鳥有鳳而魚有鯤也,士亦有之。夫聖人瑰
> 意琦行,超然獨處,夫世俗之民,又安知臣之所為
> 哉?」

The article is first composed in the structure of question/answer. The question is a lead-in to the text body, pointing out the questioner, the addressee, and the question itself. The answer, which constitutes the main body, is then arranged in an array of touching (referring to who spoke) and spreading (referring to what was spoken of). What was spoken of is introduced by the utterance "(a)buse me indeed they do" as a gesture of acknowledgement, which is in turn followed by the words "but pardon my boldness, and I will explain" to euphemistically bring forward his explanation of the dishonor. This is the general part. The answer to the question of dishonor, which constitutes the detailed part, is on the other hand arranged in the structure of 'guest/host'. The 'guest' part consists of three passages from "a stranger was singing in one of our villages" to "what can the minnow of a puddle know of the depth of the sea". The first passage, namely Guest I, paves the way for the 'host' by using music as a metaphor to suggest, through contrasting loftier songs with vulgar ones, that the higher one reaches, the less followers one has. The second passage, namely Guest II, prepares further for the 'host' by using birds as a metaphor to signify, through the contrast between sky and ground, the shallowness and ignorance of the ordinary man. The third passage, namely Guest III, furnishes yet again the host part with the metaphor of fishes to indicate, through contrasting, that the ordinary man is too narrow-sighted to measure the great man's deeds.

The host part, on the other hand, begins with the sentences "there are phoenixes and leviathans, not only among birds and fishes, but among men", which connects the preceding and the following remarks. What follows is a distinction between men in relation to the metaphorical contrasts raised above. Thus, there is, on the one hand and corresponding to the classical music, phoenixes and leviathans, symbolizing the great man 'full of nervous thought and of unsullied fame, who dwells complacently alone', and on the other hand, corresponding to the minnow of a puddle, the hedge quail, and 'the music of the masses', symbolizing the vulgar people who 'know nothing of me'. In this way the speaker, by analogizing himself to the great man who never caters to the vulgar tastes, not only answers the Prince's question but also satirizes those who criticize him. As Lin Xizhong acclaimed, "A virtuous man is understood only by his kind; how can he be judged by the laymen? The King certainly asked an improper question, but Song Yu wittily replied in such a way as to not only earn himself, through the three metaphors, a higher status but also to reprehend the ruses and senses of the vulgar mass. How gratifying it is!"[20]

The structure of the article is diagrammed on the next page. Here is a simplified chart representing its compositional levels.

Top Level   L2   L3   L4   L5   L6   L7   Base Level

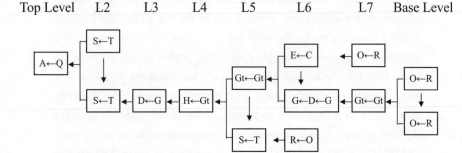

From the diagrams we can see that this article employs six rules of (con)textual construction, including 'question/answer', 'touching/ spreading', 'general/detail', 'guest/host', 'cause/effect', and 'positive/negative'. The replacements and shifts of these find their rhythm in concerted strata to create a musical structure. They are given different significance, though. Subsidiary to the core structure are structures based on 'question/answer', 'pointing/spreading', and 'general/items', which are used as bridges in the text. The core

20 Lin Yunming, *Expositions of Ancient Texts* (古文析義合編), vol.3 (Taipei: Guangwen Bookstore, 1965), p.126.

structure that gives form to the structure of duality, on the other hand, lies in that of 'secondary/primary' as it organizes the main body of the article. Based on the core structure, the text employs subsidiary ones to unite and organize its substrata, giving rise to its multiplicity. Furthermore, the guest and the host part are supported respectively by a threefold set of negative and positive

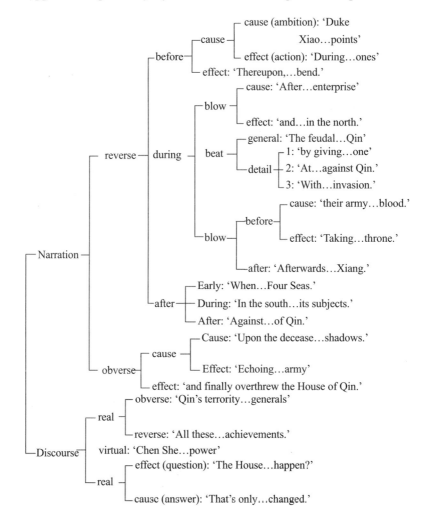

examples and a one-fold set of positives and negatives, both giving a masculine feel to the dual structure of the text through the tension of the contrasts. The masculinity is stylistically implied in the speaker's euphemistic, hence 'soft', answer and embodied in his satiric yet strong criticism of his accusers, which in turn is reached by way of using the dual structure as a medium for moving from M up to S(N), ending at the speaker's theory that a virtual man cannot be understood by the unrefined people. The stylistic implication of strength in softness actually agrees with the holistic arrangement of the text, as Zhang Da-zhi acutely mentioned, 'Song Yu's indirect reply to the Chu prince in fact tactfully suggests his grievance against the political frustration he had endured.' [21] He Wooxiou also points out that 'the text is structured in a novel way by starting with a question and ending with another. The Prince of Chu asked a question to disguise his intention to reprove *via* others' words, a question with something of a cunning hint; Song Yu replied with a question to conclude his defense through the interplay of hardness and softness, a question flowing with saddening sentiments and a sense of conceitedness and self-admiring.' [22] The remarks concur with ours on the implication of strength in softness, which can be uncovered with the help of the logic structure of 'M/D/S(N)'.

Now, take Jia Yi's 'A Critique on Qin'.

Duke Xiao of Qin and his ministers defended the territory of Yong against the natural shield of Yao Mountain and the barrier of Hangu. He constantly pried about the Chou kingdom, venturing on wraping the world into his mat, enveloping the

---

[21] See *General Dictionary for Admiration of Ancient Texts* (古文鑑賞大辭典)(Hungzhou: Zhejiang Education Publishing, 1998), p.151.

[22] See *Dictionary for Admiration of Ancient Texts* (古文鑑賞辭典)(Nanjing: Jiangsu Arts Publishing, 1987), p.176.

world with his power and seizing the Four Seas to the farthest eight cardinal points. During that time, Lord Shang was his counselor, advising the duke to issue laws and measures, to encourage agriculture and weaving, to renew the army and its strategies, and to make coalitions with stronger states to defeat the weaker ones. Thereupon, the state of Qin almost effortlessly occupied the territory west of the Yellow River bend.

After Duke Xiao, Prince Huiwen, Prince Wu, and Prince Zhao Xiang inherited the enterprise and extended the state's dominion to the middle Han in the south, the lands of Ba and Shu in the west, fertile lands of the east and strategically located counties in the north. The feudal princes were so terrified that they united and allied against Qin with the help of able and loyal masterminds that they recruited with bounteous rewards of wealth, valuables, and lands. At that time, Lord Mengchang of Qi, Lord Pingyuan of Zhou, Lord Chunshen of Chu, and Lord Xinlin of Wei—the four noblemen were both intelligent and devoted. They respected virtuous men and trusted them with major positions. Allied with other anti-Qin princes, they managed to gather armies from states of Han, Wei, Yen, Zhao, Qi, Chu, Song, Wei, and Zhong Shan. Ministers of the Six States planned for their lords and journeyed to and fro to form connections among them, while generals led armies of the states to battles against Qin. With territories ten times bigger than the Qin state and with an army outnumbering Qin's by hundreds of thousands, the Six States once reached the Pass at Qin's border for a massive invasion. Their army, however, collapsed once Qin sent their legions out. The anti-Qin ally crumbled as the princes rushed to cede lands to appease Qin. Those disobedient to its will were smashed up, their armies being slaughtered while retreating. The corpses piled up in hundreds of thousands, with scattered shields floating in the streams of their blood. Taking advantage of the occasion, Qin was able to dominate over other princes, snatching their lands, surrendering the strong to its will, subjecting the weak to its throne.

Afterwards, the state underwent no major changes during the short reigns of Prince Xiao Wen and Prince Zhuang Xiang. When the time came to the First Emperor, he made even more effort to pursue the enterprise than the six rulers of Qin before him. He brandished the mighty whip to command the world, devoured the two houses of Zhou and extinguished the feudal lords. Holding cane and cudgel, he scourged all under heaven and spread terror within the Four Seas. In the south, he conquered the territory of the Hundred Yue barbarians and installed the commanderies of Guilin and Xiangjun. The rulers of the Hundred Yue put a rope around their necks to express their submission even to the lowest of Qin's officials. The First Emperor sent Meng Tian to erect the Great Wall in the north in order to protect the border regions. He drove back the Hun hordes more than seven hundred miles away. The Non-Chinese peoples did not even dare to come to the south to pasture their horses, and their soldiers did not even risk to span their bows to take revenge. The First Emperor then departed from the virtuous way of the former kings and burned the writings of the Hundred Schools of Thinking only to make the black headed people stupid. He devastated great cities and executed heroes and leaders; he gathered all weapons in the empire and had them sent to the capital Xianyang. He had all arrow-heads melted to cast twelve bronze statues, all to weaken the people. Against the natural walls of the Huashan ridge, and bordered by the Yellow River as its natural fosse, defended by outstanding generals and selected soldiers with powerful crossbows and sharp-edged spears, and ministered by trustworthy officers, Qin surely had made the first empire that no reasonable minds would dare to defy. When the empire was appeased, the First Emperor thought that the territory west of the Hangu Pass would be safe, and inside his metal wall of a thousand miles, he wanted to establish an eternal rule of his sons and grandsons of the house of Qin.

Upon the decease of the First Emperor, while his power remained threatening across borders, a man called Chen She, a penniless nobody, a serf in lifelong servitude, an exiled minor officer in a border region, led several hundreds of tired and scattered soldiers to attack the government. This man, having less skills than an average person, no intellect and virtue comparable to that of Confucius and Motze, and certainly no wealth one ten-thousandth of that of Tao Zhu and Qi Dun, chopped trees to make weapons and used bamboo poles to uplift banners, and followers from everywhere flocked together like clouds, carrying foods to tread after him like his shadows. Echoing his venturous cause, heroes from the east of Huashan rose and wielded their army against the House of Qin.

Qin's territory was neither small nor weak. Yongzhou remained vast, while the Yao mountain and the Hangu Pass stood firm and solid as before. On the other hand, Chen She bore no comparison with the princes of the Nine States. Their iron hoes were far less sharp than spears and lances. Soldiers banished to the border regions were by no means of same quality as the States' army. Nor could their strategies and tactics bear the least comparison with those famous counselors and generals. All these were, however, overshadowed by their reversed achievements. Chen She would have stood no chance or whatsoever had the states east of Huashan and he been placed side by side for a comparison of their strengths and power. The House of Qin, after having commanded the feudal princes for more than one hundred years and finally conquered all the land under heaven, was nevertheless overthrown upon Chen's uprising, its ancestral temples destroyed, its emperor murdered, and its falling sneered at by the whole world. Why would this happen? That's only because the virtuous and righteous way of ruling was abolished and the conditions of expansion and conservation had changed.

秦孝公據殽函之固，擁雍州之地，君臣固守，以窺周室；有席卷天下，包舉宇內，囊括四海之意，并吞八荒之心。當是時也，商君佐之，內立法度，務耕織，修守戰之具，外連衡而鬥諸侯。於是秦人拱手而取西河之外。

孝公既沒，惠文、武、昭襄，蒙故業，因遺策，南取漢中，西舉巴蜀，東割膏腴之地，北收要害之郡。諸侯恐懼，會盟而謀弱秦，不愛珍器重寶肥饒之地，以致天下之士，合從締交，相與為一。當此之時，齊有孟嘗，趙有平原，楚有春申，魏有信陵；此四君者，皆明智而忠信，寬厚而愛人，尊賢重士，約從離橫，兼韓、魏、燕、趙、齊、楚、宋、衛、中山之眾。於是六國之士，有寧越、徐尚、蘇秦、杜赫之屬為之謀；齊明、周最、陳軫、召滑、樓緩、翟景、蘇厲、樂毅之徒通其意；吳起、孫臏、帶佗、兒良、王廖、田忌、廉頗、趙奢之倫制其兵。嘗以十倍之地，百萬之眾，叩關而攻秦。秦人開關延敵，九國之師，逡巡遁逃而不敢進。秦無亡矢遺鏃之費，而天下諸侯已困矣。於是從散約解，爭割地而賂秦。秦有餘力而制其敝，追亡逐北，伏尸百萬，流血漂櫓；因利乘便，宰割天下，分裂河山，強國請服，弱國入朝。施及孝文王、莊襄王，享國日淺，國家無事。及至始皇，奮六世之餘烈，振長策而馭宇內，吞二周而亡諸侯，履至尊而制六合，執捶拊以鞭笞天下，威振四海。南取百越之地，以為桂林、象郡；百越之君，俛首係頸，委命下吏；乃使蒙恬北築長城而守藩籬，卻匈奴七百餘里；胡人不敢南下而牧馬，士不敢彎弓而報怨。於是廢先王之道，燔百家之言，以愚黔首；墮名城，殺豪俊，收天下之兵，聚之咸陽，銷鋒鏑，鑄以為金人十二，以弱天下之民。然後踐華為城，因河為池，據億丈之城、臨不測之谿以為固。良將勁弩，守要害之處；信臣精卒，陳利兵而誰何？天下已定，始皇之心，自以為關中之固，金城千里，子孫帝王萬世之業也。

始皇既沒，餘威震於殊俗。然而陳涉，甕牖繩樞之子，甿隸之人，而遷徙之徒也，才能不及中人，非有仲尼、墨翟之賢，陶朱、猗頓之富，躡足行伍之間，倔起阡陌之中，率罷散之卒，將數百之眾，轉而攻秦；斬木為兵，揭竿為旗，天下雲集而響應，贏糧而景從。山東豪俊，遂並起而亡秦族矣。

且夫天下非小弱也，雍州之地，殽函之固，自若也；陳涉之位，非尊於齊、楚、燕、趙、韓、魏、宋、衛、中山之君也；鋤耰棘矜，非銛於鉤戟長鎩也；謫戍之眾，非抗於九國之師也；深謀遠慮，行軍用兵之道，非及曩時之士也；然而成敗異變，功業相反也。試使山東之國，與陳涉度長絜大，比權量力，則不可同年而語矣；然秦以區區之地，致萬乘之權，招八州而朝同列，百有餘年矣；然後以六合為家，殽函為宮，一夫作難而七廟隳，身死人手，為天下笑者，何也？仁義不施，而攻守之勢異也。

This essay consists of two parts: narration and discourse. The narration part, including the first four paragraphs, employs the structure of contrasts to narrate the difficult rising of Qin and the easy falling of Qin. First, from a reverse angle, paragraphs 1 to 3 deal with the labor-taking process leading to Qin's power and prosperity. The process begins with a description of cause and effect: Establishing a stronghold between Yao Mountain and Hangu Pass, and motivated by his ambition to conquer the world "to the farthest eight cardinal points", Duke Xiao went out "to make coalitions with stronger states to defeat the weaker ones." –This passage describes the cause. The effect, on the other hand, is narrated in the sentence

"Qin almost effortlessly occupied the territory west of the Yellow River bend". The style in this paragraph is concise and direct.[23]

In paragraph 2 the author narrates the progressive rising of Qin by employing a rhythmic structure composed of three repeating elements: blow/beat/blow. (See Ch.3 for detail—translator) It begins with the passage from 'the decease of Duke Xiao' to 'strategically located counties in the north', which concisely describes the succeeding princes' follow-up to angle for the Six States, and which constitutes the first 'blow'. Then a second passage from "The feudal princes were so terrified" to "(the Six States) reached the Pass [...] for a massive invasion" accounted in detail for the feudal lords' anti-Qin strategies, manpower, and doings, with special emphasis on the individuals involved into this enterprise—including state counselors, distinguished generals, armies, and masterminds and diplomats. This passage constitutes the 'beat' of the narration.[24] At the end, and to conclude what precedes, a third passage describing how the anti-Qin ally broke down "once Qin sent its legions out" and how Qin took the advantage to increase its power, and thus constitutes the final 'blow'.[25] Compared to paragraph 1, this section produces a manifold picture of Qin's development.[26]

....

23 See Chen Manming, 'On the techniques of cropping and trimming literary texts (談辭章剪裁的手段), in Discourses on Chinese Teaching: Second Collection (國文教學論叢續編)(Taipei: Wanjuanlou, 1998), p.439.

24 'Beat' is equal to what literary critics usually call 'off-setting by contrast'. For example, Wang Wenju comments on the passages about the anti-Qin feudal princes by saying, '(The author) made a sudden shift to the princes in order to set off the mighty Qin by contrast.' and '(The author) greatly praised the feudal lords for their successful enlisting of talented helpers, only to set off, in the coming passages, Qin's greater success against their surprising defeat.' See Expositions of Ancient Texts, op. cit., in note 20, pp.6~7.

25 See Chen Manming, 'On several special textual laws', in Bulletin of Chinese, no.31 (Taipei: Taiwan Normal University, 2002), p.216.

26 Chen, op. cit., in note 23 above, p.441.

Paragraph 3 is used to narrate the apex of Qin's power and is divided into three passages: from "the state underwent no major changes" to "(barbarian) soldiers did not even risk to span their bows to take revenge" is a passage describing the falling of all the land under heaven into Qin's hand; from "(t)he First Emperor then left the virtuous way of the former kings" to "all to weaken the people" is another passage depicting how Qin ruled its subjects by depressing them for any possible rebellion; and from "(a)gainst the natural walls of Huashan" to "eternal rule of [...] the House of Qin" is yet another passage aimed to describing how the First Emperor intended to make an eternal empire of Qin. Going through these three passages, the narration switches from a spatially-based perspective to a temporally-based one in picturing, in detail again, an empire that first expanded outwards, then wielded power inwards, and tried to extend forever.[27]

Preceded by the first three paragraphs which narrates from the reverse side the rising of mighty Qin, paragraph 4 deals with the fall of Qin, which gives the subject of the *Critique*, hence its obverse side. The paragraph is arranged in a causal relation, of which the cause is represented by Chen She's uprising as described in the passage from "the decease of the First Emperor" to "tread after him like his shadows" and the effect in the sentence depicting Qin's fall: "(H)eroes rose [...] against the House of Qin". In contrast with the reverse part, the stylistically concise presentation here makes Qin's fall look dramatically quick and abrupt.[28]

The discourse part begins where the narration ends. In the last paragraph, the author re-appropriates material from the preceding

---

27 The narration part, including the first four paragraphs, employs the structure of contrasts to narrate the difficult rising of Qin and the easy falling of Qin. First, from a reverse angle, paragraphs 1 to 3 deal with the labor-taking process leading to Qin's power and prosperity. Chen, *op. cit.*, in note 23 above, p.442.

28 See Chen, *op. cit.*, in note 23 above, p.442.

sections to make comparison between the Six States and Chen She (and, implicitly and indirectly, between Chen She and Qin) and from it inferred that the Six States should have defeated Qin and Qin should have defeated Chen She. The fact that, on the contrary, it is Qin that defeated the Six States and Chen She who defeated Qin begs the question of why? Then the concluding remarks, "the virtuous and righteous way of ruling was abolished and the conditions of expansion and conservation had changed," tactfully brings in focus the theme of the whole essay. From the point of view of textual construction, the content of the discourse goes along with the structure of factual/counterfactual/factual. The passage from "Qin's territory" to "their reversed achievements" refers to the first fact. It is then followed by a counterfactual comparison in the sentence beginning at "Chen She would...," which would anticipate exactly the opposite, i.e. Chen She's total defeat. The virtual comparison notwithstanding, a second fact concludes the discourse by bringing out the question and then the answer, hence manifesting a structure of effect/cause.

Put together, in order to argue for the theme that Qin's fault lies in its departure from the virtuous and righteous way and the change of the conditions for attack and defense, the author accounts for 'expansion' in paragraph 1, 2, 3(first half), and discuss 'conservation' in paragraph 3(second half) and 4, while mentioning the fact of betraying the way of virtuous ruling in paragraph 3 and what it had resulted in in paragraph 4. It is not until the very end of the essay that the author had brought forth its key message—only after a counterfactual comparison between the parties in order to highlight their reversed achievements in paragraph 5.

From the point of view of its eventual message, this essay should contain two axes: namely, the departure from the virtuous and righteous way and the change of the conditions of expansion and conservation. Given that 'A Critique on Qin' has been regarded as representative of the inductive writing since the ancient times, there should be two lines of arguments going through the text. However, this is not the case. The problem consists in paragraph 3 and 4 as they, in contrast with 1 and 2 describing the conditions of expansion, are to be concerned with self-protection and yet overlaps the illustration of betraying the virtuous and righteous way. To explain away such confusion of description, it is best for us to view the overlap as hinting at a hidden yet integrated message, namely, the fault of Qin rests with its failure to conserve its empire in the virtuous and righteous way. Viewed from the positive side, this hidden message implies that the conservation of the throne must be done through applying the virtuous and righteous way of ruling. Obviously, the author was using Qin's misfortune to mock at today's royal house. It can be argued that our discussion presented here demonstrates that the structural analysis of (con)text is useful for identifying the real message conveyed in a text. On the following page is shown the diagram of structural analysis of the *Critique*. Immediately here is a simplified chart representing its compositional levels.

Top Level   L2   L3   L4   L5   Base Level

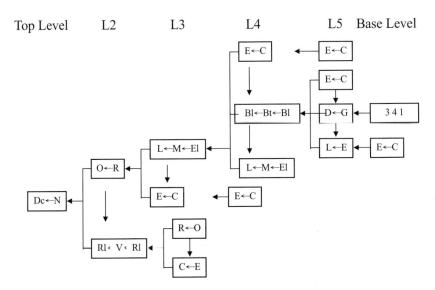

From this we can see that the 'Critique' employs eight rules of textual construction to form its substructures, namely 'narration/discourse', 'contrasts'(obverse/reverse), 'virtual/real', 'beat/blow', 'general/detail', 'cause/effect', 'spatial/temporal' and 'apposition' (side by side). Substructures that find their manifestation at the second and lower levels belong to M in the M/D/S(N)

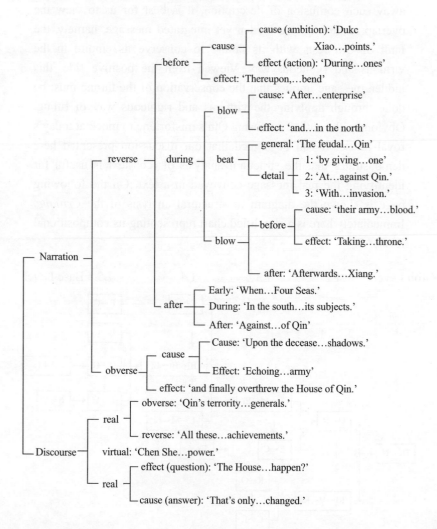

structure of the essay. They are attached to, and hence developed from, what constitutes D at level one, i.e., 'narration/discourse'. Level 1 is also where the forces of yin/yang reside, with discourse representing yang and narration yin: from here, the text goes down to realize its multiplicity and, at the same time, connects up the single real message the author intended to convey. Out of the upward connection is given the S(N) structure, manifested in the form of the absentee theme: conservation by carrying out the virtuous and righteous way of ruling. The hidden message owes its power not only to the discourse of which it is implied, but also to the narration part, which, though inclining to the character of yin as it were, builds its core structure out of tension-abounding 'contrasts'. This explains why the essay has long been appraised as 'teeming with vigor of style'[29] and 'heaved with untamed waves of writing'.[30]

Now, let us turn to Li Wenshao's 'A Lesson on Frugality'.

Frugality is a virtue, yet belittled by customs.

The poor man envies the rich man when seeing him; the rich man envies the richer man on seeing him. A meal costs ten pieces of gold; a dress costs one hundred; a house one thousand—how can this not lead to destituteness? It is commonly seen in neighborhoods that fathers and elders live a simple and plain life, satisfying their own needs by themselves, while sons and youngsters, thinking of this as vulgar and unrefined, go to great lengths to change their ways, ending up wiping wealth of generations out in their hands. Moreover, one who spends freely

....

29 Wu Chucai & Wang Wenju, *Elaborate Commentary on and Collation of Guwen Guanzhi* (精校評注古文觀止) (Taipei: Zhonghua Bookstore, 1972), p.10.

30 Li Fujio, *A Hundred Examples of Ancient Literary Writing* (古文筆法百篇) (Xian: Sanqin Publishing,1998), pp.67~74.

must desire greedily, haggling over every penny and digging for every opportunity. In the end, bribing, lying, fawning, swindling—shameless and immoral, all become something he cannot do without. How can this be better than avoiding overspending and enjoying benefits of the constant satisfaction? To be sure, what I call 'frugality' does not mean to deny any spending. Articles for sustenance and funeral, demands of felicitating and condoling, all these pertain to humanity and cannot be abandoned. Bestowing under proper considerations can assure one not to go so far as to be obstinate.

This article aims to encourage people to pursue the virtue of frugality and is written in the deductive structure of generalization/itemization. The first paragraph constitutes the generalization by coming straight to the point that frugality is a virtue (the obverse) and yet belittled by customs (the reverse). It is like an umbrella covering the coming paragraphs. What is itemized starts from the reverse side with a discussion of the belittling of frugality by customs in the second paragraph, followed by a positive exposition of the virtuous application of frugality in the final paragraph. In the second paragraph, the author uses the first sentences beginning from '(t)he poor man envies...' to explain how being extravagant can 'lead to destituteness'. Following it is the middle part 'It is...in their hands' which illustrates the waning of a rich family due to extravagance. This is then furthered by a quick mentioning in the next two sentences of the never-ending desire of one who over-consumes and his becoming shameless and unscrupulous and ended in the last sentence of '(h)ow can this be...'with returning back to the positive side of a frugal lifestyle. The final paragraph on the virtuous application of frugality begins with the author's presuming a plausible questioning for being parsimonious and hence brings out the emphasis on the 'humane'

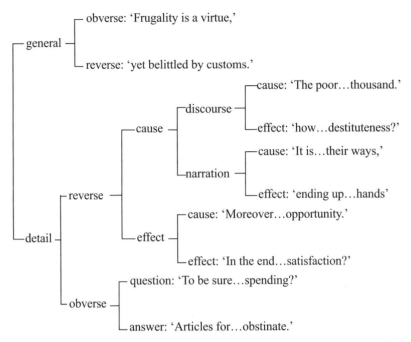

side of controlled spending. The structure of the essay is represented as follows.

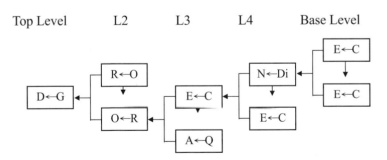

The author, on the one hand, sets off what is positive (obverse) by what is negative (reverse), both carried out through the generalization and the itemization part; on the other hand, he deploys structures units of 'cause/effect', 'narration/discourse', 'question/answer' across the paragraphs to form consonance via pairing and echoing. In this way the text attaches consonance to contrast, making its parts stylistically cohere. In correspondence with the M/D/S(N) structure, substructures that manifests at level 3 and 4 belong to M. The substructure of 'general/items,' as it represents the force of yin/yang that communicates between the levels and thus forms the core structure, belongs to D. The theme of frugality as a virtue accentuated by the combination of imagery thinking and logical thinking, plus the solemn and moderate style, pertains to M.

To turn to prosodic writings, here is Du Fu's 'On Hearing about the Army Taking Back Henan and Hebei':

劍外忽傳收薊北，(Rushed from out of Jianmen is news of Jibei's recovery,)初聞涕淚滿衣裳。(On hearing of it I wet my clothes with tears.)卻看妻子愁何在，(Turning about did I see wife worry no more,)漫卷詩書喜欲狂。(While packing up books untidily with ecstatic joy.)白日放歌須縱酒，(On a bright day for singing aloud and drinking at will,)青春作伴好還鄉。(It's in spring when we'll travel in company back home,)即從巴峽穿巫峽，(Sailing right from the Ba Gorge and passing through the Wu Gorge,)便下襄陽向洛陽。(Upon reaching Xiangyang shall we head south for Luoyang.)

This poem portrays the author's ecstasy at the imperial government's recovery of his hometown and is written in a pattern of 'Item(Factual)/General/Item(Counterfactual)'.

The author expresses in the first couplet how he wept with joy ('effect') when hearing of the imperial army taking back Henan and Hebei (or together as Jibei) ('cause'). The expression 'rushed' and 'on hearing of' shows its surprising nature, which led one to cry happy tears. The second couplet switches the subject from that of the narrator ('host') to his wife ('guest'), to use his preoccupied concern about her response ('turning back') to technically make the careless packing of books stand out. Up to this point the poem provides the factual description of the cause and the poet's overjoyed reaction, which constitutes 'Item 1'. Right after this is put forward the theme of the ecstatic joy which constitutes 'General' as in the phrase 'with ecstatic joy'. The 'real' is then replaced by the 'virtual' in the third couplet, of which 'singing aloud and drinking at will' corresponds to 'ecstasy', and 'travel in company back to homeland' to 'wife'— together illustrating virtually the plan of going home when spring comes (hence 'time'). Paired with this planning for time is another virtual description of that for the route (hence 'space') in the concluding couplet. The second half of the poem thus writes about 'ecstasy' from a virtual point of view, giving rise to 'Item 2'. In this way, a linear flow of emotion from 'rushed' to 'on hearing', 'turning about' to 'packing untidily', 'a bright day' to 'in spring', and 'sailing right from' to 'on reaching' goes through the poem[31], vividly picturing his and his wife's overjoyed emotion.[32]

The diagram of structural analysis on the next page shows that the poem is configured globally in the pattern of 'item(real)/general/ item(virtual)' and locally in the structure of 'cause/effect' and 'time/space'. In this way, the poem is made coherent by, on the local plane, echoing 'Item(real)' with 'Item(virtual)', 'cause' with 'effect', 'guest' with 'host', 'time' with 'space' and by, on the global plane, covering the two 'Items'—one real, one virtual'—, and hence uniting the horizon of the poem, with'General', i.e., 'an ecstasy'.

....

31 Zhao Shanlin views this as an assemblage of successive images. See his *A Discourse on the Art of Poetic Works* (詩詞曲藝術論)(Hangzhou: Zhejiang Education Publishing House, 1998), p.124.

32 The discussion presented here is also seen in Chen Manming, *New Perspectives into Theory of Textual Construction* (章法學新裁) (Taipei: Wanjuanlou, 2001), p.383..

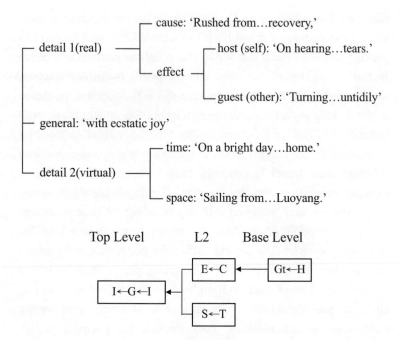

Viewed from the perspective of the M/D/S(N) scheme, the consonant structure consisting of the binary operations of 'cause/effect', 'time/space', and 'guest/host' belongs to M, while the changing structure of General/Item, as it constitutes in itself yin/yang and hence communicates between the levels, belongs to D. The theme of 'ecstatic joy' and its stylization with 'a state of ease full of verve and satiation' [33] are in line with S(N).

It is worthy to note here that, contrary to the commonly held interpretation, it is, in my belief, the wife, instead of the poet himself [34], that arranges bookcases in disorder. The wife's careless

....

33   See Zhao, op. cit., in note 31, p241.

34   Shi Shuangyuan, for example, argues that, when he turned to his wife and children, he saw joy and delight instead heavyheartedness on their faces, which in turn magnifies his excitement so much as to roll up and wave his book like in a

and unmindful packing rightly gives evidence to the poet's judgment that she worried no more. This, added to the portrayal of the poet's own 'wetting clothes with tears', is conducive to a picture of a family in overjoyed celebration. To approach the poem from the changing perspective of the host (the poet) and the guest (his wife) seems to better balance its two halves and fulfill the principle of coherence by liking up its parts through one single line of unity.

Ci, or lyric poems, a type of classical poetry that is always written to an existing tune, is exemplified for the structural analysis with Xin Qiji's 'Congratulations on the Groom'.

> From the trees is heard the cry of shrikes.
> What is more unbearable is,
> When partridges stop crowing,
> Hastier would the cuckoo wail.
> When spring leaves will all crying stop,
> As if they were regretting the withering blossoms.
> Yet with parting between men none of these could be compared.
> In company with a *pipa* on a horse,
> And the utter dark at a frontier fortress,
> The fragrant carriage had long left the imperial palace.
> Away rows of swallows flew,
> And on her way home the concubine was seen off.
> With a body so tired and a reputation deeply scarred,
> Standing on the bridge and looking back ten thousand miles far,
> The veteran general could never win his old friend back.
> Alongside the Yi River chill winds blew westward.

....

dance. See *Dictionary for Appreciation of Chinese Poems* (中國古詩文鑑賞辭典) (Nanjing: Jiangsu Ancient Books Publishing, 1988), p.68. Huo Songlin holds a similar reading on the verse. See *A Grand Sight of Tang Poetry* (唐詩大觀) (Hong Kong: The Commercial Press, 1986), p.543.

In snow-like white guests present were dressed.
The saddening song sung by the hero
Seemed not to be finished up ever.
Had the crying birds realized this kind of ordeal,
Blood instead of tears they would have wept.
In whose company
Shall I get drunk under the moon?

This lyric is subtitled as 'Farewell to my 12th younger cousin Maojia'. As far as this title is concerned, it is written in a structure of 'guest and host', although it can be said to be 'host and guest' if looked at from the theme (see further below).

The guest part is divided into three sections, covering the most of the lines. The first consists of the lines from '(f)rom the trees' to 'withering blossoms', and leads the reader to enter the poem's prospect from a side perspective, that is, using the cry of one bird after another (*items*) until the leave of spring to foreground 'regretting'(*general*); this gives rise to the first 'beat'. In the second section from '(y)et with parting' to 'finished up ever', which is aimed to describe the regretting of man, the metaphor of birds is then replaced by their human counterpart, illustrated by two women, namely Wang Zhaojun (of which the 'fragrant carriage' is a metonym) and the homecoming concubine in a classical legend, and two men, Li Ling referred to by the 'general' and Jin Ke by the 'hero'. The arrangement here is twofold in terms of textual structuration: on the one hand, the sequence of women followed by men goes in line with the structure of reverse/obverse; and on the other, it first lifts the examples of parting on the same level and then converges all on the significance of the last one[35] to bring into the

....

35 See Chen Manming, 'On the textual structure based on Leveling and Convergin' (談「平提側收」的篇章結構), *op. cit*, in note 32, pp.435～459.

picture something deeper and wider than the parting motif (as in '(t)he saddening song...finished up ever'), that is, as hinted by the strong contrast between the general's treason and the hero's sacrifice, the partisan turmoil in the imperial government of the author's time.[36] Interpreted this way this part forms the core, the 'blow', of the poetic lyric inasmuch as it brings out the thematic expression of the poet's lament for the nation's tragedy. The guest part then ends in the third section at a returning back to the side perspective of the crying birds, hence conducive to the second 'beat', this time being virtually (counterfactually) predicting the birds' deeper regrets of weeping 'blood instead of tears'.

After the guest part comes the host, which in the final clause beginning '(i)n whose company' signifies the poet's sentiments for leaving his cousin. It also echoes what Su Dongpo, another Sung Dynasty poet, depicted as the 'longing no one sees'[37]. The structural analysis of 'Congratulations' is represented on the next page, which is followed by a chart of its compositional levels.

With 'consonance' (including guest/host, beat/blow, virtual/real, general/item, leveling/converging, earlier/later) is contained 'contrast' (reverse/obverse); in its development lies 'change'(beat/blow/beat). The fact that the part of change extends across the most of the poem with the structure of contrast placed at the textual center

....

36 See Chen Manming, 'Selected works of Ci in the periods of Tang and Sung' (唐宋詞拾玉), in *Chinese Bulletin* (國文天地), vol.12, no.1(Taipei, 1996), pp.66~69. See also Gong Bendong, *A Critical Biography of Xin Qiji* (辛棄疾評傳) (Nanjing: The Press of Nanjing University, 1998), pp.400~401.

37 Su Shi wrote in a lyric during his stay at Dinghui Temple:
   Startled, she gets up, looks back
   With longing no one sees
   And will not settle on any of the cold branches
   Along the chill and lonely beach.
   See *Dongpo Ballads* (東坡樂府箋)(Taipei: Huazhen Books, 1978), p.168.

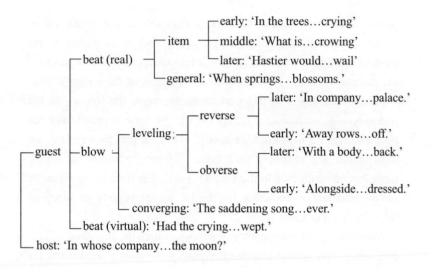

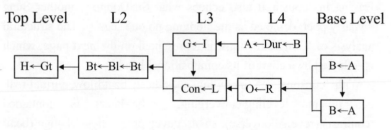

makes it possible for all the constituent substructures of the concordance part to serve for the core message. The arrangement of many 'satellites' surrounding 'a star' is conducive to the *Ci* poem's style of 'dismal and bleakness infused with leaping disturbance'.[38]
It also helps reveal the underlying structure of M/D/S(N) in the lyric: M refers to the manifestation of leveling/appending, general/item, reverse/obverse, and earlier/later; D to that of beat/blow (as in guest/host) as the medium for coherence of the global text; and, finally, S(N) to the theme of lamenting for the nation's tragedy and

....

38 Chen Tingchuo, *Comments on Ci from Baiyu Zhai*(白雨齋詞話), vol.1(Taipei: New Wenfeng,1988), p.3791.

the style of 'dismal and bleakness infused with leaping disturbance'. The discussion presented in this section so far has demonstrated the universality of the 'M/D/S(N)' structure in Chinese thinking across philosophy, aesthetics, and literature. Applied onto literary texts, it not only helps explain the four laws of textual construction— ordering (shifting) and changing (twisting) as Multeity; cohering (concordance or contrast by way of yang and yin, or hard and soft, to go up and down between structural levels) as Duality; unifying (theme and style, rhythm, atmosphere, realm, etc.) as Singularity (Naught)—but also is germane to the stracturation of individual artifacts. As we have seen in the above-mentioned examples of prose and prosodic writings, they are unexceptionally organized around a binary operation leading either to concordance (feminine and softness) or to contrast (masculinity and hardness), whose textual manifestations can make the text cohere globally by going up and down between the structural levels, and which therefore pertains to D. Around the core structure of binary operation further lie the satellite structures which in the whole pertain to M. Last but not least, the interplay between D and M in a text artifact leads structurally to a unified yet sometimes hidden theme belonging to the structure of S(N).

II. Styles of the structure of "many, two, one/zero"

Literary styles vary greatly according to genres, writers, schools, times, regions, nations, and individual text artifacts. Even when it comes to one single text we have to look at the difference between the style of its content and of its form. The formal (artistic) style can itself be analyzed from different perspectives of grammar, rhetoric, and textual (local and global) construction. Based upon the binary operation and complying with the logic of M/D/S(N), different ways of textual construction must be stylized in close relation to the structures of concordance and contrast, or feminine softness and masculine hardness, and their shifting and twisting. The key to the stylization is the D of M/D/S(N) as it, while functioning as a hinge for the connection between the upper and lower levels, signifies the feminine-soft or masculine-hard nature of a core structure. Put differently, the binary structure is in a position from which the text, under the support of the satellite, multiple structures, is both decentralized locally and centralized globally to create either the character of softness or that of hardness. In this section, more examples of Chinese poetry will be scrutinized with an aim to comprehend the tendency of how the characters of softness and hardness rise and fall according to particular textual structuration.

1. The formation of the styles of the structure of "many, two, one/zero"

In terminology, style refers to 'attitudes, appearances, inclinations—the synthetic expression of characters' pertaining to a variety of artifacts ranging from architecture, sculpture, music, costumes, through to literature. [39] As far as literary style is concerned, genre, writer, school, time, region, ethnicity, works—all these are sources of stylistic differences. [40] Even for one single literary work, its content and form differ in their stylistic expression.

China has a fairly long history of the theorization of literary styles. Indebted to the beginners like Tsao Pi's Dianlun Lunwen, or 'On Literature' in *Canonical Treatises* and Liu Xie's Wenxin Diaolong, or *The heart of Literature and Carving of Dragons,* most of the literal criticism had been focused on styles of particular authors and individual works. [41] Few of them differentiated between content

....

[39] Li Yunhan, *Mandarin Styles* (漢語風格學) (Guangzhou: Guangdong Education Publishing, 2000), p.3.

[40] Zhou Zhenfu, *Illustrated Talks of Literary Styles* (文學風格例話) (Shanghai: Shanghai Education Publishing, 1989).

[41] Li, *op. cit.* in note 39, p.2.

and form for analyzing the style of individual works; still fewer, if any, are analyses that worked out the style of works from the point of view of grammar, rhetoric and textual construction.

The stylization of literary works through binary operation of yin and yang is characterized by hardness and softness. As early as in about the 510's Chinese critics began to discuss literary styles in a way that involved the concepts of hardness and softness and yet stopped short of using the very terms. Likewise, Huang Zongxi, a scholar between the Ming and Qing Dynasty, once appropriated yin and yang as a tool for commenting upon literary works, yet without direct mentioning softness and hardness. [42] It is not until 'A reply to Lu Qifei' by Yao Nai (1731~1815) that the terms had found in works of literary criticism their uses for generalizing and classifying stylistic expressions.

鼐聞天地之道，陰陽剛柔而已。(I heard that the way of heaven and earth lies in nothing but femininity(yin)/ masculinity(yang) and soft/hard.) 文者，天地之精英，而陰陽剛柔之發也(Writings, as quintessence of heaven and earth, comes directly out of the interplay of femininity and masculinity, softness and hardness.[...]) 其得於陽與剛之美者，(Those who derive its beauty from masculinity and hardness) 則其文如霆，如電，(are as powerful as thunderbolt,) as 如長風之出谷，(speedy as fine horses,) 如崇山峻崖，如決大川，如奔騏驥；(as turbulent as bursting floods, as magnificent as lofty

....

42 Yu Min & Sun Tonghai argues that the use of yin/yang, or soft/hard, in literary criticism, being there implicitly for a long time, had not seen a significant development until the period of the late-Ming and mid-Ching, when Huang Zongxi, as well as Yao Nai several decades later, began to see literary texts emblematic of the interplay of the two forces. See Principal Works of Ancient Chinese Aesthetics (中國古典美學舉要)(Hefei: Anhui Education Publishing House, 2000), p.962.

mountains,) 其光也，如杲日，如火，如金鏐鐵；(and as harsh as the sunbeam to the eye or the forge blazes to the iron.) 其於人也，如憑高視遠，(They are like a man who looks far from a height,) 如君而朝萬眾，(who ascends the throne in front of his subjects,) 如鼓萬勇士而戰之。(and who drums to lead ten thousand warriors into battles.) 其得於陰與柔之美者，(Those who derives its beauty from femininity and softness,) 則其文如升初日，(on the other hand, emerge as the rising sun,) 如清風，如雲，如霞，如煙，(the spring breeze, the clouds, the morning star, the smog,) 如幽林曲澗，如淪，如漾，如珠玉之輝，如鴻鵠之鳴而入廖廓；(the ripples and wavelets, appear as winding as streams in the shadowy woods, glows as the pearl beads, and echoes like the phoenix crying in the vault of heaven.) 其於人也，漻乎其如歎，(They can be likened to a man who is as dreary as sighing,) 邈乎其如有思，(as secluded as pondering,) 暖乎其如喜，(as mild as delighting,) 愀乎其如悲。(and as worried as saddening.) 觀其文，諷其音，(Scrutinize their wordings and recite their tones,) 則為文者之性情形狀舉以殊焉。(and one would find individuality and uniqueness in every single writer's writings.) 且夫陰陽剛柔，其本二端，(Although yin and yang, soft and hard, are two different ends,) 造萬物者糅而氣有多寡、進絀，則品次億方，以至於不可窮，萬物生焉。(they can nevertheless give rise to myriads of classes and even the creation itself This is all because the creator, while creating every single thing, mixed the two forces of a more or lesser amount, and in a progressive or regressive order. [...]) 故曰：一陰一陽之為道。夫文之多變，亦若是已。(The dissimilitude of one literary style from another results from the same cause.)
　。……

The passage is explained by Zhou Zhenfu as follows:

Yao actually generalizes literary styles into two classes; one is feminine softness; the other masculine hardness. Into the class of feminine softness are included styles of magnificence, vigorousness, sturdiness, sublimity. Into the class of feminine softness are included styles of reticence, implication, elegancy, distance and subtlety. He believes that both the personal characters and the wording and phrasing of a literary text have to do with the dichotomy between feminine softness and masculine hardness. He further points out that the changing styles of literary works are produced by mixing up the forces of yin/yang of different amounts and levels: they might rise and fall, or advance and recede, in relation to one another. Therefore, under the two classes are seen a diversity of infinitely changing styles[43].

This means that the literary style depends for its diversity on how hardness and softness increase and decrease among different texts. Yao Nai inherits this conception of softness/hardness from the ancient classics, as he claimed in the *Reply*:

惟聖人之言，統二氣之會而弗偏，(Only the ancient sages integrated the two forces in their words and were not deviated (from the middle way).) 然而《易》、《詩》、《書》、《論語》所載，亦間有可以剛柔分矣。(Yet in *Zhouyi(I Ching)*, *Shijing*, *Shangshu*, and *Lunyu* there are sometimes passages germane to the dichotomy between softness and hardness.)[44]

....

43 Zhou, *op. cit*. in note 40, p.13.

44 To integrate the two forces without deviation means to speak and act in accordance with the theorem of *Zhouyi Xici* that 'one yin and one yang is called the Way'. Xici Zhuang, or the *Treatise of Appended Words*, was usually attributed to Confucius himself. Other Confucian classics also mention concepts of the

The theory about the handing down of the yin/yang, or soft/hard, dichotomy from the ancient Confucian classics could help explain why Yao Nai himself 'upholds yang and extends hardness, while downplaying yin and retreating softness', as Confucianism is characterized by its favor to masculine hardness, in contrast with Taoism's advocacy of feminine softness. However, given that Zhouyi and Laotze offer the philosophical basis for the hard/soft stylization, one should not be biased against either of the two schools in order to be truly integrating 'the two forces' without presuppositions.

Since textual construction is based upon the binary operation of yin/yang, or soft/hard, it can be expected that the structures of textual construction are conducive to the interpretation of how the styles of softness/hardness take shape. In other words, to understand the stylization of textual construction requires us to explore the feminine softness and the masculine hardness characteristic of the structure of textual construction.

To start with, each and every law of textual construction, either concordant or contrast, comes from the binary operation of yin/yang. As a result, the quality of femininity and masculinity, softness and hardness, are inherent in textual laws themselves. Put simply, those pertaining to origin, earliness, stillness, lowness, ins, smallness, closeness, etc., are characteristic of femininity and softness; those pertaining to end, lateness, movement, highness, outs, largeness, farness, etc., are of masculinity and hardness. The *Treatise of Appended Words* of *Zhouyi* states,

The heaven is superior, and the earth is inferior, so determined are the *Qian* hexagram and the *Kun* hexagram. Low and high are in display, so established are the noble and the despicable.

....

soft/hard distinction. See Yu & Sun, *op. cit.* in note 42, p.965.

Movement and stillness act with regularity, so judged are the hard and the soft.

'The hard and the soft', undefined as they were, can nevertheless be identified on the basis of the theory of ying/yang. As Chen Wanghen argues,

> The conception of hardness and softness in *Zhouyi* does not only carry with itself the meaning of sexes but also symbolizes other oppositions as seen in sky and ground, sun and moon, day and night, king and subjects, fathers and sons. Furthermore, hardness and softness interflows with many conceptual pairs of opposites, such as movement and stillness, progress and regress, nobleness and humbleness, highness and lowness, with hardness referring to the first unit in each of the pairs and softness to the second.[45]

Applied to textual construction, the binary operation of yin/yang can function as both the foundation of and a touchstone for the textual laws as listed below:

Law of present/past: the present as masculinity and hardness, and the past as femininity and softness.
Law of distant/close: the dkstant as masculinity and hardness, and the close as femininity and softness.
Law of large/small: the large as masculinity and hardness, and the small as femininity and softness.
Law of beginning/end: the end as masculinity and hardness, and the beginning as femininity and softness.
Law of real/virtual: the real as masculinity and hardness, and the

....

[45] See *History of Classical Chinese Aesthetics* (中國古典美學史)(Changsha: Hunan Education Publishing House, 1998), p.184.

virtual as femininity and softness.

Law of guest/host: the guest as masculinity and hardness, and the host as femininity and softness.

Law of obverse/reverse: the reverse as masculinity and hardness, and the obverse as femininity and softness.

Law of construction/deconstruction: the deconstruction as masculinity and hardness, and the construction as femininity and softness.

Law of item/general: the item as masculinity and hardness, and the general as femininity and softness.

Law of effects/cause: the effects as masculinity and hardness, and the cause as femininity and softness.

On the basis of the yin/yang characters of textual laws one can move on to probe into the stylization of literary texts. Specifically speaking, how literary texts are stylistically characterized as masculine hardness and/or feminine softness can be analyzed and identified by matching the binary characterization of the textual laws with their realization in particular textual construction of the global sense of concordance (feminine softness) and/or contrast (masculine hardness). Among the laws of textual construction, some tend to give rise to contrast, such as the law of noble/humble, intimacy/ alienation, obverse/reverse, depressing/arousing, construc-tion/ deconstruction, many/few, detailed/sketchy, tension/ease, and others are more likely to produce contrasts, such as far/close, large/small, high/low, shallow/deep, guest/host, real/virtual, leveling/ converging, general/item, loosening/retrieving, cause/effects, and so on.

The analysis is then furthered on the structural level of textual construction and has to do with what is called the 'shifting' and 'twisting' of laws of textual construction and of their structures. First, with regard to the binary interplay within individual textual laws, 'shifting' means the forward or the backward movement emerging from and inherent in every single realization of a textual law in a particular textual artifact. The law of obverse/reverse, for example, can be textually manifested in either a forward flow from obverse to reverse, or a backward flow from reverse to obverse. 'Twisting', on the other hand, refers to a movement that unifies progression and regression in one particular realization of textual laws. If, so to speak, 'shifting' is a one-way, either forward or backward, ticket, 'twisting' puts the reader on a return journey, as it always flows back to where it starts. There are, diagrammatically, flows of 'host/guest/host', 'real/virtual/real', 'effects/cause/effects', and so on.

Secondly, as regards the local and global structure of textual construction, we can also distinguish between the 'shifting' and the 'twisting' movement. First, the local text might switch forwardly or backwardly from one (sub)structure of textual construction to another (sub)structure, giving rise to movements of, for example, construction/destruction to originals/ends, touching/spreading to close/distant, past/present to depressing/arousing, and so on. Connect any two instances of the 'shifting' on a higher level and repeat it backwards and then we have the global movement of 'twisting'. For example, a text may develop a local structure of obverse/reverse out of the shifting of two substructures of cause/effects and asking/answering at a lower level, and reverse, or 'twist', it at a different level of the text, hence globally, to form a complementary structure of reverse/obverse[46]. (See for information the diagram of structural analysis on page ___ of this chapter.—translator's note)[46]

To conclude, 'shifting', including forward and backward, and 'twisting' represent changes of a text in the 'momentum' of its

....

[46] See Chou Xiaoping, 'On the shifting and twisting of textual laws and its aesthetic significance' (論章法的移位、轉位及其美感), in *Selected Papers on Theory of Texts* (辭章學論文集), vol.1, *op. cit.* in note 8, pp.98~122.

internal flow (from one structural unit to another). Among them the forward 'shifting' is the weakest as it complies with the common way of reasoning. Stronger than it is its backward counterpart. And the strongest belongs with 'twisting' as it surprises the reader with a turning back to confront what is already settled. The difference surely reflects the changing style of textual construction and the accompanying sense of beauty.

In general, the structuralization of textual units relies for its momentum as the intensity of the inclination to yin/yang, or soft/hard, upon the following factors.

1. The yin/yang, or soft/hard, features of the textual law. For example, closeness, positive, and general are attributed to feminine softness, while their counterpart in textual construction—distance, negative, and item—are to masculine hardness.

2. The quality of concordance and contrast characterizing each structure of textual construction. For example, shallow/deep, guest/host, general/item are conducive to concordance, and positive/negative, depressing/rising, and constructive/destructive to contrast.

3. The local and global changes and transformations of structures of textual construction, including shifting (forward and backward) and twisting (circular). Among them the forward movement is the prototype, while the backward and the circular ones are derivative.

4. The compositional levels on which the structures and their movements are placed. They may range from the top level, level 2, 3,…through to the base level.

5. The logical structure of 'M/D/S(N)'.

The tendency of yin/yang, or softness/hardness, or momentum, which rises and falls according to these five factors, can be interpreted in the following manner.

(Artists) understand everything in the universe, especially that of/for artistic expression, as a form of existence that keeps changing and moving, as a living thing that communicates with them. They are constantly pursuing the 'tendentious momentum' inherent of objects and forms.[47]

Such pursuing relies on different grasps of the forward, backward and returning movement of the tendency:

Momentum is not only concerned with the intensity; it is also directional in its realization in individual texts. The forward, or compliant, movement goes in line with the aesthetic subject's prepositions and ways of thinking, assuring him of a feel of pleasant freedom and mind-opening self-confidence. The backward, or defiant, movement, to the contrary, confronts the object head-to-head with the admiring subject's repositions and ways of thinking. What is conflicting, disturbing and offending now dominates his psychology.[48]

Generally speaking, the 'forward momentum' leads to satisfaction and openmindedness, the 'backward momentum' leads to agitation and disturbance, and the 'returning momentum' to both of them with a greater degree. Although the tendentious momentum in itself belongs with the yin/yang categories, it does not act upon the yin/yang quality of structures of textual construction and yet is

....

47 Tu Guangshe, 'Momentum by Movement' (因動成勢) (Nanchang: Baihuachou Arts Publishing, 2001), p.256.
48 Tu, *ibid.*, p.265.

decided for its own categorization by the movements within the structures.

In order to gauge the proportion of the yin quality to the yang quality in a single text and accordingly compare the patterns of tendentious momentum across different texts, we offer a recipe for calculation based on the following rules.

1. First determine the yin/yang characterization of each element of a binary textual law, and then assign the beginner to '1(-fold)' and the finalizer '2(-fold)'.
2. Assign the interplay of 'concordance' to '1(-fold)', and that of 'contrast' '2(-fold)'.
3. Assign the forward shifting to '1(-fold)', the backward shifting '2(-fold)' and the returning twisting '3(-fold).
4. Assign the base level to '1(-fold)', and a next level '2(-fold)', a still next level '3(-fold)', and the so forth.
5. The core structure of a text receives the highest number assigned consequently, and other than that the number ('-fold') decreases by each level.

Tentative as it might look, the formula offered here allows the researcher to compare one text with another, and observe the pattern across more, against a quasi-arithmetic scale. We have hence attained three levels of the hardness to softness proportion of literary texts.

1. Pure hardness or pure softness: the figure of its momentum is between 66.66 and 71.43.
2. Weighted hardness or weighted softness: the figure of its momentum is between 54.78 and 66.65.
3. Half hardness and half softness: the figure of its momentum is between 45.23 and 54.77.

Among them the figure of 71.43 is attained from the ratio of 5 to 7 representing the yin/yang proportion of the twisting structure, which constitutes the maximum of the calculation of momentum. The number 66.66 comes from the ratio of 2 to 3 representing the yin/yang proportion of the shifting structure, which constitutes the medium of the calculation of momentum. And finally, we use 50 to denote an ideal half and half distribution between yin and yang and deduce from and add to it by 4.77, the difference between maximum and medium, to produce a range from 45.23 to 54.77, which, we believe, can better represent the changing nature of the tendentious momentum. For the sake of the convenience of discussion, the figures can be slightly adjusted to obtain the following grades.

1. Pure hardness or pure softness: the figure of its momentum ranges from 66 to 72.
2. Weighted hardness or weighted softness: the figure of its momentum ranges from 56 to 65.
3. Half hardness and half softness: the figure of its momentum ranges from 45 and 55.

Applying this formula we may expect some concrete proof of what Yao Nai said of the creator mixing 'the two forces of a more or lesser amount, and in a progressive or regressive order.'

2. A few examples of the styles of the structure of "many, two, one/zero"

A literary text is composed of a succession and strata of structures of textual construction. Each of the structures differs in its interplay of concordance and contrast, its nature of yin(soft) and yang(hard), and, finally, in its tendency emerging from the movement of shifting(backward and forward) and twisting (circular). All these are indispensable for the logical analysis of the style of textual construction. In the following, such analysis is illustrated by several poems, of which Tao Yuanming's (known also Tao Qien) 'Drinking' comes the first.

結廬在人境，I built my cottage among the habitations of men, 而無車馬喧。And yet there is no clamor of carriages and horses. 問君何能爾，You ask: "Sir, how can this be done?" 心遠地自偏。"A heart that is distant makes a remote hermitage." 採菊東籬下，I pluck chrysanthemums under the eastern hedge, 悠然見南山；Then gaze afar towards the southern hills. 山氣日夕佳，The mountain air is fresh at the dusk of day; 飛鳥相與還。The flying birds in flocks return. 此中有真意，In these things there lies a true meaning; 欲辨已忘言。I want to tell it, but have forgotten the words.

Tao wrote 20 poems entitled Drinking, all of them implying his aspiration and longings. This one comes in the fifth, aimed to express the interests of insolating oneself in the bustling world. In the first two verses it clarifies that '(a) heart that is distant makes a remote hermitage'. The subject is followed by a description of his admiring the nature in a lighthearted mood, ending with the true delight of 'forgetting words due to realizing the genuine meaning' (from Zhuang Tzu).

In detail, the first two verses write about the poet's living in solitude in the bustling world of human affairs, foregrounding with the contradiction herein the following Q & A. Moving from the supposed question to the poet's reply, the third and forth verses pick up 'the distant heart' as the spine of the poem by explaining how one's mind can set him free from mundane shackles. Following the explanation is a description in the fifth and sixth verses of the feeling of quietness and transcendence while plucking flowers and gazing afar into hills, a feeling that arises naturally from the poet's castaway heart. The seventh and eighth verses continue to portray the natural scene with the atmosphere in the mountains and the activity of flying birds. All the feelings and seeings reach at the height in the ending verses when words become unnecessary for communicating the sublime state and meaning of 'distant heart'. As Wu Qi of the Qing dynasty acutely points out, 'The word 'meaning' arises from the word 'heart' and is added to by the word 'true' to push the theme deeper. As a result, while the distant heart can be regarded as the spine of the poem, the true meaning is the marrow of it.' Fang Dongshu of Qing holds a similar view when he says that the poem's 'ambiance is presented as idle and lighthearted and the scenery is pictured beautifully, but its true meaning cannot be grasped without a distantly secluded heart.' In sum, Tao Yuanming demonstrated a creative setting in this poem, making it a temptation for readers to ponder its wordless spirit. The following diagram represents the structural analysis of the poem.

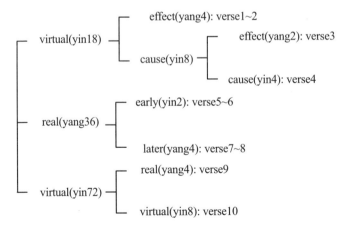

The following compositional chart represents the distribution of yin/yang across the structural units:

Top Level   L2   Base Level

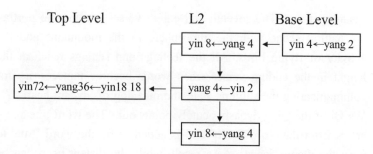

At the top level lies the core structure of the poem, represented by 'virtual/real/virtual', which twists in a circular movement from yin back to yin, and which can be converted into the number of yin90 and yang36. At the second level lie three shifts of local structures: respectively, from effect to cause (backward), from early to later (forward), and from real to virtual (backward), together represented by the number of ying18 and yang12. The shifting structure of effect/cause (hence backward) at the bottom gives the figure of yin4 and yang2. Add all these together and we have a total of yin112 and yang50 as representative of the tendentious momentum of the poem. The result shows that, implying hardness in softness as it were, the poem actually downplays the feature of masculine hardness (covering only 31% of the total compared to 69% covered by softness). Chou Zhengfu's interpretation of the poem is of relevance here:

The poem is high in its aesthetic performance. It describes the poet's resignation from office and having no visitors of high status or whatsoever, ... which shows his determination for living a hermit's life. Even if he lived in populated areas, his place looked remote to those who he kept away from through his secluded heart. This suggests his loathing toward the filthy practices within the officialdom and sets off his noble choice for a rather harsh life in the farmland. In the following verses, the image of flower plucking directs the reader to his sight of Lu Mountain and his attention to foggy air and flying birds in the mountains. What's so important about mountain air and flying birds? In a word, the imagery expresses the poet's sentiments. He first associated the clouds and fog surmounting the peaks with his earlier ideal about undertaking a government career, while the homecoming birds reminded him of his weariness toward and retiring from the officialdom. This is the true meaning of his living in retirement, a meaning that finds no words for its expression in the poem. The implicit style of mixing up imagery and affections is where the aesthetic achievement of the poem, and its ingenious setting, resides.[49]

The inference Chou draws from the mixed and implicit writing about the 'ingenious' stylization of the poem corresponds to Fan Dongshu's interpretation that the idleness must be explained away by means of the 'distant heart' in order to unveil the 'true meaning'. Either 'ingenious' or 'idle and lighthearted' belongs to a stylization characterized by and inclined to feminine softness. The question as of how inclined it is, however, needs arguably to be answered through its structures of textual construction.

Now, let us turn to Wang Wei's Seeing off Envoy Li of Zichou.

萬壑樹參天，Towering trees rise in myriads of valleys, 千山響杜鵑。Crying cuckoos are heard across the mountains. 山中一夜雨，Mountain rain continued for the whole night, 樹杪百重泉。Pouring hundreds of springs down the tree tips, 漢女輸橦布，Han Women submit flower-weaved cloth; 巴人訟芋田。The Ba people sue for disputes over taro farms. 文翁翻教授，May you revive the cultivation once carried out by Wen the Elder, 不敢倚先賢。Do not take advantage of your forerunners'

---

49 See Chou, *op. cit.* in note 40, pp.79~80.

heritage.

It is written as a gift poem and describes the costumes of Zizhou, while implying praise to its receiver.[50] It is structured by the law of real/virtual. The first three couplets consists in what is 'real', of which a scenic depiction precedes accounts of the indigenous customs. The first two verses resort to vision and sound for a long-shot of the landscape. Following it is a close-range view offered by a manifestation of the lasting/momentary structure in the third and fourth verses. The next two verses depict the local customs through the structure of obverse/reverse. What is virtual consists in the last two verses, which conclude the poem with complimentary implications. Throughout the lines is carried out a proper writing that fits the place, the thing, and the person. As Yu Shouzhen points out,

The first four verses fit the place by visualizing from afar the spectacular scenery of Zizhou. The second couplet repeats the use of mountain and tree in the first couplet. [...] The third couplet is focused on the Ba people and the women of Han ethnicity for a description of the local customs, and hence pertains to the thing. The final couplet mentions the Han Dynasty Governor Wen the Elder who succeeded in cultivating the local people. In this way the poem implies praise for Envoy Li by likening him to the famous local administrator, and hence fits the person.[51]

With the help of the elaborate interpretation, we can better understand this poem and go further with an analysis of its structures as follows.

....

50 See Yu Shouzhen, *Elaborate Analysis of The Three Hundred Tang Poems* (唐詩三百首詳析) (Taipei: Zhonghua Books, 1996), p.147.
51 Ibid., p.148.

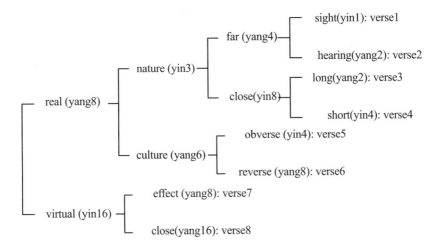

Represented in the yin/yang structure only is the following compositional chart:

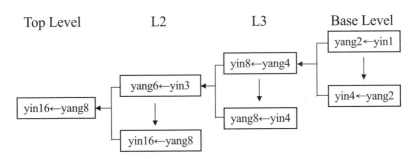

The poem is structurally composed of four levels. On the top is the core structure of real/virtual (backward shifting), the momentum of which is represented by the number of yin16 and yang8. On level 2 lie two shifting structures of scene/thing (forward) and effect/cause (backward), acquiring for their momentum the number of yin19 and yang14. Two more shifting structures are manifested on level 3, namely distant/close (backward) and obverse/reverse (forward and contrast), the momentum of which is converted into yin12 and yang12. The shifting structures of vision/sound (forward) and lasting/momentary (backward) at the bottom gives the figure of yin5 and yang4. Add together and we have a total of yin52 and yang38 as representative of the tendentious momentum of the poem. The percentage is 58% of yin and 42% of yang. This shows a pattern of half softness and half hardness with a slight tilt to the soft. We can relate this finding to Chou's accounts:

> Commenting on the first two couplets, the Qing Dynasty poet Ji Yun speaks of 'a lofty tone of the like of clouds' and another scholar Xu Yinfang says 'infusion of great strength into the brush'. It can therefore be attributed to the style of strength and hardness. It, however, is worth to note that Xu also points to the existence of both majestic satiation and freshness from afar in its stylization. The poem certainly shows implications of distant freshness as it writes about the crying cuckoos in parallel with the towering trees, and the water coming down the trees like springs after an overnight rainfall. From the picturing of the horizon of grand mountains emerges some taste of distance and briskness. Without admiring this freshness one would stop short of applauding the grandeur of nature as depicted in the poem. The poet would even not have been able to write in a strong style.[52]

It can be argued that implications count as a decisive factor for the success and failure of poetic writings. Since the poem, on the one hand, has the implications of 'freshness far away from the human world' and, on the other, is grand and satiable only in terms of its scenic depiction, its stylization goes in between feminine softness and masculine hardness with a bias in favor of the former. This kind

---

[52] See Zhou, *op. cit.* in note 40 above, p.49.

of 'coupling of hardness and softness' is of great aesthetic value.[53] The next analysis makes use of Du Fu's 'Ascending a Pavilion'.

花近高樓傷客心，Flowers close the pavilion hurt the heart of a wanderer 萬方多難此登臨。For I see, from this high vantage, calamities everywhere. 錦江春色來天地，The Jinjiang River, bright with spring, floats between earth and heaven 玉壘浮雲變古今。Like a line of cloud by the Jade Peak, between ancient days and now. 北極朝廷終不改，Though the Empire is established as firm as the North Star 西山寇盜莫相侵。And bandits dare not venture from the western hills, 可憐後主還祠廟，Yet sorry in the twilight for the woes of the late Emperor Li, 日暮聊為〈梁甫吟〉。I am singing a song by Kong Ming near the time of sunset. (Kong Ming was an able and famous premier of the Tri-kingdom periods.—translator's note)

This poem expresses Du Fu's sentiments of the upheaval of the time. He first reverses the cause and the effect by starting with his seeing and feeling, which results from his ascending the pavilion at a time of calamities. In this way the poet foregrounds the subject of a wanderer's saddened heart in the first couplet, which therefore constitutes the general part. Couplet 2 writes about the view at the high story, manifesting the part of item 1 as in accordance with the 'flowers' at the beginning, while couplet 3 brings about item 2 as it echoes with 'the calamities'. The final couplet, in a linkup with the subject of a wanderer's sadness, concludes with the poet's sorrow for the lack of a great man to defend the state, hence manifesting item 3. The poem is arranged in an orderly way, with everything falling into place under the key idea. The following is a rather elaborate and faithful comment by Yu.

....

53 See Chen, *op. cit.* in note 45 above.

The first four verses describe the view from the pavilion. The flowers nearby sadden the visiting poet due to its contrast with the barren fields in the far. Seasons change and clouds transform—both denote figuratively the disturbing times. The third couplet signifies in its first verse the gratified reaction to the recovery of the capital, and in its second the worry about non-Chinese invasion. The final couplet begins with a reminder of the late-emperor Li's fatuousness and consequences, and ends with a suggestion of the poet's own ambition to pacify everything under heaven.[54]

Now, let us turn to the diagram of the structural analysis of 'Ascending',

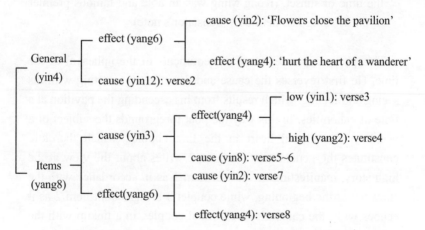

and the compositional chart that demonstrates the attribution of yin and yang across the poem.

....

54   See Yu, *op. cit.* in note 50 above, pp.233~234.

Top Level   L2   L3   Base Level

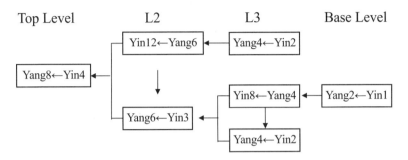

There are four structural levels, on the top of which is manifested a shift from 'lower' to 'higher', represented for its momentum by the number of yin1 and yang2. On level 3 are three shifting structures, including two plies of cause/effect (forward) and one ply of effect/cause (backward), together giving a number of yin12 and yang12. On level 2 lie one shifting structure of effect/cause (backward) and another of cause/effect (forward), together giving a number of ying15 and yang12. On the top level is the core structure manifested in the form of general/item (forward shifting), and is converted for its tendentious momentum into yin4 and yang8. The total is yin32 and yang34, in a ratio of 48% to 52%. To compare with Wang Wei's Seeing off, the poem obviously represents something close to the ideal type of the hardness-softness-balanced style. What is different is that Du Fu writes in a manner slightly inclined to what is hard rather than what is soft. Zhou offers a similar view into the style of Ascending:

The terrace offers an angle to cut across the spring scenery at Jinjiang and the floating clouds surrounding the Jade Peak. The 'wanderer's saddened heart', on the other hand, links up 'calamities everywhere' and 'bandits' from western hills, through to Zhuge Kongmin, realizing a heavyhearted line of thinking.

Among 'grandness, broadness, superior, and wholeness'--the four qualities that stylize this poem--, the 'superior' refers specifically to this sophisticated thinking, whereas the general style as well as couplet 2 belongs to a strong style.[55]

From the point of view of tendentious momentum, the strong style characterized by grandeur and wholeness is represented by the number of yang52, while 'heavyheartedness' is by ying48 as it affiliates to the poem's theme from the implicit side of feminine tenderne

Now, take Jiang Kuei's Dark Fumes as the final example.

舊時月色。The bright moonlight in the past 算幾番照我，Shined on me for many times, 梅邊吹笛。While I played a flute by plum blossoms. 喚起玉人，The melody woke up a beauty, 不管清寒與攀摘。Who joined me plucking blossoms in spite of the chill. 何遜而今漸老，Till now I have aged just like He Xun, 都忘卻、春風詞筆。And forgotten all the spring-like graces of writing. 但怪得、竹外疏花，Yet to my surprise, from the sparse blossoms out of the bamboo shrubs 香冷入瑤席。Is sent a dim and brisk fragrance into the banquet room. 江國、正寂寂。The watery countryside of Jiangnan sleeps in an utter silence. 歎寄與路遙，I'd send you a blossom and sadly the distance blocks the way, 夜雪初積。Not to mention the snowfall overnight covering the roads. 翠尊易泣，The jade vessel lures me into tears, 紅萼無言耿相憶。And the speechless red calyxes evoke old memories 長記曾攜手處，About the place where we visited hand in hand. 千樹壓、西湖寒碧。又片片、A thousand trees overlaid plum blossoms and the Xihu Lake reflected green and freezing glitters. 吹盡也，幾時見得。As of now, blossoms are blown away in batches,

....

55 Chou, *op. cit.* in note 40, p.54.

The lyrics, written in the Song dynasty, is a singing of red plum blossoms. It is arranged globally by the structure of real/virtual. The real part starts from the first line through to the second line from the end. Its first five lines describe what he used to do under the moonlight and are arranged in the early/later couple: the poet played the flute and then his mistress joined him. As a whole, this section manifests a reverse part at an upper level, in contrast to an obverse one which lasts from line 6 to line 14 and which is concerned with the situation of the present: if the reverse shows a man's vigorous past, the obverse pictures his waning at present. In doing so, it employs two substructures at the lower levels. First, in line 6 and 7, is the poet's lament on 'all' the departed graces and charms—except for one thing: the fragrance of plum blossoms that is sent in to their room through air, which evokes the poet's memories about and longing for his love. Thus, the latter part of 'remaining', as coupled with the preceding 'whole', includes in itself yet another substructure of 'smell/sight', referred to respectively by the fragrance and the vast, snow-covered lands. In describing what he recalls, line 15 and 16 manifest a 'virtual' reflection of plum trees on the lake, as opposed to the cruel 'reality' of blossoms being blown away as in line 17 and 18. What he sees virtually and factually here results from the unfolding of the poet's emotion from seeing the moon (line1) to recalling through red calyxes (line16). The substructure of cause/effect manifested herein overlaps the core structure of real/virtual on the top level, which, as we have mentioned above, invests the 'virtual' part in the final line. By asking 'when shall I see them again?' the poet again likens plum blossoms to his mistress and concluded the poem with an endless longing for her.

With intense contrasts between real/virtual, vigor/waning, before/present, Jiang Kuei expresses his nostalgia in an extremely subtle, tortuous way. Some said this poem connotes the imperial state and has to do with the kidnapping of the then father and son Emperors by northern tribes.[56] This view, we believe, is not acceptable for its lack of evidence[57.] Pan Shanchi comments justly on the poem's esthetic performance: 'The motif of the blossom cuts across the Ci poem to bring about a circular movement from the past to the present and back to the past, to express the poet's reminiscence of the gathering in the vigorous past and sorrow for the separation and the waning present. It dances like a spiraling dragon, flows like an undulating melody, and surely is made a masterpiece.'[58] The diagram below represents the analysis of the structure of "Hidden Perfumes".

....

56 For example, Sung Xiangfeng, in his *Supplementary Essays on the Yueh Fu poems*(樂府餘論)(in *Complete Anthology of Ci Comments*, op.cit. in note 38 above, p.2503) argues, 'Historically, Jiang Kuei is to the *Ci* lyrists as Du Fu is to the regular poets: both carried on the past and opened a way for future.[...] *Dark Fumes* implied the poet's sorrow for the fall of the northern territories. As with the case of Chu Yuan (屈原) and Sung Yu (宋玉), the deeper a subject is implied, the circuitous its expression becomes.' Chen Tingzhao holds a similar view by saying, 'Witnessing the empire's declination since the government's moving to the south, Jiang Kuei resorted to lyrics to imply his sorrows. In poems like *Dark Fumes* and *Sparse Shades*, indignation at the two Emperors' mishap and worries about the poorly-run government are insinuated in such a hidden and traceless way that one could hardly detect it.' See his *Talks about Ci from Baiyu Study* (白雨齋詞話), vol 2, op. cit. in note 38, p.3797.

57 Chang Guowu maintains that the lyrics, while expressing the poet's changing mood as he waved goodbye to his joyful youth and thought of his old friends, has nothing to do with the indignation about the state's tragedy. See his *A New Selection of Three Hundred Sung Ci Poems* (新選宋詞三百首)(Beijing: The People's Literature Press, 2000), p.403.

58 See *Cilin Guanzhi*(詞 林 觀 止), vol.1(Shanghai: Shanghai Ancient Texts Publishing, 1994), p.590.

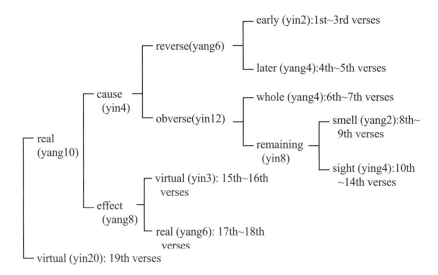

The compositional chart demonstrates the attribution of yin and yang across the poem.

Top Level   L2   L3   L4   Base Level

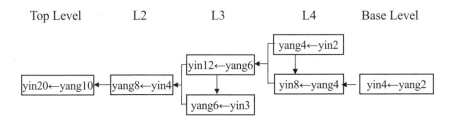

The first level of "Hidden Perfumes" represents its core structure of real/virtual (backward shifting), attributed to by the 'momentum' number of yin20 and yang10. On the second level is manifested a forward shifting structure of cause/effect, giving a number of yin4 and yang8. On the third level lie two shifting structures: reverse/obverse (backward) and virtual/real (forward), together giving a number of ying15 and yang12. Two more structures of shifting couples, early/later and whole/remaining, are seen at level 4, adding to the momentum of the poem by a number of yin10 and yang10. The shifting structure of smell/sight (backward) at the base level gives the last number of ying4 and yang2. All this adds up to a total of yin53 and yang40, or 57% of yin and 43 of yang. The number of momentum shows a style of softness containing hardness, as Chou describes:

> The yearning and affection is expressed through the extensive use of plum blossoms as a metaphor. The plum blossom is both everywhere and nowhere: it is there only in relation to the absentee lover. This shows a character of clearness. On top of it is added a touch of disturbing elegance, which comes from the poetic nature of the lyricist's strong affection.[59]

Here Chou borrows the ideas of clearness and disturbing elegance from Zhang Yen[60] and uses them to denote, respectively, the poem's style and its 'hidden message'. As Liu Yangzhong puts it,

> Jiang Kuei's works are distinct from the two trends of the historical development of the Ci poetry: he clears out the flamboyant expressionism and turns down heroic and robust behaviorism. Instead, he creates a style that transcends worldliness and outstands with calm and plain vigor, and that reveals how he thinks of his uniqueness and of his prospects for

....

[59] Zhou, *op. cit.* in note 40 above, p.76.

[60] Zhang Yen argues that the *Ci* poems would rather be transcendental than substantial. Transcendence leads to primitive simplicity and vigorousness, while substantiality leads to sophisticated rigidity and obscurity.[...] Jiang Kuei's Ci is not only transcendentally clear in its style but is elegant with a touch of unease, giving the reader an experience of intuitive transcendence. See his Origins of Ci (詞源), vol.2, in *Complete Anthology of Ci Comments, op. cit.* in note 38 above, p.259.

the nation.[61]

What Liu refers to as 'transcending worldliness with calm and plain vigor' can be seen as 'clearness', representing a prosodic style lying in between restrained graces and robust boldness. As shown in our analysis of Dark Fumes, it is better to see this as characteristic of soft and weak expressions with a hue of hardness and strength.

The poems illustrated above, as well as their stylistic performance, have been commented on by literary critics such as Chou and others from the perspective of authors' experience, content and significance, and expressional skills. Conventional criticism of this kind, however, might be caught into the dilemma of over or under-speculation. This is where the structural analysis of textual construction might be of help: it could contribute to a more objective, elaborate judgment of the stylization of literary works.

Structural analysis has its own blind spots, though. It very much depends on the perspective one chooses to cut across the text, which will certainly influence its result. This happens especially when we try to infer from structural analysis understanding of its stylistic tendencies. It is to undo this influence that we introduce the calculation of the 'momentum' of feminine softness and masculine hardness, in order to comprehend fairly fixed patterns for stylization among literary texts.

Although at a preliminary stage of its development, the calculation, as well as its theoretical basis, has proven to be a breakthrough in the study of textual construction. It is strongly suggested that, through our experimental attempts, Chinese textual analysis, including studies of textual styles, move toward a certain level of scientific systemization, making room for objective

....
61 See *Developments of Schools of Tang and Sung Ci Poems* (唐宋詞流派史) (Fuzhou: Fujiang People's Publishing, 1999), p.489.

reasoning in addition to the traditional intuitive sensibility.

III. The aesthetic effects of the structure of "many, two, one/zero"

In this section, we begin with the hypothesis that, as with the case of its philosophical origins, the logic of 'M/D/S(N)' should belong in the aesthetic due to the binary operation upon which it is based.

For a thorough investigation into the phenomenon of textual construction, it is necessary to go further from the discussion of philosophical origins to examine its aesthetic effects on the reader's psychology. The power of a text's logical structure to touch the heartstrings of its readers lies in the tempo (local) and the rhythm (global) that are produced by the structure itself. Zong, in his *Studies of Art*, explains,

> Rhythm is fundamental to both physical and mental sensibilities. Humans are susceptible to its symmetric formation as it accords with the dual nature of human parts.[62]

Li Zehou addresses this issue in his *Four Lectures on Aesthetics* by saying

> Appreciative attention first is attracted by the formal structure of the object before it is developed into psychological activities such as the permeation of emotions and imaginations. Psychological elements at this stage are infused into the formal object, perceiving its shape and pattern to the full. Attentivness is thus given to formal and structural aspects such as lines, shapes, colors,

....

62   *Collected Works of Zong Baihwa*(宗白華全集), vol. 1, op. cit. in note 10 above, p.506.

voices, time and space, tempo and rhythm, change and balance, union and harmony, etc. At the same time, those psychological factors that belong to the subject, such as feelings, imagination, ideology, wishes and expectations, are invested consciously or unconsciously into this process.[63]

Arguably, Li's remarks on formative arts apply onto our discussion of textual structure and its regularity. What he refers to as 'time and space, tempo and rhythm' involve the local shifting and twisting of textual structures, consonance and contrast, as well as the overall 'M/D/S(N)' structure; 'changes and balance, union and harmony' involve, on the other hand, the four laws of textual construction, namely, order, change, coherence and union.

Given its tendency to induce aesthetic appreciation, the structure and regularity of textual construction should also lead to some kind of aesthetic effects. As Chiu Zhengming points out in his *Psychology of Aesthetic Appreciation*,

> In the process of aesthetic appreciation, the subject either explores the aesthetic qualities of an object and levels the gap between him and the object with an aim to procure the sense of beauty, or creates his own autonomy and uniqueness of aesthetic senses through maintaining, and even strengthening, this gap. In either way, the subject undertakes a psychological process that features rhythm and regularity.[64]

The following analysis is focused on how the subject-reader can

....

[63] *Four Lectures on Aesthetics* (美學四講) (Tianjin: Tainjin Social Sciences Publishing, 2001), pp.158~59.

[64] *Psychology of Aesthetic Appreciation* (審美心理學) Shanghai: Fudan University Press, 1993), p.92.

acquire aesthetic experiences through a rhythmic and structured movement of reading led by the 'M/D/S(N)' logic.

1. The aesthetic effect of many

Multeity means variety. Ouyang Zhou *et. al.*, explains:

> 'Variety' refers to the distinction of each part that contributes to a whole. The laws illustrated in the previous passages, such as order, symmetry and balance, ratio and measure, tempo and rhythm, are included into a covering law of formal beauty, contributing its unity or appearing as its dimensions.[65]

As regards textual construction, everything outside the core structure belongs to this variety. Within it, every single structural unit, be it forward or backward, consonant or contrastive, realizes an instance of change through the shifting or twisting of its elements (e.g., obverse/reverse and obverse/reverse /obverse), and hence contributes to the tempo and order at a global level. From the perspective of the four laws of textual construction, the aesthetic effects that results from the structure of Multeity can be called 'beauty of change' and 'beauty of order'.

Generally speaking, 'order' is reflected by the uniformity or repetition of forms. As Chen Xiuefan puts it:

> The simplest of formation appears in repetition. As it is realized by repeating the same matter, it can be viewed as uniformity. Hence the law of repetition and the law of uniformity are the same. A very simple form indeed, it might be employed whenever

....
[65] Ouyang Zhou, Gu Jianhua, and Song Fansheng, *A New Compilation for Aesthetics* (美學新編) (Hangzhou: Zhejiang University Press, 2001), p.80.

a naïve pleasure is being aimed at.[66]

Ouyang Zhou *et. al.*, furthers the understanding of the law of repetition or uniformity by combining it with 'tempo and order', and argues that

agreement, unanimity, uniformity---all refer to the most commonly seen and simplest beauty of form. Its identical, unitary, and repetitive nature allows of nothing different or opposite, and hence gives an impression of order. From it is developed the beauty of uniformity, which can be perceived when colors, shapes, or sounds repeat in identical forms. Rows of rice seedlings on the farmlands, fashionable terraced houses on the street, phalanxes of soldiers treading in the same pace, and lacework that shows identical patterns in repetition—all these produce a tempo and take on the beauty of uniformity. This kind of aesthetic form induces a feeling of naivety, pureness and freshness.[67]

It clearly points out that the multiple structures can produce the sense of order due to the uniform and repetitive form of its units.

Change, on the other hand, results from the functioning of power and is the cause of the multiple structures. The *Treatise of Appended Words* of *Zhouyi* states that 'the hardness and the softness interact to generate change,[…] which is emblematic of advance and retreat' and that 'ends beget changes, changes beget openings, openings beget permanency'. Therefore, 'ending' is a condition of 'changing' and 'changing' is inseparable from symbolism. As Chen interprets,

....

66 Chen Xiuefan, *An Introduction to Aesthetics* (美學概論) (Taipei: Wenjin, 1984), pp.61~62.

67 See Ouyang Zhou, et. al, op. cit. in note 65, p.76.

the concept of change in Zhouyi has a profound influence upon Chinese aesthetics and Chinese culture as well. [...] The symbolic notions of the 64 hexagrams function to represent the changeable.[...] Change is both spatial, as of the relocation of physical objects, and temporal, as of the linear procession of time. As the Appended Words indicates, 'The greatest emblem is (that of) Heaven and Earth, and the most changeable emblem is (that of) the Four Seasons.'[68]

Given that change, as indicated in the quote, is across time and space, and that, as we have seen, textual laws are based on the time-space interface, we can interpret, through the perspective of the changeable, how the shifting and twisting structures across time and space can bear upon the reader's mentality. Chen explains this by saying

humans by nature are inclined to changing and the excitement it brings. The reason might be that changing is necessary for activities of raising and awakening one's consciousness. A stimulus lasting long enough to be stiff and dull will cause stagnation at the conscious level. Over-repetition leads to under-reaction of the brain and pushes the subject to attend to what is changing and rising instead of repeating in the surroundings.[69]

Not only rhythm of repetition may end up with new changes, but changing as such forms complicated types of rhythm. As Ouyang Zhou et. al., explains,

Rhythm takes the form of recurring changes in successive and

....

68 See *History of Classical Chinese Aesthetics, op.cit.* in note 45, p.188.
69 Chen, *op. cit.* in note 66, pp.63~64.

regular cycles.[...] Nothing in the world is rhythm-free: there is sunset and sunrise, full moon and crescent, and seasonal alternation; along with the tempo of Nature we work and rest, go out and come home, and harvest and feast; and along with the rhythm of everyday life there is the tempo of biological process found in life-surviving activities such as breath, pulse, sleeping and awakening, diets and excretion, and even emotions. Physical comfort and mental joy may arise once the rhythm prevailing in the social and natural environment somehow harmonizes with the pace and tempo of the human organism.[70]

'Mental joy' that arises from change and rhythm is exactly what we call aesthetic effects.

In order to illustrate this point, we shall now turn to the first example: 'He Man Zi' by Su Dongpo.

見說岷峨悽愴，We are talking about the wretched mountains of Min and Emei, 旋聞江漢澄清。When someone told us the pacification of Jiang and Han. 但覺秋來歸夢好，Suddenly it seemed good to dream of going home in autumn, 西南自有長城。Thanks to the able governor in the Southwest. 東府三人最少，He is the youngest among the three general chiefs of the East Palace now, 西山八國初平。While General Wei pacified the eight tribes in the West Mountain before.　莫負花溪縱賞，May he not forget seeing around the flower stream; 何妨藥市微行。Why not treading down the drug market without robes? 試問當壚人在否，Is the gifted beauty still there tending on the oven? 空教是處聞名。Don't leave their place nothing but empty fame! 唱著子淵新曲，Singing the new song by Wang Bao, 應須分外含情。I'd like to deliver this extra feeling to him.

....

[70] See Ouyang Zhou, et. al, *op. cit.* in note 65, pp.78～79.

Subtitled 'For Yizhou Governor Feng from Huzhou'71, the lyric was written for congratulating on Feng's successfully pacifying the tribal unrest in Szechuan. The first two verses point out this subject by virtually depicting the misery of the remote mountain area before its pacification like the Jianghan Plain in the ancient time. It is followed by a time dimension as of autumn in verse 3 and then a space dimension as of the Southwest in verse 4. The time and space substantiates the poet's reference to the governor Feng and, through a causal relation ('Thanks to') added on to it, brings forward his great admiration for him. After that the poem reassumes the virtual writing to describe Feng's military achievements (verse 5 & 6) and his civil administration (verse 7 to 10). The military achievements, which led him to the highest post as general chief72, are again put side by side with a past general's victory some hundred years ago; the virtual link between them requires interpretative imagination on the part of the reader. Likewise, the description of Feng's civil office invites the reader into a virtual time-space interface, to imagine the then Governor's close communication with the street people, while making out the poet's encouragement to the now General Chief of the emperor. Though communicating vividly the subject of congratulation and admiration, the verses to this point constitute only the guest part of the lyric. The host, representing the hidden

....

71 It has been noted that the subhead contradicts with the time of space of the lyric's writing: to be short, Su was in Mizhou instead of Huzhou when he composed it. See Shi Shenhuai and Tang Lingling, *Chronicle Commentaries on Dong Po's Yueh Fu Poems* (東坡樂府編年箋注) (Taipei: Huazheng Bookstore, 1993), pp.91~92.

72 The East Palace mentioned in the poem is equal to today's National Security Council of the state. During the Song Dynasty, it is of the same paramount power as the Central Secretary Department, or 中書省 *zhongshu sheng*. There were three ministers holding office at these two imperial apparatuses. Feng, the head to the East Palace, should arguably be the youngest among them. See *ibid.*, pp.93~94.

message, lies in the ending couplet. It first echoes the virtual pity in verse 9 and 10 that the gifted mistress (and her husband) had long left the now famous tavern, and moves to another classical story in verse 11 about a Han dynasty Governor Wang Bao presenting to the emperor a song for admiring one of his ministers who had recommended him. At last, in the final verse, the poet could hardly stop short of speaking away his wish for gaining Feng's same attention and recommendation. The following diagram represents the structural development of He Man Zi.

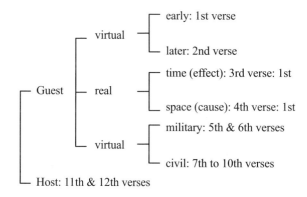

The core structure (forward shifting) consists of the guest and the host part, of which the former covers at the second level a twisting structure of virtual/real/virtual. Following it, and on the base level are realized three shifting structures of, respectively, early/later, time/space (effect/cause), and military/civil. On the local plane of the text the reader senses a returning pattern of three 'beats', each of which contains a distinct unit of two 'beats', hence the feel of change embedded in the rhythm of order. Before the beats drag to a point of falling out of the tempo, however, the poem suddenly changes it and leads the reader to a new musical 'measure' toward its very end. This time, through the coupling of guest/host is realized a tempo that not only continues the musical flow locally but reverses it globally as the lyric as a whole concludes in its paramount yet hidden motif in the final verse.

The analysis demonstrates that it is possible, and productive, to uncover the musical quality—the rhythm and tempo—of a poem through structural analysis. A poetic text can be seen as a rhythmic melody, of which changing and orderly repeating cross to motivate its content materials in different paces of tempo. In this way, it may cause resonance in the reader's mind and lead to a certain aesthetic happiness.

It is not only prosodic writing that 'plays' structurally to a tempo, though. Rhythmic analysis, so to speak, also can apply to narrative and expositional essays. Take, as an example, Ouyang Xiou's 'Preface to the Biography of Eunuchs'.

Since the ancient time, eunuchs have had endangered the state more seriously than women. Women are nothing but sexual lures; eunuchs, by contrast, pose as a more severe curse to the emperor. They do their work habitually and close by, while using their head with great attention and patience. They can please their master with trivial good, and ease his mind with petty honesty— all these make the emperor have trust in and depend on them. Once they won his trust, they control the emperor with what he likes and fears; even though loyal and able officials line up in the court, the emperor regards them as aloof and estranged, much less intimate and reliable than the servants beside him. The more intimate the servants become, the more alienated those loyal and able ministers are, and the more isolated the emperor is. As isolation worsens, the emperor's fear grows, and their control firms. Thus, the emperor's safety hinges upon the eunuchs' likes and dislikes, mishaps lurk behind the screen, and those who he used to think of as reliable are now the real phantoms. When the emperor realizes the seriousness and resorts to the alienated ministers against his intimate servants, it is already too late as a slow plan for that might continue to grow the lurking threat and a rush could goad the castrated servants into holding the emperor as hostage. At that time he can hardly consult any one even if the emperor is willing to, nor can he do anything if he plans it, neither would he succeed if he does something. Over-straining at it could only bring destruction on both sides. The gravest consequence of it is the fall of his state; a lesser one can lead to his own death. Either would give ambitious strongmen the opportunity to control the imperial house and end up with arresting and slaughtering the eunuchs' gang in order to pacify the plebs. This kind of eunuch-related disaster is recorded in the history of not one but many dynasties. It is not that emperors wished to grow their own curses from within and keep their loyal ministers away; it is the gradual worsening of the situation that caused their mishaps.

The curse of feminine lures, even if the emperor plunges into it, is limited to a point of indulgence. Once realizing its existence, pull it up and simply throw it away. The curse of eunuchs, by contrast, may grow deep to an extent that even with heartfelt regretting one couldn't undo what has been done. Emperor Zhao of Tang is a good example. This is why it is more severe than the women as sexual lures, and also why the emperor can never be too much warned.

自古宦者，亂人之國，其源深於女禍。女，色而已；宦者之害，非一端也。蓋其用事也近而習，其為心專而忍。能以小善中人之意，小信固人之心，使人主必信而親之。待其已信，然後懼以禍福把持之，雖有忠臣碩士，列於朝廷，而人主以為去己疎遠，不若起居飲食前後左右之親為可恃也。故前後左右者日益親，則忠臣碩士日益疎，而人主之勢日益孤。勢孤則懼禍之心日益

切，而把持者日益牢，安危出其喜怒，禍福伏於帷闥，
則嚮之所謂可恃者，乃所以為患也。患已深而覺之，欲
與疏遠之臣，圖左右之親近，緩之則養禍而益深，急之
則挾人主以為質，雖有聖智，不能與謀，謀之而不可
為，為之而不可成，至其甚則俱傷而兩敗。故其大者亡
國，其次亡身，而使姦豪得借以為資而起，至抉其種
類，盡殺以快天下之心而後已。此前史所載宦官之禍，
常如此者，非一世也。夫為人主者，非欲養禍於內，而
疏忠臣碩士於外，蓋其漸積而勢使之然也。
夫女色之禍，不幸而不悟，則禍斯及矣。使其一悟，捽
而去之可也。宦者之為禍，雖欲悟悔，而勢有不得而去
也，唐昭宗之事是已。故曰深於女禍者，謂此也，可不
戒哉。

The overall structure of the essay shows a flow of
leveling/siding/leveling: first lifting eunuchs and concubines to the
same level, followed by an extensive emphasis on the side of the
eunuchs, and returning back to the lifting of the two. By juxtaposing
eunuchs and concubines the author tries to make the point of the
former as graver threats to the imperial house.[73] The main part that
lays sided emphasis on the eunuchs further employs the structure of
cause/effect and of pointing/spreading in order to explore the
emperor's falling victim to the castrated servants. In the end the
curse of concubines is brought up again to not only echo with the
beginning structure but, more importantly, reemphasize the eunuchs'
menace to the emperor and the importance of being alert against it.
The leveling of eunuchs with concubines is a rhetoric technique of
contrasting that smoothly opens up the reader's horizons as the two,

....

[73] Guo Shangho mentions that the technique is 'to make the sin of eunuchs look
graver by the side of the concubines'. See his *Criticism and Comments on Ancient
Writings* (古文評注)(Taipei: Zonghe Publishing, 1969), p.6.

both historically rooted within the imperial house, are alike in their appearance. The return of the contrast toward the end also functions to conclude the discussion at a broader angle. The structuralization featuring movements of opening and converging is represented in the diagram on the next page.

'Preface' demonstrates an intensive sense of rhythm through its complex structuralization of multeity. As with the 'leveling/siding/leveling' structure on the global plane, the local textual construction is also dominated by the pattern of three 'beats' in a 'measure' (or a ply of structural unit), such as 'early/later/last' (shifting) and 'pointing/spreading/pointing' (twist-ing). Of special importance is the structure of 'early/later/last' at the base level which repeats itself in a continual session (interfered only by one sentence functioning as generalization of information) and which henceforth speeds up the pace of the reading, making the reader keen to read, or listen, through to the finale on a higher level. In addition to the intensive tempo of repetition, the twisting structure of pointing/spreading/pointing consisting almost of the main body

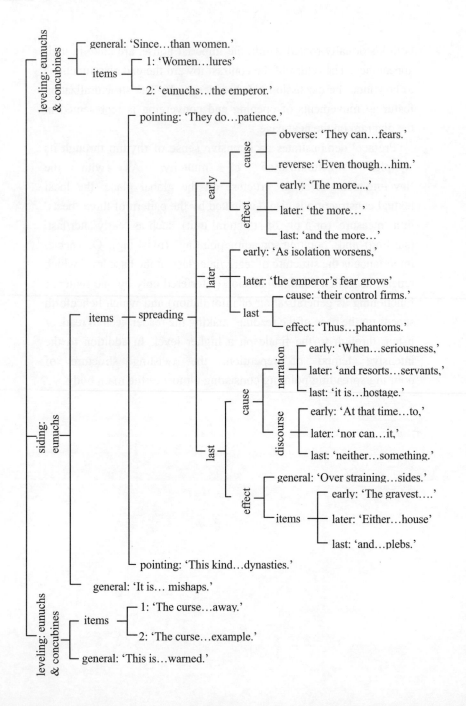

contributes to a rather moderate feel of changing as it offers in the beginning a short stop before, say, entering an allegro and finally another one for resettling down after reaching a climax. The interplay of repetition and changing is eventually contained in and transformed to the beauty of symmetry characteristic of the repeating (yet in different directions) structure of general/items before the text folds itself globally. In sum, although the structural arrangement of this essay is complex (7 layers), its tempo and rhythm is clear and forthright enough to induce joys of reading through the reader's psychological reaction.

2. The aesthetic effect of two

Duality refers to the distinction of ying and yang, which, in Chinese philosophy, pertains to everything in the world through 'binary operation'. Thus yin and yang exists in layers of operation and in nonstop interaction and circulation. In textual construction, not only each structural unit, to the extent that it abides by a certain textual law, is characterized by the yin/yang distinction; it also pairs with another unit to form a more abstract layer of the binary operation of yin/yang. This binary operation works to characterize the structure of duality either as consonant, if it belongs to the category of yin, or as contrasting, if it belongs to that of yang. From the aesthetical point of view, the consonant structure leads to the beauty of feminine softness, while the contrasting structure to that of masculine hardness. As Chen Xueifan explains,

two things of remarkable similarity coexist to form harmony, while two things of major difference standing side by side create contrast. Harmony arises when one, for example, takes pure black and black of a lesser chromatic grading and juxtaposes them. Contrast takes shape when one puts side by side the pure black and the pure white on the other end of the spectrum. [...] Those pertaining to harmony hardly entertain any visible changes, hence delivering feels and interests of consonance, elegance, calm and cool-heartedness. [...] The form of contrast, on the other hand and due to its obvious change, usually occurs with feels and interests of vividness, vigor and a leaping and open mind.[74]

The analogy of colors used here vividly illustrates the difference between consonancc and contrast, and between the 'feels and interests' respectively arising. The following remarks from Ouyang, et. al., moves on to link it up with the beauty of femininity and masculinity.

Contrast results from the process of synthesizing two confronting formal elements with remarkable differences. Heavy vs. light hues, cold vs. warm, dark vs. bright, straight vs. curvy, loud vs. silent—all these form contrasting and comparison, while at the same time making one element stand out against the other. The synthesis therefore works to bring out the best in each other. The complementary colors of red and green, for example, are commonly used to picture things of vividness, visibility, and thrust as in expressions like taohong liulu, or 'red peaches and green willows', honghua luyeh, or 'red flowers and green leaves', and 'a single red in the midst of a thousand greens'. Given its bold and inclusive handling of confronting elements, the formal beauty of contrast belongs with the masculine strength. Consonance, on the other hand, results from the process of synthesizing two confronting formal elements with no remarkable differences. At its core lies gradual blending instead of sudden opposition, and the convergence on unison among differences instead of on individualities. Rainbow gives an excellent example

....

[74] Chen, *op. cit.*, in note 66 above, pp.70~72.

of consonance as every two neighboring colors represent two adjacent quantities along the same grading system. They coordinate to create a certain degree of agreement, delivering the senses of blending and tranquility. In this light, the formal beauty of consonance belongs with feminine weakness.[75]

The explanation of the difference between consonance and contrast as two forms of beauty is helpful for understanding how the beauty of femininity and masculinity comes into existence.[76]

Dong Xiaoyu explains the beauty of the two forms of consonance and contrast from the point of view of 'foil'.

Foil, originally a skill used in Chinese brush painting to set an object off from its surroundings, can be appropriated in literary creation and refer to one thing that by contrast underscores or enhances the distinctive characteristics of another, making the appearance of the latter outstanding and eye-catching. Using foils is an important technique of literary expression borrowed from everyday life wherein things tend to set off one another in their coexistence.[77]

In our view, the binary operation of yin and yang is a form of what Chou calls 'setting off one another in everyday life'. Furthermore, we can distinguish between consonance and contrast as two abstract forms of binary operation along with different uses of foil:

....

[75] Ouyang, *et. al., op. cit.*, in note 65 above, p.81.
[76] Chou Xiaoping, *Aesthetics of the Design of Time and Space in Ancient Poems* (古典詩詞時空設計美學)(Taipei: Wenjin Publishing, 2002), pp.278~335.
[77] See Dong, *Literary Creation and Aesthetic Psychology* (文學創作與審美心理)(Chengdu: Szechuan Education Publishing House, 1992), p.338.

The use of foils to set off subjects varies with the pairings: to pair things of like quality as foils to one another, or positive foil using, so to speak, can make the description more vivid and catching, whereas negative foil using pairs the subject with those of opposite quality with an aim to service the subject only. For example, beautiful scenery can be used either to underscore and foreground the happy mood of the protagonist positively or to set off his sadness negatively. Other than these two, a third way of using foil is added a developmental dimension, with a focus on the mail plot or the climax to come and therefore a function that is always 'delayed'.[78]

The positive and 'delayed' use of foils belongs with what we call consonance, while the negative use belongs with the structure of contrast. Either side of the dichotomy, however, is conducive to the aesthetic value of beauty. Moreover, since it consists in the structure of duality, the binary operation of yin and yang at this level plays the role of bridge for the beauty of multeity, on the one hand, and the beauty of singularity (naught), on the other. Whether it is contrast or consonance, as Ouyang, et. al., points out, what is aimed at is always the synthesis of unison and change, and the beauty of both diversity and uniformity it shows.[79]

To illustrate the theory developed here, let us take a look at Xin Qiji's 'Spring in the Garden Qin'.

三徑初成，The paths in the garden have been paved, 鶴怨猿驚，Yet the crane and the monkey are complaining 稼軒未來。Because of my absence. 甚雲山自許，I have expected to live a hermit's life, 平生意氣；Daring to follow my own instincts. 衣

....

78 Ibid., pp.339~341.
79 Ouyang, *et. al., op. cit.*, in note 65 above, p.81.

冠人笑，My robes have been next to nothing but a laugh to those high rankers, 抵死塵埃。And my career hardly has achieved anything but drifted along like dirt. 意倦須還，My weary heart speaks of going home, 身閒貴早，To plan for retirement as soon as possible. 豈為蓴羹鱸膾哉。But do I quit for the thick soup and fish fillets back home? 秋江上，In the river of autumn time, 看驚弦雁避，Look at the startled geese dashing away from the bows, 駭浪船回。And the boat returning back from the rollers!　東岡更葺茅齋。On the eastern hill is built my hut. 好都把、軒窗臨水開。It's better to have windows facing the lake. 要小舟行釣，Want to row and fish? 先應種柳；Need to grow some willows by the shore. 疏籬護竹，Also needed are fences to protect the bamboo shrubs, 莫礙觀梅。But remember not to block the view of the plum blossoms. 秋菊堪餐，To cook chrysanthemums in autumn 春蘭可佩，And wear orchids in spring, 留待先生手自栽。These still await planting with my own hands. 沉吟久，Thinking again and again, 怕君恩未許，And being afraid of detainment by the Emperor, 此意徘徊。I hover.

This lyric poem is subtitled 'Finishing new cottage home by Lake Dai' and was written during Xin's second office of the Governor of Jiangxi[80]. Since the cottage home is not located where he runs his office (hence 'my absence' in line 3), the poem clearly begins with a virtual writing about his ideal space which continues to cut across almost the whole body. The subject is indicated in the first three verses, with the third one 'because of my absence' opening up the room for self-reflection in the next two couplets. The latter also

....

80 HongMai of the Song Dynasty recorded this occasion in his *A Bibliography of Jiaxuan* (稼軒記). See Deng Kuangming, *Chronicles of Xin Qiji* (Heluo Publishing, 1979), pp.82~83.

represents the poet's apology for not being able to be where he should be (the hermitage). Following it is a passage of six verses pointing out the reason, both subjective and objective, why he should and want to go. From 'the crane and the monkey' till now extends a larger part of which the poet deals with the background of the cottage home (as a hermitage). It is then paired with the cottage's prospect (even more counterfactual!) as represented in lines 14 to 22. In the ending lines the narrator suddenly jumps out of the virtual writing to express his present hesitation between career and retirement.[81] The diagram on the next page represents the structural analysis of Spring.

The core structure of virtual/real is a form of contrastive synthesis as it semantically extends an obverse/reverse coupling at a lower level where the author's yearning for a hermit's life runs counter to his real official career. This does not mechanically determine the aesthetic value of the poem, though. The virtual/real coupling is unsymmetrical in so far as the poet, after extensively describing his wishes for leaving in general and his prospect of the cottage life in particular, suddenly stops and changes to a tone of hesitation. In doing so, he sets off his dilemma by using his own imagination as a reverse foil, making a strong and vivid case of the subject of contraction[82]. However, that the hearty expectation of the life after

---

81 See Chang Kuowu, *Introduction to the Works of Xin Qiji*(辛稼軒詞集導讀)(Chengdu: Bashu Bookstore, 1989), pp.159~160.

82 Yu Chaogang maintains that the poem is concerned with the poet's contradiction between a worldly career and retirement from the world. See his *Xin Qiji and His Works* (辛棄疾及其作品)(Changchun: Shidai Literature Publishing, 1989), p.156.

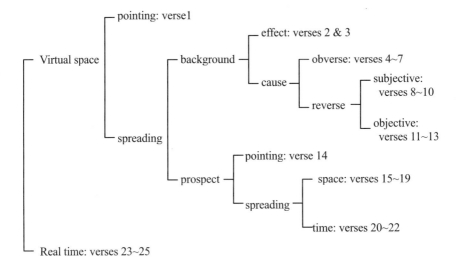

retirement ends up abruptly with an indecisive mind makes one feel pity for the poet, a feeling which certainly belongs with the feminine rather than masculine qualities. To explain this away, we need to turn to a detail in lines 11~13 about the poet's answer to why he wants to retire. Appearing, somewhat awkwardly, to express his favor to the scenery rather than cuisines mentioned in line 10, the poet actually uses geese, bows, rollers and the returning boat from the verses as metaphors for his situation in the empire's officialdom. Interpreted this way, the answer can be seen, from a global point of view, as a supportive foil through the delayed use of which the otherwise hidden message is set off in relief: it is the Emperor's favor, the only thing that could keep him in the 'river' of bureaucracy, rather than the hermit's life that the poet is longing, and sighing, for. To conclude our discussion, the lyric poem involves a twofold process of the creation of aesthetic values. First, its abrupt ending realizes a contrastive, or negative, way of using foils, producing in its appearance a surprise to the reader. This goes with the masculine form of beauty created by the structure of virtual/real.

Secondly, the delayed use of the metaphors of geese, etc., as a positive foil to the indecisiveness at the end gives a lingering sound that echoes the poet's sighing to like-hearted readers after their reading. This reminds one of the feminine form of beauty hidden in learned, yet cold-shouldered, officials'—such as Qu Yuan and Sung Yu—persistent pursuit of, or metaphorically, 'courting for', wise lords and princes.

Such an interpretation may induce aesthetic senses of both masculine and feminine beauty in the reader's mind, thanks to the sophisticated arrangement of the structural units as well as its accompanying form of rhythm. It is not exclusively realized on the level of the core structure of the poem, though. As argued in the beginning of this section, yin and yang as two forms of aesthetic beauty exist in and across layers of binary operation. The analysis of Xin Qiji's Spring shows that what is embedded among lower layers can link up with the core structure that governs the global construction of a text, forming consonance within contrast, and vice versa, with an aim at producing pleasures of reading.

Let us turn to the genre of historical writing and look at Kuei Youguang's 'Remembrance about the Map of Mount Wu'.

The two counties of Wu and Changzhou belong to the municipal government of Suzhou and are divided as two regions of administration. Mountains to the west of Suzhou sit in the Wu County. Among them the higher ones are the Vault Mountain, Mount Yang, Mount Dengwei, the West Ridge, and Mount Copper Well. The palace of the ancient state of Wu was seated in the Spiritual Rock, where one can still find traces of the beauty Xishi. Places like Tiger Hill, Sword Lake, and mountains of Tianpin, Shangfang, Zhixing—all these are famous tourist sites. Lake Tai covers an ocean-like water of 36,000 hectares, with 72 peaks sinking in it. What a spectacle within the Four Seas! My friend Wei Yonghuei was magistrate of Wu for three years, before he was promoted to the office of Jishizhong in the imperial government for his distinguished performance. Because Mr. Wei bestowed grace on the people of Wu, they tried to detain him, yet in vain. Mr. Wei could hardly let go of his people, either. Therefore, someone with an enthusiastic heart sent him a map of Mount Wu for a remembrance.

Important is a magistrate to the people! If the magistrate is able and virtuous, even the mountains and the trees under his jurisdiction are bestowed with grace and feel proud; if the magistrate is not able and virtuous, even the mountains and the trees under his jurisdiction undergo miseries and feel ashamed. Mr. Wu indeed adds gilding to the mountains of Wu. Someday our people will find a beautiful place in the mountains and enshrine him in a Buddhist or Taoist temple. This is of certainty. However, why would Mr. Wei keep thinking of the mountains after leaving Wu?

In the past Han Chi of the Sung Dynasty remembered the lands of Huangzhou forty years after he left. Su Dongpo admired his sensibilities and thus wrote a poem named Missing Huangzhou. He even carved it on a stone stela for the people of Huangzhou. From this we know that, wherever he goes, the able and virtuous man would not only make the people there remember him but also keep them in his own mind. Mr. Wei has left Wu for three years. One day in the yard, he showed this map to me, admiring it while sighing for the old days. He then asked me to write down this story. Sigh! How would the people forget him given his true thoughts for them!

> 吳、長洲二縣，在郡治所分境而治，而郡西諸山，皆在
> 吳縣。其最高者，穹窿陽山、鄧尉西脊銅井，而靈巖吳
> 之故宮在焉。尚有西子之遺跡，若虎丘劍池，及天平尚

方支硎，皆勝地也。而太湖汪洋三萬六千頃，七十二峰，沈浸其間，則海內之奇觀矣！余同年友魏君用晦為吳縣，未及三年，以高第召入，為給事中。君之為縣，有惠愛，百姓扳留之不能得，而君亦不忍於其民，由是好事者繪〈吳山圖〉以為贈。

夫令之於民誠重矣。令誠賢也，其地之山川草木，亦被其澤而有榮也；令誠不賢也，其地之山川草木，亦被其殃而有辱也。君於吳之山川，蓋增重矣。異時吾民將擇勝於巖巒之間，尸祝於浮屠老子之宮也，固宜。而君則亦既去矣，何復惓惓於此山哉？昔蘇子瞻稱韓魏公去黃州四十餘年，而思之不忘，至以為〈思黃州〉詩，子瞻為黃人刻之於石。然後知賢者於其所至，不獨使其人之不忍忘而已，亦不能自忘於其人也。

君今去縣已三年矣，一日與余同在內庭，出示此圖，展玩太息，因命余記之。噫！君之於吾吳有情如此，如之何而使吾民能忘之也。

The essay adopts the structure of flowing/addition for its global arrangement. It flows in the order of time from the history and land of Wu, through Wei's office of magistrate and the map as a remembrance, to the memory of Wei about his people.[83] In the end, it flashbacks to the very recent to add the cause for writing the narration. The flow of the narration, realized in the structure of siding/leveling/siding, begins with the lateral description of 'wise and able' used to tell the story about the map[84]; then it moves on to juxtapose officials that are wise and able and those that are not wise and able, to 'explore on two levels with one in upmost opposition to another'.[85] After that the emphasis is placed again on the side of

83　Wu Chuchai & Wang Wenru, *op. cit.*, in note 29 above, pp.34~35.
84　Wu & Wang, ibid., p.35.
85　See Li, op. cit., in note 30, p.20.

Magistrate Wei, with different material and from a different angle for another profile. The two cases of 'siding' employ different material and adopt different perspectives to bring Wei's wisdom and ability into full play.[86] The part of leveling carries out a broader horizon and makes possible the contrast between the virtuous and the not virtuous, in order to set off the importance of the former. It also works to carry on the preceding sided emphasis and make room for the one that follows. Together, the skills of siding and leveling can be interlocked in a way that brings diversity to the structural development of a text, creating in it 'ingenuity of writing that outmatches other skills for carrying on lines of argument'.[87] The structural analysis of Remembrance is offered as follows.

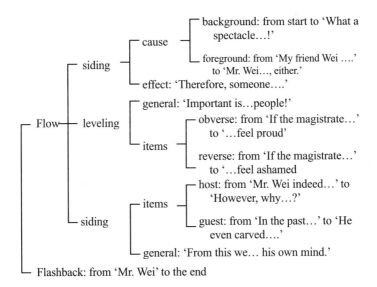

86   See Chou Xiaoping, *On the Types of Textual Structure* (篇章結構類型論)(Taipei: Wanjuanlou, 2000), p.254.

87   Li Fujiou, *op. cit.*, in note 30 above.

On the local plane of textual construction are deployed consonantly shifting structures of back/foreground, host/guest, general/items and its reverse, and cause/effect; contrastively shifting structure of obverse/reverse; and consonantly twisting structure of siding/leveling/siding. On the global plane are deployed the core structure of flow/flashback, which contributes to the consonant form of aesthetic value in the essay. Thus, there is contrast within consonance and consonance within contrast. The interlocking of the two activates the semantic content and carries with them a certain sense of beauty, in order to produce pleasures on the part of the reader.

3. The aesthetic effect of one/zero

'Singularity(Naught)', generally speaking, refers to 'unison', or the atmosphere of 'harmony' and results from the synthetic inclusion of 'multeity' and 'duality'. Applying to the aesthetics of textual construction, it arises from the process of which formal textual laws connect the tempo of repetition and/or changing within the multiple structure and the contrast and/or the consonance between hardness and softness within the dual structure, so as to string up a rhythm of reading, set off the subject, and reach a unified realm of graceful harmony. Chen discusses the formal principles of this unison or harmony by speaking of 'unity in variety'. To quote,

The form of beauty must not be in a condition of disintegration and disunity, or it will lose the aesthetic frame of mind. Therefore applies the first rule: unity is a necessary quality of the aesthetic object. Within the unity must there be a diversity of elements lest the object gets monotonous easily. Thus follows the second rule: diversity in the sense of variety is a necessary quality of the aesthetic object. What counts as beautiful consists in, on the one hand, the distinct unity and, on the other, a significant variety of elements. This does not mean the coexistence of a unity and its varieties that negates it, or whatsoever. The unity exists within the diversity. Hence the idea of 'organic unity': unity unifies diversity, while diversity diversifies unity. Understood this way, the formal principle of beauty can get rid of both the monotone and dullness resulted sometimes from unity, and the impatience and mess usually brought by diversity.[88]

The statement that 'unity unifies diversity, while diversity diversifies unity' signifies the inseparable relationship between multeity and singularity, including the dual structure functioning as an in-between 'bridge', which is suggested here by the action of unifying and diversifying.

Ouyang, et. al., pursues this discussion in more details by saying

Unification involves the common features of the form of constituent parts and the various relations of them: collocation, echoing, foil, and coordination. That is to say, every single part has to be in the service of the unity, contributing to its harmony and uniformity. To contain these parts in a unity is to avoid the disintegration characteristic of mere diversity and the monotone characteristic of mere uniformity. In so doing, it allows a dynamic coexistence between differences and sameness; it implies 'the one' in 'the many', and sees 'the many' in 'the one'; and it combines two opposite phenomena into an integrated organism, creating uniformity out of non-uniformity, and order out of disorder, arriving finally at the highest of formal beauty. [89]

The passage indicates the binary operation of singularity(naught)

....

88 See Ouyang, et. al., op. cit., in note 66 above, pp.77~78.
89 See Ouyang et. al., op. cit., in note 65 above, pp.80-81.

and multeity in a dynamic synthesis. It follows that the beauty of singularity(naught) is based upon multeity, while the beauty of multeity relies for its integrity on singularity(naught). After pointing this out, Ouyang et. al, moves on to argue that diversity and unity are usually manifested in two basic patterns of contrast and consonance, either of which requires and presupposes their dynamic combination.[90] As we have discussed above, the choice of consonance and contrast as two kinds of formal beauty is a function of duality in the form of the core structure. Again, this argument makes explicit that the structure of duality plays an important, if not fundamental, role in the creation of unity in variety.

The 'N' as included in 'S' stands for the abstract forces of the text such as style, aroma, atmosphere, realm, and the like. These forces, signified by 'naught' due to its being too abstract to be seen, is related closely to the qualities of hardness and softness. As discussed in section 5.2.1 above, Yao Nai of the Qing Dynasty 'generalizes literary styles into two classes: one is feminine softness and the other masculine hardness.' [91] Not only are softness and hardness used to characterize ways of wording and phrasing among different texts; the two abstract forces, based on the even more abstract ideas of yin and yang, are, according to Yao, mother to literary styles. That is to say, different styles, or ways of stylizing written texts, are produce of yin and yang mixed up in different amounts and on different levels. The way that the two forces 'rise and fall or advance and recede' directly determine the stylistic characters of literary writings.

On examining the bearings of the category of yin/yang on the aesthetic of Chinese literature, Wu Gongzheng points out the fact that

....

[90] *Ibid.*, p.81.

[91] The discussion of Yao Nai's viewpoints here and below is borrowed from Zhou, *op. cit.* in note 40, p.13.

from a most simplified category of yin/yang are derived a number of aesthetic classifications, such as word/will, mood/scene, gloss/plain, heavy/light, heterodox/orthodox, virtual/real, genuine/fake, and skillful/clumsy. This shows a distinct feature of Chinese aesthetics, namely, the diffusion of aesthetic elements from a fixed center. An example of its application for theoretical framing is Liu Xie's Wenxin Diaolong. Regarding the relationship between the aesthetic subject and the object of beauty, Liu argues that the mind (of the subject) winds about the object, whereas the object lingers around the mind. As regards the relationship of sensibilities and objects, he says, 'Sensibilities are susceptible to the object, so the sense must be refined in order to check them; objects are admired with sensibilities, and therefore the word must be beautiful in order to picture them.' Other categorical forms such as gloss/plain, sensibilities/words, logical/non-logical, etc. are also dealt with in pairs, taking the basic form of the binary constitution of yin/yang.[92]

This passage raises two interesting points. First, all the important categories of aesthetic activities belong with the binary operation of yin/yang. Second, through the binary operation aesthetic activities can proliferate themselves in multiple forms ('M') and at the same time return to a single, unchanged origin ('S(N)'). Yet again, the structure of 'Duality' plays a key role in bridging the 'Singularity(Naught)' and the 'Multeity'. From the point of view of the 'Naught', this ensures the unity of the beauty inherent in the 'M/D/S(N)' structure, as 'N' represents 'the origin of the origin', of which all the diffused forms of aesthetical categories find their destination.

....

92 Wu Gongzheng, *The Aesthetics of Chinese Literature* (中 國 文 學 美 學), vol.2(Nanjing: Jiangsu Educational Publishing, 2001), pp.785 786.

Two examples are given below to demonstrate the theoretical views raised so far. First, Su Dongpo's 'Washing away River Sands':

軟草平莎過雨新，Nutgrass flourish on the ground after raining, 輕沙走馬路無塵。And the horse hardly raises dust striding down the sandy road. 何時收拾耦耕身？When will I pick up everything and retire to the farmland?　日暖桑麻光似潑，The sun warms crops with pouring beams, 風來蒿艾氣如薰。While the breeze brings with it the odor of mugwort. 使君元是此中人。All this reminds me that I belonged with them!

The lyric poem was written on the way back from a lake where the poet, as magistrate to the region, presided over worship for requiting gods' bestowing rain during a draught. It begins with a perspective into the real space, portraying, from aside (grass by the road) to beneath (sand on the road), a picture of delight and freshness. What follows is a switch to the virtual time of future, to express his wish for the country life after retirement. After that, the poet returns to the immediate reality and offers a different take on the fresh scene, this time resorting to the senses of sight ('sunbeams') and smell ('odor'). Then, the poem is concluded with a fact that the poet has long forgotten due to his busy official career, and is reminded of only now: that is, he was from the countryside. His wish for a retired life in the country therefore seems ever so logical now. The structural analysis of 'Washing' is represented in the diagram below.

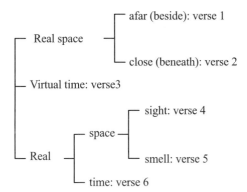

On the local plane the binary operations of far/close, sight/smell and space/time constitute the shifting structure that is of the character of consonance. On the global plane the coupling of 'virtual/real' extends itself to form a twisting structure of a consonant quality. Thus, a tiny work as it is, the lyric nevertheless organizes layers of semantic content in a way that contains change within order, and order within change, and unites them under the motif of 'retired life'. Carried along with the process of unity in variety, the reader becomes empathic with the poet and hence is bathed in a state, or aroma, of 'a rarely acquired idleness'. This, to the reader, can be a source of pleasure on reading this poem.

Let us now turn to a passage from King Hui of Liang of Mencius.

The people of Qi attacked Yen and conquered it. King Xuan asked, 'Some advise me not to occupy it, and some advise me to occupy it. For a state of ten thousand chariots to attack another of the same strength and to conquer it in fifty days, is a success beyond mere human strength. If I do not occupy it, calamities from Heaven will descend on me. What do you say to my occupying it?'

Mencius replied, 'If the people of Yen are pleased with your occupying their lands, then do so. Among the ancients there was

King Wu of Chou who acted so. If the people of Yen are
displeased with your occupying their lands, then don't do so.
Among the ancients there was King Wen of Chou who acted so.
When you attacked another state of ten thousand chariots with
yours of the same strength, and the people brought baskets of
food and pots of drink to meet Your Majesty's army, was there
any other reason for this but that they hoped to avoid the torment
of fire and water? If you make the water more deep and the fire
more fierce, they will just in like manner turn to another for help.'

> 齊人伐燕，勝之。宣王問曰：「或謂寡人勿取，或謂寡
> 人取之。以萬乘之國，伐萬乘之國，五旬而舉之，人力
> 不至於此。不取，必有天殃。取之何如？」
> 孟子對曰：「取之而燕民悅，則取之；古之人有行之
> 者，武王是也。取之而燕民不悅，則勿取；古之人有行
> 之者，文王是也。以萬乘之國，伐萬乘之國，簞食壺漿
> 以迎王師，豈有他哉？避水火也。如水益深，如火益
> 熱，亦運而已矣。」

The passage, focused on the ways of conquering, begins with
pointing to the Qi's defeat of Yen and then unfolds the argument
through a structure of question/answer. In the part of question, a
structure of leveling/siding is employed as the King first raises two
advices, namely, to occupy or not to occupy, and then put emphasis
on the side of the former, somehow revealing his priority. However,
Mencius does not follow his suggestion but uses the same skill of
leveling to take ancient kings as examples of whether to occupy a
rival state or not. In doing so, Mencius makes clear that the decision
lies not in the King's fathoming of the heavenly will but in the
support or opposition of the people. The passage then goes on to put
emphasis on occupying, claiming that the people would welcome
the army of an enemy state only if they wanted to escape from the

oppression of their own state. In other words, it is suggested that how to carry out a virtuous rule, rather than whether to occupy the state, be on the King's priority.

The parallel structure used in the King's question and Mencius's answer signals Mencius's purposeful mimicry of the King's thinking. The rhetoric strategy involved is obvious: by means of instantiating the two opposing decisions, the Confucian sage tries to add a deep value to the consideration and talk indirectly the King into the key role of the people's yearning for a virtuous and benevolent monarch. Tactical as it is, he by no means stops short of speaking out his stern admonishment. The diagram on the next page represents the structural analysis of the passage.

On the local plane the binary operations of host/guest, real/virtual, and leveling/siding, and pointing/spreading constitute the shifting structures that are of the character of consonance, while the coupling of obverse/reverse constitutes the contrastively shifting structure. On the global plane the coupling of 'question/answer' constitutes the shifting structures of a consonant quality. Thus, the essay organizes layers of semantic contents in a way that contain consonance within contrast, and contrast within consonance, and unites them under the motif of 'virtuous and benevolent ruling'. Carried along with the realization of unity in variety, the reader becomes empathic with the narrator and hence is immersed in a state of 'strong rigors and sternness'. [93] For the reader, this can be a source of pleasure of reading.

....

93 As Guo Yuheng points out, Mencius's words are filled with unstrained rigors as they are always expressive of his magnificent cause. See his *History of Chinese Essays*, vol.1 (中國散文史)(Shanghai: Shanghai Ancient Texts Publishing, 2000), p.138.

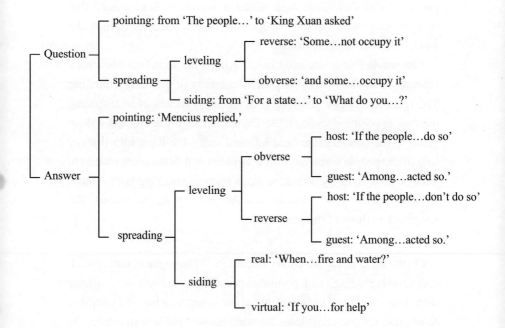

［ Appendix ］

Researches on Language Proficiency and Lexical Composition

-In Terms of the Spiral Structure of

"Many, Two, One/Zero"

Abstract

Language proficiency is natural (*a posteriori*), while the study of composition depends on human efforts.   The former refers to creative writing, presenting the logical structure of "one/zero, two, many," while the latter refers to critical reading, presenting the logical structure of "many, two, one/zero."   Generally speaking, language proficiency consists of "general capability," "special capability," and "complex ability."   In addition, the study of lexical composition is comprised by imagery, diction, rhetoric, grammar, compositional art, theme, and style.   And the former is applied to the sequential process of "from concept to likeness," while the latter focuses on the reverse process of "from likeness to conception"   Moreover, three kinds of thinking ways—"image," "logic," and "synthesis"—are combined so that natural abilities are ensured by their connection with scholarly studies, which in turn become spirits due to their connection with natural abilities.   Accordingly, it can be seen that natural abilities with scholarly studies can be fused to form the spiral structures of "many, two, one/zero."

Key Words: linguistic proficiency, composition study, thinking (image, logic, synthesis), creative power, spiral structure of "many, two, one/zero"

I. Introduction

Generally speaking, linguistic proficiency can be divided into three levels: "general proficiency" (including thinking power, observing power, memorizing power, associative power, imaginative power), "special proficiency" (including meaning establishing, expressions employing, materials selection, dictions, phrases construction and sentence organization, materials employing and composition organization, and style establishing), "complex proficiency" (including creative power).   However, the focus of these proficiencies is "thinking power."   Through the thinking power related to "image," "logic," and "synthesis," and in combination of "associative power" and "imaginative power," all kinds of proficiencies are able to produce "creative power."   Through the observation and explanation of the spiral structures of "many," "two," and "one/zero," the unity of "linguistic proficiency" and "compositional study" can be attained.

II. The Formation of the Spiral Structures of "Many," "Two," and "One/Zero"

Concerning the process of the creation of the universe, we can use the spiral structure of "many," "two," and "one/zero"[1] to portray it.

....

1   The two parties in "binary opposition" will produce the function of interaction and cycling, and then form a spiral structure.   Take love and wisdom, heaven and man, for example.   See "On the Spiral Structure of Confucius' Thinking System." (Taipei: Chinese Journal 《國文學報》 June 2000) pp.1-36.   The so-called "spiral" was originally a conception applied in the theory of educational curricula.   According to an educator of Czech, "based on ages, from shallow to deep, from simple to complex, from concrete to abstract, we use a spiral, cycling way to present the contents of ethical education."   See *Concise International*

Generally speaking, holy men in ancient times used the epistemological world to research the ontological world, and increasingly formed the reverse structure of "many, two, one/zero." And then, the ontological world was employed to explain the epistemological world, gradually constituting the sequential structure of "zero/one, two, many." Accordingly, the two-way thinking has long been explored and examined to form their all-inclusive cosmology. This sort of cosmology and world view varies all right, but in terms of similarities we can use the interaction and cycling between the structure of "zero/one, two, many," and the structure of "many, two, one/zero" to unify the spiral relations.

Concerning the formative process of this structure, we can see a brief explanation in Hsukuachuan〈序卦傳〉. Although probably "due to the order of 卦, the meaning is revealed,"[2] 卦、爻 both have a symbolic nature, serving as symbols for general conceptions, which can be generally seen as "likeness," signifying the change in life of the universe. In addition, in terms of Chouyi 《周易》 (including Yichuan 《易傳》), its 64 卦, according to their order, roughly have this feature.[3] In terms of all things and events which are put in the changing process from heaven to personnel, the

....

Education Encyclopedia. (Beijing: Sinhua Bookstore, June 1991) p.611. In addition, in contrast to humanity, the technological sector also discovered that genes and DNA contain a spiral structure.

2 Tai Lien-chang, *The Formation And Thoughts of Chouyi*《易傳之形成及其思想》(Taipei ：Wenching Publishing Company）, pp. 186～187。

3 Shu Fu-kuan, *Critical History of Chinese Nature. Chin Dynasty.*《中國人性論史・先秦篇》p. 202，"Likeness" is an imitation of the complicated objective world. In addition, likeness is the image of the objective world. However, such imitations and images are not handed down like the drawn pictures. Indeed, likeness is a symbol of the doctrines of things. 64 卦 and 384 爻 belong to these symbols. *Fen Yu-nan's Collected Papers.* 《馮友蘭選集》（Beijing: Beijing UP, 2000），p. 394。

structure of "one, two, many" is presented.   This indeed is the main contents of the first part of Hsukuachuan〈序卦傳〉. On the other hand, in terms of "from personnel to heaven," the structure of "many, two (one)" is presented as the main contents of the second part of Hsukuachuan〈序卦傳〉.   Here, "one" refers to Tai Chi; "two" refers to "heaven and earth," or "yin and yang," or "hardness and softness"; "many" refers to "all creatures" (including personnel). Although in Hsukuachuan〈序卦傳〉the concepts and functions of Tai Chi (Tao) and "yin, yang" (hardness, softness) were not clearly pointed out, they had already been conceived.   Otherwise, if "heaven and earth" lose the functions of "Tai Chi" (Tao) and "yin yang" (hardness and softness), they will not be likely to incessantly "create all creatures" (including personnel).   And here, take a look at Yichuan《易傳》.

乾知大始，坤作成物。(《周易‧繫辭上》)
一陰一陽之謂道，(One yin and one yang is called the Way, or Tao.)繼之者善也，(What is tied to it is goodness;)成之者性也。(what completes it is life.)……生生之謂易，成象之謂乾，效法之謂坤。(同上)
是故易有太極，(Therefore in *Zhouyi* there is the 'grand terminus', or Tai Chi,)是生兩儀，(which gives life to the two properties;)兩儀生四象，(the two properties give life to the four emblematic symbols,)四象生八卦。(which give life to the eight trigrams.)（同上）

According to this passage, the author of Yichuan 《易傳》used "Yi," "Tao," or "Tai Chi" to generalize "Yin" (Kun 坤) and "Yang" (Chien 乾), which serve as the source of creatures which have been incessantly growing.   As to the source, 「生生」(incessantly growing) is "Yi" 「易」.   Indeed, 「生生之謂易」(incessant birth or growing is Yi.)   In terms of 「初始」(beginning), a likeness number, it refers to Tai Chi. Thus, according to *Explicating Words* 《說文解字》, "In the beginning was Tai Chi; Tao was founded in oneness. Heaven and earth were created and separated. And all creatures were born. (note 4)」; [4] The principle of "Yin and Yang" indeed refers to Tao. 「一陰一陽之謂道」(One yin and one yang is called the Way, or Tao.) And the three items can be fused into one. As to this point, Feng Yu-nan 馮友蘭 explains "universe" and "likeness number" as follows.

The words of Yichuan have two sets. One set talks about the universe and its concrete things. The other set discusses the abstract system of likeness numbers. Sitzuchan (I) 〈繫辭傳上〉says," These words later turn out to be the basis of metaphysics and cosmology of new Confucianism. However, this is not a practical universe, but a system of likeness. According to Yichuan, these "likeness" and formulas all have exact corresponding things in the universe. The line「一陰一陽之謂道」(One yin and one yang is called the Way, or Tao.) talks about the universe all right, it can be an alternative of 「易有太極，是生兩儀」. (Therefore in *Zhouyi* there is the 'grand terminus', or Tai Chi,) (which gives life to the two properties;) Tao equals「太極」Tai Chi，while Yin and Yang do 「兩儀」two properties。According to Sitzuchuan （Ⅱ）繫辭傳下, "Great virtues of the earth and the heaven are called birth." And Sitzuchuan (I) 〈繫辭傳上〉says, " The cycle of birth is called Yi." These words also consist of two sets. The former refers to a universe, while the latter, Yi. However, both are simultaneous and reciprocal. [5]

....

4　See Huang Chin-fen, *On Chouyi*《周易縱橫談》(Taipei: Shanming Bookstore, March 1995)，pp. 33-34.

5　見 See *Fen Yu-nan's Collected Papers.* p.286。

He uses the corresponding relation between reality (universe) and fiction (likeness number) to make an explanation. In this way, the features of Chouyi are well highlighted. Thus, the positive-direction process can be presented by the "one, two, many" structure. Here, one refers to "Tai Chi," "Tao," or "Yi." Two refers to "Yin Yang," or "Chien Kun" (heaven and earth). Many refers to "all creatures" (including personnel). Corresponding to "from heaven to man" and "from man to heaven" in Hsukuachuan〈序卦傳〉, the "one, two, many" can be closely connected with the reverse-direction "many, two, one," forming a spiral structure. [6]

In this way, chouyi《周易》uses the change of "reciprocal births and oppositions" between 爻 and 爻 [7] to form a small cycle. And then the change is extended to 卦. The change of "reciprocal births and oppositions" between 卦 and 卦 can thus form a bi cycle. Furthermore, the cycling interaction between the bi cycle and small cycle forms a spiral structure. Concerning this point, Huang Ching-hsuan said.

The word chou 周 in chouyi 周易,...in a sense, means circulation. Each 卦 has six X. It begins with the first one, is divided at two, gets smooth at three, changes at four, prospers at five, and ends at above 上. This represents a small circulation of things. And then, let's take a look at 64 卦. These begins with the strength and self-reliance of 〈乾卦〉. And these come to a peaceful and harmonious state at 63 卦. Then,〈未濟〉follows.

....

6　See "On the Spiral Structure of Many, Two, One/Zero: Focus on Chouyi and Laotzu"（Taipei: Taiwan Normal University Journal. July 2003），pp. 1-24.

7　See *New Edited History of Chinese Philosophy*. (TaipeI, Shanming Bookstore, Jan. 1984) pp. 85-86. Lao Szu-kuan says, "In talking about the luck and omen of each 爻, we often point out that extremism brings about reversal. We can see this in using 爻.

It represents a cycle-we've got to resume our efforts to be strong and self-reliant. The constitution of materials, the evolution of time, and people's efforts always more forward in accordance with a definite cycle. Accordingly, life is better and civilization has increasingly been developed.[8]

The so-called "circulation", "repetition" and "flowing forward in a circular way" refers to the ever-changing spiral structure of chouyi. When corresponding to Sanyi「三易」(《易緯乾鑿度》), "many" refers to change, "two" refers to "simplicity", and "one" refers to "unchanging" Therefore, Sanyi can not any generally include the contents and features of chouyi, but present the spiral structure of "many, two, one."

We can find this kind of spiral structure in Laotzu，which may even make it more complete.

道可道，(the way gained in a usual way) 非常道；(is not a lasting way)　名可名，(being named in a usual way) 非常名。(is not a lasting name) 无，名天地之始；(being named from none seems the beginning of the universe) 有，名萬物之母。(being named from existential names is the source of all creatures) (〈一章〉)
致虛極，(doing one's best to make his heart uttermostly clear and calm) 守靜篤，(making life extremely quiet)萬物並作，(all creatures grow together)吾以觀復。(I observe the doctrine of historical cycles) 凡物芸芸，(everything common and ordinary) 各復歸其根。(returns to its root) 歸根曰靜，(which can be called quiet) 是謂復命，(can also be called a destiny) 復命曰常。(which is called truth) 知常曰明。(knowing truths is brilliance) (〈十六章〉)

....
8　See *On Chouyi*,《周易縱橫談》p. 236.

道之為物，惟恍惟惚。(Tao as a thing is unsubstantial)惚兮恍兮，其中有象。(lack of clarity consists of images) 恍兮惚兮，其中有物。(lack of clarity consists of concrete things) 窈兮冥兮，其中又精。(depth and darkness consist of essence) 其精甚真，(the essence is genuine) 其中有信。(the essence can be verified)（〈二一章〉）

有物混成，先天地生，(a being existed before the earth and heaven were created) 寂兮寥兮，獨立不改，(despite being unheard and unseen, it forever existed) 周行而不殆，可以為天下母，(incessantly repeated moves can serve as the fountain of all creatures) 吾不知其名，(I don't know its name) 字之曰道，(I named it Tao) 強為之名曰大。(it can also be named greatness) 大曰逝，(greatness moves incessantly) 逝曰遠，(moving incessantly until far away) 遠曰反。(moving far away equals coming back) （〈二五章〉）

知其雄，(knowing how to be strong) 守其雌，(I still keep soft in everything) 為天下谿；(I am willing to serve as ditches for the world) 常德不離，(eternal virtues won't be detached) 復歸於嬰兒。(being willing to be as mild as a baby) 知其白，(knowing what is clear and white) 守其黑，(being willing to go ahead in darkness) 為天下式；(being willing to be a tester for the world) 為天下式，常德不忒，(eternal virtues won't change) 復歸於無極。(returning to the original state) 知其榮，(knowing what is glory) 守其辱，(being willing to keep humble) 為天下谷；(being willing to be a nihilist) 為天下谷，常德乃足，(as a nihilist I can make virtues complete) 復歸於樸。(returning back to the original state) （〈二八章〉）

反者道之動，(moving back and forth between positive and negative is a feature of Tao's moving) 弱者道之用。(a feeble and active moving is a feature of Tao's application) 天下萬物，生於有，(all creatures come into being because of being named) 有生於无。(having names originates from none) （〈四十章〉）

道生一，(Tao is a unique unification) 一生二，(oneness gives birth to Yin and Yang) 二生三，(two begets harmony) 三生萬物。(harmony begets all creatures) 萬物負陰而抱陽，(all creatures face Yang and stand opposite Yin) 沖氣以為和。(a vibration in Yin and Yang becomes harmony) （〈四二章〉）

According to the above quotations, Laotzu holds that nothingness comes "having," and that "having" in turn comes to nothingness. "The way gained in a usual way is not a lasting way." "Tao as a thing is unsubstantial." "Tao is a unique unification; oneness gives birth to yin and yang; two begets harmony; harmony begets all creatures." "Having names originates from none." "A being existed before the earth and heaven were created....can serve as the fountain of all creatures." All of these are the sequential process "from nothingness to having." In addition, "moving back and forth between positive and negative is a feature of Tao's moving." "Returning to the original state." These are the reversely directive process "from having to nothingness." Indeed, Tao is "a fundamental power creating all creatures in the universe." In terms of the wholeness of roots and ends, Tao is a combined entity of nothingness and having. Moreover, from the perspective of "roots (origin)," since Tao is invisible and soundless, "Laotzu uses 'nothingness' to explain the feature of Tao." [9] The process from nothingness to having is a genesis "from one to many." So Tsung Pai-hua says,

The function of Tao is natural driving power, motherly power, and not man-made. Also, it is a will without any purpose. This simple and unclear entity incessantly mores, changes into all

9　See Shu Fu-kuan, *Critical History of Chinese Nature. Chin Dynasty.*《中國人性論史・先秦篇》p. 329.

creatures. Thus, we say 「 大道氾兮，其可左右」(Tao is everywhere in the universe) (chap.34), "repeatedly moving without pausing"(chap.25), " 反者道之動"(all things will return to their origin) (chap.40) and 「樸,則散為器。聖人用之，則為 官長」(simplicity is the heart of the holy man, who with the heart become the example of people.) (chap.28). The process in which the body of Tao evolves into all creatures is from one to many, from invisibility to visibility.[10]

And Hsu Fu-Kuan also says,

The process in which all creatures of the universe were created reveals the one in which Tao has been developed from non-materials to materials. But Tao is a whole and oneness. The creation and birth of Tao are a process from a whole to parts, from one to many.[11]

In terms of "from having to nothingness," that is "from many to one," Laotzu uses "returning" as a bridge to explain the philosophy. Here, "returning" means not only "coming back" but "cycling." Lao Szu-kuan explains "returning is the usage of Tao" in this way—

"Moving" is "operation"; "opposition" includes the meaning of cycling and inter-change. "opposition "is the contents of Tao. In terms of cycling and inter-change, "opposition" can be a form of Tao. In *Morality Script*(道德經)， Laotzu repeatedly explains the reason why "oppositions reciprocally exist," and why "each thing

....

10 *Anthology of Tsung Pai-hua*（Hofei: Anhei Education Publishing Company,Dec. 1994）p. 810.。

11 Shu Fu-kuan, *Critical History of Chinese Nature. Chin Dynasty.*《中國人性論 史‧先秦篇》p. 337.

and nature can turn back to the opposite side."[12]

Chiang Kou-chu also says,

The movement of Tao is a circular, repeated one. The final result of movement is a return to its root. "Return to its root;" "return to simplicity." Here, "root" and "simplicity" both refer to Tao. It produced and changes into all creatures, which through a cycling movement return to Tao. Laotzu' s thoughts are to a certain degree related to the   theory of cycling.[13]

Here "cycling" is emphasized, and is explained from the perspective of "returning."

Therefore, "mutual opposition and mutual establishment" keep a cycling process, that is, "change." And the result of "change" is the return to Tao itself. This can be said to be a cycling process whose change and order can co-exist.

So, based on *Chouyi* ; and *Laotzu*, so-called Tao, in terms of "sameness," uses the continuous cycles of "mutual opposition and mutual establishment" and "coming to origins" to connect the sequential order of "one, many" and the reversely directive "many, one" making them continually develop and cycle to form a spiral structure. In this way, the original law, by which the universe was created, conceiving all creatures, was presented.

In the process of "from one to many" (sequential) and "from many to one" (reverse) exists "tow," which serves to follow "one and to start "many" "Tao begot   one; one begot two; two begot

....

12 See Lao Szu-kuan, *New Edited Chinese Philosophy History* 《新編中國哲學史》 p. 240

13 See Chiang Kuo-chu, *History of Chinese Thoughts*《中國歷代思想史》(Taipei: Wenching Publishing Company, Dec. 1993) p.63.

three; three begot all creatures," So the "two" is the one exisiting in the cycle of "one begetting two; two begetting three" For generations, scholars have held different views of "two". Generally speaking, some orgue that "two" means nothing but a figure. For example, Chiang Si-chung and Jen Chi-yu some hold that it refers to "heaven and earth" For example, Si Tung and Kao Hen. And some think that it is "yinyang." For example, Ho Sankung, Wu Chen, Chu Chien-tze. In fact, "yinyang" is likely to be the best explanation. For Laotzu said, "All creatures bear yin and embrace yang." Although this only refers to the tributes of all creatures, Tao as the origin of all creatures must have this tribute. However, here Laotzu didn't directly point out this. Therefore, Chen Ku-yin, in explaining "Tao begot one,"says,

In the process of "from one to many" (sequential) and "from many to one" (reverse) exists "tow," which serves to follow "one and to start "many" "Tao begot　one; one begot two; two begot three; three begot all creatures," So the "two" is the one exisiting in the cycle of "one begetting two; two begetting three" For generations, scholars have held different views of "two". Generally speaking, some orgue that "two" means nothing but a figure. For example, Chiang Si-chung and Jen Chi-yu some hold that it refers to "heaven and earth" For example, Si Tung and Kao Hen. And some think that it is "yinyang." For example, Ho Sankung, Wu Chen, Chu Chien-tze. In fact, "yinyang" is likely to be the best explanation. For Laotzu said, "All creatures bear yin and embrace yang." Although this only refers to the tributes of all creatures, Tao as the origin of all creatures must have this tribute. However, here Laotzu didn't directly point out this. Therefore, Chen Ku-yin, in explaining "Tao begot one,"says, [14]

....

14 Chen Ku-yin, *Laotzu's Introduction, Explication And Notes.*《老子今注今譯及

And Huang Chuan also says,

I think one refers to original spirit 元氣, as chu chien said. "Two" refers to the spirits of yin and yang, "Three produced all creatures." This means that yin and yang are combined to produce all creatures.[15]

Despite their difference in the explanation of "one" and "three (many)," they hold the same view that "two" refers to "yin yang two spirits," which indeed can include "heaven and earth." For "heaven" as 「乾」chien is yang, while "earth" as 「坤」kun is yin. "Heaven and earth," a form of time and space, can hold and bear all creatures.[16] In addition, "yin yang" refers to "the good function of two spirits," which can be used to create all creatures. Judging from this, Laotzu's "one" is equal to Tai Chi of 《易傳》 yichuan; "two" means "yin yang" of yichuan. Here, the original structures of "one, two, many" and "many, two, one" are presented. However, it is worth mentioning that (1) although contents of "one," "two," and "many" are different from those of Chouyi (including yichuan), the structure still exists. (2) Tao in "Tao is a unique unification" is "a fundamental power creating all creatures in the universe," and "Tao itself is the manifestation of nothingness."[17]

......

評介》p. 106。

15 See Huang Chuan, *Analysis And Notes of Laotzu*《帛書老子校注析》(Taipei: Student Bookstore, Oct. 1991)，p. 231.

16 Shu Fu-kuan says, "According to Chinese conventional wisdom, earth and heaven can be said to be a form of time and space, which holds all creatures. Therefore, in terms of sequences, earth and heaven are supposedly created before all creatures. Otherwise, all creatures can be put nowhere. Therefore, by "one begets two," it means that one begets earth and heaven. See *Critical History of Chinese Nature. Chin Dynasty.* 《中國人性論史‧先秦篇》 p.335.

17 See Lin Chi-yen, *History of Chinese Academic Thoughts*《中國學術思想史 p. 34.

Therefore, Wang Pi says, "Nothingness is achieved via objects, and "having" is of no form." [18] Laotzu's Tao is essentially not "nothingness." [note 19] But it refers to "unsubstantial nothingness," serving as the "unsubstantial reason" before "one." [20] This "unsubstantial reason," if expressed in "number," may be "zero." Thus, the sequential and reversely directive structures can be adjusted, becoming "one (zero), two, many," (sequential), and "many, two, one (zero)" (reversely directive), supplementing the insufficiency of Chouyi. In this way, the sequential and reversely directive processes of genesis can become more complete.

Such a "many, two, one/zero" spiral structure reflects the sequential and reverse process in which all creatures were conceived and created so that it can be universally applied to everything, including philosophy, aesthetics and literature. In terms of compositional art, the structure based on creative writing presents a "one/zero, two, many" structure of a sequential direction. In addition, in terms of criticism, it presents a "many, two, one/zero" structure of a reverse direction.

....

[18] 見 *Laotzu Wang Pi's Notes*《老子王弼注》(Taipei: Holo Publishing Company, Oct. 1974.) p. 16。

[19] Feng Yu-nan says, "Tao is nothingness. Instead of being zero, nothingness makes a contrast to "having" in concrte things. Tao refers to the general principle of begetting all creatures in the universe. It's not zero." See *Fen Yu-nan's Collected Papers.* 《馮友蘭選集》 p.84.

[20] Tang Chun-yi says, "The so-called common principles of all creaturs can be either real resons or fictional reasons. However, they refer to fictional reasons other than real reasons. The fictional reason signifies that it can not exist alone. Although things can abide by or express it, it still can not be seen as an existing entity." See *Chinese Philosophy's Original Theory. Introduction.* 《中國哲學原論‧導論篇》p. 350-351.

III "One/Zero, Two, Many" Logical Structure of Linguistic Proficiency

Linguistic proficiency focuses on "general proficiency" of which the core is "thinking". Therefore, "thinking" can be considered the mother of all kinds of linguistic capabilities. And according to General Psychology by Peng Jan-lin, the so-called "general proficiency" refers to the capabilities shown forth in different kinds of activities. [21] In other words, it's needed not only in writing but also in learning other disciplines. So, the ability is remarkably basic and widely applied. It can include thinking ability, observatory ability, memorizing ability, associating ability, and imagining ability.

First, in terms of thinking ability, according to Language Education of Primary Schools by Chou Yuan, "Thinking is organized by language. In engaging in thinking, we've got to use vocabularies, phrases, and sentences. For the basic form of thinking, that is, general conceptions, is marked by words. And the process of judgments and reasoning is also via words. Because man used language to engage in thinking, thinking can be indirect and general. [22] In addition, because man is equipped with thinking ability, he may not be confined by space and time in human contact. Moreover, the training of thinking ability and the advancement of linguistic proficiency are closely connected. They can be interactive, cycling and progressive. In his Language Education of Primary Schools, Chou Yuan-chu said, "Language is a direct reflection of thinking> In understanding language, we are supposed to experience thinking from linguistic forms to thought contents, and from thought contents to linguistic forms. However, in expressing language, we'd

....

21 *General Psychology,* p. 392。

22 Chou Yuan, *Language Education of Primary School*《小學語文教育學》p.26.

better experience thinking from contents to forms, and from forms to contents. And in this repeated process, we should engage in analytical combination, abstract generalization, judgment, reasoning, image thinking and logical thinking."[23] Because language and thinking are closely related, we should consciously engage in a thinking training in the whole process of language teaching. The expression of a strong thinking power is the ability of abstract thinking and generalizing concepts. That is, a strong thinking power enables an individual to seek differences and similarities. In General Psychology, Peng Jan-lin even thinks that the capability of abstract thinking and generalizing concepts is the core of general abilities.[24] In language teaching, we can use the way of comparing to train students' ability of seeking differences and similarities, thus enhancing their thinking abilities.

Second, as to the observing ability, in *General Psychology*, Peng Jan-lin says," The out ward feeling receives the stimulus of the outside world, reflecting its attributes. These kinds of feelings are called outward feeling. For example, seeing, hearing, smelling, tasting, etc.... inward feeling receives the stimulus of the inside of an organism, reflecting its attributes (the exercise and state of an organism itself). This kind of feeling is called inward feeling. For example, feeling of exercising, feeling of balancing, and the feeling of internal organs.[25] Observing power means the ability to employ five outward feelings-seeing, hearing, smelling, tasting, and touching-and inward senses to gain the information of the outside world as well as the inside of an organism. A good observing ability is very important for writing, for just as Chou Yuan-chu said in *Language Education of Primary School* that observation is an

....

23 *Language Education of Primary School*
24 *General Psychology.*
25 *General Psychology*《普通心理學》p.76.

important means of gaining materials for speaking and writing. And it is also a pre-condition for an exact, vivid expression.[26]

In addition, as to memorizing power, Pen Jan-lin in *General Psychology* said, "Memory is a psychological process of accumulating and preserving the experiences of an individual via brains. That is, it is a process in which human brains number, store, and take the messages input from the outside world.... Memory is an active, energetic activity. Man is able to actively number the messages input from the outside world, making them acceptable forms for human brains. Modern psychologists think only messages being numbered can be memorized."[27] As a psychological process, memory is a process of recognition, re-recognition, and representation. It is the pre-condition on which man uses knowledge and experiences to think, imagine, solve problems, create and invent things. With memory, man can accumulate knowledge and enrich experiences. And without memory, we can not develop any psychological phenomenon. Thus, our education and teaching would be stopped.

As to associating power, Tung Ching-ping said in *Psychological Poetics And Aesthetics of Ancient Chinese.*" Association is man's psychological mechanism, mainly referring to the apparent connection of human brains. That is, when one sign or certain signs appear in consciousness, it or they will be connected with other signs.[28] For example, when we see a calendar shows February, we will think that winter has ended and spring is coming. And then, we'll think that all creatures will be revived. Accordingly, we would think of the beauty of spring scenes. Such kinds of reasoning are

......

26 *Language Education of Primary School*《小學語文教育學》p.23.
27 *General Psychology*.《普通心理學》 p.201.
28 Tung Chin-pin, *Psychological Poectis And Aesthetics of Ancient Chinese*《中國古代心理詩學與美學》(Taipei: Wanchunlo Publishing Company, Aug. 1994.) p.133.

associating power. In *Aesthetic Psychology,* Chiu Ming-cheng
divided association into "near association" similar association
"contrastive association" and "relational association."[29]
Furthermore, in terms of imagining power, Peng Jan-lin says in
General Psychology, "Imagination is a process in which we
reconstruct the already existing signs in brains to form new
images."[30] There are two directions towards the reconstruction-
regrouping and transformation. There, the richness of imagination
depends on two important factors: one is the richness of the signs
stored in brains; the other is the ability of regrouping and
transformation. Also, because the imagining power is operated in
this way, the products of imagination consist of the features of
images and innovation. This accounts for the fascination of
imagination. Take "roaring letters" in *Harry Potter,* for example.
Here, "letters" and "roaring" are regrouped to produce new signs-
roaring letters. As to certain huge monsters in fairy tales, some of
their characteristics are exaggerated-for example, rough and hard
skin, loud voices, and huge eyes. These are features trans formed via
imagination. However, in more cases, the process of imagination
contains both regrouping and transformation. The above data is
provided by prof. Chou Hsio-ping, an assistant professor at Chinese
Department of Chengkung University.

And then, in terms of the language field, "special ability" follows
"thinking power"(including "associating power" and "imagining
power"). In addition, "image thinking" "logical thinking" and
"synthetic thinking" employ "images"(including narrow definitions
and broad definitions), "diction" "rhetoric" "grammar"
"compositional art" reaffirming "topics" (guidelines) and "styles" to

....

29 Chou Ming-chi, *Aesthetic Psychology*《審美心理學》(Shanghai: Fudan UP,
    April 1993) p.179.
30 *General Psychology*《普通心理學》p.248.

enhance the study of the discipline of compositional art.

As to synthetic ability, it is general abilities to combine the above-mentioned "general ability" and "special ability." This kind of ability, resorting to "thinking power," is "creating power," Their mutual relation is like the one between "intelligence" and "wisdom." Despite the same level, their standing points are different. Peng Jan-lin says in *General Psychology,* "creative ability refers to the ability of producing new thoughts and products." Because one's creative ability is generally expressed via creative activities and the production of creative products. Thus, it's reasonable to use products to judge whether one is of creative abilities. And, in terms of writing activities, thinking about new figures images and searching for different ways of expression, and creating a complete new work combine, as a whole, to be an expression of creative ability. Moreover, in terms of whole reading activities, through different kinds of materials in contexts and various kinds of ways of expression, the creative ability highlights, "from likeness to meanings", topics and styles. This is a complete process of re-creation.[31]

Of the above-mentioned abilities, the thinking power is the focus. Indeed, "observing ability" serves "thinking ability" "Memorizing ability" is used to memorize the results of thinking. "Associating ability" is the initial expression of "thinking ability." And "imagining ability" is a further manifestation of "thinking ability" guiding three kinds of thinking, that is, thinking of "image," "thinking of logic" and "thinking of synthesis" Among these, "the thinking of image" is inclined to subjective association. The "thinking of logic" is inclined to objective association. And the "thinking of synthesis" is a combination of the two kinds of thinking.

....

31 *Reading And Writing*〈閱讀與寫作〉，*Practical Chinese Writing*《實用中文寫作學》(Taipie: Lijen Bookstore, Dec. 2004) pp.45-82.

The "thinking of synthesis" is used to express "abilities of synthesis" in an attempt to make the most of " creative ability." Their relation ship can be shown as follows.

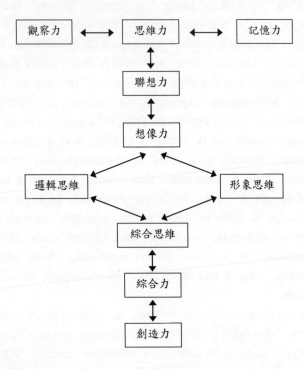

If corresponding to the sequential logical structure of "one/zero, two, many,""thinking ability" is "one/zero." "Thinking of images"(dark and soft) and "thinking of logic"(shiny and strong) combine to be "two," The "special abilities" derived from "thinking of image," "thinking of logic" and "thinking of synthesis" as well as " creative ability" combining all kinds of "special abilities" refer to "many." The process from "one/zero" to "two" then to "many" The process from "one/zero" to "two," then to "many," highlights the sequential process of creative writing.

IV. "Many, Two, One/Zero" Logical Structures

As a general rule, the rhetorical composition consists of "image thinking", "logical thinking" and "composite thinking".[32] Each of the thinking types has its own identity. When a composition intends to express certain emotion or reasoning by combining the scene or ongoing event with subjective association and imagination,[33] or the illustration of the author's descriptive skill by description of a certain emotion, reasoning, scene or event, it falls into the realm of "image thinking".　These aspects involve "conceptualization", "materialization" and "wording", and the studies associated with these aspects are imagology, lexicology and rhetoric.　If materials in scenes or events are combined with emotion and reasoning and expressed by objective associations with natural rules and the imagination, and arranged based on the principles of order, variation, consistency and unification, all this can be regarded as "logical thinking".　This process involves the gathering of material, composition layout and word structuring.　Study in these areas is a study in grammar and composition stylistics.　"Composite thinking" is a process entailing the combination of "image thinking" and "logical thinking" in search of an entity's characteristics, which involves conceptualization and character establishment. The study of these aspects would be thematology and stylistics.　The study of the whole or partial subject in these fields is rhetorical composition or essay study.

Rhetoric composition consists of contents that can be studied, as

....

32　See Wu Yin-tien, Compositional Structuralism. 《文章結構學》(Beijing: Chinese People University Publishing Company, Aug. 1989) p.345.

33　See Peng Yi-lien, *Fun in the Logic of Classic Poetry and Tzu* 《古典詩詞邏輯趣談》(Shaghai: Shanghai People Publishing Company, Sep.2001) p.13.

in the fields of academic studies, imagology, lexicology, rhetoric, grammar, composition stylistics, thematology and stylistics ... etc. Which will be further explained as follows: First, imagology.   This is one aspect of image study in terms of rhetorical composition. The image aspect in the Chinese literature had been noted for a long time. It had been regarded as the "first component in writing, most important in composition" (*The Literary Mind and the Carving of Dragons*, mind searching).   Huang Yung Wu explains "image" as "the intersection of author's senses and the display of external objects, brewed by observation, thinking and beatification, manifested as a vivid description of scene and state of mind. [34]   The object described, as explained by Chu Xi, includes events that are happening in the surrounding environment. Scenery is motionless space (static) and events are motions in time (dynamic). A complete work of literature usually consists of multiple images.   Image thinking is applied during the formation of the individual image.

Lexicology is part of linguistic studies, which studies text composition and the development of linguistics or certain languages. Zhuang Wen Chung said: "If language is a building, then text is the construction materials of this building--just like thousands of bricks and prefabricated building blocks which compose this spectacular building of literature."   Chang Zhe Gung said: "The foundation of language is text.   The functions of language (tool of socialization, tool of information propagation, tool of thinking) depend on the text to materialize.   He also said: "From the perspective of teaching, learning and applying, text is important, text is difficult." [35]   From these descriptions we may see text as the first steps in transforming

....

34   See *Chinese Poetics, Part of Design*. 《中國詩學‧設計篇》 (Taipei: Chuliu Publishing Company, June 1999) p.3.

35   See Middle School Language Teaching Study. 《中學語言教學研究》 (Kuangchou: Kuangtung Education Publishing Company, Jan. 2001) pp.29-30.

emotion, reasoning, scene and event into writing notations, which is fundamentally important in the study of rhetorical composition.

Next is the study of rhetoric. Master of rhetoric Chen Wang Tao said: "Rhetoric is a way of expressing with emphasis on reasoning and emotion. Rhetoric is simply an effort to adjust the contents of a text such that they are expressed appropriately." [36] Huang Ching Shuan thought that "the contextual substance of rhetoric is the image formed by the author." "The way of rhetoric is to design and readjust", "the principle of rhetoric is to be accurate and vivid". [37] It can be said that the rhetoric emphasized individual expression by the objective design and adjustment of the author, making it accurate and lively to intensify the appealing and persuasion of the text. This is obviously a process based upon image thinking.

The study of grammar is a study of the structure of certain languages. It includes the composition of words and their variation, the organization of idiom and sentence. Yang Zhu Snow combined the hypothesis of such scholars as Lu Shu Shiang, Chao Yuan Zhen and Wang Li in the revised edition of "The ABC of Grammar": "What is grammar? Simply put, grammar is the order in an arrangement of words. There is no set formula for the order of this arrangement. It is a rule extracted from analysis of the words of the language. This order also includes the internal structure of words and the integration of words into sentences. Therefore grammar is the set of rules governing the linguistic structure and sentence making." [38] Given these arguments, when these principles are applied to form the grammar, they are directly related to logical thinking.

Next, the composition stylistics. The so called stylistics is a

......

36 See *Retorics*, 《修辭學發凡》 p.5.
37 See *Retorics*. 《修辭學》(Taipei: Shanming Bookstore, Oct., 2002) pp.5-9.
38 See *Grammar ABC*. 《文法 ABC》 (Taipei: Wanchunlo Publishing Company, Feb., 2002) pp.1-2.

search of the logical structure of a composition. In other words, the organization of making words into sentences, combining sentences into paragraphs, and paragraphs into an essay. Even though it appeared early in the development, the actual formulation of rules in regards to its scope, contents and principles were integrated to become a system, did not happen until lately.[39] At the present time, there are approximately forty rules of stylistics which can be explained clearly. These rules evolved from the common principles of human discipline and were formed by logical thinking, all of them serving the functionality of form in order, to diversify but to interconnect so as to achieve a unified expression. Order, diversity, connection and unification are referred to as the four rules of composition stylistics. From the perspective of usage of the material, order, diversity and connection are analytic and unification is an expression of emotion and stresses continuity. This method of considering partial (material) analysis and the continuity (emotion) of the entire setup, is very comprehensive.[40] The logical thinking of the composition and wording are consistent.

....

39 Cheng Yi-Shou said, "It's fruitful for Taiwan's establishment of the discipline of compositional art. The representative work is *New Design of Compositional Art* by Chen Man-ming. A series of works are also done by his students including Chou Hsiao-ping and Chen Chiao-chun. The system and science of taiwan's compositional art might well become a discipline." (Suchou: Conference on Cross-Strait Chinese Traditional Culture and Modernization, 《海峽兩岸中華傳統文化與現代化研討會文集》 May 2002) pp.131-139. Wang Si-chieh also said, "Compositional art is a practical discipline with high academic value. It is intimately associated with rhetorics, pragmatics, aesthetics, logic. And Chen Man-ming has initially established its system." "Small Talks on Compositonal Art" 〈章法學門外閒談〉(Taipei: The World of Chinese Language and Monthly Literature 《國文天地》Oct.2000) pp.92-95.

40 See Chen Man-ming, *On Compositional Art.* 《章法學綜論》(Taipei: Wanchunlo Publishing Company, June 2003) pp.17-58.

Chen Peng Shiang stated in his "Theory and Practice of Thematology": "Thematology is a field of study in Comparative Literature. Ordinary thematic studies are studies in a single layer of the multiple layers involved in any literature creation. The objective of thematology is the study of identical themes (including verbiage, imaging and topics) in the hands of different authors at different times in an effort to understand the characteristics of an era and the intention of the author, whereas the ordinary thematic studies will concentrate on the illustration of a certain singular theme."[41] From this description we may see that theme includes "verbiage," "imaging" and "topics." In the scope of one single chapter, i.e., the expression of a particular topic, it means the language of emotion, the language of reasoning, imaging and purpose (abstract included). The language of emotion and reasoning are used to illustrate the purpose (abstract included) and should be regarded indifferently. Where the theme of a chapter is concerned, it usually means the purpose (abstract included) and imaging (generalized), which is a composite of image logic and thinking logic.

The last is stylistics. Generally speaking, there are multiple aspects of style, and this is especially true for literal style. Differences exist in writing style, author, school, time, region, ethnicity and creativity. Looking further into a composition, it has content and appearance (artistic), the content by itself being related to theme (topic, image) whereas appearance is closely related to grammar, rhetoric and order. The style of a composition is an integral presentation which is composed of content and appearance.[42] This is a combination of the author's logic and image

....

41 See Chen Pen-siang, *Theory and Practice of the Study of Themes.* 《主題學理論與實踐》 (Taipei. Wanchunlo Publishing Company, May 2001) p.238.

42 Ku Chu-chun said, "the causes of style are not necessarily individual elements of

thinking, which drives the theme with individual characteristics in grammar, rhetoric and composition for the presentation of an integrated appearance. In terms of style, the "hardness" and "softness" formed by "binary opposition of Yin and Yang" can be said to be the mother of all kinds of styles. In deed, it is not until Yao Ni of the Ching Dynasty that "hardness" and "softness" were clearly explained and used to generalized all kinds of styles. He divided styles into "hardness" and "softness. The styles such as spacious, active, open, and awesome belong to the type of "hardness." In addition, the styles such as conservative, indirect, decent, and opaque belong to the type of "softness." [43] And, the presentation of "hardness" and "softness" mainly depends on the compositional types formed by "binary opposition." [44]

As to the study of genre, the earliest discussion can be seen in Taso Pei's "On Canon" 〈典論論文〉. And in Liu Hsieh's *Literary Mind And Carved Dragon*, there are over twenty articles discussing genres. These articles make the bulk of the whole book. Since then, there have been more and more articles discussing genres. For example, in "An Introduction of Compositions," Liang Jen-fan divided articles into 84 kinds. In the Sung dynasty, *Tang Composition Essentials* 《唐文粹》 divided prose into 22 kinds. And the Ming dynasty, Wu Na's *Genre Differentiation* 《文章辨體》 divided prose into 49 genres, and divided pienwen 駢文 into five kinds. In the Ching dynasty, Yao Nai's *Anthology of Ancient*

---

the work, but an overall aesthetic view of the organic content and form of the literary work." See *New Interpretation of Literary Principles*. 《文學原理新釋》 (Beijing: People Literature Publishing Company, May 2001) p.184.

43   See Chou Chen-fu, *Examples of Literary Styles*. 《文學風格例話》 p.13.

44   Compositional art can be soft, hard, yin, and yang through the analyses of order, position, blending, contrast. See Chen Man-ming, "On the Styles of Compositional Art." *Paper Collection of Rhetoric*. 《修辭論叢》 (Taipei: Hungye Cultural Business Company, Nov. 2003.) pp.1-51.

Prose《古文辭類纂》divided genres into 13 kinds. Tseng Kuo-fan's *Compilation of Books and History* 《經史百家雜鈔》 divided compositions into three major branches and eleven kinds. All of these belong to the genre study of old schools. It's the end of the Ching dynasty that under the influence of oriental and Western literature our national genre study has changed. And then, compositions could be divided into event recording, narration, explanatory articles and argument articles (Nung Po-chun, Tang Jo-chang). And some divided compositions into application articles and artistic ones (Chai Yuan-pei). In addition, in terms of psychological analysis, compositions could be divided into articles of reasoning and articles of feelings (Szu Chi). All of these belong to "the genre study of Sinchu," [45] which influences four genres of today—narration (including description), arguments, feelings expressing, and application. Judging from this, imagery thinking and logical thinking are combined.

Indeed, the main contents of expressions and compositions are closely related to imagery thinking, logical thinking or "composite thinking." In the scope of words and sentences are images (individual), diction, rhetoric, and grammar. In the scope of paragraphs and compositions are images as a whole and compositional art. And in the scope of compositions are topics, genres, and styles. Thus, the contents of compositions are mainly images (from individual to whole, from narrow definitions to broad definitions), and within compositions topics and styles are unified.

However, its definition differs in a broader sense and narrower sense. It often means the entire content of the whole body in a broader sense, and can be subdivided into sense and appearance. The narrower sense refers to the individual, usually the partial and

....

[45] *Major Studies on Genre* 《文體論纂要》(Taiwan: Chinchung Bookstore, May 1979.) pp.1-12.

sense and appearance are treated as one. Since the entirety is the integration of partials and the partial is a part of the entirety, the two have inseparable relations. Nevertheless, even sense and appearance are a combinational representation, which often takes the meaning of partial identification. For example, the sensing images of grass and wood or peach blossom all lean toward the sensing part, since grass and wood or peach blossom lean toward the "image" by themselves. One of the representation of the peach blossom is love, and love is a sense. The sensing image of reunion or wandering lean toward "image". One image of wandering is the cloud, and the cloud is an "image". The former may be one image with multiple senses and the latter may be one sense and multiple images. Despite their differences, they are all "sensing images".

Based on images as a whole, we try to use the corresponding composite thinking to unify imagery thinking and logical thinking. In addition, we'll penetrate main contents of compositions to see the role images play in compositions.

First, in terms of the formation and expression of images, they are both connected with imagery thinking, which involves the combination and expression of "meaning" (feeling, reason) and likeness (events, landscape). The discipline of images (narrowly defined) research the combination of "meaning" (feeling, reason) and "likeness" (events, landscape). And the discipline of diction makes a study of the expression of "meaning" (feeling, reason) and "likeness" (events, landscape), just as archetypes find expressions in symbols. In addition, rhetoric uses transformation to make expressions vivid. Furthermore, the organization of images is associated with logical thinking, which involves the arrangement of images (meaning and meaning, likeness and likeness, meaning and likeness, images and images). Among these, the study of compositional art is related to paragraphs and compositions. Moreover, grammar is related to sentences. And the composite thinking involves the core meaning (feeling, reason), that is, the topic as well as "style." Judging from this, imagery thinking, logical thinking and composite thinking combine to cover the main contents of expressions and compositions, which are closely related to images. In the study of compositional art, the process from "likeness" to "meaning" abides by the reverse logical structure of "many, two, one/zero."

In short, the relation among the main contents of expressions and compositions can be shown in the following diagram.

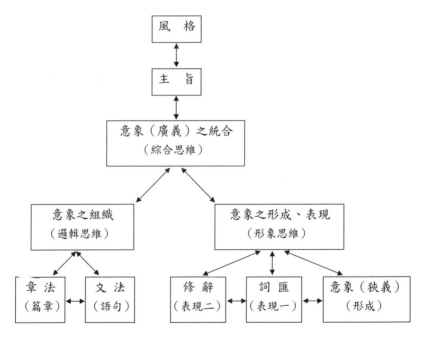

If we expand the discussion to rhetorical composition, there is the same spiral structure of multitude, two and one (0). The multitude would be the artistic representation of rhetoric, grammar, imaging and text order. "Two" means the image thinking (feminine) and logical thinking (masculine), and the reaction obtained with the connection of through and through. The "one (0)" is the "topic" and the "style" highlighted by this structure. This is the sincerity stated in *The Book of Changes*, "sincerity established by rhetoric", being the core of rhetorical composition. When rhetorical composition is dissected by "multitude, two, one(0)", the buffer effect of "two" ("image thinking"[feminine] and "logic thinking"[masculine]), the multitude (image, verbiage, rhetoric, grammar, order) may be unified with "one" (topic and style).

V. Combination of Linguistic Proficiency and Lexical Composition

In terms of these levels of proficiencies, "general proficiency" develops into "special capability," which then develops into "composite abilities," which in turn comes back to "general proficiency." These levels interact with each other, cycling and being promoted to a spiral structure. The structure diagram is as follows.

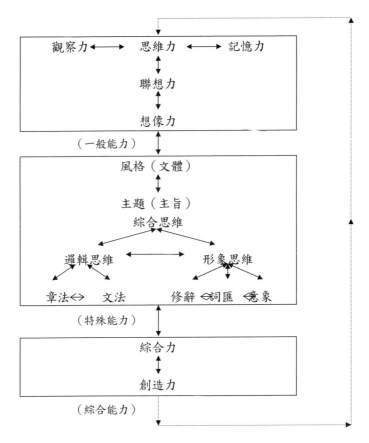

　　The capability of forming a spiral structure can be endorsed by "criticism" (reading) and creative writing.　For creative writing is from "meaning" to "likeness."　It depends on natural (empirical) abilities, and it is almost unconscious.　In addition, "criticism" (reading) is from "likeness" to "meaning."　It depends on hard study.　It uses scientific methods to analyze works, consciously affirming natural abilities.　Thus, creative writing is an expression of natural abilities, while "criticism" (reading) depends on human efforts.　Both are inseparable.

We shall use "Endless memory of love" by Bai Ju Yi as an example:

汴水流，(The Pien river flows) 泗水流，(The Szu river flows) 流到瓜州古渡頭。(Flowing onto Guachou harbor it goes) 吳山 點點愁。(My sorrow is as spacious as the mountains) 思悠悠， (Thoughts are immensely long) 恨悠悠，(Hatred is immensely deep) 恨到歸時方始休。(Hatred will not end until I go back home) 月明人倚樓。(I look forward to my hometown under the moonlight)

This poem depicts the strong emotion of separation of a wandering traveler, with the structure of "image (scenery), sense (emotion), image (scenery, event)".

For the image (scenery) part, the first three lines record the water scene (image one), the long flowing of the two rivers accentuating his lasting dismay. The two lines from the "flowing of Bien River" with the structure of "from host to guest" provided a description of the events. When put together, enhanced, lasting and lingering effects are achieved. The usage of the water scene to depict emotion has been a favorite of poets for generations. From "Early autumn of Taiyuan" by Li Po:

思歸若汾水，(thinking to return is like water flowing)無日不悠 悠。(every day my thinking endures long)

Or take "Farewell to Mr. Wang Ba one night in Baling" by Gia Zhe:

世情已逐浮雲散，(Feelings of the mundane world have faded away like floating clouds) 離恨空隨江水長。(hatred for departure is as long as the running river)

Furthermore, the author uses "flowed to the ancient pier of Guazhou" to continue the line with "Si River flows". The succeeding method is used to emphasize the emotional expression. The same rhetoric can be seen in many compositions. For example, in "Book of Poems"

威儀孔時，君子有孝子。(Among subjects of Chengwang, there were men of filial piety) 孝子不匱，(they served as models for later generations) 永錫爾類。(we needed to promote the filial piety in the court)

As stated in "Feeding a horse at the Great Wall" by an anonymous writer:

長跪讀素書，(I sincerely knelt down to read your letter) 書中竟何如？(what was told in your letter?)

In this way of modifying with the succeeding method, the two lines are connected seamlessly for a unified lingering effect. Moreover, the word "flow" is used three times in three consecutive lines, which makes the flow of the river even more endless, and thus the special lingering effect.

After the author describes watery scene in such fashion, he uses "tiny bitsy glooms of the Wu hills" to portray the hills as seen through his eyes (scene two). Here, the author uses "from host to guest" to express the scenery mixed with his mood. The words "tiny bitsy" being used to paint the not-so- tremendous but numerous hills of Jiang Nan, they were also used to express the gloomy mood felt by the author.

楚天千里清秋，(on the immense land of the southernnation autumn arrives) 水隨天去秋無際。(waters flow to the horizon

of heaven, and the autumn scene is so spacious) 遙岑遠目，
(looking far into the sky)獻愁供恨，(sorrow and hatred are
presented) 玉簪（尖形之山）羅髻（圓形之山）。(on small
mountains)

Xin Qigi of the Southern Song Dynasty states in his poem, "Chant
of the Water Dragon"

琵琶起舞換新聲，(with the new music of the string instrument)
總是關山離別情 (the music stirred up the feelings of
homesickness)

In this way, the gloomy mood is enhanced by the long and slow-
flowing waterways, and multiplied by many a "tiny bitsy" of them;
the so-called "hills hang with a separating dismal and broken heart,
the gurgling water carries the sound of farewell and flows into a
dream" (Lo Yin, poem for the Tsai brothers at Mien Valley), the
emotional expression thereby making an even deeper impression.

Next, looking at the role of sentiment (emotion), it uses the three
lines from "lingering thoughts" to express the emotion underyling
the scene, i.e., to describe the lingering gloomy mood after viewing
the scenery. In the two lines from "lingering thoughts" the author
uses overlapping characters [words] and repeated rhymes to
correspond with the flowing of Bien river, Si River and the "tiny
bitsy" of the Wu hills in order to create the integrated effects of
"lingering". The use of "thought" (meaning emotion, a gloomy
mood) and the gloomy mood draws out the dismal thinking
(sentiment) previously mentioned. And "this dismay [that]will not
end until the time to go home" not only reacts to the previous two
lines to enhance the lingering dismal mood, but also pushes the time
frame from present (reality) to future (virtual), which escalates the
feeling of gloom. We can see the same method used by Jimmy Tu

in his poem, "Moonlit night":

何時倚虛幌，(when can we both stand leaning by the gauzy veils) 雙照淚痕乾。(our faces'll shine with tears that have become dry trails)

These two phrases which describe the elation of reunion in the future (virtual) to compliment the bitterness of the present suffering from love (reality), match exactly the mood described by "this dismay [that] will not end until the time to go home". Bai Ju Yi pushed the time frame into the future, achieving the same effect as Tu, the emotion aspect of the poem having been strengthened.

At the end the "image (scenery, event)" portion will be discussed. There was only one sentence, "a man is leaning on a building under the bright moonlight". From a grammatical perspective, this sentence contains the attitudinal statements of "bright moonlight" and the narrative sentence of the "man leaning on the building" with the same structure of "from subject to predicate", only the predicate of the latter contains the predicate and the premised object, and there is only a slight difference. And even though "a man is leaning on a building under the bright moonlight" is only one sentence, it controls the entire poem. It makes the reader see the author as this "man" leaning on a building under the bright moonlight, facing the scenery of the waterways and far hills, while thinking thoughts provoked by his gloomy, dismal mood. This greatly demonstrates the sentiment brought forth by this scene (event). Everybody knows that one of the best ways to conclude a rhetorical composition is to combine the emotion with the scenery. For instance, take the "auspicious dragon chant" by Chow Ban Yen: "Spring field trips are full of the sadness of departing", which concludes the field trip on a spring day. It continues with the following after pointing out the topics:

官柳低金縷，(the willow tree besides the path bow down) 歸騎晚、(I rode a horse coming late) 纖纖池塘飛雨，(slim rain is flying upon the pond) 斷腸院落，(I am so sad in the empty yard) 一簾風絮。(wind blows through willow trees and lonely curtains.)

It is obvious that the evening scene in late spring (objects) highlights the sad feelings for departure. (meaning) In this way, the objects express the feelings (meaning). And Pai Chu-yi has ever used 「月明人倚樓」 (under bright moonshine man leaned against the building) to conclude his poem.　Here, the moonshine (object) is used to highlight the meaning of hatred. For ages, moon has been used to highlight "memory" (feelings for departure).　Also, take Li pai's poem, for example.

我寄愁心與明月，(I gave my feelings to tonight's bright moon) 隨風直到夜郎西。(hopefully, my feelings could fly on wind to a foreign nation in the West) P54

Another example is from the poem "Good Bye by the Ancient Road" by Meng Jiao

別後唯所思，(after departure we missed each other) 天涯共明月。(although we lived so far apart, we shared the same bright moon)

There are numerous examples similar to this.

The author uses the structure of "image (scene), sentiment (emotion), image (scene-event)", to arrange the sequence of "water", "hills", "moon", "man"--namely the scene he had seen under the moonlight, and the feeling that had arisen from seeing such a scene, making a special impression that lingers on and on.　There are sayings that this is a poem which describes the feelings of a married woman, which is acceptable--the beauty of the poem remains unchanged.　The following is the structural analysis:

Such examples are numerous.

Accordingly, the author uses the structure of "first dye (likeness/landscape, meaning/feeling)　and　then　dot (likeness/landscape, event) to arrange and organize "likeness," such as "water," "mountains," "moon," and "people."　In other words, the likeness is what the protagonist saw under the moon.　And then, the likeness is combined with "meaning (hatred)," making the significance more profound.　Some hold that the poem is about the remembrance and feelings of a household woman.　The structure diagram of images (including compositional art) is as follows.

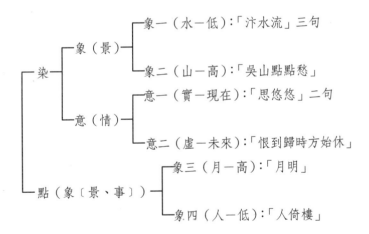

In an attempt to highlight hardness and softness, each level can be shown as follows.

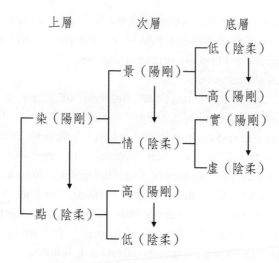

The topic of this Tzu is the long hatred of departure, which is placed in the middle of the composition. Its style is inclined to be "dark and soft," for in terms of hardness and softness of each level of the structure, except for the bottom level which is inclined to be sunny and strong based on the sequence "from low to high," other levels are all "dark and soft." Especially, its core structure of "first landscape and then feeling"[46] is inclined to be "dark and soft." Thus, the tendency is naturally inclined to be "dark and soft."

Based on this, in terms of all levels of abilities, this Tzu can be concluded as follows.

㈠ First, let's look at the "general proficiency." The selection of individual images (narrowly defined), such as flowing water, dotted mountains, and bright moon, mainly depends on observation and memory. In addition, the formation, expression, and organization of the images as a whole (broadly defined) mainly depend on association and imagination. And observation, memory, association

....

46 *On the Core Structure of "Many, Two, One/Zero" in Compositional Art.*

and imagination are connected with thinking.

Second, let's take a look at special proficiency.

Generally speaking, this poem used individual sensing images such as "water flow", "tiny bitsy hills", 'bright moon light" and "a man leaning on a building" and integrated them with "long lingering" "dismal", resulting in a huge effect by "different material of identical structure". From the perspective of "verbiage and phrase", the different phrases ad were formed by the emotions felts (sentiment) and scenery seen (event)(image). From the aspect of rhetoric, the watery ways were presented by a succeeding method and the hills were portrayed by personification, which made the water and hills filled with lingering sentiment to enhance the affection of this literary work. The author's image thinking can be seen from these points, and from the distinguishing characteristics of the forming and presentation of the sensing image. From the perspective of grammatical analysis, all of the phrases used were of the subjective predicate structure, which organizes thed individual concepts to form different images in a presentation of verbiage of logical structure. From the point of chapter order, the entire all poem has used methods of "scene sentiment", "high- low" and "reality and the virtual" to sequentially string the images together and form the logical structure of the chapter order. Finally, in terms of "synthetic thinking," it combines such delicate designs as "images" (individual), "diction," "rhetoric," "grammar," and "compositional art" to fully express the topic of long hatred and the dark, soft style with harmonious acoustics like beautiful pearls .[47] Man would be moved by such beauty.

And then, in terms of "composite abilities," it unifies "general

....

47　Chao Jen-kue, Li Chien-yin, Tu Yuan-ping, *Translation And Analysis of 300 Tzu of Tang And Five Dynasties* 《唐五代詞三百首譯析》(Changchun: Chilin Publishing Company, Jan. 1997) p..148.

proficiency" and "special proficiency" to fully exert the author's creative power from words to sentences, and from paragraphs to compositions.

Judging from this, compositional arts are inseparable from the formation (narrowly defined image), expressions (diction , rhetoric), and organization (grammar, compositional method) of images. This is the so-called "many". And the combination of "imagery thinking"(dark and soft)and "logical thinking"(shiny and strong) refers to "two". Furthermore, the highlighting of the topic and style refers to "one/zero." Actually, in terms of creative writing (linguistic proficiency), this structure is presented by "one/zero, two, many." And, in terms of "the study of compositional arts "(criticism), this structure is presented by "many, two, one/zero." As to the same work, when the author engages in sequential creative writing (one/zero, two, many) from "conception" to "likeness," he will repeatedly examine the reverse structure of "many, two, one/zero" from "likeness" to "conception" as the reader will. Likewise, when the reader engages in a reversely inductive criticism of "many, two, one/zero" from "likeness" to "conception" he will repeatedly study the sequential deductive structure of "one/zero, two , many" as the author will. The two-way interaction can be cycled and promoted to form a spiral structure, achieving the best world. In this way, "linguistic proficiency" (writing) and "the study of composition and expressions" are combined.

VI. Conclusion

Generally speaking, the application of "language usage" from "image" to " likeness" is almost unconscious. In addition, the efforts of "studying compositions and expressions" from "likeness" to "conception" are completely self-conscious". The former presents the sequential deductive process of "one/zero, two, many," while the latter presents a reversely inductive process of "many, two, one/zero." In these processes, both of them keep interacting and cycling, thus being promoted to form a spiral structure of "many, two, one/zero. "Gradually, "unconsciousness" is transformed into "self consciousness" in order to achieve a world of unification. Accordingly, natural language application and the man-made researches on lexicalcompositions and expressions can be connected and affirmed. Furthermore, thanks to the connection, the man-made researches on compositions and expressions can come back to life. This indeed the common goals of lexicographers and lexical researchers.

References

Wang, P. (1974). *Laotzu Wang Pi's notes.*《老子王弼注》Taipei: Holo Publishing Company.

Wang, S. (2002). Small talks on the arts of composition. 〈章法學門外閒談〉, *The World of Chinese Language and Monthly Literature.*《國文天地》 pp.92-95.

Wu, Y.(1989). *Compositional structuralism.*《文章結構學》Beijing: Chinese People University Press.

Tsung, P.(1994). *Anthology of Tsung Pai-hua.*《宗白華全集》Hofei: Anhei Education Publishing Company.

Chou, M.(1993). *Aesthetic psychology.*《審美心理學》Shanghai: Fudan University Press.

Chou, Y.(1992). *Language education of primary School.*《小學語文教育學》.

Chou, C.(1989). *Examples of literary styles.*《文學風格例話》Shanghai: Shanghai Education Publishing.

Lin, C.(1999), *History of Chinese academic thoughts.*《中國學術思想史》Taipei:Bookman Books.

Chiang, K.(1993), *History of Chinese thoughts.*《中國歷代思想史》Taipei: Wenching.

Tang, C.(1966), *Chinese philosophy's original theory. introduction.*《中國哲學原論・導論篇》Taipei:Living.

Shu, F.(1978), *Critical history of chinese nature. Chin dynasty.*《中國人性論史・先秦篇》Taipei: The Commercial Press.

Chen, K.(1985), *Laotzu's introduction, explication and notes.*《老子今注今譯及評介》Taipei: The Commercial Press.

Chen, M.(2000).On the spiral structure of Confucius' thinking system. *Chinese Journal*.《國文學報》pp.1-36.

Chen, M. (2003). *On compositional arts*.《章法學綜論》Taipei: Wanjuan Lou Publishing Company.

Chen, M. (2003). On the spiral structure of many, two, one/zero: Focus on Chouyi and Laotzu. *Taiwan Normal University Journal. 48*(1)，pp. 1-24.

Chen, M. (2003). On the core structure of many, two, one/zero in Chinese composition . *Taiwan Normal University Journal. 48*(2)，pp. 71-94.

Chen, M. (2004). Reading and writing〈閱讀與寫作〉, *The proceedings of applied Chinese and writing strategies.*《實用中文與寫作策略研討會論文集》.Tainan: Cheng Kung University.

Chen, P.(2001), *Theory and practice of the study of themes.*《主題學理論與實踐》Taipei: Wanchunlo Publishing Company.

Fen, Y.(2000), *Fen Yu-nan's collected papers.*《馮友蘭選集》Beijing: Beijing University Press.

Lao, S.(1984), History of Chinese philosophy: A new compilation.《新編中國哲學史》, vol. 1.Taipei：San Min Bookstore.

Huang, Z.(1991), *Commentary on annotations to the silk-copy Lao Tzu.* 《帛書老子校注析》Taipei: Students' Bookstore.

Huang, C.(1995), *On Chouyi.*《周易縱橫談》Taipei: Shanming Bookstore Publishing Company.

Tung, C.(1994), *Psychological poectis And aesthetics of ancient Chinese.*《中國古代心理詩學與美學》Taipei: Wanjuan Lou Books.

Peng, Y.(2001), *Fun in the logic of Classic poetry and Cu.*《古典詩詞邏輯趣談》Shaghai: Shanghai People Publishing Company.

Huang, Y.(1999), *Chinese poetics, part of design.*《中國詩學‧設計篇》Taipei: Chuliu Publishing Company.

Huang, T.(2002), *Rhetorics.*《修辭學》Taipei: Shanming Bookstore.

Yang, L.(2002),*Grammar ABC.* 《文法 ABC》.Taipei: Wanjuan

Lou Books.

Chao, J., Li C., Du Y.(1997), *Tang Wu Tai 300 Tze Translation and Analysis.*《唐五代詞三百首譯析》Changchun: Chilin Literature and History Publishing Company.

Jiang, P.(1979), *Major Studies on Genre.*《文體論纂要》Taiwan: Chinchung Bookstore.

Li, Y.(2000), *Mandarin styles.*《漢語風格學》Guangzhou: Guangdong Education Publishing.

Tai, L. (1986), *The formation and thoughts of Chouyi*《易傳之形成及其思想》Taipei：Wenching.

Ku, C.(2001), *New interpretation of literary principles.*《文學原理新釋》Beijing: People Literature Publishing Company.